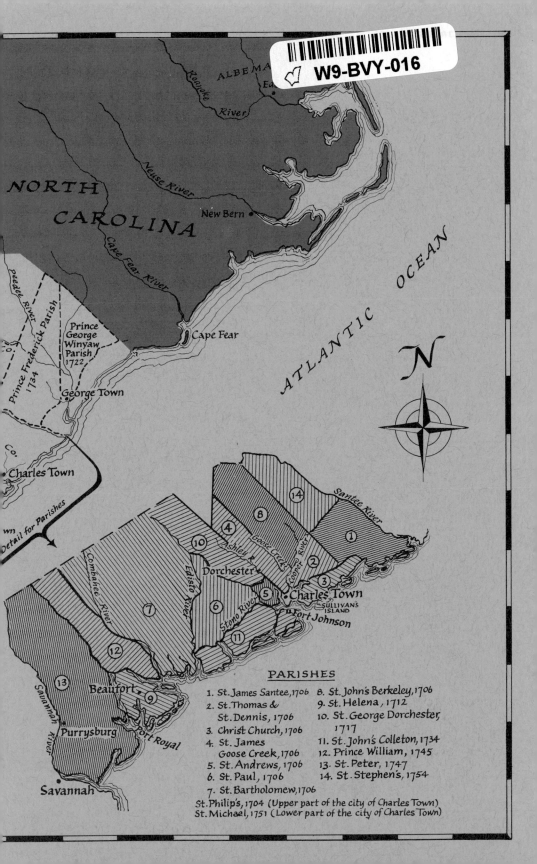

NORTH
CAROLINA

ALBEMA

Roanoke River

Neuse River

New Bern

Cape Fear River

Cape Fear

ATLANTIC OCEAN

N

Peedee River

Prince Frederick Parish 1734

Prince George Winyaw Parish 1722

George Town

Co.

Charles Town

wn Detail for Parishes

Santee River

14

8

4

10

Ashley R.

Goose Creek

Cooper River

1

2

Dorchester

Combahee River

Edisto River

5

3

Charles Town

7

6

SULLIVAN'S ISLAND

Stono River

Fort Johnson

11

12

13

Beaufort

9

Savannah River

Purrysburg

Port Royal

Savannah

PARISHES

1. St. James Santee, 1706
2. St. Thomas & St. Dennis, 1706
3. Christ Church, 1706
4. St. James Goose Creek, 1706
5. St. Andrews, 1706
6. St. Paul, 1706
7. St. Bartholomew, 1706
8. St. John's Berkeley, 1706
9. St. Helena, 1712
10. St. George Dorchester, 1717
11. St. John's Colleton, 1734
12. Prince William, 1745
13. St. Peter, 1747
14. St. Stephen's, 1754

St. Philip's, 1704 (Upper part of the city of Charles Town)
St. Michael, 1751 (Lower part of the city of Charles Town)

COLONIAL SOUTH CAROLINA

A Political History, 1663–1763

The Institute of Early American History and Culture is sponsored jointly by the College of William and Mary and Colonial Williamsburg, Incorporated.

COLONIAL
SOUTH CAROLINA

A POLITICAL HISTORY
1663–1763

By M. EUGENE SIRMANS

Foreword by Wesley Frank Craven

PUBLISHED FOR THE
Institute of Early American History and Culture
AT WILLIAMSBURG, VIRGINIA
By The University of North Carolina Press · Chapel Hill

TO SYLVIA

FOREWORD

Marion Eugene Sirmans, Jr., was born in Moultrie, Georgia, on January 27, 1934. He died in Atlanta on August 30, 1965. His many friends will remember him for the good company he repeatedly gave them, and even more for his extraordinary courage. Despite the knowledge he had after 1957 that his life was likely to be short, Gene sustained a remarkably buoyant view of life and spent the time allotted to him working in his chosen field. He experienced no defeat.

Mr. Sirmans had graduated from Emory University in June 1955, had enrolled at Princeton University in the following fall as a graduate student in the Department of History, and had qualified for the M.A. degree in June 1957. He won the Ph.D. degree in 1959, with a dissertation entitled "Masters of Ashley Hall: A Study of the Bull Family in Colonial South Carolina, 1670–1737." The excellence of this dissertation led to his appointment from 1959 to 1962 as a Fellow of the Institute of Early American History and Culture, and in that capacity he taught for three years as an instructor in history at the College of William and Mary. In 1962 he returned to Emory University, where at the time of his death he was an Assistant Professor of History.

Studies by Mr. Sirmans which previously have been published include:

"The South Carolina Royal Council, 1720–1763," *William and Mary Quarterly*, 3d Ser., XVIII (1961), 373–92

"The Legal Status of the Slave in South Carolina, 1670–1740," *Journal of Southern History*, XXVIII (1962), 462–73

"Politicians and Planters: the Bull Family of Colonial South Carolina," *Proceedings* of the South Carolina Historical Association for 1962 (1963), 32–41

"Charleston Two Hundred Years Ago," *Emory University Quarterly,*
XIX (1963), 129–36
"Politicians in Colonial South Carolina: the Failure of Proprietary
Reform, 1682–1694," *William and Mary Quarterly,* 3d Ser., XXIII
(1966), 33–55

The last item in the list was adapted for publication in the *Quarterly*
from the manuscript of the book which follows.

In view of the length of Mr. Sirmans' final illness, he left a manuscript that was remarkably complete. As an old friend who long had
been familiar with his working habits, and as a reader for the Institute, I was satisfied that only in the case of some of the earlier chapters
had he been denied the time he needed for the final revision of his
text. In those chapters there were sections obviously drafted with a
view to their subsequent condensation, contradictions with judgments
clearly stated in later parts of the text, even an occasional misstate-
ment of familiar facts—the kind of mistake one makes when depend-
ing upon his memory in the expectation that any error will be caught
in a final check. The argument from the beginning to the end was
persuasively consistent, and none of the difficulties presented by the
manuscript seemed to be more serious than are those often ironed out
in last minute consultations between an author and his editor. I
recommended publication, though well aware that the decision to
publish would place upon James M. Smith, book editor for the Institute, a heavy responsibility. The decision to publish, of course, depended upon more than my own recommendation.

Happily, Mr. Smith had been closely identified with the project
since its inception. The two of us agreed to collaborate, one as the
supervisor of the dissertation which first enlisted Mr. Sirmans' interest
in South Carolina's history, the other as a colleague in the Institute of
Early American History and Culture who gave his encouragement to a
more ambitious development of that interest. Smith has carried the
main responsibility. I have served as backstop to him, and we have
concurred on the revisions which have been made in the manuscript,
all of them minor except for a substantial reduction in the length of
the earlier chapters. Our confidence that Mr. Sirmans would have
approved the changes is strengthened by the generous agreement of his
wife that we should have a free hand in the revision. In return, we
have sought to avoid every debatable revision, whether of fact or
interpretation. For example, we have wondered if he might have
wished to soften his judgment of some of the earlier political leaders in
view of the tolerance he showed later in the text for other self-seeking

men, but we have left the judgments as he chose to make them. We have decided too against undertaking to write any such summary conclusion as Mr. Sirmans might have been persuaded to add. As a result, the book ends abruptly, but at the logical terminal point for the story it tells. In its own way the study of a century of political life in colonial South Carolina is as complete as it is full of useful information for students of early American history.

No other scholar has written a comparably revealing and convincing account of South Carolina's early political history. The book promises to be the standard study of the subject for many years to come, or else the work which stimulates other students to improve upon it.

It has been said that the "great use of a life is to spend it for something that outlasts it." This Eugene Sirmans did.

WESLEY FRANK CRAVEN

Princeton University

PREFACE

This book attempts to relate the political history of South Carolina from the issuance of the first proprietary charter in 1663 to the end of the French and Indian War a century later. My interest in colonial South Carolina developed in a somewhat roundabout fashion. Politics has always fascinated me, and I acquired an equal fascination for the eighteenth century as a college freshman. In graduate school my interest in eighteenth-century politics began to focus on the American colonies, and when I discovered that almost nothing had been written on the political history of colonial South Carolina for fifty years, the selection of a thesis topic was simple. My dissertation attempted to describe the political careers of the first two generations of the Bull family of South Carolina, but while working on it I realized that a more general study must precede any meaningful biographical work. I therefore broadened my subject into a general political history of the colony while I was a Fellow at the Institute of Early American History and Culture in Williamsburg, Virginia.

Readers who are familiar with the literature on colonial South Carolina know that Edward McCrady, William Roy Smith, and David Duncan Wallace have already written political histories of the colony, and some may wonder why anyone should write a new book on the same subject. My answer is simply that I am not satisfied with any of the existing histories. All of them suffer from a general failure to relate the internal history of the province to other events in the British empire, particularly to Indian affairs on the southern frontier. Additional, and even more compelling, reasons for a new study appear when the various periods of the colony's history are examined. To begin with, the accounts of the proprietary period by McCrady and Wallace badly need to be revised. They present the early history of South Carolina as a struggle between colonists who wanted only to

defend their liberties and proprietors who alternated between despotism and greed. Such an interpretation not only misrepresents proprietary policy, especially the Fundamental Constitutions of Carolina, but
it also neglects the key role of the faction known as the Goose Creek
men.

The older generation of historians have treated the period from
1712 to 1743 in a much more satisfactory manner. I have found
repeatedly in dealing with those years that I have little to add to what
has already been written. Indeed, there is not much any modern
historian can add to Francis Yonge's account of the rebellion against
the proprietors, which was written in 1721, or to the several accounts
of South Carolina's disputes over paper money, which were written in
the 1730's. I have, however, modified considerably the older studies of
South Carolina's land boom in the 1730's and early 1740's. An entirely
different situation exists for the period from 1743 to 1763. No previous
historian has ever written a comprehensive narrative for that era.
McCrady, Smith, and Wallace were all aware of the most significant
event of that time, the rise of the Commons House of Assembly, but
they did not describe it in any detail. Jack P. Greene has recently
published an excellent work on the rise of the lower houses of assembly in the southern royal colonies, a study which supplies a wealth of
detail on the South Carolina Commons House, but his approach is
topical while mine is chronological. Because historians have relatively
neglected this period of the colony's political history, more work
remains to be done on it than any other time. In particular, we need a
comprehensive analysis of the membership and power structure of the
assembly and biographical studies of the leading politicians, notably
Governor James Glen.

Some mention should be made of the point of view from which this
study is written. I believe that politics at its best is the art of the
possible, the art of accommodating contrary interests in a manner
acceptable to all parties or factions. I therefore respect most highly
those political leaders who were able to adjust conflicts rather than
those who initiated them. Prominent in this group are Governors
John Archdale, Francis Nicholson, Robert Johnson, and William Bull,
Sr.

Several stylistic practices should also be explained. I have expanded
all abbreviations in quotations, but I have retained the original spell-
ing, punctuation, and capitalization. I have not tried to convert Old
Style dates to New Style, but I have treated January 1 as the beginning
of each year. I have referred to Indians by the names that were given

them by the English colonists, rather than the Indian versions of their names, because the English names are easier to remember; for example, I have used the name Little Carpenter in preference to its Cherokee equivalent, Atta kulla kulla.

Like most other historians, I wish to thank the many persons who have helped me in one way or another. Professor Wesley Frank Craven of Princeton University directed my dissertation and has been a constant source of advice and encouragement even after I left Princeton. I owe a special debt to the staff members of the Institute of Early American History and Culture, especially Lester J. Cappon and James M. Smith, for their counsel and assistance while I was an Institute Fellow. Jack P. Greene of the Johns Hopkins University has helped me in several different ways, particularly in discussing political developments in South Carolina. The late J. H. Easterby of the South Carolina Archives Department introduced me to the colony's records, advised me several times on their use, and took a special interest in my project. The staffs of the various libraries and manuscript depositories I visited always treated me courteously, especially Mrs. Mary Granville Prior of the South Carolina Historical Society and Howard H. Peckham of the William L. Clements Library. The Emory University Research Committee paid for the typing of the manuscript. Finally, I wish to thank my wife, Sylvia Lanham Sirmans, for her critical appraisals of my work, her assistance in typing, and most of all for goading me into finishing the book.

TABLE OF CONTENTS

COLONIAL SOUTH CAROLINA
A Political History, 1663–1763

CHAPTER I

ENGLISH BACKGROUND
1663–1670

In the sultry dog days of August 1669, three ships rode at anchor in the Downs off the southeastern coast of England. There were two frigates, the flagship *Carolina* and the *Port Royal,* and a sloop, the *Albemarle,* all waiting for a favorable wind to carry them to the Carolina coast. The fleet's commander, Captain Joseph West, had orders from his employers, the True and Absolute Lords Proprietors of Carolina, to sail by way of Barbados to a harbor in Carolina called Port Royal. There Captain West and the fleet's passengers planned to found a new colony, a settlement to which men later gave the name of South Carolina. For more than six years the proprietors had worked to secure a clear title to their possession of Carolina, devise a plan of development, and recruit settlers. Yet, for six years their plans had persistently gone awry, and at one time they had seemed ready to abandon the whole scheme. It was not until 1669, the year Captain West's fleet was fitted out, that the Carolina venture took a turn for the better.

I

That project was to place the English far to the south of their earlier settlements on the North American mainland in a new projection of an old contest between England and Spain. Heretofore the main center of conflict in the New World had been the Caribbean, and there the story of South Carolina logically begins. On the island of Barbados the change to large-scale sugar production, combined with the rapid expansion of the slave labor system, had effected an agricultural revolution which placed the small planters at a competitive disadvantage. By the decade of the 1660's, Barbados had a surplus population which was not only ready to consider emigration to other West Indian islands but to the mainland as well.[1]

Sir John Colleton, who took the initiative in securing the Carolina charter, was one of the most enterprising of the Barbadian planters. He had served as a colonel under John Berkeley, Baron Berkeley of Stratton, in the royalist army during England's Civil Wars, but after Charles I's execution he migrated to Barbados, where he had become embroiled in a series of political intrigues involving royalists and Parliamentarians. Colleton had normally—although not always—supported the royalist faction, and immediately after the Restoration of 1660, like so many other royalists, he set out for London to claim his reward. His connections in London were excellent; several of his relatives were London merchants, his friend Lord Berkeley enjoyed favor with the new government, and his distant cousin George Monck, Duke of Albemarle, was the hero of the Restoration. When Lord Berkeley presented a memorial to the King in Colleton's behalf, Charles II not only knighted Colleton but also promptly appointed him to the Council for Foreign Plantations.[2]

Among Colleton's colleagues on the Council for Foreign Plantations were men knowledgeable about colonial settlement in America and influential in formulating colonial policy. Sir William Berkeley, governor of Virginia, was appointed when he returned to London in 1661. His brother, Lord Berkeley, was important in naval affairs and very close to the Duke of York, Lord High Admiral and heir to the throne. Sir Anthony Ashley Cooper, later to become the Earl of Shaftesbury, was a former owner of Barbados property. Others included Edward Hyde, Earl of Clarendon, Charles II's first minister, and Sir George Carteret, vice chamberlain of the royal household and treasurer of the navy.

It was while he was working with these and other influentially placed men that Sir John Colleton seems to have conceived his idea of the Carolina proprietorship. His hope was to secure a royal charter, and for the achievement of this purpose he became associated with several of the most powerful men in the kingdom. He apparently

[1] Vincent T. Harlow, *A History of Barbados, 1625–1685* (Oxford, 1926), 152–53, 169–73.

[2] *Ibid.*, 69, 119–21, 128, 130; William S. Powell, *The Proprietors of Carolina* (Raleigh, 1963), 47–49.

turned first to his influential kinsman, the Duke of Albemarle, and to his friend, Lord Berkeley, who brought into the project his brother, Governor Berkeley. In addition four other men were recruited: the Earl of Clarendon; William Craven, Earl of Craven; Anthony Ashley Cooper; and Sir George Carteret.[3] The Carolina proprietors were intimately associated with the economic expansion of Restoration England. Six of the eight men became adventurers in both the Royal African and Hudson's Bay Companies; two of them—Carteret and Lord Berkeley—became the proprietors of New Jersey, and in 1670 the King granted the Bahama proprietary to them and four other Carolina proprietors. On the policy-making level five of the original proprietors were members of the Council of Trade and six were members of the Council for Foreign Plantations.[4]

On March 24, 1663, the Crown issued a charter giving the eight proprietors title to the land lying between 31° and 36° north latitude —including most of present-day North Carolina, all of South Carolina, and virtually all of Georgia—and stretching from the Atlantic Ocean to the "South Seas." Two years later, on June 30, 1665, the proprietors secured a second charter which extended their grant southward two additional degrees into Spanish Florida, and northward to 36° 30'. This latter extension was designed to make certain that all of Albemarle Sound and the settlement recently begun there by Virginians was included.[5]

During the early years of the proprietorship Sir John Colleton and the Duke of Albemarle assumed the leadership of the venture, hoping ultimately to profit from Carolina without bearing the actual cost of its settlement. Their plan was to attract experienced colonists from the older settlements into Carolina by the promise of generous land grants and comparably liberal concessions of religious and political rights. It was expected that the colonists themselves would meet the main costs of settlement, and eventually compensate the proprietors for their

[3] Charles M. Andrews, *The Colonial Period of American History*, 4 vols. (New Haven, 1934–38), III, 185–87; Herbert R. Paschal, Jr., Proprietary North Carolina: A Study in Colonial Government (unpubl. Ph.D. diss., University of North Carolina, 1961), 70–74.

[4] Powell, *Proprietors*, 12–49; Wesley Frank Craven, *The Southern Colonies in the Seventeenth Century, 1607–1689*, in Wendell H. Stephenson and E. Merton Coulter, eds., *A History of the South*, I (Baton Rouge, 1949), 322–23; Elizabeth Donnan, ed., *Documents Illustrative of the History of the Slave Trade to America*, 4 vols. (Washington, 1930–35), I, 169–70 and *n;* Charles M. Andrews, *British Committees, Commissions, and Councils of Trade and Plantations, 1622–1675* (Baltimore, 1908), 67–68.

[5] Andrews, *Colonial Period*, III, 187–92; Mattie E. E. Parker, ed., *North Carolina Charters and Constitutions, 1578–1698* (Raleigh, 1963), 74–104.

efforts by the payment of rents. They planned to establish not just one colony but several "colonies," each with its own government consisting of an appointed governor and council and an elected assembly. There was no thought of undertaking the expense of colonizing from England.

For a time, the proprietors' hope for a maximum return on a minimum investment seemed entirely feasible. In 1663 the proprietors instructed Governor Berkeley of Virginia, in his capacity as a Carolina proprietor, to organize a government for the Virginians settling around Albemarle Sound, which was done in 1664. New Englanders had already established a colony at the mouth of the Cape Fear River, and there was every prospect of recruiting settlers from Barbados. When the New Englanders abandoned the Cape Fear after only a few months, the proprietors in 1665 granted the sole right to settle on that river to a Barbadian company known as the Adventurers of Barbados, which founded a colony there immediately.[6]

In spite of the very real promise of the Carolina venture in 1665, the whole project nearly collapsed within the next four years. Although the Albemarle Sound colony endured, the Barbadian Adventurers, beset by bad luck and lack of supplies, abandoned the Cape Fear settlement in 1667. In England, the proprietors lost their first leaders when Colleton died and Albemarle's poor health forced him to retire from public life. Clarendon soon fell from power and fled into exile, and other members of the group lost interest. The proprietors could claim to have accomplished little more than the exploration of the area south of Cape Fear, the region that later became South Carolina, and for this the Barbadians seem to have been mainly responsible.[7]

II

The Carolina proprietorship was rescued from failure by the dedication of one man—Anthony Ashley Cooper. Baron Ashley reinvigorated the faltering project, impressed upon it the force of his own personality and philosophy, and gave proprietory policy a new direction. Forty-seven years old when he assumed the leadership of the Carolina venture, Ashley was an accomplished, even a slippery,

[6] Craven, *Southern Colonies*, 324–32; Louise F. Brown, *The First Earl of Shaftesbury* (New York and London, 1933), 152–55; Concessions and Agreements, Jan. 7, 1665, Parker, ed., *N. C. Charters and Constitutions*, 109–27.

[7] Edward McCrady, *The History of South Carolina under the Proprietary Government, 1670–1719* (N. Y., 1897), 79–93; Brown, *Shaftesbury*, 155; Craven, *Southern Colonies*, 329–34.

politician who had held office under Charles I, Parliament, Cromwell, and Charles II. In 1669 his political career was approaching its peak; in 1672 Charles II made him the first Earl of Shaftesbury and appointed him Lord High Chancellor. More significantly for Carolina, Lord Ashley's knowledge of colonial affairs matched his political acumen. He had taken an active interest in England's colonies for many years. During the Protectorate he had served on the select committee of the Council of State for Plantations, and after the Restoration, he became a member of all the various committees and councils dealing with the colonies and trade. He also invested in companies trading overseas.[8]

Ashley first asserted his leadership at a meeting of the proprietors on April 26, 1669, when he persuaded the proprietors that they must abandon their parsimonious policy and assume more of the financial burden of settling Carolina. The proprietors agreed to contribute £500 sterling each to start a new settlement and pledged further contributions for support of the colony, although they hoped to limit any additional outlay to £200 each. Impressed by reports of earlier explorations of the coast below Cape Fear, they decided to locate their settlement at Port Royal. Ashley continued to expect that most of the settlers would be recruited from other colonies, especially Barbados, but he partially reversed that policy by proposing the enlistment of some of the first settlers in England. Once the other proprietors had agreed to his plans, Ashley moved fast. Within three months he had recruited more than a hundred prospective colonists in England, purchased three ships and outfitted them, and appointed Captain Joseph West to command the expedition. By the first of August in 1669, the fleet was ready to sail.

Although preparations for the Carolina expedition occupied much of Ashley's attention between April and August, he also found the time during the summer of 1669 to draft a remarkable document for the guidance of the revived project: the Fundamental Constitutions of Carolina. In composing it he had the assistance of John Locke, then thirty-seven years old and just beginning to mature as a philosopher. While in his twenties, Locke had become an Oxford don but had grown dissatisfied with academic life and turned to the study of medicine. In July 1666, he had met Ashley while Ashley was visiting

---

[8] The best biography is Brown, *Shaftesbury;* on his colonial interests, see pp. 128–34, 150–51. To avoid confusion about Anthony Ashley Cooper's several titles, I have referred to him throughout as Lord Ashley, the title he held while he was active in Carolina affairs.

Oxford before going to nearby Astrop to try the waters for a liver infection. Locke, who had several flasks of the water, brought them to Ashley; in the conversation that followed Ashley had been impressed with Locke's intelligence as well as his knowledge of medicine. In 1667 Locke moved into Ashley's home as his personal physician, and subsequently supervised an operation on Ashley's liver which probably saved the baron's life. The grateful Ashley rewarded Locke with several offices. By 1669 he had become tutor to Ashley's children, secretary to the Council for Trade and Plantations, and secretary to the Carolina proprietors, in addition to serving as Ashley's personal secretary and physician.[9]

The fragmentary sources still surviving and the intimate association between Ashley and Locke make it difficult to determine how much the latter actually contributed to the Fundamental Constitutions of Carolina. The earliest known version of the Constitutions, dated July 21, 1669, is in Locke's handwriting,[10] and several contemporaries believed Locke was the chief draftsman of the document. Sir Peter Colleton, who had inherited his father's proprietorship, in a letter of 1673 to Locke referred to the Constitutions as "that excellent forme of Government in the composure of which you had soe great a hand." [11] Locke himself occasionally seemed willing to take credit for the Constitutions, but he never made a clear-cut statement one way or the other.[12] On the other hand, internal evidence in the first extant draft of the Constitutions indicates that Ashley dictated the document to Locke. Locke's draft contains a number of clerical errors that were later corrected, errors that a secretary might easily make when taking dictation or in copying from a not too legible draft.[13] Moreover, there is evidence that in 1669 Locke was going through a transitional period in his thinking, under the tutelage of Ashley.[14] That there was collaboration between the two men in the composition of the

[9] *Ibid.*, 156–61; Craven, *Southern Colonies*, 334–36; Maurice Cranston, *John Locke, A Biography* (N. Y., 1957), 57–67, 93–95, 103–4, 111–13.

[10] This version of the Constitution is in Parker, ed., *N. C. Charters and Constitutions*, 132–52.

[11] Colleton to Locke, [1673], Lovelace Manuscripts, c. 6, fol. 216, Bodleian Library, Oxford University; I have used the microfilm at the Institute of Early American History and Culture, Williamsburg, Va. It should be noted, however, that Colleton was in Barbados when the Constitutions was written, and he was never a close friend of either Locke or Ashley.

[12] Introduction to John Locke by Peter Laslett, ed., *Two Treatises of Government* (Cambridge, Eng., 1960), 29–30.

[13] Parker, Introduction to Fundamental Constitutions, *N. C. Charters and Constitutions*, 128–29.

[14] Laslett, Introduction to Locke, *Two Treatises*, 19–21, 25–30.

Fundamental Constitutions seems likely, but the weight of the argument indicates that the ideas were mainly Ashley's.

Ashley and Locke completed the document in July 1669 and after correcting Locke's clerical errors and revising it in a few details, they sent it to Carolina with Captain West. The other proprietors had not approved the Constitutions, however, and when Ashley submitted the document to them they insisted on several amendments. Not until March 1, 1670, was a revised draft approved. The proprietors intended the Fundamental Constitutions to be a permanent frame of government for Carolina and had several copies made and bound.[15]

Historians have subjected the Fundamental Constitutions to much unsympathetic criticism, asserting that it had little, if any, effect on the subsequent development of South Carolina. Such criticism usually centers around the futility of trying to transplant an elaborate feudal system in a frontier community.[16] Criticism of this nature, however, apparently stems from a misunderstanding of the Fundamental Constitutions and its role in South Carolina's history. To begin with, Lord Ashley and the other proprietors were not impractical utopians bent on establishing feudalism in a virgin land. The Constitutions said nothing at all about vassalage, oaths of homage, military duties, or any of the other characteristics of feudalism. Rather, Ashley hoped to set up a variant form of the manorial system in Carolina; the Constitutions provided for manors, manorial courts, and the equivalent of serfs. But the Carolina proprietors had no intention of imposing such an elaborate system upon the frontier settlement immediately. They regarded the Constitutions not as a plan for instant application, but, in Ashley's words, as "the compasse [we] are to steere by." [17] Ashley and his fellow proprietors planned to put all of the provisions of the "Grand Model," as it was often called, into operation only after Carolina had passed the frontier stage of its development.

As for the second general criticism—that the Fundamental Constitu-

---

[15] Journal of John Locke, Apr. 18–24, 1673, Lovelace Mss., c. 30, fol. 3, Bodleian Lib.; Parker, Introduction to Fundamental Constitutions, *N. C. Charters and Constitutions*, 130–31; the revisions of 1669 and the version of 1670 are in *ibid.*, 153–64, 165–85.

[16] See, e. g., McCrady, *Proprietary Government*, 94–109; Herbert L. Osgood, *The American Colonies in the Seventeenth Century*, 3 vols. (N. Y., 1904–7), II, 208–12; David D. Wallace, *South Carolina: A Short History, 1520–1948* (Chapel Hill, 1951), 25–26.

[17] Ashley to Maurice Mathews, June 20, 1672, Langdon Cheves, ed., *The Shaftesbury Papers and Other Records Relating to Carolina . . . prior to the Year 1676*, in South Carolina Historical Society, *Collections*, 5 (1897), 399, hereafter cited as Cheves, ed., *Shaftesbury Papers*.

tions had little effect on South Carolina—it, too, is misleading in at least two respects. In the first place, the Constitutions provided for a policy of religious toleration in Carolina that profoundly affected the colony's history for half a century by attracting many religious dissenters to it. In the second place, the land system proposed in the Constitutions had far-reaching effects. Ashley hoped to foster a landed aristocracy in the colony, and by the middle of the eighteenth century a landed gentry had emerged. Because a similar society developed in Virginia without such assistance, it might be argued that a landed gentry would have developed without the aid of the Fundamental Constitutions. Nevertheless, no one can deny that the Constitutions, with its provisions for a local aristocracy and incredibly large land grants, speeded the development of a landed gentry in South Carolina.

III

At the heart of the Fundamental Constitutions lay Lord Ashley's dream of creating in Carolina his version of the perfect society, one in which power and property preserved "the Balance of Government" between aristocracy and democracy. Ashley set forth his social and political theories in the preamble, proposing to maintain "the interest of the Lords Proprietors with Equality" by avoiding the dangers of "erecting a numerous Democracy"; such a balanced government would be "most agreeable to the Monarchy under which we live." "It is as bad," he wrote later, "as a state of Warr for men that are in want to have the makeing Laws over Men that have Estates." [18] At the same time, Ashley could not tolerate the possibility that the government of Carolina might fall into the hands of an irresponsible upper class, and he tried to devise a system that would force the nobility which exercised political leadership to develop a sense of *noblesse oblige*. He agreed with the political philosopher James Harrington, who believed that "a nobility of gentry overbalancing a popular Government is the utter bane and destruction of it, as a nobility or gentry in a popular Government not overbalancing it, is the very life and soul of it." [19]

Ashley proposed to create an aristocracy that would include both the proprietors in England and a local nobility in Carolina. He would have preferred that the proprietors migrate to America and take their places at the head of the ruling class, but he realized that such a

[18] Ashley to Governor and Council, June 10, 1675, *ibid.*, 468; Parker, ed., *N. C. Charters and Constitutions*, 132.
[19] Andrews, *Colonial Period*, III, 213 n.

development was unlikely. As a compromise, he undertook to give each proprietor a direct voice in the government of the colony through the agency of a deputy. The oldest proprietor would automatically assume the office of palatine, the chief position among the proprietors, and his deputy would become the governor in America. As for the local aristocracy, the royal charter of 1665 empowered the proprietors to grant titles of nobility and the Fundamental Constitutions provided for the creation of two orders of nobles, the higher rank to be called landgraves and the lower cassiques. In order to force these noblemen to accept their responsibilities in making and enforcing laws, the Constitutions established penalties for those who refused to do so; irresponsible nobles might lose the income from their estates or even forfeit their estates and their titles.[20]

One of the primary responsibilities of the nobility was the administration of the colony, for which Ashley devised an elaborate scheme of eight administrative courts. Seven were to manage specific executive matters, such as finance and defense; each would be composed of a proprietor or his deputy and six councilors, all of whom were required to be noblemen. The highest court was to be the palatine's court, and its members were to be the eight proprietors or their deputies; this court was to supervise the work of the other courts. All members of the eight administrative courts—the palatine, the other proprietors, and the forty-two councilors—would form the Grand Council, which would settle disputes between courts and prepare legislation for the parliament.

The system of land ownership provided for in the Fundamental Constitutions reflected a corollary to Ashley's aristocratic preference. He accepted Harrington's dictum that power follows landed property, and when he formulated a land system for Carolina, he tried to make sure that the nobles would be large landowners.[21] The Constitutions directed that Carolina be divided into counties, each consisting of 480,000 acres. Each county in turn would be divided into forty 12,000-acre tracts. Each of the eight proprietors was to own one 12,000-acre seignory in every county. In each county there was to be a resident aristocracy of one landgrave, who was entitled to four baronies of 12,000 acres, and two cassiques, each of whom was to receive two baronies. Thus, the nobility would own two-fifths of the land in every

[20] Unless otherwise noted, this description of the Fundamental Constitutions applies equally to the original draft, Ashley's revisions in 1669, and the version of Mar. 1670. All quotations are from the first draft.

[21] On Harrington's influence, see H. F. Russell Smith, *Harrington and His Oceana* (Cambridge, Eng., 1914), 157–61.

county, and the remaining three-fifths of the land was reserved for the people. The people's land would consist of twenty-four 12,000-acre tracts called "colonies," and every group of six colonies would be organized as a precinct. All land was to be held in free and common socage and granted by deed. The grantee could bequeath or convey his rights to someone else, but each freeholder had to pay the proprietors a quit rent of 1d. per acre every year. The Constitutions stated further that freeholders must pay their rents in silver and that the first rent payments were due in 1689.

Similarly, the Carolina judicial system represented another phase of Ashley's attempt to establish an aristocratic government. His hope was to keep the judiciary from falling into the hands of lawyers, who might otherwise usurp the prerogatives of the nobility. The Constitutions banned the professional practice of law, deeming it a "base and vile thing." [22] In order to keep the laws relatively simple, the Constitutions declared that all legislation would automatically become void sixty years after enactment; it also prohibited legal commentaries, because "multiplicity of Comments, as well as of laws, have great inconveniences, and Serve only to obscure and perplex." [23] In short, Ashley hoped to establish a legal system simple enough to be administered by aristocrats untrained in the law.

Ashley modified his aristocratic system somewhat when he came to local courts. The Constitutions provided for manorial courts on every barony or seignory for the tenants he expected to settle there, but he also provided for precinct and county courts in the areas occupied by freeholders, with membership open to freemen, provided only that they meet minimum property qualifications. But the county and precinct courts were weakened by provisions stripping them of the traditional administrative duties of local courts in England. The Constitutions entrusted all executive responsibilities to the administrative courts, which were made up only of nobles; Carolina's local courts were to be limited to the trial of civil and criminal cases.

When Lord Ashley was working on the Fundamental Constitutions, he was trying to establish a balanced government, one which not only guaranteed the rights of the aristocracy but which also protected the rights of all men, even from encroachment by the proprietors. Ashley believed that the Constitutions would achieve exactly that kind of balanced government. "By our Frame," he observed a few years later,

[22] Parker, ed., *N. C. Charters and Constitutions*, 145.
[23] *Ibid.*, 147.

"noe bodys power noe not of any of the Proprietors themselves were they there, is soe great as to be able to hurt the meanest man in the Country." [24] The Fundamental Constitutions carefully enumerated such judicial rights as trial by jury and freedom from double jeopardy. Despite the proprietors' fear of "a numerous Democracy," they gave freemen a limited share in the legislative process. Freeholders who owned at least fifty acres could vote for representatives to the Carolina parliament, but the delegates were required to own a minimum of 500 acres. The parliament, which would be composed of the eight proprietors or their deputies, one landgrave and two cassiques from each county, and one freeman from each precinct, would sit together as a unicameral assembly. Although each man would have one vote, the distribution of membership tipped the scales toward the nobility rather than the people's representatives. With four precincts in each county, freemen would always outnumber the local nobles, but the proprietors or their deputies and the nobles acting together could command a majority in the parliament until the time when nine or more counties had been created. The Constitutions limited the power of the popular element in parliament in other ways as well, for it could only accept or reject laws proposed by the Grand Council; it could not amend them or initiate legislation itself. Moreover, any legislation enacted by parliament could be disallowed by the palatine's court. Finally, the parliament would have no executive powers, which were entrusted solely to the administrative courts.

Although the Fundamental Constitutions thus limited the political power of the freemen, Ashley opposed absolutely rigid class lines and made it possible for an ambitious man to rise socially. If a freeman accumulated an estate of at least 3,000 acres, he could petition the proprietors to proclaim his estate a manor and grant him manorial rights. Should a vacancy occur in the ranks of the landgraves and cassiques, a lord of a manor would be eligible for elevation to the nobility.

Two classes of inhabitants in Carolina were to enjoy not even the limited rights of freemen. In addition to tenants who were expected to occupy the manorial estates, Ashley assumed that the great feudal domains would be inhabited in part by leetmen bound to the land for life in a status not unlike that of a medieval serf, men whose children

[24] Ashley to Maurice Mathews, June 20, 1672, Cheves, ed., *Shaftesbury Papers*, 399.

would inherit their father's status and whose service would be part of any transfer, by sale or otherwise, of the estate from one manor lord to another. It is not clear why Ashley assumed that there would be candidates for this social station among colonists who were to be recruited chiefly from the West Indian and other American colonies. Perhaps he had doubts himself, for when he revised the Constitutions in 1669 he amended it to make sure that no man became a leetman except by his own consent.[25] At the bottom of the social scale were the slaves, who recently had come to play an important role in the economy of the West Indian colonies and Virginia. Ashley, who had earlier invested in slave-trading ventures, inserted in all drafts of the Fundamental Constitutions a provision which became of crucial importance in shaping the development of Carolina. "Every Freeman of Carolina," it was stipulated, "shall have absolute power and authority over his Negro Slaves, of what opinion or Religion soever." [26]

Finally, a significant feature of the Fundamental Constitutions was the care which Ashley took to identify Carolina with the principle of religious toleration. Colonists in Carolina had only to "acknowledge a God, and that God is publicly and Solemnly to be worshipped." If seven persons agreed to form a church and to state their doctrines publicly, the proprietors would allow them to worship as they pleased. The policy would apply to all religions, even to "heathens, Jews, and other dissenters," but the promise of religious freedom did not end there. Every political office was to be open to members of every religion; registries of births, marriages, and deaths were to be kept by the agencies of the secular government, instead of by the church, as in England; the Constitutions forbade the use of "reproachful, Reviling, or abusive language against the Religion of any Church or Profession"; and the Constitutions permitted men to meet the requirement for an oath of office and testimony in a trial by making an affirmation rather than by swearing an oath, this last a point of particular importance for the rapidly growing sect of Quakers.[27] Unfortunately, not all of the proprietors shared Ashley's religious liberalism, and when they reviewed the Constitutions in 1670 they insisted on adding a clause proclaiming the Church of England to be the "National Religion" of Carolina and empowering the Carolina parliament to levy taxes for its support.[28] Even so, Carolina still offered a greater

[25] Parker, ed., *N. C. Charters and Constitutions*, 155–56.
[26] *Ibid.*, 164; the words "power and" were added in Ashley's revisions of 1669.
[27] *Ibid.*, 148–50.
[28] *Ibid.*, 181.

degree of religious freedom than England or any other American colony, with the single exception of Rhode Island.[29]

The Fundamental Constitutions was a plan for the future, and the proprietors, being practical men, accepted it as such. In 1669 and 1670, while the Constitutions was still under consideration, the proprietors turned to the problem of a temporary government. They set up the palatine's court in London on October 21, 1669, with the Duke of Albemarle as the first palatine and Ashley as chief justice,[30] but they left the rest of the Constitutions for later implementation. Sketching the framework of a temporary government, their instructions to the first governor ordered him to set up a temporary Grand Council which would include the governor, the proprietary deputies, and five freemen to be chosen by parliament from its own membership; twenty freemen were to be elected to form with the council a parliament as soon as the settlers had landed in Carolina. The parliament would have the power only to approve legislation proposed by the Grand Council; all other powers of government were vested in the council, including all judicial powers and, if necessary, the right to issue decrees which would have the force of law.[31]

In no way did the proprietors display their practical knowledge of colonial affairs more than in their provisions for the distribution of land. They understood the attraction land would have for prospective colonists, and they offered liberal terms of settlement by authorizing the governor and council to make headright grants on a sliding scale. Every settler in the first fleet was entitled to 150 acres of land for each adult male he took to Carolina, including himself, and 100 acres for each female and for each male under sixteen. Colonists who arrived during the first year of settlement would receive 100 and 70 acres, respectively, while men arriving after that could claim 70 and 60 acres. As a further inducement, the proprietors promised to accept quit rent payments in commodities, rather than silver. The proprietors also directed the governor and council to force the people to settle in towns, as in New England, rather than allowing them to disperse on isolated farms. Township settlement, according to Lord Ashley, was

[29] John Lawson, *Lawson's History of North Carolina* . . . , ed. Frances L. Harriss (Richmond, 1937), xxvii. This work is best known under Lawson's original title, *A New Voyage to Carolina* . . . (London, 1709); it is hereafter cited as Lawson, *Carolina*, ed. Harriss. [Thomas Nairne], *A Letter from South Carolina* (London, 1710), 18.

[30] Minutes of Proprietors' Meeting, Oct. 29, 1669, Cheves, ed., *Shaftesbury Papers*, 155.

[31] Instructions to Governor and Council, July 27, 1669, *ibid.*, 119–21.

the "Cheife thing that hath given New England soe much the advantage over Virginia," and he especially wanted Carolina to avoid the "Inconvenience and Barbarisme of scattered Dwellings." [32]

IV

While Lord Ashley and the other proprietors carefully considered their plans in the summer of 1669, Captain West's fleet dropped down from London to the Downs, where contrary winds forced them to lie at anchor for about ten days. Finally, some time after August 17, the winds changed and the *Carolina,* the *Port Royal,* and the *Albemarle* sailed to Kinsale, Ireland, where Captain West hoped to recruit a number of servants. He not only failed to enlist anyone, but lost four passengers who ran away. The fiasco at Kinsale set the pattern for the rest of the voyage. The fleet arrived at Barbados without incident, but there in November a gale blew the *Albemarle* aground and sank it. Sir John Yeamans, the leader of the earlier Barbadian colony on the Cape Fear to whom the proprietors had sent a blank commission for the governor's post in the new colony with instructions to fill in his own name or that of another of his choice, now replaced West as commander of the expedition. Yeamans rented another sloop, the *Three Brothers,* and set sail for Carolina. This time a severe storm separated the ships, wrecking the *Port Royal* in the Bahamas and blowing the *Carolina* to Bermuda, the *Three Brothers* to Virginia. In Bermuda, the command suddenly shifted again, when Sir John Yeamans decided to return to Barbados and named William Sayle, a Bermudian, to take his place as governor. In February 1670 the settlers and their new governor left Bermuda, but bad weather again battered the fleet. Not until March 1670 did the tempest-tossed emigrants finally reach Port Royal, their ranks reduced to less than a hundred colonists. Two months later the *Three Brothers* limped into port after losing its way again. It had missed the settlement and sailed south to that part of the coast which later would be Georgia, where Spanish soldiers captured the ship's captain, Lord Ashley's deputy, and several other passengers. Everything considered, it was not an auspicious beginning for the new colony. [33]

[32] *Ibid.,* 121–23; Ashley to Sir John Yeamans, Apr. 10, Sept. 18, 1671, *ibid.,* 315, 344.
[33] Craven, *Southern Colonies,* 342–44; McCrady, *Proprietary Government,* 115–25.

Part I

THE AGE OF
THE GOOSE CREEK MEN
1670–1712

Very soon after the first settlement of South Carolina the government of the colony came to be dominated by a group of men known eventually as the Goose Creek men—immigrants from Barbados who had settled near Goose Creek, a tributary of the Cooper River. Representing the largest immigration into the colony during its first decade, and contemptuous of less experienced colonists, they undertook to retain control of the provincial government and so determined the course of South Carolina's politics for almost half a century. The Goose Creek men, who belonged to the Church of England, quickly encountered political opposition from a group of religious dissenters, who had been attracted to South Carolina by the proprietors' guarantee of toleration. Proprietary policy changed markedly between 1670 and 1712, but the antagonism between these two factions remained constant.

Throughout the seventeenth century the Goose Creek men consistently opposed proprietary policy. They had no sympathy for Lord Ashley's plans for Carolina, including religious toleration, but were concerned mostly with making their own fortunes. They also engaged in several practices that the proprietors condemned, notably an Indian slave trade and a trade with pirates. By contrast, the dissenters supported the proprietors and were willing to accept Ashley's Fundamental Constitutions in order to secure religious toleration in the colony. The proprietors tried repeatedly to break the power of the

Goose Creek men by replacing them with dissenters and other proprietary men, but their attempts to reconstruct the provincial government merely provoked political disorder. The proprietors finally were forced to compromise with the Goose Creek men in the last years of the century so that they could restore order to the government.

After 1700, the proprietors reversed their policy on religious toleration, and launched a concerted effort to establish the Church of England as the state church of South Carolina. By doing so they revived factionalism in South Carolina and forced a realignment of the parties, the dissenters going into opposition and the Goose Creek men switching to support the proprietors. Once again, however, the proprietors discovered that they could not force their wishes upon the colony, and once again they were forced to compromise, this time with the dissenters.

CHAPTER II

THE RISE OF THE BARBADIANS
1670–1682

For seven months the colonists who landed at Port Royal in March
1670 had been continuously at sea, except for short layovers at Ireland,
Barbados, and Bermuda. Nor was the stay at Port Royal long, for on
the advice of friendly Indians they immediately moved northward to
Albemarle Point on the west bank of the Ashley River, where they
began to build the town which the proprietors named Charles Town.[1]
It had been a wearying experience, but the settlers turned to the tasks
of colonizing with optimism. "Though we are (att present) under
some straight for want of provision . . . ," Governor Sayle reported,
"yet, we doubt not (through the goodness of God) of recruits from
sundry places," and one of the colonists, happy that the long journey
from England had ended, recklessly predicted that "this is likely to bee
one of the best setlements in the Indies." [2] In time it would be, but first
many difficulties had to be overcome.

I

The colonists fully realized, as one of them observed, that they had
"settled in the very chaps of the Spaniard." [3] The Carolina settlement

[1] Nicholas Carteret's Relation, 1670, Ashley to Joseph West, Nov. 1, 1670, Cheves,
ed., *Shaftesbury Papers*, 168, 210. It was not until 1680, at the direction of the proprietors, that the colonists moved the town to the peninsula between the Ashley and
Cooper rivers, the site of modern Charleston.
[2] Sayle to Ashley, June 25, 1670, Stephen Bull to Ashley, Sept. 16, 1670, Cheves,
ed., *Shaftesbury Papers*, 171, 193.
[3] Joseph Dalton to Ashley, Sept. 9, 1670, *ibid.*, 183.

lay much closer to the Spanish fort at St. Augustine than to the Virginia settlements on the Chesapeake, or even to the recently established community of Englishmen on Albemarle Sound. The new colony had extended the frontier of England's possessions in North America far to the south, an exposed outpost on a new frontier of international conflict. The governor of Spanish Florida was quick to accept the challenge. In the summer of 1670 he dispatched three ships and a large Indian war party, reportedly led by a Spanish friar, for the purpose of expelling the interlopers at Albemarle Point. Fortunately, a storm drove off the ships, and the Indians withdrew without a skirmish. Abortive though it was, the Spanish attack underlined the need for continuing efforts to strengthen the colony's defenses, a task to which the colonists thereafter devoted much of their time. The proprietors had sent an ample supply of arms and ammunition, and by autumn the settlers had built a palisade which surrounded the town at Albemarle Point. To make the best use of the men available the governor and council divided the population into militia squads, assigned each unit a rallying point in the event of an attack, instructed the colonists in the use of arms, and imposed a fairly effective discipline on the militia.[4] Such measures gave the English settlers at least a greater sense of security, but the specter of a major Spanish invasion still haunted the colony.

Of continuing concern too was the shortage of food. Most of the first settlers were townsmen who knew "nothing of planting." Thomas Newe, who migrated to Carolina in 1682, reported accurately that "the first Planters . . . were most of them tradesmen, poor and wholy ignorant of husbandry . . . their whole business was to clear a little ground to get Bread for their Familyes."[5] Drought and crop failure added to their difficulty, and not until 1674 did the colony enjoy a good harvest. In the winter of 1672 the council limited each man to five quarts of peas a week and prohibited all non-agricultural work. To alleviate the shortages, the proprietors advanced food and other supplies on credit. Even the most prominent among the colonists went heavily into debt; a list of debtors in June 1672 included a majority of

[4] Governor and Council to Proprietors, Sept. 9, 1670, *ibid.*, 178–79; Verner W. Crane, *The Southern Frontier, 1670–1732* (Durham, 1928), 10–11; Oct. 26, 1671, June 28, 1672, Alexander S. Salley, Jr., ed., *Journal of the Grand Council of South Carolina, 1671–1692*, 2 vols. (Columbia, 1907), I, 10–12, 35–37.

[5] Henry Brayne to Ashley, Nov. 9, 1670, Cheves, ed., *Shaftesbury Papers*, 214; "Letters of Thomas Newe, 1682," Alexander S. Salley, Jr., ed., *Narratives of Early Carolina, 1650–1708*, in *Original Narratives of Early American History*, ed. J. Franklin Jameson (N. Y., 1911), 184.

the deputies, half of the council, and a third of the parliament. The accumulating indebtedness became an early irritant between colonists and proprietors, especially when the settlers refused to post bonds.[6]

Carolina's inability to produce its own food also helped to frustrate the proprietors' hopes for the prompt development of a marketable staple. They well understood the importance of finding some staple crop, like tobacco or sugar, which could easily be marketed in England. Accordingly, they had directed Joseph West in 1669 to set up an experimental farm to be staffed with thirty servants at their own expense. They had also furnished cotton and indigo seed, ginger roots, sugar cane, vines, and olive sets for testing. Other colonists had arrived with seedlings for orange, lemon, lime, pomegranate, and fig trees.[7] Except for indigo, the early experiments failed, and it would be many years before the Carolina settlers could compete successfully with the established indigo producers of the West Indies. As Sir Peter Colleton, Barbadian heir to the Colleton share in the proprietary, pointed out, the colonists, as long as they had to struggle to produce their own food, would never be able to spare the time for serious experimentation with staple crops.[8]

Agricultural failure was not the only problem of the Charles Town settlers. Governor William Sayle, an old Puritan, was distressed by the low moral standards of his people, and in his first letter to Lord Ashley he expounded at length on the need for a "Godly and orthodox" minister. The council shared Sayle's distress; when it learned in July 1670 "how much the Sabboth Day was Prophanely violated, and of divers other grand abuses, practised by the people, to the greate dishonour of God Almighty," it immediately adopted an ordinance regulating conduct on the Sabbath, the first law passed in South Carolina.[9] The governor and council were even more concerned about losing population than about loose morals. Many colonists, discouraged by the lack of food and difficult living conditions, deserted the colony as soon as they could. Running away, even by proprietary deputies, reached such alarming proportions that the council was

[6] Feb. 10, June 6, 1672, Salley, ed., *Grand Council Journal*, I, 26–27, 34; Abstract of Joseph West to Sir Peter Colleton, Sept. 15, 1670, Cheves, ed., *Shaftesbury Papers*, 264.

[7] Instructions to West, [July 1669], Stephen Bull to Ashley, Sept. 16, 1670, Cheves, ed., *Shaftesbury Papers*, 125–27, 193; Craven, *Southern Colonies*, 336–37.

[8] Colleton to John Locke, Mar. 3, 1673, Lovelace Mss., c. 6, fol. 213, Bodleian Lib.; see also Lewis Cecil Gray, *History of Agriculture in the Southern United States to 1860*, 2 vols. (Washington, 1933), I, 291.

[9] Sayle to Ashley, June 25, 1670, Council to Proprietors, Mar. 21, 1671, Cheves, ed., *Shaftesbury Papers*, 171–73, 291.

forced to take action. In 1671 it ordered all shipmasters entering Carolina to post bond that they would not carry off any inhabitant without a special license. The next year the council decreed that every person planning to leave Carolina must give twenty-one days' notice.[10]

For all of Carolina's hardships, the colony grew. The proprietors had launched a vigorous campaign to recruit settlers which was especially successful in attracting immigrants from the older colonies. As early as February 1671, 110 Barbadians moved to Carolina, the vanguard of a large and significant migration. Before the year was out they were joined by 96 settlers from New York. By January 1672 the population had nearly quadrupled, the council's secretary reporting that the population had grown in less than two years to a total of 406, which included 69 women and 59 children.[11] Each year thereafter brought more immigrants.

Another development of significance was the beginning made in trade with the Indians. The English exchanged trinkets, guns, ammunition, clothing, and rum for deer and beaver skins, which became the first staple in Carolina's export trade. At first the Carolinians traded with the loosely allied coastal tribes of the Cusabos and Coosas, who had been fighting a losing war against the well-armed Spaniards and the Westoes, a large and reputedly man-eating Indian nation living along the Savannah River which had acquired arms and ammunition through trade with Virginia. The Cusabos and Coosas quickly agreed to an alliance with the English but were not always reliable; in 1671 the Coosas stole so much corn that the governor and council declared war on them. But an English expedition captured a few Indians, and the chastized Coosas became more amenable.[12]

In dealing with the Indians the colony's most valuable agent was Dr. Henry Woodward, who started South Carolina's Indian trade almost single-handedly.[13] A young English surgeon, he had accompanied Captain Robert Sandford on his exploration of the South Carolina coast in 1666 and had volunteered to remain at Port Royal to learn the

---

[10] Dec. 23, 1671, May 26, 1672, Salley, ed., *Grand Council Journal*, I, 20, 32–33.

[11] Joseph West to Ashley, Mar. 2, 1671, Locke's Memoranda, [1671], Joseph Dalton to Ashley, Jan. 20, 1672, Cheves, ed., *Shaftesbury Papers*, 266–67, 352, 381–82.

[12] Chapman J. Milling, *Red Carolinians* (Chapel Hill, 1940), 35–36, 39–40, 47; John R. Swanton, *The Indians of the Southeastern United States* (Smithsonian Institution, Bureau of American Ethnology, *Bulletin*, no. 137 [1946]), 124, 129; on the trouble with the Coosas, see Sept. 27, Oct. 2, 1671, Salley, ed., *Grand Council Journal*, I, 8–9; Ashley to Thomas Gray, June 20, 1672, Cheves, ed., *Shaftesbury Papers*, 400.

[13] Crane, *Southern Frontier*, 6–7; Herbert E. Bolton and Mary Ross, *The Debatable Land: A Sketch of the Anglo-Spanish Contest for the Georgia Country* (Berkeley, 1925), 29–31, 46.

Indians' language while Sandford returned to England. Woodward lived with the Indians for four years before joining the settlement at Charles Town, and then acted as the colony's interpreter in negotiating alliances and trade agreements with the Indians.

In 1674 Woodward was instrumental in extending South Carolina's Indian trade beyond the small coastal tribes. Trade with the large Westo nation held out the promise of larger profits, but relations between Charles Town and the Westoes were poor because of the English alliance with the Coosas and Cusabos. In 1672 rumors of an attack by the Westoes had led the council to dispatch an expedition of thirty men, and the council in 1673 had actually voted in favor of a war against the tribe. In 1674, however, Lord Ashley ordered Henry Woodward to seek a treaty with either the Westoes or the Kasihtas, another large tribe which lived between Carolina and Florida. In October, shortly after receiving Ashley's letter, Woodward accidently met a party of Westoes and made a daring journey alone with them deep into their own country. There he signed a treaty of alliance against Spain and opened the way for a large trade in deerskins, furs, and Indian slaves.[14]

The Westo treaty of 1674 marked a turning point in South Carolina's early history. Freed from the fear of war, the colonists expanded their Indian trade and finally mastered the techniques of frontier agriculture. Although subsistence farming was the general rule, they managed to produce some surplus food for export, specializing in cattle, which they raised by the thousands. The settlers also learned to extract profits from the pine forests which surrounded them; in addition to barrels and other lumber products, they began on a small scale to make pitch, tar, and other naval stores. By 1680 South Carolina had developed an intricate pattern of production and trade, selling their furs and naval stores to England and shipping meat, lumber, and Indian slaves to the West Indies in exchange for rum and sugar. Since the colony's production of naval stores was limited, the Indian trade was the key to the colony's emerging prosperity, because furs were the only export that commanded a ready market in England.[15] As South Carolina's prosperity increased, so did its

[14] Salley, ed., *Grand Council Journal*, July 2, 1672, Oct. 4, 1673, I, 38, 64; Crane, *Southern Frontier*, 16–17.

[15] Alexander Hewatt, *An Historical Account of the Rise and Progress of the Colonies of South Carolina and Georgia* (London, 1779), in Bartholomew R. Carroll, ed., *Historical Collections of South Carolina*, 2 vols. (N. Y., 1836), I, 88–90. On the importance of the Indian trade, see Earl of Craven to [Lords of Trade, July 1687], *Records in the British Public Record Office Relating to South Carolina, 1663–1710*, 5 vols. (Columbia, 1928–47), II, 200, hereafter cited as *S. C. Pub. Recs.*

population. By 1683 there were about 1,000 men in the colony, with some 200 families living in Charles Town. [16]

Although the colony was beginning to prosper from its rather diversified economic activity, both colonists and proprietors still hoped to develop an especially profitable staple, and farming experiments continued. When the first substantial group of Huguenots arrived in 1680, they came with a special commission from the proprietors to begin the production of silk and wine.[17] Perhaps it was this preoccupation with the search for a profitable staple that accounts for South Carolina's unusual preference for Negro labor long before a plantation economy had developed. In other English colonies on the mainland, including Virginia, the preference at first had been for white servants and they turned to Negro labor only after many years had passed. In South Carolina the order was reversed with proprietors and colonists alike giving early recognition to the part that Negro labor might play in the development of the colony. There can be little doubt that the experience of many of the Carolina settlers in the West Indies counted heavily, as is suggested by the guarantee in the Fundamental Constitutions that no emigrant to Carolina would lose authority over his Negro slaves. That experience had demonstrated that Negro labor was cheaper; not only was the Negro commonly bound to a lifetime of servitude but his owner could skimp on the cost for his maintenance, especially for his clothes.[18] Whatever the colonists' reasons, Carolinians expressed their preference for Negro slave labor far in advance of the development of a major agricultural staple. "Without [Negro slaves] a Planter can never do any great matter," the author of a promotional tract wrote in 1682, and a settler reiterated the same theme when he told a friend that "negroes were more desirable than English servants." [19]

Even so, South Carolinians did not import Negroes in large numbers until after the introduction of rice in the 1690's; most of those in the colony prior to that time were brought from Barbados by their owners. Instead, the colonists met the demands for cheap labor by exploiting

[16] John Crafford, *A New and Most Exact Account of the Fertile and Famous Colony of Carolina* (Dublin, 1683) , 4–5.

[17] Craven, *Southern Colonies*, 355–56.

[18] Wilson, "An Account of Carolina," in Salley, ed., *Narratives of Carolina*, 172; on slavery in Barbados, see M. Eugene Sirmans, "The Legal Status of the Slave in South Carolina, 1670–1740," *Journal of Southern History*, 28 (1962) , 462–64.

[19] Samuel Wilson, "An Account of the Province of Carolina" (London, 1682), in Salley, ed., *Narratives of Carolina*, 174; "Letter from Edmund White to Joseph Morton," Feb. 29, 1688, *South Carolina Historical and Genealogical Magazine*, 30 (1929) , 2.

the native Indian population. Indian slavery was known in all of the colonies, but South Carolina enslaved far more Indians than did any other English colony. The whites usually acquired these slaves by persuading their Indian allies to make slave raids on other tribes, but the Carolinians were not above making an occasional raid of their own. Although the colonists exported most of the captured Indians to the West Indies, they kept many of them for service in the colony.[20]

II

Throughout the early years of failure the Carolina proprietors never lost faith in their colony. In fact, adversity only strengthened the determination of the leading proprietors. Lord Ashley grew so enamored of the Carolina venture that he once referred to the colony as "my Darling." Sir Peter Colleton remained optimistic even in 1673, when the food shortage was at its worst. He compared Carolina with the Chesapeake and New England colonies and predicted that "our being able to produce many comodityes that they cannot, and all their own cheaper than they can, must force them in time all to come to us." [21] Some of the proprietors were less enthusiastic. Lord Berkeley, the Earl of Craven, and Carteret attended meetings of the palatine's court regularly, but they left most of the work to Ashley and Colleton. The heirs to the Albemarle and Clarendon shares attended none of the meetings, but they, along with the others in England, agreed in 1674 to invest £100 each per year in the development of the colony.[22] Sir William Berkeley, governor of Virginia, was the only completely inactive proprietor. An agreement was made with him in 1672 by which he would receive sole title to the Albemarle Sound region and relinquish his share in the rest of Carolina. The deal apparently fell through, however, because Berkeley's widow inherited his proprietorship after his death in 1677.[23]

The palatine's court in London functioned much more smoothly than did the provincial government in Charles Town. William Sayle's appointment as governor had not been popular; his age (nearly

[20] Almon W. Lauber, *Indian Slavery in Colonial Times within the Present Limits of the United States* (N. Y., 1913) , 105–6, 240.

[21] Ashley to Colleton, Nov. 27, 1672, Cheves, ed., *Shaftesbury Papers*, 416; Colleton to Locke [1673], Lovelace Mss., c. 6, fol. 216, Bodleian Lib.

[22] Ashley to William Sayle, Apr. 10, 1671, Articles between the Lords Proprietors, May 6, 1674, Cheves, ed., *Shaftesbury Papers*, 311, 432; on attendance, see Locke's Journal, Lovelace Mss., c. 30, *passim*, Bodleian Lib.

[23] Locke's Journal, Mar. 29, 1672, Lovelace Mss., c. 30, fol. 2, Bodleian Lib. Powell, *Proprietors of Carolina*, 9.

eighty), his ill health, and his dissenting religion stirred dissatisfaction. Some of his associates charged that his zeal for the spiritual
welfare of the colony led him to ignore the settlers' physical needs.[24]
William Owen, later deputy of Sir Peter Colleton, and William
Scrivener, deputy for Lord Berkeley, led the opposition. They had
objected while still in Bermuda on the way to Port Royal to Sayle's
appointment and had even tried unsuccessfully to persuade their
fellow passengers to sue Sir John Yeamans for turning over the command to Sayle. It is significant that when the governor, after the land-
ing in Carolina, called the freemen of the colony together to elect five
members to serve on the council with the proprietary deputies, the
voters rejected Owen in favor of other men. The unhappy Owen
challenged the legality of the election, but he found no opportunity to
win the following he desired until Sayle and the council decided
against calling an election for a parliament. This decision depended
upon the argument that as yet there were not enough freemen in the
colony to meet the requirement, in the governor's instructions, that a
parliament include twenty elected members. Owen accused the
governor of dictatorial repression, scheduled an election on his own,
and as self-constituted clerk recorded the results. The election returns
proved the governor's point; Owen could find only eighteen freemen,
including himself, to sit in the parliament, and when he tried to fill up
the house by declaring two indentured servants elected, he lost his
following. The governor and council, which included the five freemen
earlier elected to it, continued to promulgate orders having the force
of laws while promising a parliament at the first opportunity. Owen
tried again in February 1671, this time telling the people that the
governor and council lacked the power to grant land, but Sayle refuted
the charge by producing his instructions. William Scrivener, Lord
Berkeley's deputy, argued Owen's case so heatedly that he was
suspended from the council by his fellow councilors.[25] It is difficult to
determine Owen's reasons for causing as much fuss as he did, but his
primary motive seems to have been religious. He was an Anglican who
apparently resented living under a dissenting governor, and he
complained especially about Sayle's attempt to improve the moral tone
of South Carolina. Owen also liked to pose as a champion of the rights
of the people, but in the long run he fooled no one. The members of

[24] Sayle to Ashley, June 25, 1670, Stephen Bull to Ashley, Sept. 12, 1670, Cheves,
ed., *Shaftesbury Papers*, 171–73, 195.

[25] Council to Proprietors, Mar. 21, 1671, *ibid.*, 290–95; David D. Wallace, *The
History of South Carolina*, 4 vols. (N. Y., 1934), I, 78–79; for a different view of
Owen and Scrivener, see Osgood, *17th Century*, II, 213–14.

the council were probably correct in dismissing him simply as one who was "alwaies itching to bee in Authority." [26] After the death of Governor Sayle on March 4, 1671, Owen quickly lost his role as a serious troublemaker.

On his deathbed Governor Sayle had picked Joseph West to succeed him as temporary governor until the proprietors made a permanent appointment, and the council approved. Like Sayle, West was a dissenter—probably a Quaker—but he was a practical man who had useful connections with the mercantile community in London; his primary interests lay in developing South Carolina's economy, not in reforming its morals. Everyone recognized his ability, and when he and the council promised to call a parliament as soon as the planting season ended, Owen's bid for power collapsed.[27]

Although Owen remained quiet, Governor West soon had to contend with a much more serious threat to his authority. In a move that foreshadowed the history of South Carolina politics for the next four decades, the Barbadian immigrants in the colony showed an early desire to take over the provincial government. The Barbadians, who by 1671 constituted nearly half the population, were ambitious, experienced, and occasionally unscrupulous men who had little interest in Lord Ashley's dream of erecting a perfect society in Carolina. Trained in the island colony to be enterprising and self-reliant, they were primarily concerned with making their own fortunes. They held West and other proprietary agents who had come from England in contempt, regarding them as inexperienced men who were unfit to manage a colony. The nucleus of a Barbadian party took form early in 1671 around Maurice Mathews, Thomas Gray, and Henry Brayne, a group which received the support, for what it was worth, of the discredited Owen and Scrivener. At first the Barbadians did nothing more than criticize Governor Sayle, Governor West, and other Englishmen who held office, and recommend to the proprietors that these officeholders be replaced by more competent persons. Significantly, all the men they recommended were Barbadians.[28]

[26] Council to Proprietors, Mar. 21, 1671, Cheves, ed., Shaftesbury Papers, 291; see also Owen to Robert Blayney, Mar. 22, 1671, ibid., 300–7.

[27] Council to Ashley, Mar. 4, 1671, Council to Proprietors, Mar. 21, 1671, Cheves, ed., Shaftesbury Papers, 275–77, 295; on West, see Henry A. M. Smith, "Joseph West, Landgrave and Governor," S. C. Hist. Mag., 19 (1918), 189–93; Mabel L. Webber, "Joseph West, Landgrave and Governor," ibid., 40 (1939), 79–80; Byrle J. Osborn, "Governor Joseph West, A Seventeenth Century Forgotten Man Rediscovered," New York Genealogical and Biographical Record, 65 (1934), 202–5.

[28] Henry Brayne to Sir Peter Colleton, Nov. 20, 1670, Thomas Colleton to Sir Peter Colleton, Nov. 23, 1670, Cheves, ed., Shaftesbury Papers, 235–37, 240–41.

When in the summer of 1671 Sir John Yeamans arrived in South
Carolina with about fifty new immigrants from Barbados, he promptly
assumed command of the faction. Yeamans, the son of a Bristol
brewer, had fought in the royalist army during the English Civil Wars
and had attained the rank of major. After the execution of Charles I,
he had moved to Barbados, where he became a leading planter and
politician. No other Barbadian, unless it be Colleton, had been more
forward in promoting earlier efforts to settle Carolina from Barbados.[29] That the proprietors recognized the importance of his earlier
services is nowhere better illustrated than by the blank commission
they had sent by Captain West to Yeamans in 1669 with instructions
that he fill his own name in as governor of the new colony, or that of
another of his choice. After apparently accepting the assignment for
himself, he finally had made Sayle his choice, with results none too
happy for the colony. Perhaps it was this experience which explains
the disenchantment with Yeamans that was expressed by Ashley in the
following words: "If to convert all things to his private profitt be the
marke of able parts Sir John is without a doubt a very judicious
man." [30] But Sir John also had offsetting advantages. He enjoyed the
support of Peter Colleton, and he had been made a landgrave of
Carolina.

Yeamans expected to become governor of South Carolina immediately upon his arrival. As a landgrave he held the highest rank of
any man in the colony, and the Fundamental Constitutions provided
that if none of the proprietors were present in the colony, the senior
landgrave should be the palatine's deputy. West refused to surrender
his office until he received instructions from the proprietors, on the
ground that the Constitutions had not yet been implemented fully.
Yeamans made his next move when West, because of the increase in
population, requested the freemen to elect twenty delegates to a
parliament in July 1671. Yeamans was elected to the parliament and
then chosen speaker. Using his position to attack the governor, he
charged that West's election was unconstitutional and that the existing
council lacked the legal power to pass laws. The parliament broke up
without dislodging West, and Yeamans began to organize a "Barbados
Party" with the assistance of Maurice Mathews, Thomas Gray, and

[29] John P. Thomas, Jr., "The Barbadians in Early South Carolina," S. C. Hist.
Mag., 31 (1930) , 79, 81; Yeamans to Sir Peter Colleton, Nov. 15, 1670, Cheves, ed.,
Shaftesbury Papers, 221–22.

[30] Ashley to Colleton, Nov. 27, 1672, Cheves, ed., Shaftesbury Papers, 416; see also
Ashley to Joseph West, Apr. 27, 1671, ibid., 317; Colleton to Locke, July 22, 1674,
Lovelace Mss., c. 6, foll. 217–18, Bodleian Lib.

William Owen.[31] Yeamans tried again in December 1671, when he went before the council and demanded that it recognize him as governor because he was the only landgrave in Carolina. Although Barbadians controlled the council, it unanimously refused to unseat West until it heard from the proprietors. In accordance with the Fundamental Constitutions, the proprietors decided that a landgrave should be preferred to a commoner and commissioned Yeamans as governor; but they also rewarded West by elevating him to the rank of cassique.

On March 26, 1672, the council proclaimed Yeamans as governor and he assumed the office he had sought for nearly a year.[32] But circumstances kept him from consolidating the position of his party. The colony's food supply ran so low in 1672 and 1673 that the people almost revolted. Yeamans could find no solution except to import more food on the proprietors' account and sell it to the settlers on credit. The proprietors blamed Yeamans for the increasing debt, and Ashley complained that "since he came in we cann hear of nothing but wants and suplys."[33] The proprietors also alleged that Yeamans had charged exorbitant prices for supplies he sold the colonists and that he had tried to reduce the authority of the proprietary deputies. Dissatisfied with Yeamans' administration, the proprietors decided in 1674 to replace him with Joseph West, whom they raised to the dignity of a landgrave in order to re-appoint him governor. Before this news reached South Carolina, however, Governor Yeamans had died, and the council had elected West to succeed him on August 13, 1674.[34]

For a decade thereafter South Carolina was to be relatively free of factional politics. In a remarkably operative truce, West remained undisturbed as governor, while the Barbadians dominated the council and parliament. Their strength in these centers of influence increased during the later years of the decade, as the islanders continued to emigrate in large numbers to Carolina. Among them were such men as James Moore, Arthur Middleton, Robert Daniel, Robert Gibbes, and Bernard Schenkingh, each of whom quickly established himself as a leading figure in local politics. Significantly, nearly all of the Barbadian immigrants were Church of England men.[35]

[31] Locke's Memoranda [1671], Cheves, ed., *Shaftesbury Papers*, 349–50; on the parliament of 1671, see West to Ashley, Sept. 3, 1671, *ibid.*, 337–38.

[32] Dec. 16, 1671, Mar. 26, 1672, Salley, ed., *Grand Council Journal*, I, 18, 29.

[33] Ashley to Colleton, Nov. 27, 1672, Cheves, ed., *Shaftesbury Papers*, 416; see also Hewatt, *Historical Account*, in Carroll, ed., *Hist. Collections of S. C.*, I, 61–62.

[34] Ashley to Yeamans, June 20, 1672, Proprietors to Governor and Council, May 18, 1674, Cheves, ed., *Shaftesbury Papers*, 397, 435–38; Salley, ed., *Grand Council Journal*, Aug. 13, 1674, I, 70.

[35] Thomas, "Barbadians in S. C.," *S. C. Hist. Mag.*, 31 (1930), 88–89.

III

Although the political truce between Governor West and the Barbadians restored harmony to the government of South Carolina, it failed to improve relations between the colonists and the proprietors. During the eight years of West's second administration, from 1674 to 1682, the provincial government repeatedly ignored the proprietors' instructions. As a result, the proprietors became more and more disgusted with the government of the colony, though they made little effort to correct the situation. The discontent of the proprietors was centered on three issues: the repayment of debts to the proprietors, the distribution of land, and the conduct of Indian affairs.

On the question of the debt, the proprietors proposed that the settlers repay them by assuming the responsibility for paying the governor's salary of £100 a year. The plan was sensible, but the colonists ran into trouble when they tried to implement it. The council offered to pay West in land, but he refused. Later he agreed to the council's alternate suggestion of paying him in commodities, but West and the debtors never could agree on the market value of commodities. Thus the debt problem remained unsolved.[36]

The second area of conflict involved the land system. The proprietors had set down the rules for land distribution in their instructions to the surveyor general and in the so-called Agrarian Laws which they had promulgated in 1672, directing the surveyor general to lay out counties along the major rivers with each county containing two 12,000-acre seignories for proprietors, two 12,000-acre baronies for the nobility and six 12,000-acre colonies for the people. The proprietors also had established the procedures for granting land under the headright system. After the colonist had selected an unoccupied tract, he was to inform the governor and council, who would then direct a warrant to the surveyor general ordering him to survey the tract and return a certificate that indicated its location, boundaries, and acreage. When the surveyor returned this plat, the governor and council would examine it to make sure all rules had been obeyed and then issue a grant to the claimant. Finally, the provincial secretary would make the grant official by affixing the great seal of the colony.[37]

[36] Instructions to West, [1674], Proprietors to Governor and Council, Apr. 10, 1677, S. C. Pub. Recs., I, 26–27, 53–59; Sept. 11, Oct. 7, 1675, Salley, ed., Grand Council Journal, I, 75–78; Wallace, History of S. C., I, 94.

[37] Commission to Surveyor General, [July] 1669, Cheves, ed., Shaftesbury Papers, 130–32; Agrarian Laws, June 21, 1672, in William J. Rivers, A Sketch of the History of South Carolina to . . . 1719 (Charleston, 1856), 355–59.

At first the proprietors' trouble with the land system was simply a question of personnel. Florence O'Sullivan, the first surveyor general, was lazy and incompetent, a "very dissencious troublesome Mann," according to one settler, an "ill natured buggerer of children," according to another.[38] O'Sullivan laid out only a few lots in Charles Town and did such a poor job that the council resorted to the expedient of allowing O'Sullivan to continue in office while John Culpeper, a more competent surveyor, did the actual work. The two men were to split O'Sullivan's fees.[39] Culpeper later succeeded O'Sullivan as surveyor, but he turned out badly, too. Distressed by South Carolina's food shortage, he ran away from the colony in July 1673. South Carolina's search for a competent surveyor ended when the council commissioned Stephen Bull, Stephen Wheelwright, and John Yeamans (the governor's son) as surveyors for the colony. Stephen Bull did most of the work and with the help of Yeamans and Wheelwright restored order to the land office.[40]

Although the land system did not function as planned in many areas, one part of it—the headright system—achieved outstanding success. The liberality of the proprietors in providing for headright grants was undoubtedly a major attraction for many immigrants. Some of them received substantial grants of more than 1,000 acres for bringing large numbers of servants with them. Most settlers, however, received grants of 300 acres or less for themselves and their families. The smaller grants dominate the land records of the first decade and bear witness to the fact that South Carolina was a land of small farmers in its early years.[41] The headright system seems to have been administered efficiently and honestly, although a recent historian has charged that the settlers abused the system by taking out several different land warrants for the same servant. At first glance the accusation seems to be true; Stephen Bull, for example, received warrants for the same five servants on two different occasions. A closer look at the warrants, however, reveals that the council directed the first group of warrants to O'Sullivan and the second group to John

[38] Stephen Bull to Ashley, Sept. 12, 1670, Locke's Memoranda [1670], Cheves, ed., *Shaftesbury Papers*, 195, 248.

[39] Council to Proprietors, Mar. 21, 1671, *ibid.*, 286; Aug. 25, 1671, Salley, ed., *Grand Council Journal*, I, 5.

[40] July 12, 1674, Salley, ed., *Grand Council Journal*, I, 61; Sir Peter Colleton to Locke, [1673], Lovelace Mss., c. 6, foll. 215–16; on Bull's work as surveyor, see M. Eugene Sirmans, Masters of Ashley Hall: A Biographical Study of the Bull Family of Colonial South Carolina (unpubl. Ph.D. diss., Princeton University, 1959), 49–53.

[41] Craven, *Southern Colonies*, 338, 350–52; Alexander S. Salley, Jr., ed., *Warrants for Land in South Carolina, 1672–1711*, 3 vols. (Columbia, 1910–15), I, *passim.*

Yeamans.⁴² Apparently, two sets of warrants exist because O'Sullivan and Culpeper left the land office in such a mess that the council had to issue new warrants to Bull, Yeamans, and Wheelwright.

The system of headright grants was the only part of the proprietors' plan for land distribution that the colonists followed. Most notably, Lord Ashley's plan of dividing the colony into 12,000-acre seignories, baronies, and colonies failed completely. The coast of South Carolina is, as the council reported, too chopped up by rivers, bays, and inlets to permit such a precise division of the land as the proprietors proposed. The colonists, and particularly the surveyors, regarded Ashley's plan as impractical. When Sir John Yeamans once directed John Culpeper to lay out three colonies of 12,000 acres each, Culpeper ignored his orders and no one else bothered to try. The proprietors later attempted to implement their plans by granting 12,000-acre colonies to private companies with the provision that the owners obey the proprietors' instructions, but this scheme failed, too.⁴³ Nor could the proprietors ever persuade the colonists to settle in townships. At first the settlers huddled together near Charles Town, but after a year or two they began to spread out, looking for the most fertile high ground and ignoring both the proprietors' instructions and the swampland that subsequently gained so much value with the introduction of rice. In vain the proprietors protested against the dispersion to widely scattered farms. Even the reduction of headright grants would not make people move closer together. Indeed, nothing seemed to work, and Charles Town, relocated in 1680 at the juncture of the Ashley and the Cooper rivers, remained the only town in South Carolina.⁴⁴

A third failure in the land system disturbed the proprietors less than the first two. Many colonists claimed land without bothering to get a clear title to it. Sometimes they took out a warrant, had the land surveyed, and then failed to have a grant issued; occasionally they just claimed their land by squatters' rights.⁴⁵ The proprietors did not object to this practice at first, probably because they did not intend to

---

⁴² Marshall D. Harris, *Origin of the Land Tenure System in the United States* (Ames, Iowa, 1953), 231; Salley, ed., *Land Warrants*, I, 5-6, 70-71.

⁴³ Council to Proprietors, Mar. 21, 1671, Cheves, ed., *Shaftesbury Papers*, 284; Apr. 23, 1672, Salley, ed., *Grand Council Journal*, I, 31; on grants of colonies, see, e. g., the grant to John Berkeley and others, June 13, 1676, *S. C. Pub. Recs.*, I, 43-47.

⁴⁴ Craven, *Southern Colonies*, 347-49; Hewatt, *Historical Account*, in Carroll, ed., *Hist. Collections of S. C.*, I, 101; Proprietors to Governor and Council, May 19, 1679, *S. C. Pub. Recs.*, I, 82-83.

⁴⁵ May 26, 1672, Salley, ed., *Grand Council Journal*, I, 32. Numerous examples of this practice can be found in the following articles by Henry A. M. Smith: "Old Charles Town and Its Vicinity . . . ," *S. C. Hist. Mag.*, 16 (1915), 1-15, 49-67; "Charleston and Charleston Neck . . . ," *ibid.*, 19 (1918), 3-76.

collect quit rents until 1689 and assumed that land claimants would complete their titles by then.

The frustrations of the land system, combined with the failure of the colonists to repay their debts, so distressed the proprietors that Lord Ashley decided to start a new colony that would be governed strictly according to the Fundamental Constitutions. He planned to establish his new settlement on the Edisto River at a place he named Locke Island, and he sent over an agent in 1675 to make preparations for the colony. As far as Ashley was concerned, the colonists at Charles Town could go their own way until they reformed. In a stinging letter of rebuke to Governor West and the council, he recapitulated all of South Carolina's failings, complaining that the proprietors had spent £9,000 or £10,000 on Carolina but had "purchased nothing but the charge of maintaineing on 5 or 600 people who expect to live upon us." [46] Despite Ashley's new plans, he never followed up his Locke Island project, perhaps because English politics came to absorb so much of his time.

By 1680 the conduct of the Indian trade overshadowed other proprietary complaints. The specific point of conflict was the trade in Indian slaves, which the proprietors, though by no means wholly innocent in its beginnings, condemned as foolish and immoral. Ashley argued that the best Indian policy would be "to get and continue the friendship and assistance of the Indians and make them useful without force or injury"; the alternative might be a major Indian war. The proprietors had gone on record as early as the Agrarian Laws sent to the colony in 1672 in opposition to the enslavement of Indians "upon any occasion or pretence whatsoever." [47] The South Carolina traders had ignored these orders, however, and the proprietors were in a position to insist upon their own right to control the Indian trade. A further inducement to undertake the establishment of such a control came from the prospect that thereby they might recoup some part of their investment in the colony. When trouble developed between the colonists and the Westoes in 1677, the proprietors took this opportunity to proclaim the establishment of a seven-year monopoly of trade with the Westoes and the Kasihtas which could have left the colonists nothing but the limited trade with the coastal Indians.[48]

The attempted proprietary monopoly only caused more trouble, for

[46] Ashley to Governor and Council, June 10, 1675, Cheves, ed., *Shaftesbury Papers*, 466–68; see also Instructions to Andrew Percival, May 23, 1674, *ibid.*, 439–47.

[47] Ashley to Stephen Bull, Aug. 13, 1673, *ibid.*, 427; Agrarian Laws, June 21, 1672, in Rivers, *Hist. of S. C.*, 358.

[48] Crane, *Southern Frontier*, 17–19.

it thoroughly outraged the Indian traders of South Carolina. At the end of the decade, they forced the colony into war against the Westoes, and before the proprietors could intervene, the Indians had been crushed, most of them being killed or captured as slaves. Since the war eliminated the Westoes as a nation, it also ended the proprietary trade monopoly with the tribe. The traders then made treaties with two other large tribes, the Savannahs and the Yamasees, establishing a monopoly for themselves. A recent immigrant to South Carolina, Thomas Newe, reported in 1682 that many colonists objected to the behavior of the Indian traders, but most officeholders followed Governor West's lead; whatever their private thoughts, they held their tongues and their jobs.[49]

IV

Considered separately, the three areas of conflict between colonists and proprietors were matters of grave concern. Considered together, they became even more serious. The proprietors had sunk nearly £10,000 into Carolina without seeing a penny in return. If the colonists could ignore the palatine's instructions on debts, Indian trade, and land distribution, the proprietors could never be sure that any of their orders would be obeyed. Thus, by the end of the first decade of active settlement the proprietors faced nothing less than the collapse of all their plans for Carolina. Their only choice lay between writing off South Carolina as a total loss or trying to revitalize the colony through drastic action of some kind.

[49] *Ibid.*, 19–21; "Letters of Newe," Salley, ed., *Narratives of Carolina*, 183.

CHAPTER III

THE FAILURE OF PROPRIETARY
REFORM
1682–1694

The Carolina proprietors in the early 1680's confronted the problem of a colony that returned neither profits nor obedience to its owners. The proprietors met the challenge by launching two campaigns in 1682, one to recruit new immigrants and the other to reform the government of the colony. They persuaded hundreds of families, mostly religious dissenters, to settle in South Carolina, but their political reforms succeeded only in stirring up an anti-proprietary faction in the province. This Goose Creek party, named for the area where many of its leaders lived, was composed mostly of Barbadians. The ensuing conflict between the proprietors and the Goose Creek men plunged South Carolina into a decade of political chaos, while the colony floundered aimlessly without effective leadership from either party.

I

By 1682 the Carolina proprietorship had changed greatly since Lord Ashley had dispatched the first fleet in 1669. Ashley himself had fallen upon hard times. For his opposition to King Charles he had been imprisoned in the Tower of London on a charge of treason, but he was allowed to escape and fled to Holland for safety in 1682. There he died early the next year. Without Shaftesbury's strong guiding hand, the

35

proprietary venture nearly collapsed. But it was salvaged by two proprietors, the Earl of Craven and a new partner, John Archdale, who carried on when the others died or faltered. Although seventy-six years old in 1682, Craven performed his duties with a sprightliness that belied his age. He outlived the other original proprietors by nearly two decades and kept alive much of the spirit of the early years. Craven was devoted to the English monarchy and opposed to the anti-Catholic Test Act. His devotion to James II was so great that a few years later, during the Glorious Revolution, he was the last of the King's followers to surrender to William of Orange. Archdale, a Quaker who in 1678 had purchased Lord John Berkeley's proprietorship in trust for his infant son, stood at the opposite end of the religious spectrum.[1] Significantly, although Craven and Archdale could scarcely have differed more in their personal, political, and religious beliefs, both favored toleration.

Under the leadership of Craven and Archdale, the proprietors decided they could no longer tolerate their unprofitable and disobedient colony. As a first step they undertook a promotional campaign to recruit new settlers, hoping that the new colonists might not only prove more amenable to proprietary instructions but that they would also stimulate the provincial economy. Between 1682 and 1685 the proprietors commissioned at least ten promotional pamphlets, publishing six in London, two in Dublin for distribution in Ireland, and two in Holland for distribution among the French Huguenots, who had fled France after Louis XIV's revocation of the Edict of Nantes in 1685.[2] The appeal to the Huguenots typified the proprietors' special appeal to persecuted religious minorities, whether in England or on the Continent. English dissenters were more than ready to listen to the promoters' description of Carolina as a religious haven, because Charles II's decisive victory over the Whig party in the early 1680's apparently meant still more religious harassment.

The promotional campaign of the proprietors achieved an extraordinary success. Some five hundred English Presbyterians and Baptists immigrated to South Carolina between 1682 and 1685, settling primarily below Charles Town in Colleton County. In 1684 a group of Presbyterian Scots founded a colony at Port Royal. These groups were led by some of the richest and most prominent dissenters in England and Scotland. Two of the English leaders were Benjamin Blake and

---

[1] Powell, *Proprietors of Carolina*, 25–29, 51–52.

[2] Paschal, Proprietary North Carolina, 163–65. The pamphlets directed to the Huguenots were written in French.

Daniel Axtel; Blake was a younger brother of Oliver Cromwell's naval commander, Admiral Robert Blake, while Axtel was the son of a convicted and executed regicide. The founder of the Scottish colony was Henry Erskine, third Baron Cardross, who came to South Carolina shortly after his release from a four-year term in an English prison for maintaining a Presbyterian chaplain in his household.[3] The dissenters' migration lasted only until 1685, when King James II's pro-Catholic policy began to make life in England easier for Protestant dissenters, too, and their situation was further improved by the passage of the English Act of Toleration in 1689. As the immigration of English dissenters slackened, the revocation of the Edict of Nantes in 1685 made French Huguenots South Carolina's chief source of dissenting immigrants. Perhaps as many as five hundred of them were living in the colony at the end of the century.[4]

As part of their promotional campaign the proprietors twice revised the Fundamental Constitutions of Carolina of 1669, adopting a minor revision on January 12, 1682, which scarcely changed the Constitutions at all, and approving on August 17 a second version that incorporated at least three major changes. The first alteration set up South Carolina's unique system of selecting juries. After a list of all eligible jurymen had been made, each name would be written on a separate piece of paper, and a child would draw the names of the jury from a box. South Carolina adopted this system and preserved it until after the American Revolution. The second change clarified parliamentary procedure and increased the power of the freemen. While Grand Councilors, noblemen, and representatives of the people would still sit together in one house, all laws were to be passed by a majority of each of the three groups in parliament, creating in effect a tricameral assembly. Another important change was designed to appeal to dissenters. Although the Constitutions continued to affirm the primacy of the Church of England, the dissenters were now assured that they would not be taxed for its support. Instead, each congregation, regardless of sect, would have the right to tax its own members. Once more, the proprietors had committed themselves to a broad policy of religious toleration.

[3] Wallace, *History of S. C.*, I, 95–96; Langdon Cheves, "Blake of South Carolina," *S. C. Hist. Mag.*, 1 (1900), 153–57; see also R. C. Browne in DNB s.v. "Axtel, Daniel," and T. F. Henderson in *ibid.* s.v. "Erskine, Henry, third Lord Cardross."

[4] Arthur H. Hirsch, *The Huguenots of Colonial South Carolina* (Durham, 1928), 13–20. Hirsch's estimate is somewhat higher than Wallace's; Wallace, *Hist. of S. C.*, I, 153–54 n. For a contemporary estimate of Huguenot population, see Edward Randolph to Bd. of Trade, Mar. 16, 1699, ed. Robert N. Toppan, Prince Society, *Publications*, 28 (1899), 200.

As before, the proprietors did not demand that the Constitutions be given full effect at once. They again adopted a set of temporary laws for the government of the colony until the Constitutions became fully effective. A major innovation in the temporary laws directed the governor to organize the first institutions of local government in South Carolina. The surveyor general was ordered to lay out three counties: Berkeley, which included Charles Town and was bounded by the Stono River on the south and the Sewee River on the north; Craven, which lay to the north of Berkeley; and Colleton, which lay to the south. The governor and council were to establish a county court in Berkeley at once and to provide similar courts in the other counties when their populations were large enough.[5] Unfortunately, the move toward the development of local agencies of self-government would prove abortive.

The proprietors knew that neither the revision of the Constitutions nor the encouragement of immigration would offer a panacea for South Carolina's troubles. They therefore decided to undertake a number of reforms. They were particularly disturbed by the traffic in Indian slaves, believing that Governor Joseph West was "swayed and governed" by the colony's slave traders—men who boasted that they could "with a bole of punch get who they would Chosen of the parliament and afterwards who they would chosen of the grand Councell." In 1682 they dismissed West and appointed Joseph Morton, a leader among the English dissenters migrating to the colony and a man who was related to both the Axtel and Blake families. The temporary laws of 1682 continued the prohibition against Indian slavery.[6]

At the same time the proprietors moved to correct deficiencies in the administration of the Carolina land system, directing the surveyor general to adhere absolutely to the Fundamental Constitutions in surveying the new counties. They also ordered him to lay out a township on every navigable river and to divide each county into 12,000-acre tracts for seignories, baronies, and colonies.[7] The instructions to the surveyor general contained little that was new, but the proprietors departed radically from their earlier practices when they drew up new rules for the payment of quit rents. Although the

---

[5] Parker, ed., *N. C. Charters and Constitutions,* 186–233; Instructions to Joseph Morton, May 10, 1682, *S. C. Pub. Recs.,* I, 138–57.

[6] Proprietors to Joseph West, Mar. 13, 1685, Proprietors to Governor and Council, Mar. 13, 1685, *S. C. Pub. Recs.,* II, 27, 33; Commission to Joseph Morton, May 18, 1682, *ibid.,* I, 158.

[7] Instructions to Surveyor General, May 10, 1682, *ibid.,* I, 130–37.

proprietors had promised earlier that they would accept rent payments in commodities, they now ordered payment in specie only. This would not have imposed a great hardship on the colonists at that time, because South Carolina, thanks in large part to a flourishing trade with pirates, had an ample supply of silver coins in the 1680's.

A more controversial innovation involved the legal form of land grants; the proprietors substituted an indenture for the simple deed that they had been using. The deed had required only the signatures of the governor and council, but the new indenture did not become valid until the grantee himself signed what was called the counterpart of the indenture. The counterpart contained a re-entry clause, in which the grantee promised to pay quit rents within six months of the date due or forfeit his claim. As an enforcement measure, the proprietors ordered the provincial secretary not to issue a survey warrant until the claimant had agreed to sign the counterpart, and they ordered the surveyor general not to sign a grant until the counterpart was signed. In the event that either official failed to obey these orders, the proprietors directed the governor to suspend him from office.[8] While attempting to strengthen provisions for the collection of rents, the proprietors also liberalized their land policy by offering land for the first time at outright sale. For those who wished to secure large tracts of land without being encumbered with the payment of large rents or being forced to import a great number of servants at one time, the proprietors offered two ways to purchase land. Men who planned to move to South Carolina but were still in England could buy land directly from the proprietors themselves at the price of 1s. per acre. Those who already lived in South Carolina had to pay the same price plus the amount of peas and corn grown on three acres in one year. In either case the grantee was obligated to pay the proprietors only a token quit rent of one peppercorn annually.[9]

In addition to their land reforms, the proprietors turned to the embarrassing problems arising from Carolina's trade with pirates, who put into Charles Town to buy supplies. Many of the pirates had been privateers during the conflicts with Spain and the Anglo-Dutch wars of the 1660's and 1670's, and after the wars they had stepped over the thin line between privateering and piracy. Such men had nearly always been welcome in the colonies, because their raids had been tradi-

---

[8] Form of Indenture, Nov. 20, 1682, Instructions to Governor, Sept. 10, 1685, *ibid.*, I, 228–31, II, 93–95; on specie supply in the 1680's, see *An Essay on Currency, Written in August 1732* (Charles Town, 1734), 6–7.

[9] Instructions to Surveyor General, Mar. 13, 1685, Instructions to James Colleton, Aug. 30, 1686, *S. C. Pub. Recs.*, II. 29, 161–63.

tionally against the Spanish and because they paid for their supplies in gold and silver. Several South Carolinians—most of them Barbadians—had discovered the profits in the pirate trade, and Charles Town had become a frequent port of call for the freebooters. When the Lords of Trade first inquired about the trade in 1684, the proprietors tried to deny its existence. After additional reports reached England, however, the Crown put pressure on the proprietors, and they began to issue directives that forbade the trade.[10]

The proprietors' attempts to reform South Carolina provoked a bitter factionalism, with the colony's leadership dividing into proprietary and anti-proprietary political factions. The basic conflict was between the old settlers and the new immigrants. The proprietors themselves later blamed party politics on "some of the first settlers, who if we are rightly informed have omitted no endeavours to discourage any people of worth that have come amongst you." [11] Most of the old settlers were Barbadian Anglicans, while most of the recent immigrants were English and Scottish dissenters. Where a man came from, when he came, and how he worshiped thus became matters of importance in South Carolina politics. Established political leaders particularly resented the new men who threatened to take over power with the backing of the proprietors.

The proprietary party was usually led by the English dissenters, particularly by members of the Blake and Axtel families, by Landgrave Joseph Morton, and by Landgrave Thomas Smith. Stuart Town, the Scottish settlement at Port Royal, was small and short-lived—the Spaniards destroyed it in 1686—but it contributed one person of importance in provincial politics. He was John Stewart, a man blessed with the gift of invective who became the proprietary faction's most effective polemicist. The dissenters supported the proprietors for three basic reasons. They were grateful for the policy of toleration that had given them a place of refuge. As newcomers to the colony none of them was as yet involved with the traffic in Indian slaves or the trade with pirates, and they could therefore support proprietary reform without sacrificing their own economic interests. Moreover, they were not

[10] Shirley C. Hughson, *The Carolina Pirates and Colonial Commerce, 1670–1740* (Baltimore, 1894), 13–20. Most South Carolina historians have tried to minimize the extent of the colony's trade with pirates; the best such defense of the colony is Wallace, *History of S. C.*, I, 113–14, 221–24. Wallace based his conclusions largely on a letter from the Earl of Craven to the Lords of Trade, May 27, 1684, *S. C. Pub. Recs.*, I, 284–85. In the letter Craven denied that South Carolina traded with pirates, but Wallace overlooked the fact that Craven and the other proprietors admitted the existence of the trade in later correspondence; see, e. g., Instructions to James Colleton, Mar. 3, 1687, *ibid.*, II, 177–83.

[11] Proprietors to Andrew Percival, Oct. 18, 1690, in Rivers, *Hist. of S. C.*, 412.

averse to seeing those policies enforced, if only to clear their path to political office and open the doors of the Indian trade in its legitimate phases. Their settlements in Colleton County and at Port Royal placed them closer to the Indians than other colonists and gave them an advantage over the established traders. Lord Cardross and his Scots were especially eager to break into the Indian trade and claimed a monopoly of the trade in the Port Royal area for themselves; in 1685 they arrested five English traders who had wandered into Scottish territory.[12]

The chief source of strength for the anti-proprietary party was the immigrant group from Barbados. Because many of them had settled on Goose Creek, a tributary of the Cooper River, they soon became known as the "Goose Creek men." Their leader was Maurice Mathews, with James Moore as second in command, and some of John Stewart's most biting insults referred to these men. Stewart called Mathews "Mine Heer Mauritius" and "his Welsh Highness," claimed that Mathews was "hel itself for Malice, a Jesuit for Designe politick," and labeled Moore "the heating Moor" and "the next Jehu of the party." [13] Mathews was one of the leading dealers in Indian slaves, and Moore was mixed up in that activity as well as the traffic with pirates. Other major Barbadian politicians emulated them. For example, Arthur Middleton and John Boone dealt in Indian slaves, and Boone also traded with the pirates.

Knowing that their reform program could never succeed as long as the increasingly anti-proprietary Barbadian immigrants controlled the government of South Carolina, the proprietors decided to replace as many of them as possible with men who would "stand by . . . [us] in the Seizeing of Privateers . . . And are not for sending away the poor Indians [as slaves] And are affectionate to our Interest." [14] Having dismissed Governor Joseph West and appointed Joseph Morton in 1682, three years later they fired the incumbent surveyor general, Maurice Mathews, an Indian slave dealer, and replaced him with Stephen Bull, an experienced surveyor and a loyal proprietary man.[15]

The Goose Creek men wanted fundamentally to preserve the status quo in South Carolina. They controlled the local government,

[12] Depositions of Henry Woodward and John Edenburgh, May 5, 1685, S. C. Pub. Recs., II, 61–64.
[13] Stewart to William Dunlop, Apr. 27, June 23, 1690, "Letters from John Stewart to William Dunlop," S. C. Hist. Mag., 32 (1931) , 3–4, 96.
[14] Instructions to James Colleton, Mar. 3, 1687, S. C. Pub. Recs., II, 181.
[15] Commission to Joseph Morton, May 18, 1682, Instructions to Surveyor General, Mar. 12, 1685, ibid., I, 158, II, 26.

and they saw nothing objectionable in their Indian slave trade or their trade with the pirates. They evidently regarded proprietary reform as an unwarranted attempt by a distant and uninformed authority to meddle in affairs that were purely local in character; in their complaints to the proprietors they adopted the view that if the proprietors could learn the truth about conditions in South Carolina they would change their policies.[16] Until changes were made, however, the Goose Creek men were determined to resist every innovation. They opposed land reforms in order to protect their land claims and to avoid quit rent payments in specie; they opposed the proprietors' efforts to stop the Indian slave trade and the trade with pirates in order to protect their profits; and they came to hate their new rivals, the dissenters, and to fight them at every step. Although the ultimate motives of the Goose Creek men were open to question, they presented themselves as the defenders of provincial liberties and enjoyed a considerable amount of popular support in the colony.

That the anti-proprietary faction was more Barbadian than Anglican is suggested by the fact that Anglican immigrants from England were divided in political allegiance. Those who had immigrated in the 1670's tended to support the proprietors, probably because they resented the Barbadian domination of public office. In this group were men like Stephen Bull, Paul Grimball, and Richard Conant, all loyal proprietary men. There were some important exceptions to this rule, however; Robert Quary, who was involved in the pirate trade, worked with the Goose Creek men, and Andrew Percival started out as a proprietary man and Lord Ashley's deputy but later changed sides. English Anglicans who immigrated in the 1680's came from a country torn by religious strife, and they sided with their fellow Anglicans, the Barbadians. Among them were Ralph Izard, Benjamin Waring, Job Howes, and George Muschamp. There were also a few Barbadian dissenters in South Carolina, and, like the English Anglicans, they seem to have been divided politically. For example, James Stanyarne favored the Goose Creek men, but his brother John supported the proprietors. The newly arrived Huguenots were also divided. Some favored the proprietors and some remained neutral, but a substantial number of Huguenots—perhaps a majority of them—opposed the proprietors.[17] Finally, a few individuals fell into no pattern what-

---

[16] See especially the Address to Seth Sothel, [1690], in Rivers, *Hist. of S. C.,* 418–30.

[17] On the Huguenots, see Hirsch, *Huguenots,* 104–5; Proprietors to M. Trouillard and others, Apr. 12, 1693, *S. C. Pub. Recs.,* III, 103–4.

soever. Bernard Schenkingh, another Barbadian Anglican, fell out with the Goose Creek men for personal reasons and became a proprietary man. Charles Colleton, although a Barbadian Anglican, came from a proprietary family and joined the proprietary party when his cousin James became governor.

II

The proprietors' attempt to reform South Carolina misfired at first. Although the worst of the Indian slave traders, including Maurice Mathews and James Moore, were suspended from office, the Goose Creek men still controlled parliament and Governor Morton could not break their power. The proprietors tried to solve the problem by appointing a governor from abroad, Sir Richard Kyrle of Ireland in 1684, but he died shortly after arriving in the colony. Robert Quary, who succeeded to the governorship, was dismissed for trading with pirates, and Joseph West then wrestled unsuccessfully with the complicated political tangle for a year before abandoning the job and the colony. In 1685 Morton returned to the governorship, only to find that Mathews and Moore were back in office; they had been elected to the parliament, and the parliament had elected them to the council.[18] The governor, finally convinced that he could do nothing to control the Goose Creek men, gave up on the Indian slave trade and openly condoned the traffic with pirates. Under pressure from the proprietors he did induce parliament to pass a law in 1685 that was supposed to stop the pirate trade, but the statute had so many loopholes in it that it was meaningless.[19] The proprietors at the end of 1685 had very little to show for three years of trying to change the colony. The surveyor general, Stephen Bull, had surveyed county boundary lines and the governor had established a county court at Charles Town, but that was all. Even this much was not wholly satisfactory to the proprietors, because Bull had not laid out any seignories, baronies, or colonies, and he had failed to survey a single township.

Although Governor Morton ignored his instructions on several points, he made one real effort to advance the proprietors' interests. When the parliament met on November 19, 1685, he informed it and the council that they must subscribe to a special oath of allegiance to

[18] Hewatt, *Historical Account*, in Carroll, ed., *Hist. Collections of S. C.*, I, 85; Proprietors to Morton, Sept. 9, 1685, *S. C. Pub. Recs.*, II, 82–84.

[19] Hughson, *Carolina Pirates*, 20–26; Instructions to Colleton, Mar. 3, 1687, *S. C. Pub. Recs.*, II, 179–80; Thomas Cooper and David J. McCord, eds., *The Statutes at Large of South Carolina*, 10 vols. (Columbia, 1836–41), II, 7–9.

the Fundamental Constitutions of 1682. The council—which had been purged of Goose Creek men—readily agreed, as did eight members of parliament. The remaining twelve members, a majority of the house, refused to sign and were excluded from the parliament. In a joint declaration they observed that they had previously subscribed to the original Constitutions of 1669; they were also "ready willing and desirous again to swear faith and allegiance" to James II, to swear fidelity to the Lords Proprietors, and to maintain the government established under the Constitutions of 1669. But they refused to subscribe to the revised Constitutions of 1682, because a constitution that changed whenever the proprietors changed their minds was "contrary to the nature of a fundamentall sacred and unalterable law." [20]

In 1686 Morton had a chance to restore his dwindling prestige, when Spanish troops from Florida invaded South Carolina in retaliation for English-backed Indian raids into Florida. The Spaniards viewed the establishment of the Scots settlement at Port Royal in 1684 as a new intrusion, and were especially aroused when Lord Cardross stirred up the Yamasee Indians to raid the mission province of Timucna. In August 1686 they launched a surprise attack on the exposed settlement at Port Royal, destroyed the Scottish settlement at Stuart Town, and after sacking and burning the home of Governor Morton on the Edisto River, they headed for Charles Town. Only a "wonderfully horrid and destructive" hurricane, which hit with "dismall dreadful and fatall consequences," halted the Spanish advance on Charles Town, forcing the invaders to turn back. Governor Morton sent a detachment of 100 militiamen to meet the invasion, but the Spaniards retreated so hurriedly that the English soldiers failed to catch them.[21] Morton began to prepare for a major military expedition against Florida, but if he was entertaining dreams of martial glory they ended prematurely. A new governor, James Colleton of Barbados, the younger brother of proprietor Sir Peter Colleton, arrived in November and disbanded the expedition on the ground that neither England nor Spain had formally declared war.

James Colleton followed his instructions from the proprietors more faithfully than did any other governor of South Carolina in the 1680's.

[20] Declaration of Twelve Members of the Commons, Nov. 20, 1685, *S. C. Pub. Recs.*, II, 107–11; the oath and the names of those who signed it are in Rivers, *Hist. of S. C.*, 334–35.
[21] Herbert E. Bolton, "Spanish Resistance to the Carolina Traders in Western Georgia (1680–1704)," *Georgia Historical Quarterly*, 9 (1925), 120–24; "Spanish Depradations, 1686," *S. C. Hist. Mag.*, 30 (1929), 81–89.

In order to prevent a repetition of the Spanish attack he reopened communications with the governor of Florida and even persuaded him to pay for ten slaves who had been captured by Spanish troops in 1686.[22] Colleton moved against the trade with pirates and abuses in the Indian trade with equal determination. An occasional pirate may have slipped into an unguarded harbor, but Colleton spoke the truth in 1688 when he boasted, "Since I came to the Government there have been no pirates nor other Sea Robbers admitted nor had any reception in this province without being brought to condigne punishment." [23]

Colleton was more of an administrator than a politician, however, and he never adjusted to the give and take of provincial politics, even though he had served in the assembly of Barbados. He was no match for the Carolina parliament, which was controlled by Goose Creek men who outwitted him handily in their first encounter. In 1686 they offered to raise the governor's salary by levying an excise tax on all liquors and sugar. Colleton took the bait, and when the council opposed the tax he alienated several proprietary men by insisting that they vote for the bill. When Colleton formally proposed the tax to the parliament, the Goose Creek men turned on him and denounced his "extreme Avarice," arguing that if parliament passed the tax, Colleton "would leave no money in any mans pocket in Carolina but his owne." Parliament defeated the bill, and Colleton suddenly found himself at odds with nearly every politician in the colony.[24]

The next year, in 1687, the Goose Creek faction challenged Colleton's authority by denying the very legality of his administration. Since the majority of parliament had refused to subscribe to the Fundamental Constitutions as revised in 1682, successive governors had attempted to achieve that goal. In 1687 Governor Colleton, with two councilors and four representatives, attempted to work out a compromise, but the committee broke up after angry discussions, the members of parliament reaffirming their decision to abide by the Fundamental Constitutions of 1669. When Colleton received a letter from the proprietors which "utterly denied the Fundamental Constitutions of July, 1669, declaring them to be but a copy of an imperfect original," Maurice Mathews drew up a resolution which declared that

---

[22] Proprietors to Colleton, Mar. 3, Oct. 10, 1687, Commission to Benjamin Blake, Oct. 10, 1687, *S. C. Pub. Recs.*, II, 186–87, 227, 239–40; "William Dunlop's Mission to St. Augustine in 1688," *S. C. Hist. Mag.*, 34 (1933), 1–30.

[23] Instructions to William Dunlop, "Dunlop's Mission," *S. C. Hist. Mag.*, 34 (1933), 2; see also Hughson, *Carolina Pirates*, 26–27; on Colleton's suppression of the Indian slave trade, see Proprietors to Colleton, Oct. 18, 1690, *S. C. Pub. Recs.*, II, 292–93.

[24] Proprietors to Philip Ludwell, Apr. 12, 1693, *S. C. Pub. Recs.*, III, 85–86.

the only legal foundation for the government of South Carolina was the royal charter granted to the proprietors in 1665. The resolution concluded that all laws and instructions issued under the authority of the Fundamental Constitutions were illegal. The charter bill thus denied the constitutionality of every one of the proprietors' reforms, from their strictures against the Indian slave trade to their rules for granting land. Under the leadership of Job Howes, parliament passed the charter bill, but the council rejected it. The Goose Creek men undoubtedly knew the bill would never pass the council, but by introducing it they had served their purpose. Many colonists now believed that the proprietors were trying to force an illegal government on the people, and the governor's reaction to the charter bill confirmed the popular view. Colleton decided he could not work with the parliament and refused to call it into session again. Such an ill-advised action accomplished nothing and lent support to the opposition's argument that the proprietors and the governor were capricious tyrants.[25]

South Carolina remained in an unsettled state for the next two years. Nothing much happened, except that Colleton steadily lost support because of his refusal to call another parliament. Former Governor Morton, who may have resented Colleton's presence, and other dissenters, including the Blake family, went over to the side of the Goose Creek faction. Colleton was fortunate enough, however, to keep Landgrave Thomas Smith and many other dissenters on his side. Meanwhile, the Goose Creek men recruited an important new member, Sir Nathaniel Johnson, former governor of the Leeward Islands and a man of wealth and prestige who came to South Carolina in 1689; Maurice Mathews and James Moore quickly won him over.[26]

In 1689 the situation became critical. News of the Glorious Revolution in England had reached South Carolina, along with reports of successful rebellions in other colonies against their governors. The uncertain state of affairs was exacerbated by rumors that a French invasion of South Carolina was imminent. The war between England and France had touched off a conflict in America known as King William's War, and French forces had already captured the English port of St. Christopher's. South Carolinians feared they would be the next target, and the provincial government was in a state of virtual

25 Address to Seth Sothel, [1690], in Rivers, *Hist. of S. C.*, 422–23; John Stewart to William Dunlop, Apr. 27, 1690, "Stewart Letters," *S. C. Hist. Mag.*, 32 (1931), 12; McCrady, *Proprietary Government*, 226.

26 John Stewart to William Dunlop, Apr. 27, June 23, 1690, "Stewart Letters," *S. C. Hist. Mag.*, 32 (1931), 23–24, 84, 84 n.

paralysis. Laws were beginning to expire because the parliament had not met, including the law governing the defense of the colony. The situation was potentially more explosive because proprietary quit rents were falling due for the first time, just when the legality of the instructions calling for their collection had been openly challenged.

Governor Colleton belatedly woke up to the need for action. At John Stewart's urging, he asked the proprietors to suspend land grants by indenture and to allow rent payments in commodities. Early in 1690 the governor had Stewart write an answer to the anti-proprietary attack. Stewart's tract argued that the charter bill had raised a false issue, and then compared the charter of 1665 with the revised Fundamental Constitutions of 1682 article by article in an attempt to prove there was no essential difference between them. Although the pamphlet also discussed the external threat to South Carolina, it emphasized even more strongly the point that suspension of the Fundamental Constitutions would endanger South Carolina's religious freedom. "If fundamentals be thrown by," he wrote, "as the [charter] bill Imports, then the wofull consequence is apparent to Aliens and dissenters: farewell then Liberty of Conscience [and] Naturalization." Colleton had Stewart's tract translated into French and distributed to the Huguenots, while Stephen Bull circulated the English version among the English dissenters in Colleton County. Stewart's defense of the proprietary government had the desired effect. Many dissenters, including Joseph Blake, returned to the proprietary party, while some of the less rabid Goose Creek men, among them Robert Quary and Ralph Izard, suggested that the two parties try to reach a compromise.[27]

Governor Colleton might have resolved South Carolina's difficulties through compromise at that time, but several of the proprietary men believed compromise was out of the question, and one of them, Landgrave Thomas Smith, drew up a petition asking the governor to declare martial law. Assisted by Paul Grimball, Stephen Bull, and Charles Colleton, Smith obtained 150 signatures to the petition from the inhabitants of Charles Town and Colleton County. The Goose Creek men and the Huguenots in Craven County refused to sign. Governor Colleton nevertheless decided to grant the petition, and he proclaimed martial law on February 26, 1690. In March he forbade any trade with the Indians except under his personal direction, an ineffective attempt to halt the remaining trade in Indian slaves, and he

[27] Stewart to Dunlop, Apr. 27, 1690, *ibid.*, 7–10, 14–15, 28; the quotation is from p. 13.

ordered all landowners to start paying quit rents at once. The more moderate of the Goose Creek men still hoped for a compromise and suggested that the governor call a parliament, but he refused. Extremists on both sides rejected compromise, however, and Maurice Mathews and James Moore defied the governor publicly by sending a trading party to the Cherokee Indians.[28]

Whether the Goose Creek opponents of the governor might ultimately have resorted to open rebellion can be debated, for they quickly found a more legitimate way to get rid of the governor. Their opportunity came in the summer of 1690 when one of the proprietors, Seth Sothel, arrived unexpectedly in South Carolina. Sothel was an English adventurer who had purchased the Clarendon proprietorship in 1677 and been appointed governor of the Albemarle settlement in 1678. Algerian pirates had captured him on his way to America and his assumption of office had been postponed until 1683. As governor there he had antagonized the colonists, and the assembly of North Carolina had forced him to leave the colony. Since Sothel could claim the governorship of South Carolina on the grounds that as a proprietor he outranked Colleton, the Goose Creek men, setting aside their objections to the Fundamental Constitutions, obtained 500 signatures on a petition asking him to do just that. Sothel complied and claimed the governorship publicly, to the dismay of Colleton and his party. Colleton and the council denied the validity of Sothel's claim and tried to call out the militia, but they were outnumbered, and Sothel took over the government of South Carolina without bloodshed.[29]

Because the overthrow of James Colleton's government came on the heels of the upheaval caused in the English-speaking world by the Glorious Revolution, it invites comparison with other colonial rebellions, particularly those which had occurred in Massachusetts, New York, and Maryland. The rebellion in South Carolina, like that in Massachusetts, followed an attempt by the superior authority in England to tighten its control over the colony, though that authority in one instance was proprietary, in the other royal. In each instance, as in New York also, the rebels were able to identify their cause with some recent denial of the rights belonging to an elected assembly. But there were differences, too, and not merely of circumstances. The contrast with the Maryland revolution is especially sharp, for the Protestant Association of Lord Baltimore's opponents undertook to

28 Stewart to Dunlop, Apr. 27, June 23, 1690, *ibid.*, 11, 105, 107–8; Proprietors to Andrew Percival, Oct. 18, 1690, in Rivers, *Hist. of S. C.*, 412–13.

29 Powell, *Proprietors of Carolina*, 68; Address to Sothel, [1690], in Rivers, *Hist. of S. C.*, 428–29.

use their rebellion for the purpose of overthrowing the proprietorship itself. In South Carolina the aim seems to have been nothing more than to get rid of an unpopular governor and to restore power to those who formerly had held it.[30]

III

Seth Sothel and his collaborators moved rapidly to consolidate their victory. The new governor threw Paul Grimball into jail for refusing to surrender the great seal of the colony, dismissed the proprietary officeholders, although most of them held deputations from the proprietors, and sent Maurice Mathews to England to present the case of the Goose Creek men to the proprietors.[31]

In December 1690 a parliamentary session passed punitive legislation against Governor Colleton and his party. Colleton was barred from holding any political office thereafter, banished from the colony, and ordered to go to England to answer the charges brought against him. Four proprietary men—Landgrave Thomas Smith, Stephen Bull, Charles Colleton, and Paul Grimball—were also barred from political office for life because of their part in the proclamation of martial law. To prevent the officeholders whom Sothel had dismissed from reclaiming their posts, another statute made it a felony for anyone to contend that a commission was legal if signed by less than all eight proprietors; Sothel, who had signed none of the commissions, thus gained the power of veto. In addition, the parliament passed a law designed to win the support of the Huguenots. Although the Fundamental Constitutions had permitted foreigners to inherit real estate if the original owner had sworn to uphold the Constitutions, the Goose Creek faction seemed to feel that its attack upon that document made some further assurance desirable. The new law therefore granted denizenship to all French and Swiss Protestants residing in South Carolina, provided they registered with the provincial government within six months. The law apparently served its purpose, for a

[30] On the rebellions in Massachusetts, New York, and Maryland, see Michael G. Hall, *Edward Randolph and the American Colonies, 1676–1703* (Chapel Hill, 1960), 98–128; Lawrence H. Leder, *Robert Livingston, 1654–1728, and the Politics of Colonial New York* (Chapel Hill, 1961), 57–76; Michael G. Hall, Lawrence H. Leder, and Michael G. Kammen, eds., *The Glorious Revolution in America: Documents on the Colonial Crisis of 1689* (Chapel Hill, 1964). For a brief appraisal of the rebellion in North Carolina, see Hugh F. Rankin, *Upheaval in Albemarle: The Story of Culpeper's Rebellion, 1675–1689* (Raleigh, 1962).

[31] Commission to James Colleton and others, May 13, 1691, Proclamation of Proprietors, May 11, 1693, *S. C. Pub. Recs.*, III, 6–7, 105–6.

majority of the Huguenots seem to have supported Sothel's administration.[32]

The Goose Creek men soon began to wonder about the wisdom of
their collaboration with Sothel, whose chief concern seemed to be the
increase of his personal fortune. During his two-year term of office, he
signed only three land grants, two for himself and one for Sir
Nathaniel Johnson. He pushed through parliament the first of South
Carolina's laws regulating the Indian trade, one which levied export
duties on furs and skins and granted to the governor one-third of all
duties and fines. The law also prohibited trade except with the coastal
tribes, thus cutting off the more profitable trade with the most distant
nations. Perhaps Sothel intended later to set up a monopoly of trade
with those tribes for himself. More acceptable to the Goose Creek
faction was Sothel's reopening of the trade with the pirates. He traded
with them on his own account, and during his administration the
trade flourished more than ever before.[33] On the question of quit rents
there was no help except that the proprietors agreed that they might
be paid in commodities fit for the English market.[34]

The proprietors at first showed surprisingly little resentment about
the overthrow of Colleton, for they believed that he had erred badly
when he declared martial law. Although they appointed an investigating committee, they censured no one. "All Partys," the third Earl of
Shaftesbury explained, "and almost all Perticulars have been soe
equally guilty." But when news of Colleton's banishment reached
England in May 1691, the proprietors reacted quite differently.
Shaftesbury described banishment as an act of "Inhumanity or
Unchristianity," and to one of the Goose Creek men he wrote: "In an
Illegall and absurd manner you prosecute a Man not Farther capaci-
tated to doe you Harme." [35] As further news of the irregularities in
Sothel's administration arrived, the proprietors turned against the
governor and his Goose Creek allies, suspended Sothel from office, and
appointed Philip Ludwell as governor in November 1691. All laws
passed during Sothel's administration were set aside, a committee of

[32] Cooper and McCord, eds., Statutes, II, 44–50, 58–60, 70–71; on the Huguenots,
see Proclamation of Proprietors, Apr. 12, 1693, S. C. Pub. Recs., III, 81–83.

[33] Cooper and McCord, eds., Statutes, II, 64–68; Crane, Southern Frontier, 141;
Hughson, Carolina Pirates, 29–30.

[34] Salley, ed., Land Warrants, II, 214–15; Proprietors to Andrew Percival, Oct. 18,
1690, in Rivers, Hist. of S. C., 412.

[35] A[nthony] A[shley Cooper, third Earl of Shaftesbury] to [Andrew] Percival, May
1691, Shaftesbury Papers, 30/24, 23–42, Public Record Office, London, (microfilm at
Institute of Early American History and Culture) ; the quotations are from pp. 28,
34.

proprietors was established to investigate his conduct, and the Goose Creek members of the council were replaced by the same men who had held office under Colleton. The proprietors then urged the Carolinians, as Shaftesbury wrote to his new deputy, Stephen Bull, "to Imbrace an Amicable Composition of matters." [36]

In the hope that it might help to bring an end to the dangerous factionalism in South Carolina, the proprietors suspended the Fundamental Constitutions and ordered several significant changes in the government. For the old council, with its partially elected membership, they substituted an appointed council composed solely of proprietary deputies. Coupled with this action was an order that thereafter the elected members of the provincial parliament would sit and act as a separate house of assembly. Such a practice had been followed more than once before, but it was this order which formally gave to South Carolina a bicameral legislature in which the Commons House of Assembly was ultimately to have the dominant voice. Perhaps the proprietors, who may have been placed at some disadvantage by the Earl of Craven's Toryism, should be credited with a desire to fall in line with the Revolution in England where parliament had prevailed, and with the common practice of other English colonies in America where the bicameral assembly was coming to provide the standard arrangement.[37]

The proprietors entrusted their plans to their new governor, Philip Ludwell, an Englishman who had lived in Virginia for thirty years. Although he had supported Governor William Berkeley during Bacon's Rebellion, and later had married Berkeley's widow, he had become a leader in opposition to Berkeley's successor as governor. The proprietors had appointed him governor of North Carolina in 1689 to replace Seth Sothel, and they now turned to him to clean up after Sothel for the second time. Ludwell arrived in Charles Town in the spring of 1692, and on April 9 he presented his commission to Sothel in the presence of the men Sothel had thrown out of office. Sothel's selfishness had cost him most of his popularity, and the Goose Creek men did not try to resist Ludwell even though his arrival meant that several of them would lose their jobs. Sothel himself did not give up

---

[36] Cooper to Bull, June 1, [1691], *ibid.*, 30/24, 43; see also Proprietors to Governor, Sept. 22, 1691, Commission to Ludwell, Nov. 2, 1691, Proprietors to Sothel, Nov. 8, 1691, *S. C. Pub. Recs.*, III, 31–32, 33, 37–38; Alexander S. Salley, Jr., ed., *Commissions and Instructions from the Lords Proprietors . . . , 1685–1715* (Columbia, 1916), 7–9, 26–27.

[37] Instructions to Ludwell, Nov. 8, 1691, William L. Saunders, ed., *The Colonial Records of North Carolina*, 10 vols. (Raleigh, 1886–90), I, 375–84.

so easily, and he and a couple of his adherents tried throughout the summer of 1692 to deny the validity of Ludwell's appointment. They had no luck, however, and Sothel appears to have left South Carolina in the fall.[38]

Governor Ludwell's task called for more talent than he possessed, and he soon found himself in the impossible position of trying to mediate among the proprietors, Colleton's party, and the Goose Creek men. Most of the old proprietary men, led by Paul Grimball, had suffered at the hands of the Goose Creek men, and they wanted revenge now that they were in power. At the other extreme were the irreconcilable Goose Creek men; James Moore inherited the leadership of the faction after Maurice Mathews left for England, and Moore had the assistance of Andrew Percival and Robert Quary. Fortunately for Ludwell, there was in the colony a growing party of moderates, which included Joseph Blake and Stephen Bull from the proprietary party and Ralph Izard, Jonathan Amory, Benjamin Waring, and Robert Gibbes from the Goose Creek faction. When the proprietors suggested that the governor select some of these men and "raise them to Office by degrees," [39] Ludwell appointed Waring and Gibbes to judicial offices. The other moderates were already in either the assembly or the council. Unfortunately Ludwell could not organize his moderate faction quickly enough. When he called his first assembly in June 1692, the council and assembly agreed on nothing, not even a date for adjournment. When the assembly reconvened in the fall, the two houses disagreed about an act of indemnity; the lower house wanted to pardon everyone who had participated in the overthrow of Colleton's government, while the council wanted to punish some of the leading rebels. Again the assembly broke up without accomplishing anything. The proprietors solved this crisis themselves by granting full pardon to everyone except those accused of high treason.[40]

Although the proprietors generally favored compromise, they refused to alter their rules for granting land, and Governor Ludwell was caught in the middle. The assembly did not like the indenture form of land grants because of the re-entry clause; it was equally unhappy

[38] See Marshall DeLancey Haywood in *DAB* s.v. "Ludwell, Philip"; see also Salley, ed., *Commissions and Instructions*, 24–25; Apr. 22, July 13, 19, Aug. 20, 22, 1692, Salley, ed., *Grand Council Journal*, II, 12–13, 48, 55–56.

[39] Proprietors to Ludwell, Apr. 12, 1693, *S. C. Pub. Recs.*, III, 94; on the leadership of the irreconcilable faction, see the same letter, *ibid.*, III, 84–90.

[40] June 1, 21, July 15, 22, 1692, Salley, ed., *Grand Council Journal*, II, 33, 42–43, 50, 53; Oct. 14, 1692, Alexander S. Salley, Jr., ed., *Journal of the Commons House of Assembly of South Carolina, 1692–1735*, 21 vols. (Columbia, 1907–47), *1692*, 24–25; Proclamation of Proprietors, Apr. 12, 1693, *S. C. Pub. Recs.*, III, 74–79.

because quit rents could be paid only in specie or commodities fit for the English market; and many people refused to pay their quit rents. The proprietors failed to offer practical concessions on any of the land issues. Although they did make 12,000 acres of land available for outright sales, this so-called concession did not even touch upon the basic issues. The proprietors unrelentingly ordered Ludwell to obey his instructions, directing him to prosecute James Moore for the full amount of his quit rents, including arrears; if Moore paid, the proprietors directed Ludwell to prosecute Percival and Quary.[41]

Preoccupation with more urgent business kept Ludwell from doing much about the pirate trade, but he handled Indian affairs quite well. When he took office he learned that "the Indian affaires are in very great disorder" because of a minor outbreak of fighting between Indians and white traders.[42] Ludwell and the council ordered all Indian traders to stay in Charles Town and clamped down on the slave trade. The chiefs of the tribes under the colony's protection were then brought to town for a conference, where Ludwell's tactics evidently succeeded, for there were no more complaints about Indian affairs during his administration.[43]

IV

Ludwell's failures outweighed his success with the Indians, however, and the proprietors replaced him in May 1693 with Landgrave Thomas Smith, a wealthy dissenter and proprietary man. Smith took office at a bad time; not long afterwards he expressed despair over the continued factionalism in South Carolina. He told the proprietors that many colonists, himself included, were thinking about moving somewhere else. Smith's pessimism was short-lived, however, for two of the chief troublemakers, Andrew Percival and Robert Quary, left the colony, and James Moore made his peace with the proprietors by paying his quit rents.[44] With the irreconcilable triumvirate no longer

[41] Jan. 18, 1693, Salley, ed., Commons Journal, 1693, 17; Proprietors to Ludwell, Apr. 12, 1693, S. C. Pub. Recs., III, 87–90; Land Grants, [1670]–1775, XXXVIII, 149, South Carolina Archives Department, Columbia, S. C.

[42] May 28, 1692, Salley, ed., Grand Council Journal, II, 31; on Ludwell's lassitude toward the pirate trade, see Hughson, Carolina Pirates, 31.

[43] Apr. 21, May 28, June 23, 1692, Salley, ed., Grand Council Journal, II, 12, 31, 45–46.

[44] Proprietors to Smith, Nov. 29, 1693, Apr. 24, May 19, 1694, S. C. Pub. Recs., III, 108, 119, 129; John Stewart to William Dunlop, Oct. 20, 1693; "Stewart Letters," S. C. Hist. Mag., 32 (1931), 171; on Smith, see George Howe, History of the Presbyterian Church in South Carolina, 2 vols. (Columbia, 1870–83), I, 128–29.

an obstacle, Governor Smith was soon able to make progress with the land system. The assembly passed its first rent collection law in 1694, and in the same year the provincial secretary reported collections of £73. Meanwhile, many settlers decided to buy their land outright and avoid quit rents entirely. By 1695 more than 16,000 acres of land had been purchased, for which the colonists paid over £800. Money from quit rents remained in South Carolina to pay salaries, but proceeds from land sales went directly to the proprietors, who saw some return on their investments for the first time in three decades. South Carolina's land system remained unsettled, but a start had been made.[45] Smith did well in other areas, too. He had no trouble about the Indian slave trade, and he became the first governor to enjoy a lasting success in suppressing the pirate trade. Shortly before his untimely death in November 1694, he reported to the proprietors that the colony was moving in the direction of peace and prosperity.[46] Governor Smith's optimism may have been a bit premature but it was well-founded.

[45] Cooper and McCord, eds., *Statutes*, II, 79; Proprietors to Paul Grimball, Apr. 12, 1695, *S. C. Pub. Recs.*, III, 156; Report of Paul Grimball, [1695], in Wills, Inventories of Estates, and Miscellaneous Records [title varies], 1671–1868, LIV (1694–1704), 84, Office of Judge of Probate Court, Charleston County Courthouse, Charleston, S. C.

[46] Hughson, *Carolina Pirates*, 37; Proprietors to John Archdale, Jan. 10, 1695, *S. C. Pub. Recs.*, III, 151.

CHAPTER IV

PEACE AND PROSPERITY
1695–1700

The colony of South Carolina had known little else besides political discord and economic hardship since its founding. For all the idealism of Shaftesbury and Locke, the proprietors had failed to create a colony that was either stable or profitable, while the colonists had failed to find an easy route to economic success and had divided into constantly bickering factions. Yet within a few years the colony changed dramatically. The introduction of rice culture and expansion of the Indian trade set the colony on a firm economic foundation, while the dedicated efforts of Governor John Archdale did much to settle the government. Other politicians carried on Archdale's work of conciliation, and the Commons House of Assembly emerged as a major political institution under moderate leadership.

I

The people associated with South Carolina—proprietors as well as settlers—had long dreamed of growing an agricultural staple that would guarantee their economic security. For a quarter of a century planters had experimented fruitlessly with every likely looking product. Finally, at about the middle of the last decade of the century, the colony found its staple when it began to cultivate and market rice successfully. Rice was one of the crops planters experimented with from the first, but they had no success until a ship from Madagascar happened to put into Charles Town for repairs. The ship's captain gave a small bag of Madagascar rice seed to a local planter, and he and his friends experimented with it until they discovered the best method of cleaning and husking it. Once they had made this discovery, rice cultivation expanded rapidly and soon became the main staple of the colony.[1]

This much of the story is indisputable, but there is a question as to just when rice production became profitable.[2] The cultivation of rice was certainly still in the experimental stage in 1690, when John Stewart reported that planters had not yet found the proper way to cultivate it. It is equally certain that the experiments had succeeded by the end of the decade. Edward Randolph, who had visited South Carolina in 1697 and 1698, reported in 1700 that the planters had not only found "the true way of raising and husking Rice," but that they had also exported at least 330 tons of it in 1699.[3] It therefore seems likely that rice cultivation began to return profits to the planters at some time in the middle of the 1690's.

At the same time that the planters were beginning to grow rice profitably, the colony's Indian traders were rapidly expanding their business. The South Carolinians had made themselves, in the words of one visitor, "absolute Masters" over the nearby Indians, and what is more important, they were carrying their trade, in the first significant English penetration into the interior of the North American continent, as far west as the Mississippi River.[4] The leader in expanding the trade was Landgrave Joseph Blake, a dissenter who held the governorship twice, in 1694 and 1695 and again from 1696 to 1700. Blake invested heavily in the Indian trade himself, and he used all the political power at his disposal to support expansion. At first the English traders competed only with Spanish traders from Florida, but a new and stronger competitor appeared in 1699 when France founded the colony of Louisiana. Although French trade did not expand actively until a few years after the turn of the century, the English

[1] Alexander S. Salley, Jr., *The Introduction of Rice Culture into South Carolina* (South Carolina Historical Commission, *Bulletin*, no. 6 [1919]). For 18th-century accounts of the introduction, see Hewatt, *Historical Account*, in Carroll, ed., *Hist. Collections of S. C.*, I, 109–10, and [Fayrer Hall], *The Importance of the British Plantations in America to this Kingdom* (London, 1731), 18–19.

[2] Salley dates the Madagascar captain's visit between 1685 and 1690; see *Introduction of Rice*, 11; Carl Bridenbaugh says that South Carolina did not produce rice profitably until about 1710; see his *Cities in the Wilderness: The First Century of Urban Life in America, 1625–1742* (N. Y., 1938), 32.

[3] Stewart to William Dunlop, June 23, 1690, "Stewart Letters," *S. C. Hist. Mag.*, 32 (1931), 85–86; Randolph to the Board of Trade, May 27, 1700, *S. C. Pub. Recs.*, IV, 189–90.

[4] Lawson, *Carolina*, ed. Harriss, xxviii.

colonists realized that France would become a more formidable antagonist than Spain, and they worried about maintaining their influence with the Indians.[5]

The expansion of their Indian trade introduced the settlers of South Carolina to the four great Indian nations that dominated the southern frontier in the eighteenth century, the Cherokees, Creeks, Choctaws, and Chickasaws. The Cherokees had a population of more than 11,000 persons, with over 3,500 warriors. They lived in sixty towns which straddled the southern Appalachian range. The towns were divided into three groups: the lower towns in the foothills, the middle towns in the mountains, and the overhill towns on the western slopes of the Appalachians. The Cherokees had little central government worthy of the name, although they all honored the overhill town of Chota as their "mother town," and authority was centered in the three main divisions. At first, South Carolina paid little attention to the Cherokees. The Carolina traders were more interested in the Creeks, who lived in what is now western Georgia and eastern Alabama. An energetic, warlike people, the Creeks numbered about 10,000, with some 2,000 warriors. They lived in forty towns or so and, like the Cherokees, were bound together only in a loose political union. All the towns recognized a supreme chief, whom the English called "emperor," but he had little real authority. Power actually resided in the four main Creek tribes: the Ocheses, whom the English referred to as the Lower Creeks, and the Talapoosas, Coosas, and Alabamas, who were known collectively as the Upper Creeks. The largest nation of all was that of the Choctaws, who counted some 15,000 inhabitants. They lived on the lower Mississippi River, and after France founded Louisiana they allied themselves with the French. The Chickasaws, a small but extremely militant nation with a population of only 2,000, lived on the Mississippi just north of the Choctaws. They were traditional enemies of the Choctaws and when the Choctaws formed their alliance with France, the Chickasaws became England's most loyal Indian allies.[6]

The new rice culture and the expanded Indian trade together brought South Carolina the prosperity it had not previously known. In 1699 the province achieved a favorable balance of trade for the first time, exporting more than it imported, and for the next two decades it

[5] Crane, *Southern Frontier*, 38–46; Edward Randolph to Bd. of Trade, Mar. 16, 1699, ed. Robert N. Toppan, Prince Society, *Publications*, 28 (1899), 195.
[6] Crane, *Southern Frontier*, 129–36; Swanton, *Indians of Southeastern U. S.*, 110–19, 121–23, 153–54.

continued to enjoy a favorable balance. Although the colony produced more than thirty marketable items by the end of the century, nothing approached the importance of rice and the Indian trade. In 1700 a visitor reported that South Carolina carried on a considerable trade with Europe and the Indies and was "in as thriving Circumstances . . . as any Colony on the Continent of English America." [7]

Life in South Carolina reflected the new prosperity in many ways, not the least of which was the decline of the pirate trade. The colonists had developed legal and more profitable sources of income, and their own rice shipments became targets for the buccaneers. Most people in South Carolina therefore turned against the pirates, and Charles Town was no longer safe for them. In an act symbolic of South Carolina's changing attitude, the colony hanged seven pirates in 1700.[8] Edward Randolph, His Majesty's Surveyor General of Customs in America, charged that Governors Archdale and Blake permitted a clandestine trade with some pirates, but the charges rested on the testimony of an unreliable and prejudiced witness, and it does not seem likely that the accusations were true.[9]

Prosperity could be seen in the colonists' style of living as well as their dress. Dr. Francis LeJau, who had just come from the West Indies and Virginia, remarked, "For Gentility politeness and a handsome way of Living the Colony exceeds what I have seen." John Lawson, another observer, said, "Their [militia] Officers, both Infantry and Cavalry, generally appear in scarlet Mountings, and as rich as in most Regiments belonging to the Crown." [10] The Carolinians promised to make Charles Town one of the most attractive colonial towns by building their homes along wide and well-planned streets, by

---

[7] Lawson, *Carolina*, ed. Harriss, xxvi–xxvii; see also Edward Randolph to Bd. of Trade, Mar. 16, 1699, and "Memorandum," 1706, *S. C. Pub. Recs.*, IV, 91–93, V, 152–54; W. Noel Sainsbury *et al.*, eds., *Calendar of State Papers, Colonial Series, America and the West Indies, 1574—*, 43 vols. to date (London, 1860—), 1702, 69; Curtis P. Nettels, *The Money Supply of the American Colonies before 1720* (Madison, 1934), 156.

[8] Salley, ed., *Commissions and Instructions*, 133–35; see also Hughson, *Carolina Pirates*, 43–45; Feb. 5, 1696, Salley, ed., *Commons Journal, Jan.–Mar. 1696*, 17.

[9] Randolph's informant was Peter Jacob Guerard, a Huguenot who not only had reason to resent the anti-Huguenot policies of Archdale and Blake, but who had lost a profitable position in the customs office during Blake's administration. See Randolph, "Narrative of His Survey," Nov. 5, 1700, and Randolph, "Crimes and Misdemeanors Charged upon the Governors of the Proprietary Governments in America," Mar. 24, 1701, ed. Toppan, Prince Soc., *Publications*, 28 (1899), 220–21, 264–65.

[10] LeJau to the Secretary of the Society for the Propagation of the Gospel, Dec. 2, 1706, Frank J. Klingberg, ed., *The Carolina Chronicle of Dr. Francis LeJau, 1706–1717* (Berkeley, 1956), 18; Lawson, *Carolina*, ed. Harriss, xxvii.

cleaning out such eyesores as weed-infested vacant lots, and by lining the streets and roads into town with pine, cedar, and cypress trees. They also took their first hesitant steps toward serious intellectual activity. Thanks to gifts made by Dr. Thomas Bray, founder of the Society for the Propagation of the Gospel, a public library was founded in Charles Town. A small group of residents, including such political leaders as Sir Nathaniel Johnson and Thomas Nairne, developed an interest in botany and reported their findings to the Royal Society in England.[11] But these were only beginnings. There were no schools in Charles Town. The town did nothing to prevent fires and epidemics, and both ravaged the colony between 1697 and 1706. Edward Marston, the Anglican rector in Charles Town, wrote Dr. Bray to thank him for the library but added, "the generality of people here are more mindful of getting money and their worldly affairs than they are of Books and Learning." [12] One of those who had an interest in natural history expressed the same regret when he described politician James Moore as "a verry ingenious Gentleman sure enough, but I fear hee will not make a good philosopher, being otherwise full of Employment." [13]

South Carolina's prosperity did not extend to all the colony's inhabitants. Small farmers in outlying areas did not benefit from either rice cultivation or the Indian trade, and they remained poor. As Charles Town grew in size and wealth, the number of people who lived in poverty and often depended upon charity increased.[14] Together the small farmers and the poor of Charles Town constituted a kind of lower class in the colony. At the same time the more successful men in South Carolina began to become conscious of themselves as a separate group, and references to a local gentry began to appear for the

[11] Bridenbaugh, *Cities in the Wilderness*, 150, 154, 170, 295–96; "Early Letters from South Carolina upon Natural History," *S. C. Hist. Mag.*, 21 (1920), 3–9, 50–51; W. H. G. Armytage, ed., "Letters on Natural History of Carolina, 1700–1705," *ibid.*, 55 (1954), 59–70; Edgar L. Pennington, "The Beginnings of the Library in Charles Town, South Carolina," American Antiquarian Society, *Proceedings*, 44 (1935), 159–87.

[12] Edward Marston to Dr. Thomas Bray, Feb. 2, 1702, Manuscripts of the Society for the Propagation of the Gospel, Ser. A, I, no. 60, Society for the Propagation of the Gospel, London (microfilm and transcripts in the Library of Congress, Washington, D. C.), hereafter cited as S.P.G. Mss.; see also Bridenbaugh, *Cities in the Wilderness*, 121, 212, 240.

[13] Edmund Bohun to James Pettiver, Apr. 20, 1700, "Letters upon Natural History," *S. C. Hist. Mag.*, 55 (1954), 65.

[14] Samuel Thomas to Sec. S.P.G., Mar. 10, 1704, "Letters of Rev. Samuel Thomas, 1702–1710," *ibid.*, 4 (1903), 281; Francis LeJau to Sec. S.P.G., July 3, 1707, Klingberg, ed., *LeJau Chronicle*, 29; Cooper and McCord, eds., *Statutes*, II, 593–98.

first time. The word "gentry" was generally used to mean only "our most Considerable Men"; other considerations seem not to have been given very great weight.[15] As class distinctions began to appear at the end of the seventeenth century, a man's material achievement in the new world seemed to count most of all.

The most impressive evidence of a South Carolinian's prosperity was the number of Negro slaves he owned. Sir Nathaniel Johnson became the first of the great slaveowners when he brought more than a hundred Negroes into the colony in the early 1690's. Rice planting later required a large labor force, and the profits derived from rice, plus liberal extensions of credit in London, enabled the planters to pay for the slaves they needed. Other planters emulated Johnson's example, especially after 1698 when Parliament opened the African trade to independent traders outside the Royal African Company. The Negro population grew so fast that as early as 1699 Edward Randolph estimated that there were four Negroes in South Carolina for every white. A more accurate count made by the council listed 4,220 whites, 3,250 Negroes, and 800 Indian slaves in a total population of 8,270 in 1703.[16]

The rapid increase in the Negro population troubled the colonists, who were most concerned about the failure of white immigration to keep up with the pace of Negro importation. As early as 1698 the assembly feared that "the great number of negroes which of late have been imported into this Collony may endanger the safety thereof." [17] By 1708 the Negroes very slightly outnumbered the whites by 4,100 to 4,080. The growth of the Negro population was accompanied by a decline in the number of white servants and Indian slaves employed by the colonists. The planters regarded white servants as completely unfit for rice planting. In 1703 there were only 210 white servants and in 1708 only 120. Indian slaves seemed to be more satisfactory, and some planters used them in the rice paddies until they could afford to buy Negroes. Although many Indian slaves died in the 1690's of smallpox and other European diseases, they still totaled one-fifth of the slave force as late as 1708.[18]

[15] Dr. Francis LeJau used the word "gentry" in this way; see, e.g., LeJau to Sec. S.P.G., Feb. 1, June 13, 1710, Klingberg, ed., *LeJau Chronicle,* 69, 78.

[16] Edward Randolph to Bd. of Trade, Mar. 16, 1699, *S. C. Pub. Recs.,* IV, 88; all population statistics cited in this and the following paragraphs are taken from Governor and Council to Proprietors, Sept. 17, 1708, *ibid.,* V, 203–4; on Johnson, see Salley, ed., *Land Warrants,* II, 212, 215.

[17] Cooper and McCord, eds., *Statutes,* II, 153.

[18] Lauber, *Indian Slavery,* 244–45, 284–88, 302; on the rice planter's aversion to white servants, see LeJau to Sec. S.P.G., Sept. 15, 1708, Klingberg, ed., *LeJau Chronicle,* 41.

II

With economic progress came an improvement in the political situation, a change due in no small part to John Archdale, who became governor in 1695. Landgrave Smith, in a moment of pessimism, had suggested that the appointment of one of the proprietors would help to overcome the colony's difficulties, and Archdale, who still acted for his young son, accepted the assignment. Although his own sympathies were with the Colleton group, he made reconciliation of factional differences the keystone of his policy.[19] Fortunately, the disadvantages of continuing the old feuds were becoming so obvious that even the Goose Creek men were eager to cooperate. The new governor received bipartisan support from such former factional opponents as James Moore, Joseph Blake, Ralph Izard, and Paul Grimball.

When Archdale reached South Carolina in the fall of 1695, he found to his dismay that the colony was embroiled in a new controversy. During King William's War, a wave of Francophobia had swept the colony, and many of the English colonists objected particularly to the presence of Huguenots in the assembly, complaining that they thought it "very hard that the French who are refugees and ought to be Subject to our Lawes are permitted to be Law Makers." [20] At that time Berkeley and Colleton counties each elected seven representatives to the assembly and Craven County elected six. Since Craven County's population was almost entirely Huguenot, this practice gave the French nearly one-third of the seats in the assembly, although they numbered hardly more than one-tenth of the population; there were only about 400 or 500 Huguenots in a white population approaching 4,000. Increasingly, anti-Huguenot sentiment centered in the old proprietary faction led by the dissenters, chiefly because Colleton's followers could not forgive the Huguenots for having supported Sothel. Moreover, the Huguenots hurt themselves when many of them, still hoping to return to France, refused to swear allegiance to the king of England.[21]

[19] Archdale's Commission and Instructions, Aug. 31, 1694, Proprietors to Thomas Smith, Aug. 31, 1694, S. C. Pub. Recs., III, 135, 140–42, 138–39; Archdale, "New Description," in Salley, ed., Narratives of Carolina, 295–96, 305.

[20] Salley, ed., Commissions and Instructions, 81.

[21] Nathaniel Johnson to Archdale, Jan. 10, 1706, John Archdale Papers, 1690–1706, no. 9, Lib. Cong.; Hirsch, Huguenots, 115–18; Salley, ed., Commissions and Instructions, 100; on the Huguenot population, see Edward Randolph to Bd. of Trade, Mar. 16, 1699, Toppan, ed., Prince Soc., Publications, 28 (1899), 200. Wallace, Hist. of S. C., I, 153–54 n, says that antagonism between the dissenters and Huguenots did not develop until after 1700.

English resentment of the Huguenots had been strongly expressed in February 1695 in a case before the Charles Town court of vice-admiralty; the defendants were naturalized French Protestants from New York. Both the judge in the case, Stephen Bull, and the attorney general, Edmund Bellinger, had been members of the proprietary faction, and Judge Bull refused to recognize the Huguenots as English denizens despite their naturalization. He condemned a ship belonging to the Huguenots on the ground that it was not English-owned (a condition fixed by the Navigation Acts for trade with the colonies), a ruling subsequently disallowed by the proprietors. When Archdale landed at Charles Town the next fall, the council presented a petition demanding an end to the Craven County representation in the assembly, and a town meeting in Charles Town drew up a petition asking for an assembly with twenty members from Berkeley County and ten from Colleton County.[22] At first Archdale took the side of the Huguenots and dissolved the existing assembly for "being Enemies to the French," but later, realizing he could accomplish nothing if he insisted on full political rights for the Huguenots, he reversed himself and issued new election writs for an assembly composed of twenty men from Berkeley County and ten from Colleton. Hoping to settle "all matters relating to the French" when the new assembly met, he tried to persuade the other proprietors to support his actions. But they refused to abandon the ideal of Carolina as a haven for religious and political refugees and insisted that the Huguenots should have full political rights.[23] Neither side yielded until after Archdale left the colony.

On other issues the governor had won a decided advantage by catering to the local Francophobia. The new assembly convened in January 1696, and Archdale moved promptly to capitalize on his harmonious relations with the colonists. On February 6 he proposed a compromise of the differences separating proprietors and colonists, particularly those involving the land system. For the next month and a half he and the Commons House of Assembly hammered out the details of legislation that came to be known as Archdale's Laws, which embodied concessions by both sides. On the critical issue of the indenture, Archdale insisted on keeping that form of land grant, but he promised that the proprietors would not alter any forms of grants for a specified length of time—fifteen years on headright grants—and

[22] Proprietors to Archdale, Jan. 29, 1696, *S. C. Pub. Recs.*, III, 166–67; Salley, ed., *Commissions and Instructions*, 84–85, 90.

[23] Archdale to Proprietors, n.d., Archdale Papers, no. 11, Lib. Cong.; Proprietors to Archdale, Jan. 29, 1696, *S. C. Pub. Recs.*, III, 167.

that the assembly would have a year's notice in advance of any changes. The laws also introduced new terms for land grants. Carolinians now could buy land at £20 per 1,000 acres, with a quit rent of 1s. per 100 acres, and the governor promised that the form of the grant for such purchases would remain unchanged for six years. Archdale also agreed to accept quit rent payments in commodities fit for the South Carolina market, rather than the English market, and pledged that the proprietors would incorporate this condition into all future grants. He promised too that the proprietors would remit all arrears if the assembly would provide for future payments, pay the debt the colony owed the proprietors, and build a new fort at Charles Town. The assembly readily agreed, but it found the provincial records in such disorder that it could not compute an accurate estimate of either rent arrears or debts owed the proprietors. Therefore the assembly and governor worked out another compromise. Archdale agreed for the proprietors to remit three years of arrears on lands held by grant, which committed him on half the amount owed, and to remit four years of arrears on land held only by survey, provided that the landholders took out full grants immediately. The assembly agreed to build the fort and, in lieu of paying off the proprietary debt, to pay the salary arrears owed by the proprietors to Governors Morton, Colleton, and Smith. The assembly also passed a strict law for the collection of quit rents, which required landholders to pay their arrears by December 1, 1697. Thereafter they were to pay quit rents on December 1 of every year. If any landholder did not pay up within thirty days, the proprietors could reclaim his land. Archdale agreed that all rent payments would remain in South Carolina to pay the governor's salary.[24] Since both governor and assembly wanted their settlement of land problems to be permanent, the statutes included the vital provision that the proprietors could not change Archdale's Laws without the assembly's consent.

South Carolina enjoyed the benefits of Archdale's Laws without serious complaint for two decades, and the colonists regarded the statutes as part of the basic law of the colony. The proprietors never gave their written assent to the laws, but they allowed them to continue in force, which had the same effect. Passage of the laws produced almost immediate results. Landholders paid their back rents and gave every indication that they would continue to pay them

[24] Feb. 5, 6, 29, Mar. 4, 5, 12, 1696, Salley, ed., *Commons Journal, Jan.–Mar. 1696*, 16–17, 19, 28–30, 32–35, 37, 41–42; Cooper and McCord, eds., *Statutes*, II, 96–104; Proprietors to Archdale, June 17, 1696, *S. C. Pub. Recs.*, III, 174.

regularly. Many men who claimed land without the formality of a legal grant decided to abandon their claims rather than pay the quit rent arrears on them. Attracted by the relatively low quit rent of 1s. per 100 acres under Archdale's Laws, most landowners agreed to purchase their holdings from the proprietors at £20 per 1,000 acres. In addition, the proprietors sold a large amount of unclaimed land at the same rate.[25] Though the reformed land system worked well, it did not work perfectly. The receiver general fell behind in the collection of quit rents, and the proprietors refused to grant land except under the headright system from 1699 until about 1704. Landholders also found a way to avoid some payments of rent. Until they were established as planters, they did not pay rents and this ordinarily took six or seven years, but the proprietors apparently approved of the practice.[26]

After agreeing on issues affecting the land system, the governor and assembly turned to the question of slavery. As late as 1696, despite the growing number of Negro slaves in South Carolina, there was no comprehensive statute defining the legal status of slaves or regulating their conduct, an omission which was due largely to the Barbadian influence on the colony. The people of Barbados preferred that the institution of slavery be governed by custom rather than law, and they had always been reluctant to enact legislation defining the slave's status. Barbadian slave laws normally dealt only with the policing or control of the slave instead of his legal status, a practice which enabled a master to impose upon his slaves the conditions of servitude he desired without interference from English authorities. In 1668, however, the Barbadian assembly had legally defined slaves as real estate. The people of South Carolina had been content to adapt the practices of Barbados. They had carefully distinguished between Negro slaves and white servants without passing any laws that would have institutionalized this distinction. The only slave law enacted in South Carolina prior to 1696 had been passed in 1690 by Seth Sothel's assembly. Like the Barbadian statute of 1668, the law of 1690 had defined slaves as real estate, but the proprietors had disallowed it along

[25] Salley, ed., *Commissions and Instructions*, 92; Archdale's Account with Proprietors, 1697, *S. C. Pub. Recs.*, III, 222–28. Many examples of the surrender of land previously claimed only by survey can be found in the following articles by Henry A. M. Smith: "Old Charles Town and Its Vicinity," *S. C. Hist. Mag.*, 16 (1915), 1–15, 49–67; "Charleston and Charleston Neck," *ibid.*, 19 (1918), 3–76; "The Ashley River: Its Seats and Settlements," *ibid.*, 20 (1919), 3–51, 75–122.

[26] Proprietors to John Ely, Sept. 21, Oct. 19, 1699, *S. C. Pub. Recs.*, IV, 109, 119; Proprietors to Governor and Council, Sept. 21, 1718, Records in the British Public Record Office Relating to South Carolina, 1663–1782, 36 vols., VII, 159, S. C. Archives, hereafter cited as S. C. Pub. Recs.; [Nairne], *Letter from S. C.*, 47.

with the other acts passed during Sothel's administration and the assembly had not attempted to replace it. Although most South Carolinians would probably have been content to do without a law defining the legal status of the slave, they felt differently about the need for legislation to control the conduct of the unfree population, whether white servants or nonwhite slaves. South Carolina had enacted laws regulating the conduct of white servants and the assembly had subsequently extended those laws to cover Negroes. But the colony did not really need a slave law as such until it began to produce a marketable staple that required a large slave labor force. Then the increased importation of African slaves, who resented their depressed condition and were often rebellious, made additional legislation imperative, but the assembly had not attempted to reinstate the act of 1690 at the time of Governor Archdale's arrival in 1695.[27]

On March 16, 1696, the assembly enacted South Carolina's first comprehensive slave law, relying upon the comprehensive Barbados slave code of 1688 for the preamble and three-fourths of the provisions relating to police control of the slave. The preamble stated that special legislation was necessary to govern the Negro slaves, because they had "barbarous, wild, savage, Natures" and were "naturally prone and inclined" to "Disorders, Rapines, and Inhumanity." The police clauses of the slave code required slaves to obtain written permission to leave their masters' residences, directed masters to make regular searches of slave quarters for weapons, and established punishment for slaves who ran away or struck their masters; among the punishments were whipping, branding, nose-slitting, and emasculation. Another clause tried to eliminate potentially dangerous slave assemblies by directing the constables of Charles Town to break up such gatherings on the Sabbath.[28]

The most unusual feature of the South Carolina slave law was its definition of a slave: "All Negroes, Mollatoes, and Indians which at any time heretofore have been bought and Sold or now are and taken to be or hereafter Shall be Bought and Sold are hereby made and declared they and their Children Slaves to all Intents and purposes." This definition, vague to the point of being cryptic, adopted and extended the customary reluctance of Barbados and other island colonies to define slavery in a specific manner. Under the terms of the law, South Carolinians seem to have treated their Negroes as personal

---

[27] Sirmans, "Legal Status of Slave," *Jour. of So. Hist.*, 28 (1962), 462–65.
[28] This and the following paragraph are based on *ibid.*, 465–68; the slave code of 1696 is in Governor Archdale's Laws, foll. 60–66, S. C. Archives.

chattels. The surviving court records attest to this custom, and they are supported by the remarks of contemporary observers. John Norris, writing in 1712, noted, "When these people [Negroes] are thus bought, their Masters, or Owners, have then as good a Right to and title to them, during their lives, as a Man has here to a Horse or Ox, after he has bought them." In 1725 Arthur Middleton, acting governor of the colony, asserted flatly that slaves "have been and are always deemed as goods and Chattels of their Masters." [29]

It seems likely that the harsher police provisions of the code were not always strictly enforced, but running away to Spanish Florida remained an unpardonable sin, and slaves who tried it were severely punished. For example, three slaves who had run away were caught before reaching St. Augustine and returned to Charles Town in 1697. They were emasculated on orders from the assembly, and one of them died as a result.[30]

Governor Archdale had accomplished much in bringing the proprietors' policies into line with the desires of the colonists. On his return to London in October 1696, he even persuaded the proprietors to confirm the legislation depriving Craven County of its representation in the assembly. The proprietors justified their decision on the ground that the population of that county was too small to merit assembly representation. But the issue remained a live one in the colony. When a group of Huguenots petitioned the assembly in 1697 for full privileges and promised to swear allegiance to England, the assembly granted the request and extended the same opportunity to all foreigners who petitioned the governor within three months. This action tended to pacify both the Huguenots and their enemies, but despite this concession many Huguenots resented the way they had been treated. Their resentment deepened subsequently when the provincial government refused to let them build or purchase ships, even though they had been naturalized. The government contended, on rather shaky legal grounds, that foreign-born ownership of vessels violated the Navigation Acts.[31]

[29] The quotations are from Archdale's Laws, fol. 60, S. C. Archives; John Norris, *Profitable Advice for Rich and Poor* (London, 1712), 17; Journal of the Council of South Carolina, Sept. 10, 1725, Colonial Office Papers, 5/428, fol. 108, PRO (microfilm in Lib. Cong.).

[30] Nov. 12, 1697, Salley, ed., *Commons Journal, 1697*, 20; Sept. 9–10, 1702, *ibid., 1702*, 99–101; [Nairne], *Letter from S. C.*, 31; Norris, *Profitable Advice*, 31; Frank J. Klingberg, *An Appraisal of the Negro in Colonial South Carolina: A Study in Americanization* (Washington, 1941), 60.

[31] Proprietors to Archdale, Apr. 25, 1697, *S. C. Pub. Recs.*, III, 195; Cooper and McCord, eds., *Statutes*, II, 131–33; Edward Randolph to Bd. of Trade, Mar. 16, 1699, ed. Toppan, Prince Soc., *Publications*, 28 (1899), 198–99.

The Commons House of Assembly, though it generally approved the Archdale settlement, petitioned for further political reforms in 1698. It asked that the proprietors increase the authority of the local government by empowering the assembly and governor to repeal existing laws, a right not previously allowed in the case of statutes approved by the proprietors. It also objected to the practice of plural officeholding, requested the right to coin money in the colony, and asked the proprietors to furnish a copy of the royal charter. Finally, it announced its opposition to large land grants by seeking the reduction of the size of baronies and the limitation of future grants to 1,000 acres.[32]

These requests for additional reforms should not be allowed to obscure the political achievement of John Archdale. Because of his interest and his willingness to compromise, the government of South Carolina began functioning for the first time in a manner acceptable to both colonists and proprietors, and for the first time in more than a decade the provincial government was free of vindictive factionalism. In short, Archdale had helped South Carolina to grow up.

III

Throughout Archdale's brief administration and after, the official voice of the people of South Carolina was the Commons House of Assembly. Through it the colonists expressed their desires, their grievances, and their prejudices, and the governor and proprietors had no choice but to listen. Earlier, the elected branch of the legislature had been assigned a very limited role, and not until the middle of the eighteenth century would it acquire extensive power. But the emergence of the Commons House of Assembly as a distinct political institution represents a significant advance for representative government. Before the 1690's the elected members could only ratify or reject the statutes proposed by the Grand Council. Not only did the proprietors recognize for the first time the elected members as a separate house in Governor Ludwell's instructions of 1692, but during Smith's administration they accepted its right to initiate legislation, a right confirmed by the final revision of the Fundamental Constitutions in 1698.[33]

The proprietors and the Commons House agreed on several basic rules during the 1690's. According to a law passed in 1694, a new

[32] Nov. 18, 1698, Salley, ed., *Commons Journal, 1698,* 34–36.
[33] Fundamental Constitutions of 1698, *S. C. Pub. Recs.,* IV, 28–29; May 15, 1693, Salley, ed., *Commons Journal, 1693,* 22.

assembly was to be elected every two years, and there was to be no more than one year between assembly sessions. Archdale confirmed this practice.[34] The house at first consisted of twenty members with the three counties electing representatives. As a result of the anti-Huguenot sentiment in the middle of the decade, however, Craven County lost its representatives and Berkeley County elected twenty members while Colleton County chose ten. Members of the house were elected by a very broad electorate, the franchise apparently extending to all freemen, that is, all white adult males who were not servants.[35]

One of the first steps taken by the new house was to work out legislative procedures suitable to South Carolina. The Commons House adopted its first set of rules of order in 1692, a sign of its growing independence in the decade of the nineties. The rules were subject to change at any time by simple majority vote until 1698, when the assembly adopted a permanent set of rules of order. One rule prohibited the reintroduction of defeated bills in the same session. Another directed the speaker "not to Sway the House with arguments or Disputes," and members were prohibited from using "Reflecting words" about the governor. Smoking during sessions was also banned. A quorum of sixteen members was set to transact business and ten to adjourn the house. When votes were taken the yeas stood while the nays remained seated. There is, regrettably, no indication of what a member did if he wished to abstain from voting.[36]

The Commons House did much of its most important work in committees, and by the end of the century it had established two standing committees. The committee to examine the statutes was charged with the responsibility of determining what laws were expiring, deciding which of them should be re-enacted, and preparing new bills for that purpose. The committee to examine public accounts was responsible for auditing the accounts of officials who reported to the assembly. All other committee work was handled by *ad hoc* committees appointed for specific purposes, administrative and judicial as well as legislative. Special committees prepared bills, investigated petitions and complaints, supervised the administration of some public works, and adjudicated the division of estates.

In general both the Commons House and the council, acting in its

[34] Cooper and McCord, eds., *Statutes*, II, 79–80; Mar. 12, 1696, Salley, ed., *Commons Journal, Jan.–Mar. 1696*, 41–42.

[35] Norris, *Profitable Advice*, 32; see also Albert E. McKinley, *The Suffrage Franchise in the Thirteen English Colonies in America* (Philadelphia, 1905), 130, 132, 136 n.

[36] Sept. 23, 1692, Salley, ed., *Commons Journal, 1692*, 6–7; Sept. 13, 1698, *ibid.*, *1698*, 8–10.

legislative capacity, tried to pattern their procedures after Parliament. For example, each assembly opened with a speech by the governor, the local equivalent of a speech from the throne. He usually welcomed the assembly and then tried to indicate the nature of the most important legislative business. From the beginning, however, the elected representatives thought they knew what their rights should be. As a former assemblyman put it, they were "imitating the House of Commons in England, as nigh as possible," and they sometimes referred to their house as "This House of Comons."[37] The governor and council generally accepted comparisons between the Commons House of Assembly and the House of Commons without argument. Perhaps they, too, had no other model than Parliament. Curiously enough, however, the council made little effort to identify its rights with those of the House of Lords.

Occasionally the assembly found it inconvenient to imitate Parliament, most notably in the passage of bills. Every bill was read and voted on by each house three times, which was customary, but the South Carolina legislature sent the bill under debate from one house to another after each reading.[38] The Commons House and the council communicated with each other by specially appointed messengers, usually the members most concerned about the message or bill. When the houses were not able to agree on a bill, each appointed members to a conference committee, again usually the men most concerned. Under normal conditions the houses remained completely separate, but on special occasions the lower house would adjourn and meet with the upper house. It normally did so to hear a speech by the governor, but occasionally both houses entered into joint debate.

A major concern of the Commons House of Assembly during the 1690's was the establishment of its rights and privileges, especially in disputes with the governor and council. Although South Carolina's legislative system was comparatively new, especially the clear distinction between houses, the members of both houses had considerable political experience. Conflicts between houses were therefore a natural outgrowth of political development, and it would be unwise to overemphasize such disputes, especially when neither house was disposed to carry their disagreements to the point of disrupting public business.[39]

By the end of the century the Commons House had successfully

[37] [Nairne], Letter from S. C., 21–22; Oct. 30, 1700, Salley, ed., Commons Journal, 1700, 5.

[38] Sept. 5, 1702, Salley, ed., Commons Journal, 1702, 94.

[39] See, e.g., Nov. 2, 4, 1700, ibid., 1700, 9–10; Aug. 22, 23, 25, 1701, ibid., 1701, 15–19.

established its claims to a number of parliamentary rights, including one of the most important legislative prerogatives: control over its own membership. In 1698 the sheriff of Colleton County was elected to the assembly, but the Commons House refused to seat him, because the election law prohibited sheriffs from standing for assembly elections. In the same election two men were tied for the last place in the Berkeley County delegation, and the house solved the problem by choosing one of the men itself.[40] Within another two years the house had gained the exclusive right to nominate the officials who handled public funds. There were two such offices at that time, the public receiver of revenue and the powder receiver. The council and the governor had the right to approve the appointments, but they did not propose candidates themselves. The Commons House protected its rights and privileges in other ways, too. It refused to admit that English statutes were in force in South Carolina unless they had been re-enacted by the assembly. It was also careful to protect the dignity of its members. When a representative was the victim of malicious gossip in 1701, the house investigated the incident, discovered the guilty party, and forced him to apologize in front of the entire house.[41]

Membership in the Commons House of Assembly was highly valued in South Carolina. Political service was time-consuming, yet candidates campaigned hard, attended sessions regularly. The house never had any trouble maintaining a quorum, and no one ever refused a seat in the assembly. The turnover in membership was slow, too. For example, a majority of the representatives elected in 1700 and 1702 served at least three terms in the Commons House. Six of these men served five terms or more, while only seven were elected for just one term.

The leadership of the Commons House reflected the moderate tone of South Carolina politics at the turn of the century. Nineteen men can be identified as assembly leaders in the period from 1692 to 1703, and that number included representatives of all religious and political factions in the colony. Most of the leaders were Anglicans associated at some time or another with the Goose Creek faction, but at least seven dissenters also qualified as assembly leaders. Six men emerged as the most active and influential members of the house at this time. Jonathan Amory, Job Howes, Ralph Izard, and Robert Stevens dominated the assembly's affairs for a decade; James Moore and

---

[40] Sept. 13–14, 1698, *ibid., 1698,* 5–8, 10; in later years the house called for a new election in the event of a tie vote.

[41] Nov. 1, 2, 1700, *ibid., 1700,* 5, 9; Aug. 15, 1701, *ibid., 1701,* 7–8.

Landgrave Edmund Bellinger occupied positions of equal importance prior to their elevation to the council. Bellinger was a dissenter and proprietary man, Stevens was an Anglican from Goose Creek who later opposed the Goose Creek faction, and the others were former anti-proprietary men who had made their peace with the proprietors. Although assembly leadership thus included all religious and political factions, with some emphasis on Anglicans and former Goose Creek men, the geographic distribution of leaders was not at all uniform. Berkeley County men ran the house, even before 1696, when they composed only a third of its membership. Fifteen of the nineteen leaders and all six of the strongest leaders represented that county. There is no ready explanation for the dominance of Berkeley County, but the advantage of living close to the seat of government must have been a factor; it was easier for Berkeley County representatives to attend sessions faithfully than men from the outlying counties.[42]

As for the economic interests of the assembly leaders, most of them seem to have been planters. One or two leaders were merchants, two were lawyers, and one was a physician, but the rest seemed to have been most interested in farming. It should be noted, however, that the economy of South Carolina had not yet matured enough to produce a high degree of occupational specialization. Rather than designating assemblymen as merchants, planters, or lawyers, it might be more accurate to say that, with a few exceptions, the leaders of the Commons House were men who were not devoted exclusively to particular occupations but were eager to make money in any legal way they could. Like most Carolinians of that era, the assembly members were primarily farmers, but they sought to supplement their income by trading with Indians and by seeking offices of profit under the provincial government.

IV

When Governor John Archdale departed from South Carolina in 1696, he picked Joseph Blake as his successor. Then, believing that his own experience proved the value of a resident proprietor as governor,

---

[42] The assembly leaders, in addition to those named in the text, were John Ash, John Ashby, John Boyd, Charles Burnham, Daniel Courtis, Robert Fenwicke, Robert Gibbes, Robert Hall, John Morton, Serurier Smith, Landgrave Thomas Smith, Nicholas Trott, and Henry Wiggington. This list is taken from Jack P. Greene, *The Quest for Power: The Lower Houses of Assembly in the Southern Royal Colonies, 1689–1776* (Chapel Hill, 1963), 457–88; I have included only those men whom Professor Greene designates as leaders of the "first rank."

he arranged for the sale of his son's proprietorship to Blake. Joseph Blake was the son and heir of Benjamin Blake, one of the leading dissenter immigrants of the 1680's, and he was related by marriage to the other leading dissenter families, the Mortons, the Axtels, and the Bellingers.[43] In order to secure his political power Blake needed assistance in England, and he allied himself with proprietor Thomas Amy and proprietary secretary William Thornburgh. According to Edward Randolph, this triumvirate monopolized the profitable offices of Carolina. The men associated with Blake in South Carolina formed a small clique. Besides Blake its members were his relatives and fellow dissenters, Landgraves Joseph Morton and Edmund Bellinger, and James Moore, who continued his policy of peaceful coexistence with his onetime enemies. Other men, such as Speaker Jonathan Amory and Thomas Broughton, may also have been included in the clique. Blake took advantage of his position to find other sources of profit, and he and his friends soon came to monopolize the profitable new trade with the western Indians.[44] Blake could be quite ruthless in the pursuit of a profitable office. When Nicholas Trott, the provincial attorney general and naval officer, criticized Joseph Morton's conduct as judge of the court of vice-admiralty in 1699, Blake suspended Trott from both his offices and then arrested him on a charge of breach of the peace. The governor then replaced Trott with a couple of his friends.[45]

Previous administrations had spent their energies trying to punish their enemies and even to harry them from the colony. In contrast, Blake simply wanted to exploit the perquisites of office and enrich himself, his relatives, and his friends. He was not guilty of graft, but he made sure that the rewards of office went only to his followers. He did not care what became of his enemies so long as they were not able to interfere with his plans. His political ambitions may not have raised the moral tone of government in South Carolina, but they helped to eliminate the vindictive spirit—except for the Trott incident—that had previously characterized local politics.

Governor Blake's fellow proprietors in England rarely caused him trouble, but during his administration they did make their last

[43] Cheves, "Blake of S. C.," *S. C. Hist. Mag.,* 1 (1900), 153–57.

[44] Randolph to William Blathwayt, Apr. 8, 1699, ed. Toppan, Prince Soc., *Publications,* 31 (1909), 553–55; Statement of Robert Crown, William Owen, and Joseph James, n. d., Archdale Papers, no. 9, Lib. Cong.

[45] Case of Nicholas Trott, Apr. 7, 1702, Council Minutes, Aug. 17, 1700, Jan. 20, 1701, *S. C. Pub. Recs.,* V, 49–51, 54–55, 61; Randolph, "Narrative of His Survey," Nov. 5, 1700, ed. Toppan, Prince Soc., *Publications,* 28 (1899), 228–29.

serious effort to secure the adoption of the Fundamental Constitutions. They instructed Blake to work toward this end in 1697, and the following year they drew up a new version of the Constitutions, somewhat shorter than the earlier drafts but without significant changes. When Blake submitted the Constitutions to the assembly, it was rejected because the South Carolinians opposed the establishment of a provincial house of nobles.[46] After this defeat the proprietors abandoned the Constitutions for all time.

The only serious challenge to Blake's power in South Carolina came from the Crown and Parliament. In 1696 Parliament, tired of colonial evasions of the Navigation Acts and disturbed by the threat of Scottish competition, passed a new Navigation Act designed to improve the methods of enforcement by introducing new agencies of control and vesting primary responsibility for enforcement in the Commissioners of Customs in England, who appointed customs collectors in the colonies. At the same time the law required colonial governors to take a special oath to enforce the Navigation Acts and to post bonds of £1,000 sterling, which they would forfeit if they failed to do so; it also reaffirmed the power of the governor to appoint a naval officer in his colony to keep detailed records concerning vessels and cargoes that entered and cleared each port; the naval officer, of necessity, cooperated with the customs collectors even though he was not involved in the collection of duties. In addition, Parliament provided for the establishment of new courts of vice-admiralty in the colonies giving them authority to try all maritime cases without juries and making them responsible to the High Court of Admiralty in England instead of the governor.[47] To supervise the new policy of trade regulation, King William III created a new agency, the Lords Commissioners of Trade and Plantations, soon known simply as the Board of Trade. Because proprietary colonies had often been guilty of flagrant violations of the Navigation Acts, Parliament extended the new law to cover proprietary colonies and required proprietary governors to obtain the Crown's approval before taking office.

In the 1690's South Carolina's economy continued to expand; King William's War created a new interest in naval stores, and Randolph reported that the people were actively promoting the production of pitch, tar, and turpentine. When Randolph departed in the spring of

[46] Instructions to Joseph Blake, Apr. 25, 1697, S. C. Pub. Recs., III, 197; Nov. 11, 1698, Salley, ed., Commons Journal, 1698, 29–30; this version of the Constitutions is in Parker, ed., N. C. Charters and Constitutions, 234–40.

[47] Andrews, Colonial Period, IV, 151–77, 222–27, 272–94; Hall, Randolph, 154–66.

1699, he left with the impression that South Carolina would soon be one of the most prosperous colonies in America.[48] Randolph's successor, Robert Quary, a former Goose Creek man, also praised the work of Blake and his associates. In 1705, early in the War of Spanish Succession, Parliament offered a bounty on naval stores produced in the colonies, and South Carolina production spurted ahead. The proprietors encouraged the new industry, creating the port of Beaufort on Port Royal Sound in 1711 in order to facilitate the production of naval stores in Granville and Colleton counties.[49] By the end of the war naval stores had become a principal and continuing source of profit for the colony. It was a fortunately timed development, for the rice trade had declined briefly at the beginning of the eighteenth century when Parliament in 1704 put rice on the list of enumerated commodities. Since that action eliminated exports to the former markets in Portugal and Holland and restricted shipments thereafter only to England, profits from the export of rice dropped for a time.[50]

V

Thanks largely to the tact and flexibility of Governor John Archdale, South Carolina had managed to compromise its political differences after a decade of controversy. Archdale had settled the land question through the land law of 1696, the proprietors had bowed to the anti-French sentiment of the dissenter party by depriving the Huguenots of their assembly representatives, and the assembly had enacted a slave code of major importance. Governor Joseph Blake had carried on Archdale's policy of maintaining harmony, even though he had built up a political faction of his own. At the same time, South Carolina was enjoying the first real economic prosperity in its history because of the introduction of rice and the expansion of the Indian trade. With its political differences composed and its economy booming, South Carolina's prospects were excellent in 1700.

[48] Hall, *Randolph*, 191–92; Nov. 18, 1698, Salley, ed., *Commons Journal, 1698*, 36; Randolph to Bd of Trade, Mar. 16, 1699, ed. Toppan, Prince Soc., *Publications*, 28 (1899), 193–200; Randolph, "Narrative of His Survey," Nov. 5, 1700, *ibid.*, 220–21.

[49] For Quary's view, see Sainsbury *et al.*, eds., *Cal. St. Papers, Col., Amer. and W. Indies, 1701*, 483; for the Proclamation of Proprietors, see Jan. 17, 1711, S. C. Pub. Recs., VI, 1–3, S. C. Archives.

[50] Gray, *Hist. of Agriculture*, I, 153–55; Nettels, *Money Supply*, 155–56; Andrews, *Colonial Period*, IV, 95.

CHAPTER V

THE RENASCENCE OF FACTIONS

1700–1712

During the first thirty years after the founding of South Carolina, religious factionalism remained a relatively minor matter in provincial politics. Although the proprietors had announced their preference for the Church of England, they also wished to establish a haven of religious toleration, and for eighteen of the thirty years they accepted dissenters as governors of their colony. The absence of organized congregations in the early years, the remoteness from religious antagonisms in England, and common grievances against the proprietors led the settlers to subordinate religious animosities to other issues in the colony. Although the religious differences between Anglican and dissenter had contributed to the political strife of the 1680's, other considerations seem to have been more fundamental and Governor Archdale was undoubtedly correct in reporting that "religious differences did not yet peculiarly distinguish the parties." [1] Reconciliation on the fundamental issue of land policy in the 1690's brought an easy collaboration among men of different faiths, and the Carolina assembly in 1697 confirmed toleration for all but Roman Catholics as the official policy of the colony. Political office was open to dissenters of varying views, including those who regarded oaths of office as blasphemous swearing; the latter were allowed to affirm their loyalty and their intention to perform the duties of their office, even though this practice was contrary to English law. During the administration of dissenter Joseph Blake in 1698 dissenters joined Anglicans in the

[1] Wallace, S. C.: Short History, 66.

75

Commons House of Assembly in resolving unanimously that the public should pay an annual salary of £150 to the Anglican rector in Charles Town.[2]

I

The renascence of factions in South Carolina was triggered by the death of Governor Blake in 1700 and the choice of an Anglican over a leading dissenter as governor. After Blake's death the council met on September 11 to select one of themselves to act as governor until the proprietors made a new appointment. The logical candidates were the two landgraves present, Joseph Morton and Edmund Bellinger, both dissenters, and the council promptly elected Morton. But James Moore, a high Anglican, and his good friend, Robert Daniel, opposed Morton's election and pointed out that a year earlier the proprietors had objected because Morton and Bellinger held royal commissions for offices in the court of vice-admiralty at the same time that they held proprietary commissions as deputies. Moore and Daniel now contended that Morton's royal commission made him ineligible for the governorship of the proprietary colony. A majority of the council accepted the conflict-of-interest argument and voted Moore into the governor's post. The proprietors did not issue a commission to Moore, but Lord Granville, now the palatine of Carolina and an aggressive Anglican, let him keep the job temporarily, in order to keep out the dissenter Morton.[3]

The elevation of Moore over Morton was the prologue to a bitter conflict between Anglicans and dissenters in which religion became the primary divisive force in South Carolina politics. Other issues—notably the need to reform the Indian trade and the claims of the Commons House of Assembly to control administrative agencies—influenced politics in the first years of the eighteenth century, but the key question was whether the rejuvenated Goose Creek faction would be able to impose the establishment of the Church of England upon the dissenters in the colony.

At the turn of the century no one of the religious groups greatly outnumbered the others. In a total white population of about 4,200,

[2] Feb. 25, 1697, Salley, ed., *Commons Journal, 1697*, 7; Sept. 20, 1698, *ibid., 1698*, 14; for dissenters making affirmations, see, e.g., Aug. 19, 1701, *ibid., Aug. 1701*, 11, Aug. 26, 1702, *ibid., 1702*, 79–80.

[3] Proprietors to Joseph Blake, Sept. 21, 1699, Council Minutes, Sept. 11, 1700, *S. C. Pub. Recs.*, IV, 101, V, 70–71; Hewatt, *Historical Account*, in Carroll, ed., *Hist. Collections of S. C.*, I, 131.

there were some 2,000 dissenters, of whom about 1,000 were Presbyterians and the rest Baptists, Quakers, and other sectarians. The Church of England could claim approximately 1,800 adherents. The remainder of the population were French Huguenots. Although technically dissenters, they had always tended to side with the Church of England, and after the dissenters had led the move to deprive the French immigrants of their political privileges in 1695 and 1696, the Huguenots definitely threw their support to the Anglicans. Some of them even began to convert to the Church of England.[4]

For the religious antagonisms that wracked South Carolina in the early eighteenth century Lord Granville, the Carolina palatine, seems to have been largely responsible. Described as one who had "distinguished himself as an inflexible bigot for the High-church," he began to press for the establishment of the Church of England in South Carolina and for the exclusion of dissenters from political office.[5] The Society for the Propagation of the Gospel in Foreign Parts was organized in 1701, and the first S.P.G. missionary in South Carolina landed in 1702, bringing the promise of additional assistance in meeting the spiritual needs of the colony. Men of genuine piety feared that without this help South Carolina might sink into a state of moral degeneration. There was some cause for their alarm. Streetwalkers and prostitutes were common in Charles Town, and the first S.P.G. missionaries found the colony suffering from religious lethargy, occasional atheism, and a common disregard for the blue laws on the statute books. One of the missionaries later summed up the general attitude of the people of South Carolina at this time: "Religion was the thing [about which] they troubled themselves the least. Sunday was only distinguished from other days because it was a day of rest and Pleasure."[6]

Although the issue of establishment dominated political debate in the early eighteenth century, the need to reform the colony's Indian trade caused an almost equal furor. Indian traders of that time were a

[4] Hirsch, *Huguenots*, 113–14; the population statistics were compiled from this source and from the following: [Nairne], *Letter from S. C.*, 41, 44, 46; Governor and Council to Proprietors, Sept. 18, 1708, *S. C. Pub. Recs.*, V, 203–4; Edward Randolph to Bd. of Trade, Mar. 16, 1699, ed. Toppan, Prince Soc., *Publications*, 28 (1899), 200.

[5] Hewatt, *Historical Account*, in Carroll, ed., *Hist. Collections of S. C.*, I, 131.

[6] Francis Varnod to Sec. S.P.G., Apr. 3, 1728, S.P.G. Mss., A 21, Carolina Letters, no. 1; see also Francis LeJau to Sec. S.P.G., Feb. 9, Apr. 2, 1711, Klingberg, ed., *LeJau Chronicle*, 86, 88; Gideon Johnston to John Chamberlain, May 28, 1712, Frank J. Klingberg, ed., *Carolina Chronicle: The Papers of Commissary Gideon Johnston, 1707–1716* (Berkeley, 1946), 110–11; Bridenbaugh, *Cities in the Wilderness*, 222, 227.

particularly odious lot. They habitually swindled and debauched the Indians with whom they traded and contrived to get the Indians into their power by letting them run up large bills until the redmen were in debt for life. Many whites recognized the injustice and the folly of such a trading system, fearing that the Indians must sooner or later revolt against it. The assembly had begun consideration of trade reform as early as 1697, and the Commons House had resolved in 1698 that "the Indian trade as it is now Managed be a grieveance to this Settlement and Prejudiciall to the safety thereof." [7] Both sectional and religious factors influenced the debate. Nearly all the leading reformers lived near the southwestern frontier of South Carolina, the most exposed area in the colony. If war came with the Indians or if England went to war with France again or with Spain, the southwest would be most exposed to attack. Colleton County in the southwest was also the home of nearly all the leading dissenters in the colony, a circumstance which led most dissenters to support demands for reform. At the same time control of the Indian trade was passing from dissenters to Anglicans after the death of Joseph Blake. The new magnates of the trade were James Moore and Thomas Broughton, both Anglicans and Goose Creek men. This shift in control made the dissenters more willing to reform the trade, and gave to some Anglicans a vested interest in the status quo.

When the political leaders of South Carolina began to take sides on these issues, they almost invariably regrouped themselves according to earlier factional divisions. To a man the surviving Goose Creek leaders —James Moore, Sir Nathaniel Johnson, Ralph Izard, Job Howes, and Robert Daniel, to name a few—supported the Anglican party. They were joined by more recent immigrants from the West Indies, including Nicholas Trott and Johnson's son-in-law, Thomas Broughton. Thanks to the dissenter leadership of the anti-Huguenot movement in the 1690's, the Anglicans could now rely on complete Huguenot support.

Anglicans and Huguenots together accounted for over half the population of South Carolina, and if the Anglicans had been united the Church party would have controlled the province. The fact was, however, the Anglicans were anything but united, and a significant number rejected the leadership of the Church party under Governor Moore and his successor, Sir Nathaniel Johnson. Appalled by the

---

[7] Crane, *Southern Frontier*, 141–42; the quotation is from Sept. 23, 1698, Salley, ed., *Commons Journal, 1698*, 18.

desertion of the dissident Anglicans, the Church party castigated them as "Designing persons" and "half faced Christians" who were motivated by "Mammon, or the hopes of getting themselves into . . . places of Profit."[8] Actually, the chief interest of the dissident Anglicans was reform of the Indian trade; living for the most part in the southwestern part of the colony, they shared the fears of the dissenters in that area. The reform-minded Anglicans distrusted Governors Moore and Johnson because they thought the two men were so involved personally in the Indian trade that they would never consent to an effective reform. The leaders of the dissident Anglicans took a particular interest in the S.P.G.'s program for the conversion of Indians, which they hoped would solidify South Carolina's alliance with the neighboring Indians. Robert Stevens, a former leader of the Commons House of Assembly and an Anglican communicant in Goose Creek Parish, became a spokesman for the Anglicans who favored an establishment of the Church of England but wanted to make it as painless as possible for dissenters. He especially opposed political discrimination against the dissenters, because "such rigid practices do not appear to me to be convenient, necessary or prudent." Suspecting that the Church party's "Zeal for settling the Church" was "only a Cloak for other designs," he charged that Governor Johnson wished to establish a monopoly of the Indian trade. For his part Stevens tried to help the S.P.G. with its plan for converting Indians.[9]

While the basic political divisions in South Carolina were old, many of the political leaders of the early eighteenth century were newcomers. The Church party especially benefited from the arrival of recent immigrants. Chief among these was Nicholas Trott, the most learned man in the colony. Trott was a lawyer who later edited several collections of laws, including a two-volume edition of the statutes of South Carolina. In his spare time he worked on a commentary on the Hebrew text of the Old Testament. In 1702 the governor and council restored him to his former positions as naval officer and attorney general at the insistence of the assembly, and the proprietors promoted him to chief justice the following year. But for all his learning, Trott bordered on being a religious bigot: He believed that all dissenters were unfit to hold political office and thought they were trying to

[8] Nicholas Trott to S.P.G., Sept. 13, 1707, S.P.G. Mss., A 3, no. 152; Gideon Johnston to the Bishop of Sarum, Sept. 20, 1708, Klingberg, ed., *Johnston Chronicle*, 27.

[9] Stevens to Sec. S.P.G., Feb. 3, 1708, S.P.G. Mss., A 4, no. 19; see also Stevens to Edward Marston, n. d., Stevens to Sec. S.P.G., Feb. 21, 1706, *ibid.*, A 2, nos. 156, 158.

undermine all religion in South Carolina.[10] The other leading Anglican at this time was Sir Nathaniel Johnson, who had immigrated to the colony in 1689 but had not taken an active part in government. A professional soldier and a devout Anglican, Johnson had been a member of Parliament and later a governor of the Leeward Islands before coming to South Carolina. After the Glorious Revolution he remained loyal to James II, and until 1702 he refused to take the newly required oath of allegiance. His acceptance of the governor's post seems to have been inspired chiefly by his desire to exclude dissenters from political office and to secure the establishment of the Church of England.[11]

Although most of the members of the old proprietary party had died or left the colony, their sons and relatives had replaced them. The most important men among this second generation were English dissenters: the second Landgrave Thomas Smith, the second Landgrave Joseph Morton, and Landgrave Edmund Bellinger. The proprietary party of fifteen years earlier had also included a small number of English Anglicans who had immigrated in the 1670's, and Stephen Bull, the lone survivor in 1700, continued to oppose the Goose Creek men and to assist the dissenters. During the 1690's, the dissenter party had been strengthened by the immigration of several parties of New England Congregationalists. The largest such group, consisting of 158 people, migrated in 1697 and founded the town of Dorchester.[12] The dissenters from Barbados had been divided in the 1680's, but after 1700 such families as the Stanyarnes and Elliotts consistently allied themselves with the English dissenters.[13]

Both of the principal leaders of the dissenters, John Ash and Landgrave Thomas Smith, were too hotheaded to be effective politicians. Ash was one of the New England Congregationalists who settled at Dorchester, apparently attracted to South Carolina by its policy of toleration; proposals to establish the Church of England threw

[10] See Theodore D. Jervey in *DAB* s.v. "Trott, Nicholas"; Trott to S.P.G., Sept. 13, 1707, S.P.G. Mss., A 3, no. 152; Jan. 20, 24, 1702, Salley, ed., *Commons Journal, 1702,* 9, 20–21.

[11] See Hayes Baker-Crothers in *DAB* s.v. "Johnson, Sir Nathaniel"; Gideon Johnston to the Bishop of Sarum, Sept. 20, 1708, Klingberg, ed., *Johnston Chronicle,* 25; Edward Marston to Dr. Thomas Bray, Feb. 2, 1702, S.P.G. Mss., A 1, no. 60.

[12] Babette M. Levy, "Early Puritanism in the Southern and Island Colonies," Amer. Antiq. Soc., *Proceedings,* 70 (1960), 265–67; Francis Varnod to Sec. S.P.G., Apr. 3, 1728, S.P.G. Mss., A 21, Carolina Letters, no. 1.

[13] The best single source for determining political loyalties at this time is Feb. 23, 1703, Salley, ed., *Commons Journal, 1703,* 52–53; on that day the dissenter party walked out of the assembly while the Anglicans remained.

him into a frenzy. At one point in the debate he even tried to curry favor with the proprietors by attempting to persuade the assembly to approve the Fundamental Constitutions, but Nicholas Trott and Job Howes blocked this maneuver.[14] Landgrave Thomas Smith was an exception to some of the generalizations that can be made about the dissenters. Most significantly, he did not actively support reform of the Indian trade, probably because he carried on an extensive traffic with the northern Indians. Smith's ideas on political tactics were also somewhat peculiar, to say the least. Whenever the provincial government did something he disliked, his normal reaction was to try to disrupt the machinery of government. Occasionally he would go about preaching disobedience to the law, but more often he withdrew from the government in a huff and tried to persuade his friends to do the same.[15]

Probably the ablest, and certainly the most admirable, politician of the day was the leader of the dissident Anglicans, Thomas Nairne, a planter living on the southwestern frontier of the colony and the leading advocate of the S.P.G. program to convert the Indians. Trade reform was his special interest, but he also spoke out for the political rights of the people and the assembly. He wanted to protect England's interest on the frontier and later proposed a scheme for English colonization of the borderland. A far-sighted imperialist, Nairne was also an able teacher. His frontier and Indian policies attracted some of the brightest young men in the colony. Among his close associates were John Barnwell, George Chicken, Tobias Fitch, and William Bull (who had married Nairne's step-daughter). This group of men originated every constructive development in South Carolina's Indian policy for the next generation.[16]

II

In an age when religious fanatics were coming to dominate Carolina politics, Governor James Moore stands out as something of an exception. Although he got the council to set aside the election of the dissenter Morton as governor, Moore seemed more interested in the perquisites of office than in imposing Anglicanism on the dissenters.

[14] Representation of Assembly Members from Colleton County, June 26, 1703, in Rivers, *Hist. of S. C.*, 457; Aug. 31, Sept. 1, 1702, Salley, ed., *Commons Journal, 1702,* 88–89, 91.

[15] He was the great-grandfather of Robert Barnwell Rhett; on his Indian trade, see Crane, *Southern Frontier*, 120.

[16] See Verner W. Crane in *DAB* s.v. "Nairne, Thomas."

An Irish adventurer who had made good, he was disarmingly candid and never denied that his chief interest in politics was money. He once justified himself to the assembly by explaining, "I have the most Numerous Family of Relations and Children in the Collony." [17] He wanted his relatives and friends to occupy the most profitable offices, and he wanted to protect and expand England's interest on the southern frontier. His enemies—and he had many—thought him an unprincipled crook, but his interest in English expansion and in reform of the Indian trade seem to have been genuine.[18]

South Carolina's dissenters worried because Moore was the first Anglican governor in nearly a decade, but most of them were disposed to try to get along with him. Wanting above all to keep the peace in South Carolina, Moore went out of his way to pacify potential enemies. For example, he dealt with the assembly in a conciliatory fashion and skillfully avoided disputes with the Commons House.[19] A few politicians, however, refused to accept conciliation. Morton declined to forget past grievances. He criticized Moore's administration, charging it with evasion of the Navigation Acts, and made such a nuisance of himself that Moore finally suspended him from the council. Nor could Nicholas Trott forget the way he had been treated by Governor Blake and his friends. Trott frequently criticized the way Joseph Morton and Edmund Bellinger ran the court of vice-admiralty, and he once angered Bellinger so much that the two men fought in public. Moore's friends sometimes caused as much trouble as his enemies. When Robert Daniel, Moore's closest associate, offended the assembly by illegally arresting several men, the Commons House denounced him as "a person of notorious ill fame and Conversation" and demanded that Moore suspend him from all his offices.[20]

For the first year and a half he was in office, Governor Moore and the assembly spent much of their time trying to find an acceptable method of regulating the Indian trade. They made some progress, appointing by legislation an agent to regulate trade among the Upper Creeks and designating three other men to perform similar, but temporary, duties among other tribes; the assembly also tried to

[17] Apr. 2, 1702, Salley, ed., Commons Journal, 1702, 48.

[18] Crane, Southern Frontier, 75–76, 144; see also Hayes Baker-Crothers in DAB s.v. "Moore, James"; for criticism of Moore, see John Ash, The Present State of Affairs in Carolina (London, 1706), in Salley, ed., Narratives of Carolina, 270, 272.

[19] See, e.g., Nov. 4–6, 1700, Salley, ed., Commons Journal, 1700, 10–11.

[20] Sainsbury et al., eds., Cal. St. Papers, Col., Amer. and W. Indies, 1701, 483, 651; Joseph Morton to Proprietors, Aug. 29, Sept. 25, 1701, S. C. Pub. Recs., V, 17–19; Nov. 8, 15, 1700, Salley, ed., Commons Journal, 1700, 15–16, 19–21; the quotation is from Nov. 15, 1700, ibid., 21.

punish some of the more offensive Indian traders. The province seemed to be slowly moving toward a regulatory system which would be directed by the assembly and enforced by a single agent, but for some reason the governor and the assembly could not agree on a general Indian code. John Ash later charged that Moore wanted to monopolize the trade for himself, but it seems more likely that there was an honest disagreement on the most suitable form of control. Moore apparently favored a public monopoly of the trade, while the Commons House preferred a private trade under a strict licensing system.[21]

James Moore's policy of conciliation came to an abrupt end in the winter of 1702, when external necessities began to overshadow his desire for internal peace. For over thirty years the English had contested Spanish control of the Florida borderland and the interior, but not until the end of the seventeenth century did France and England collide on the southern frontier. After the Peace of Ryswick in 1697 brought a temporary end to hostilities between England and France, the French, in a move to outflank the southwestward march of the Carolina traders, founded Louisiana in 1699, creating a new zone of Anglo-French rivalry for the Indian trade. In his message to the Commons House of Assembly in 1701, Governor Moore cautioned that in "warr or peace we are sure to be always in danger and under the trouble and charge of keeping out guards, even in time of Peace, so long as those French live so near us." [22] By February 1702 a formal declaration of war against Spain and France was expected at any moment, and Moore saw the approaching war as an opportunity to advance England's imperial interests. He hoped to dislodge the French on the Gulf Coast and to remove Spain from the international competition for control of the southern frontier. Despite the lack of any official notice of the outbreak of hostilities in Europe, he asked the assembly for support, at least to the extent of preparing the colony's defenses for war. But he failed to persuade the Commons House of the urgency of the situation, and when it refused to appropriate funds for adequate defenses, Moore dissolved the assembly on February 2, 1702, and called a new election for March 11.[23]

The assembly election seems to have been an especially wild affair in

[21] Crane, *Southern Frontier*, 144 and *n;* Aug. 27, 28, 1701, Salley, ed., *Commons Journal, Aug. 1701*, 24, 31; Jan. 29, 1702, *ibid., 1702*, 25–26; Ash, *Present State of Affairs*, in Salley, ed., *Narratives of Carolina*, 270.

[22] Aug. 14, 1701, Commons Journal, cited by Crane, *Southern Frontier*, 74–75.

[23] Crane, *Southern Frontier*, 75; Apr. 1, 1702, Salley, ed., *Commons Journal, 1702*, 42.

Berkeley County, where Moore and his opponents worked hard to win votes. John Ash later charged that Moore rigged the election there and "so Influenc'd the Sheriff, that Strangers, Servants, Aliens, nay Malatoes and Negroes were Polled." [24] Other irregularities may have occurred. As soon as the assembly met on April 2, it received petitions charging that the elections of three men were invalid because unqualified Frenchmen had voted. Although Moore undoubtedly campaigned for men who would support his imperialistic policies, he did not win control of the Berkeley County delegation or of the assembly.[25] Led by John Ash, the Commons House ignored Moore's pleas for military preparations and launched a full-scale investigation of the election, calling in forty-one voters and demanding that they prove their qualifications for the franchise. At least twenty-nine of them were French, and one, a man called "Black Natt," may have been a Negro or mulatto.[26]

The investigation enraged Governor Moore, who thought the assembly should be preparing for war. He may also have feared the investigation would turn up something embarrassing to him. Moore therefore prorogued the assembly until May 5. When it reconvened, the Commons House not only continued the investigation but expanded it. A group of petitioners charged that three additional men had been elected fraudulently, and the Commons ordered a total of eighty-three men to prove their right to vote. This was too much for Moore, who promptly prorogued the assembly until August.[27]

When the assembly reconvened in August South Carolina knew unofficially that England and her allies had declared war against Spain and France. The Commons House dropped its investigation of the election and turned its full attention to military affairs. Moore presented his plan for an expedition against St. Augustine and urged the assembly to act before Spain reinforced Florida, but the Commons House initially insisted it should first attend to the colony's defenses. The dissenters, in particular, opposed the expedition, because they suspected everything Moore proposed, and John Ash called the expedition "a Project of Freebooting under the specious Name of War." Actually, Ash was too suspicious of Moore. The governor

[24] Ash, *Present State of Affairs,* in Salley, ed., *Narratives of Carolina,* 271.

[25] Of the 21 men elected from Berkeley County, six sooner or later opposed Moore, including the leading votegetter, Dr. Charles Burnham. The others were Stephen Bull, Abraham Eve, George Smith, Landgrave Thomas Smith, and Henry Wiggington. There were 21 members of the delegation, because two men tied for the 20th position and the Commons House seated both of them.

[26] Apr. 2, 4, 6, 1702, Salley, ed., *Commons Journal, 1702,* 46, 51–54.

[27] May 14–16, 18–19, 1702, *ibid.,* 55–59, 61–63.

sincerely wanted to advance England's interests, although he probably helped himself later to a little loose church silverplate on his invasion of Florida.[28] Fortunately for Moore not all the dissenters shared Ash's extreme views, and when official news of the declaration of war reached Charles Town on August 26, a majority of the Commons House voted in favor of the expedition. After that the only stumbling block was the question of who would command the forces. Moore wanted to appoint Robert Daniel, who commanded the provincial militia, but the Commons House still distrusted Daniel for his earlier arbitrary arrests. It asked Moore to take personal command of the expedition. Moore refused at first because of the pressure of business at home, another indication that he had no ulterior motive in planning the attack. The assembly prevailed, however, and Moore agreed to take command himself.[29]

Invading Florida in October, Moore and his troops easily took possession of the town of St. Augustine and drove the inhabitants into the Castillo de San Marcos. But the size and strength of the Spanish fort surprised and dismayed Moore. Not expecting such a formidable structure, he had not brought along the cannon needed to besiege it properly. After settling down to the weary business of trying to starve the Spanish into submission, he sent Daniel to New York to get larger cannon. The siege lasted a month and a half; it ended when Spanish reinforcements in the form of two men-of-war showed up before Daniel returned. Moore burned both the town and his boats, then retreated overland in December.[30] Although the English had failed to take the fort, they had pushed the Spanish frontier farther south.

Moore's return to Charles Town was as turbulent as it was ignominious. The dissenters thought he had bungled the invasion, and the Commons House began an investigation. One dissenter accused Moore of having been drunk at St. Augustine; tempers grew hot, and fists as well as insults flew. A majority of the assembly favored Moore, however, and on January 27, 1703, the assembly gave him a formal vote of thanks for his leadership of the expedition.[31] Moore's expedition had cost South Carolina £4,000 sterling more than the assembly had authorized, and he proposed that the colony pay its creditors with

[28] Ash, *Present State of Affairs*, in Salley, ed., *Narratives of Carolina*, 272; Crane, *Southern Frontier*, 75–76.

[29] Aug. 26, 28, 29, Sept. 1, 1702, Salley, ed., *Commons Journal, 1702*, 80, 84–87, 89.

[30] Charles W. Arnade, *The Siege of St. Augustine in 1702* (Gainesville, 1959).

[31] Jan. 15, 16, 20, 22–23, 27–28, Feb. 5, 1703, Salley, ed., *Commons Journal, 1703*, 6, 8, 13–14, 25, 30, 35–36.

bills of credit. He also indicated that he wanted to embark on a more grandiose expedition against St. Augustine, Pensacola, and the new French post on the Mississippi, which would involve still greater expenditures. The dissenters disliked Moore's latest proposals, but they saw in the governor's financial distress an opportunity to advance some of their own ideas. John Ash introduced three bills in February, one to regulate assembly elections, one to revise the law on naturalization, and the third to regulate the Indian trade. The Commons House quickly passed all three bills. None of the texts of these bills has survived, but it seems likely that the election bill was designed to prevent future election frauds. The naturalization bill possibly made it more difficult for Huguenots to obtain citizenship, and the trade bill probably followed the assembly's preference for a licensed private trade.[32] Ash undoubtedly hoped that Moore would compromise, giving his support to Ash's measures in return for dissenter support of Moore's bills of credit.

Governor Moore, who was in no mood to trade votes with the dissenters, persuaded the council to delay action on Ash's proposals until the bill to emit £4,000 in bills of credit had been passed. On February 23 sixteen members of the dissenter party in the lower house walked out of the house in protest and left it without a quorum. The next day they returned and offered to sit longer if the remaining members would join them in protesting the council's action, but the other assemblymen refused to readmit those who had bolted and adjourned the assembly for a month. Governor Moore's followers immediately started a series of riots, during which voters threatened the lives of dissenter leaders but did them no actual harm.[33]

III

While the riots were going on, Sir Nathaniel Johnson replaced Moore as governor. The proprietors had never confirmed Moore, though they had allowed him to serve temporarily. On June 18, 1702, they commissioned Sir Nathaniel Johnson as governor, but when his instructions arrived he was suffering from an illness which caused him

[32] Feb. 11, 13, 22, 1703, *ibid.*, 39, 42; on the election bill, see Feb. 13, 1703, *ibid.*, 42; on the trade bill, see Jan. 20, 1703, *ibid.*, 15; on the naturalization bill, see Representation of Assembly Members from Colleton County, June 26, 1703, in Rivers, *Hist. of S. C.*, 457.

[33] Feb. 22-23, 1703, Salley, ed., *Commons Journal, 1703*, 52-53; Representation of Assembly Members from Colleton County, June 26, 1703, in Rivers, *Hist. of S. C.*, 457.

to lose the use of his limbs temporarily. He therefore refused to accept his commission until he had recovered sufficiently to exercise authority, as well as his muscles.[34] Completely recovered by early March 1703, Johnson then took over the governorship from Moore, who became attorney general. As a professional soldier Johnson shared much of Moore's concern about South Carolina's exposed position as an outpost of the English empire. He helped Moore arrange an expedition against the pro-Spanish Apalache Indians in 1704, and Moore recouped his military reputation by nearly exterminating the Apalaches. Smaller expeditions followed Moore's and by 1710 the Spanish had lost control of Florida, except for St. Augustine and a few neighboring villages near the Atlantic coast. Governor Johnson was equally concerned about South Carolina's defense posture and persuaded the assembly to fortify Charles Town. When Spanish retaliation came South Carolina was prepared. A Spanish fleet of five ships landed troops at three places near Charles Town on August 27, 1706, but the provincial militia and some friendly Indians easily drove the invaders back. The Spaniards lost forty men dead and 230 captured, while only one South Carolinian was killed.[35]

Although Johnson guided South Carolina ably in its military preparations, he usually acted in internal affairs as if he thought dissenters were as great a menace as Spanish soldiers. From the time he took office he aimed at the establishment of the Church of England. His first act as governor was to dissolve Moore's assembly and call new elections for March 31, 1703. Although Colleton County returned its usual slate of dissenters, the Anglican party won control of the assembly by sweeping the elections in Berkeley County. Johnson took no action against the dissenters for a year, although he obtained passage of Moore's proposal to emit bills of credit. Then in the spring of 1704 he executed a well-planned coup. The assembly was recessed and stood adjourned until May 10, when Johnson suddenly issued a call for an emergency meeting of the assembly on April 26. Before all the dissenters from Colleton County could reach Charles Town, the Anglican delegation from Berkeley County squeezed through by one vote an act of exclusion, barring dissenters from the assembly by requiring all members to swear either that they took communion in the Church of England or that they conformed to Anglicanism and had not taken communion in any other church for a year.

[34] McCrady, *Proprietary Government*, 389–90; Edward Marston to Dr. Thomas Bray, Feb. 2, 1702, S.P.G. Mss., A 1, no. 60.
[35] Crane, *Southern Frontier*, 78–81, 86–87; Francis LeJau to Sec. S.P.G., Dec. 2, 1706, Klingberg, ed., *LeJau Chronicle*, 17.

A member of the Anglican party, Job Howes, later tried to excuse the exclusion act by saying it was necessary "to quell all factions which so much disturb'd the peace of the Government," although there had been no internal disturbances in South Carolina for a year.[36] The true motives of the Anglicans became apparent when they promptly passed an act establishing the Church of England as the state church of South Carolina and providing that the Book of Common Prayer would be the official form of worship. The affairs of the church were to be governed by twenty commissioners named in the act, including Johnson and his principal supporters. The law refused legal recognition to marriages performed by dissenting clergymen and gave Johnson a veto on the acts of the church commission for as long as he remained governor. It also created seven parishes and directed that the public treasury would pay the salaries of Anglican ministers and underwrite the construction of Anglican churches. The Anglican freeholders in each parish had the right to elect rectors, but the church commissioners retained the right to suspend any clergyman.[37]

The colony's dissenters promptly dispatched a special agent to England to secure the disallowance of these two laws. John Ash, the first agent, died soon after his arrival, and the dissenters sent Joseph Boone in his place. Less excitable than Ash, Boone made a better agent. Despite the work of the agents, however, the proprietors ratified both laws. John Archdale and Maurice Ashley, Shaftesbury's grandson, voted against the acts, but Lord Granville cast his own vote and the proxies of two absent proprietors in favor of them and persuaded Sir John Colleton to vote with him. Joseph Boone then appealed to the House of Lords, hired several pamphleteers, including Daniel Defoe, to present the case for the dissenters in polemical writings, and won the support of the S.P.G., which objected to the powers vested in the church commission. The House of Lords heard Boone's petitions on February 28, 1706, and after questioning Archdale and Granville, it resolved on March 9 that the Carolina legislation was repugnant to the laws of England. On March 12, the Lords presented an address asking Queen Anne to relieve the people of South Carolina from the "arbitrary oppressions," and the Crown directed the proprietors to disallow the acts.[38]

[36] Howes to John Archdale, Jan. 15, 1706, Archdale Papers, no. 55, Lib. Cong.; see also Petition of Joseph Boone, Feb. 28, 1706, in Leo F. Stock, ed., *Proceedings and Debates of the British Parliaments Respecting North America, 1542–1754,* 5 vols. (Washington, 1924–41), III, 117; Cooper and McCord, eds., *Statutes,* II, 232–35.

[37] Cooper and McCord, eds., *Statutes,* II, 236–46.

[38] Stock, ed., *Proceedings and Debates,* III, 115–26; on S.P.G. opposition to the laws, see Governor and Council to S.P.G., Sept. 19, 1707, S.P.G. Mss., A 3, no. 153.

In South Carolina the dissenters had already set about trying to win back their political rights. In February 1705 the Commons House passed a bill repealing the exclusion act, but the council rejected it. In an assembly election that year voters disregarded the act of exclusion by electing a majority of dissenters. The Commons House, under their domination, refused to qualify itself under the act of exclusion, and Governor Johnson dissolved it. The dissenters tried again at the elections of February 13, 1706, but this time the Anglicans carried the Commons House, and over the opposition of several dissenters, the assembly qualified itself according to the exclusion act. The Church party wanted to stay in power as long as possible, so it quickly pushed through a self-perpetuating law which provided that the present assembly would continue at least another two years if Johnson remained governor. If Johnson were to die or be replaced, the assembly was to sit another eighteen months after such a change.[39]

When the assembly met in November 1706, news had reached the colony of the Crown's opposition to the acts of establishment and exclusion and of the proprietors' recommendation that the laws be repealed. With some reluctance Johnson suggested the repeal of the establishment measure and the law excluding dissenters from office but recommended the passage of a new act of establishment with a less powerful church commission. The assembly followed his advice, and dissenters again became eligible for all political offices. In drafting the new act of establishment Johnson's followers inadvertently made an error which later plagued them; they provided for ten parishes but set exact boundaries for only four: St Philip's in Charles Town and the three parishes in Colleton and Craven Counties. Until boundaries were set, the other six parishes—all in Berkeley County and including the great majority of the colony's Anglicans—could not be organized, because vestries could not be elected. Since the three parishes in Colleton County were settled largely by dissenters, St. Philip's in Charles Town seems to have been the only parish fully organized before the assembly corrected its error in 1708. One or two other parishes in Berkeley County were organized informally, however, with S.P.G. missionaries serving as rectors.[40]

After the passage of the new act of establishment, the church controversy waned but the bitterness of the ecclesiastical dispute carried over to other issues as interest shifted chiefly to the Indian trade. Thomas Nairne, who was elected to the assembly in 1706,

[39] Feb. 9, 1705, Journals of the Commons House of Assembly, 1705–1775, I, 20, 22, S. C. Archives; Mar. 7, 8, 14, 1706, Salley, ed., *Commons Journal, 1706*, 9–13, 15, 27; Cooper and McCord, eds., *Statutes*, II, 266–67.

[40] Cooper and McCord, eds., *Statutes*, II, 281–94.

spearheaded the drive to regulate the trade, and even Governor Johnson paid lip service to the need for regulation. But the issue turned on whether the Commons House or the governor and council should control the administration of Indian policy. At stake also were the perquisites of control: should the Indian presents to the South Carolina government go to the governor, as they had in the past, or to the public treasury? The customary presents from the Indians, Governor Johnson noted, were the only "considerable source of his income," suggesting that they exceeded his £200 sterling annual salary.[41] For that reason—and perhaps because he feared reform would hurt the trade of his merchant son-in-law, Thomas Broughton—the governor opposed assembly control. Nevertheless, the Commons House passed a bill to regulate the trade on December 7, 1706, entrusting trade regulation to commissioners appointed by the Commons and providing a £200 annual grant to the governor in lieu of the presents he received from friendly tribes. Both Johnson and the council objected to the bill. Johnson rejected the bill's offer of £200 as penurious and insisted that he must receive more money to compensate him for his loss of the presents, which may have been, in effect, a polite request for a bribe. Johnson only made the Commons House angry. Denouncing the council's opposition to the bill, which it blamed on "the Interest that the Upper House have had in the Indian trade," it threatened Johnson with an appeal to the proprietors if he rejected the bill. After the Christmas recess, on January 31, 1707, Johnson, ranting about the assembly's "harsh and unmerited treatment" of him, insisted that he must have a veto over the Indian trade commission. Realizing it could do no more, the Commons House tabled the trade bill. Disregarding the self-perpetuating act, Johnson dissolved the assembly a week later.[42]

Johnson had blundered. His opposition to trade reform, his apparent demand for a bribe, and his illegal dissolution of the assembly alienated many Anglicans who had previously supported him. The governor did not call new elections until May 31, 1707, but even then his opponents swept the elections. The dissenter party, including Thomas Nairne's group of dissident Anglicans, won at least twenty-five of the thirty seats in the Commons House.[43]

Johnson was in a dilemma, and his opponents knew it. As Johnson

41 McCrady, *Proprietary Government*, 453.

42 Dec. 20, 1706, Jan. 31, Feb. 8, 1707, Salley, ed., *Commons Journal, 1706–7*, 35–37, 39–43; see also Crane, *Southern Frontier*, 146–48.

43 Nicholas Trott to S.P.G., Sept. 13, 1707, S.P.G. Mss., A 3, no. 152; for list of members, see June 5, 1707, Salley, ed., *Commons Journal, June–July 1707*, 3–5.

explained in his speech opening the session on June 5, the colony had to pay the public debts incurred in the war, it had to provide adequately for defense, and it needed to re-enact a number of laws which had expired. Johnson could not afford to dissolve another assembly, so under the leadership of Thomas Nairne, the Commons House adopted the time-honored strategy of delaying the laws the governor wanted until Johnson consented to an Indian trade bill. Although the assembly ignored the subject of religion, it left the act of establishment ineffective by refusing to set parish boundaries.[44]

The assembly session of June 1707 quickly degenerated into a political brawl between Johnson and his opponents. The Commons House immediately launched an attack on Johnson's trusted lieutenant, Chief Justice Nicholas Trott, claiming that his appointment as a deputy was irregular and demanding that Johnson dismiss him from the council. At the same time the house began making plans to introduce another Indian trade bill. Johnson's opponents thought they had him cornered, but the governor was a shrewd politician, and the day the lower house was scheduled to begin debate on the trade bill, he raised a new issue, one that was sure to sidetrack the assembly. In the annual tax bill, the lower house, as was customary, had nominated a public receiver and a controller, but Johnson and the council scrapped the assembly's nomination and claimed the sole right to appoint both officers. At the same time the council rejected a new elections bill, saying the existing law was entirely adequate.

Johnson's stratagem worked. The Commons House dropped both the attack on Trott and the Indian trade bill until the dispute over the revenue officers was settled. The Commons maintained that it had the right to nominate both the public receiver and the controller because their duties were concerned with the purse, the traditional prerogative of the House of Commons; the argument soon focused on the question of who the new public receiver would be. Johnson and the council proposed Alexander Parris, the lower house George Logan. Johnson consented on June 27 to let the receiver and controller be nominated as before, provided that someone other than Logan was named receiver. Logan solved the problem himself by withdrawing on July 2, and the next day the Commons House nominated George Smith, who then received the approval of the upper house. To guard against the

[44] This account of the assembly session of June and July 1707 is taken from Salley, ed., *Commons Journal, June–July 1707, passim;* see also Crane, *Southern Frontier,* 148–49; on the failure to set parish boundaries, see William Dun to Sec. S.P.G., Nov. 24, 1707, S.P.G. Mss., A 3, no. 154.

revival of this dispute the assembly passed a law—drawn up by Thomas Nairne—asserting the Commons House's sole right to nominate the receiver and controller.[45]

The Commons House still had not passed revenue or defense bills, and Johnson's tactics had only delayed the main issues. On July 4 the council rejected the first trade bill, which provided that the Indian trade be managed by the Commons House with the profits to go into the public treasury; the council said the bill would create a government monopoly. The Commons informed the council that it had misunderstood the bill, but the council said it would consider a new bill proposed by Nairne. The next day Johnson and the council refused to accept the new bill, turned down the elections bill again, and insisted that no further business be transacted until a tax bill was passed.

The impasse lasted until July 12, when Johnson finally made a deal with the leaders of the Commons House. He agreed to approve the rejected bills, and the Commons promised to present him a gift of £400 for doing so. Because the council had formally rejected the Indian trade, elections, and militia bills, the assembly could not consider the bills again in the same session. The governor prorogued the assembly over the weekend of July 12, and the bills were reintroduced on Monday, July 14. They met no further serious opposition, and in a burst of activity on July 18 and 19, the governor and assembly passed the Indian trade bill, the revenue bill, the militia bill, and the elections bill into law. Johnson had achieved only two things; he was £400 richer, and the attack on Trott had petered out.

Under the new Indian bill, the governor was given no authority at all over the trade, but he received £100 annually in lieu of presents. Except for the trade with Indians living within the area of English settlement, the lower house controlled the trade through its appointment of nine commissioners and an agent. All traders were required to take out annual licenses, for which they paid £8, and on penalty of stiff fines they were forbidden to indulge in such abuses as selling rum to Indians, selling arms and ammunition to hostiles, seizing friendly Indians as slaves, or obtaining goods by threats. The nine commissioners were in charge of general regulation of the trade and issuing licenses, but the burden of enforcement fell upon their agent, Thomas Nairne, the natural choice for the job. For £250 a year Nairne was supposed to live ten months of every year among the Indians in order to redress grievances and supervise trade. He was also supposed to

[45] Cooper and McCord, eds., *Statutes*, II, 299.

serve as political adviser on Indian affairs to the provincial government.[46]

IV

With the passage of the Indian trade act the major political issues in South Carolina were settled, and the colony should have been able to enjoy a few years of peace and quiet. Lord Granville died in 1707 and was succeeded as palatine by William, Earl of Craven, a more tolerant man who persuaded the proprietors to urge the colony to follow a policy of leniency and toleration. In South Carolina the governor and assembly temporarily laid aside their differences in the fall of 1707 and began to plan an attack on the French settlement at Mobile. Both parties favored the expedition, but the colony abandoned the plan after several delays.[47]

South Carolina's prospects for an end to factional strife were defeated by the extremists on both sides. The first disruption came from the dissenters, led by Landgrave Thomas Smith. Assisted by his brother George and the widow of Joseph Blake, Smith told other dissenters that the new act of establishment would be disallowed, too, because it discriminated against the Presbyterian Church and therefore violated the recent Act of Union between England and Scotland. Smith urged his clique to ignore the church act and to keep the Anglicans from putting it into operation. Following his own advice, Smith refused to pay when the collector of church taxes for St. Philip's Parish called, and he threw the man out of his house.[48]

In the summer of 1708 Governor Johnson's smoldering resentment against Thomas Nairne, who had engineered his defeat over the Indian trade bill, burst forth when Indian agent Nairne prosecuted the governor's son-in-law, Thomas Broughton, charging him with responsibility for the enslavement of a number of friendly Cherokees and for illegally seizing 1,000 deerskins belonging to the public.[49]

[46] *Ibid.*, II, 309–16; Crane, *Southern Frontier*, 149–51.

[47] Hewatt, *Historical Account*, in Carroll, ed., *Hist. Collections of S. C.*, I, 170–71; Crane, *Southern Frontier*, 89–91.

[48] Francis LeJau to Sec. S.P.G., Apr. 15, 1707, Klingberg, ed., *LeJau Chronicle*, 32 and *n*; Governor and Council to S.P.G., Sept. 17, 1707, S.P.G. Mss., A 3, no. 153.

[49] Johnson had shown his antagonism to the trade law in the fall of 1707 by arguing with the assembly about its enforcement. Oct. 28–29, 1707, Commons Journal, I, 118, 121–23, S. C. Archives. This paragraph and the one that follows are based on the Documents Relating to the Case of Thomas Nairne, Henry E. Huntington Library and Art Gallery, San Marino, Calif.; the Huntington Library was kind enough to furnish the author with a microfilm copy of this collection. See also Crane, *Southern Frontier*, 92.

Governor Johnson found a way out of his troubles by arresting Nairne on a trumped-up charge of treason. The governor and his son-in-law arranged for two men, both employees of Broughton and both of unsavory reputation, to testify that Nairne favored the restoration of King James II to the English throne, and Johnson accepted their testimony. Sixty-two inhabitants of Colleton County came to Nairne's defense with a petition to the governor asking for the Indian agent's release. They pleaded that he was needed among the Indians and guaranteed his bail to the amount of £10,000. Johnson rejected their petition and refused to accept a bond of £20,000. When three recently appointed council members from the dissenter party, Thomas and George Smith and Richard Beresford, demanded that Johnson allow the council to examine the documents in the case, Johnson refused and suppressed the evidence against Nairne.

While Nairne was in jail, Johnson dissolved the old assembly and called new elections. With their leader under arrest for treason, the dissenter party was able to carry only Colleton County, and the Church party dominated the Commons House. The new assembly met on November 24, 1708, and elected James Risbee, a trusted Johnson lieutenant, as speaker. Nairne had been elected from Colleton County, and Johnson released him long enough to allow him to appear at the opening session. The Commons House quickly lined up in support of Johnson by refusing to seat Nairne and by removing him from the Indian agency.[50]

Although Nairne was eventually cleared, he had lost his latest political battle with the governor. Johnson controlled the assembly, and both the Church party and the Indian traders took advantage of the situation for their own purposes. The assembly passed a measure setting parish boundaries, which allowed the act of establishment to become effective. It also made one concession to the dissenters by abolishing parish taxes and giving complete financial responsibility for the established church to the provincial treasury. The commissioners of the Indian trade and the assembly tried to correct the abuses in the trade, but Nairne's successor as agent, John Wright, was ineffective. The whole system broke down when the traders refused to take out licenses, and the commissioners could not enforce the licensing requirement. The traders continued to mistreat the Indians, and the Indians' debts grew larger.[51]

After the Nairne affair died down, politics in South Carolina

---

[50] Nov. 24, Dec. 3, 11, 1708, Commons Journal, III, 375, 383–84, 390, S. C. Archives.

[51] Crane, *Southern Frontier*, 92 and *n*.

entered upon an uneasy armistice. The old antagonisms were sputtering, but they had not gone out. The extreme dissenter faction, led by Joseph Boone and Landgrave Thomas Smith, had not given up hope of repealing the act of establishment; they drew up new petitions in 1709 and considered sending agents to England again. Johnson tried to stop them, but both his efforts and the new petitions failed.[52] The continual controversies under Johnson had finally exasperated the proprietors, who tried to restore tranquility in December 1708 by appointing a new governor, Edward Tynte. When Nairne was released from jail, he went to England in 1710 and the proprietors not only cleared him of Johnson's charges but appointed him as judge of vice-admiralty.[53]

Governor Edward Tynte arrived in November 1709 and died on June 26, 1710. When the council met to elect a successor, the leading candidates were Robert Gibbes and Thomas Broughton, loyal Goose Creek men and supporters of Johnson. Gibbes won the election by bribing a councilor, and the followers of Broughton armed themselves and were ready to fight the Gibbes forces when Broughton withdrew on July 12, in order to preserve peace and probably to keep the Church party intact. After Gibbes called an assembly election, the dissenters, hoping to take advantage of the rift in the Church party, waged a hard-fought campaign. In the face of this threat, the Anglicans reunited. With Johnson no longer a factor, Nairne in England, and new trade regulations passed, many of the old anti-Johnson Anglicans voted for the Church party, and the Church party swept all twenty seats in Berkeley County by wide margins.[54]

Refusing to accept defeat, Landgrave Thomas Smith tried to persuade all dissenters to refuse to serve in the assembly as a means of protest against the Anglican establishment. But Thomas Nairne, who returned to the colony in October 1711, was more influential. Nairne did not favor obstruction for its own sake, and after his election to the assembly he seems to have persuaded the dissenters to abandon their futile resistance,[55] marking the end of organized opposition to the establishment of the Church of England. Thereafter, dissenters ac-

[52] *Ibid.*, 152–53; Cooper and McCord, eds., *Statutes*, II, 328–30, 338–42; Lauber, *Indian Slavery*, 180.

[53] Francis LeJau to Sec. S.P.G., Feb. 1, 1710, Klingberg, ed., *LeJau Chronicle*, 71; Oct. 19, Nov. 5, 1709, Commons Journal, III, 440–46, 463–67, S. C. Archives.

[54] Gideon Johnston to Sec. S.P.G., July 15, 1710, Jan. 20, 1711, Klingberg, ed., *Johnston Chronicle*, 54–55, 71–73; LeJau to Sec. S.P.G., July 14, 1710, Klingberg, ed., *LeJau Chronicle*, 83.

[55] Henceforth, no dissenter refused to serve in the assembly. Dec. 5, 1710, Jan. 12, 31, May 15, June 13, Oct. 10, 1711, Commons Journal, III, 493, 498–99, 511–12, 551, 557, 577–78, S. C. Archives.

cepted establishment as an accomplished fact, and as one colonist said, "Now the resentments on both sides begin to abate." [56]

Robert Gibbes held the governorship of South Carolina for nearly two years, but his bribery cost him the respect of everyone associated with the colony. The Anglican Commissary Gideon Johnston observed that "the present Governor is scarce owned or regarded as such either at home or here." During Gibbes's administration the provincial government came to a halt, while everyone waited for the arrival of a new governor from England.[57]

When the new governor, Charles Craven, landed in March 1712, he lived up to the colony's expectations, taking a position on religion that probably reflected the views of most Carolinians. Although an Anglican himself, Craven promised the assembly he would "show the greatest Tenderness" to dissenters and do nothing to endanger religious toleration. Both governor and assembly went to work seriously, and in 1712 alone they enacted forty-three laws, including statutes on such vital matters as regulation of the courts, defense, slavery, education, and finance. They also wrote into South Carolina law nearly two hundred English statutes, most of which related to legal procedures.[58]

V

When the political battles over religion had ended, the Church of England remained as the established church of South Carolina and was integrated into the government of the colony. It was supported by the public treasury, it operated according to laws passed by the assembly, and the parish became an important unit of local government.

Central supervision of the church's affairs was supposed to be supplied by the church commission. Of the twenty-one commissioners, all named in the act of 1706, most were leaders of the Church party, but there were also a few anti-Johnson Anglicans. The commissioners were directed to meet twice a year to authorize expenditures of public funds for religious purposes, to grant licenses to Anglican ministers,

[56] Gideon Johnston to Sec. S.P.G., Jan. 20, 1711, Klingberg, ed., *Johnston Chronicle*, 75.

[57] LeJau to Sec. S.P.G., Jan. 4, 1712, Klingberg, ed., *LeJau Chronicle*, 103; Johnston to Sec. S.P.G., Nov. 15, 1711, Klingberg, ed., *Johnston Chronicle*, 100; the quotation is from *ibid.*, 103.

[58] Apr. 2, 1712, Commons Journal, IV, 2–3, S. C. Archives; Cooper and McCord, eds., *Statutes*, II, 366–604.

and to assign rectors to parishes. Actually, the church commissioners failed to develop much authority in South Carolina, and their function became limited to the supervision of expenditures. Although they assigned rectors to parishes, they had no way to make the parishioners accept the assigned minister. Until 1711 they did not even meet regularly, but in that year a statute changed the time of their meetings to coincide with court sessions, when most of the commissioners were in Charles Town anyway.[59] They seem to have met regularly after that. To the central authority of the commission the Church of England in 1707 added a commissary, the provincial representative of the Bishop of London. He supervised the clergy and generally acted as the bishop's assistant but lacked the powers of ordination and confirmation.[60] Like the church commission the South Carolina commissary did not operate effectively at first, and it was not until the 1720's that a commissary used his authority fully.

The real seat of power in the establishment in South Carolina was the parish vestry. The act of 1706 provided for ten parishes: one, St. Philip's, in Charles Town, six others in Berkeley County, two in Colleton County, and one in Craven County. After enactment in 1708 of the law setting definite parish boundaries, the parishes were organized. The Anglican freeholders of each parish met every Easter Monday and elected seven vestrymen and two churchwardens. The vestry in turn selected a sexton and clerk. The vestry was responsible for providing a register of births, marriages, and deaths, and for the supervision of parish finances and church repairs.

The parish, acting through its vestry, also became the only unit of local government to acquire any significant authority in South Carolina before the American Revolution. South Carolinians knew well the role of the parish in England and Barbados and realized at an early date that the parish would be an important unit of local government.[61] The Barbadian vestry was responsible for poor relief, education, and the punishment of some crimes, and it had the power to levy parochial taxes; the parishes also served as the electoral units for the assembly. South Carolina parishes never became that important, but they did increase their responsibilities in the area of local government. For example, an act of 1712 entrusted poor relief to the churchwardens and to special commissioners of the poor chosen by the

[59] Johnston to Sec. S.P.G., July 5, 1710, Klingberg, ed., *Johnston Chronicle*, 59; Cooper and McCord, eds., *Statutes*, II, 366–76.

[60] Klingberg, ed., *Johnston Chronicle*, 4 n.

[61] Cooper and McCord, eds., *Statutes*, II, 338–46, 593–98, 683–91; on Barbadian parishes, see Harlow, *Barbados*, 331–33.

vestry, and an act of 1716 transferred assembly elections from the counties to the parishes and made the churchwardens responsible for the conduct of elections.[62] Later in the century parish vestries assumed the primary burden of establishing public schools. On the other hand, the South Carolina assembly retained control over parish finances and never allowed church officials to collect taxes. Once the dissenters accepted establishment of the Church of England, they supported the vestry in its function as an agency of local government and were frequently elected vestrymen and churchwardens, although this was contrary to law. Even Landgraves Thomas Smith and Joseph Morton served on parish vestries.[63]

Most South Carolina Anglicans took a congregationalist attitude toward church government and were determined to uphold the power of the parish against all outside interference. The act of establishment gave parishioners, through the vestry, the sole power to appoint rectors, and if a minister displeased his parishioners he suffered for it. As one minister reported, "They have in this Country the ambition to rule and Command their Ministers." [64] An obstacle to this ambition was that the parish could not dismiss a rector once it had appointed him. That power was vested only in an ecclesiastical court or the Bishop of London. But Carolinians got around this difficulty by appointing rectors only on a temporary basis. South Carolina Anglicans extended their independence even into dogma. The first commissary declared that there was scarcely a person in the colony who "has not some religious Whim or Scruple peculiar to himself." [65]

Anglican ministers depended upon the public treasury for most of their incomes. Each rector received an annual salary of £100 current money. The parish furnished a house for the rector and a glebe, varying in size from twenty-six acres in St. Andrew's Parish to 600 acres in St. Paul's. A minister might also receive voluntary contributions from his congregation, but such gifts were rare. The vestry of St. Andrew's reported in 1716 that its rector had never received any

[62] Robert Stevens to Sec. S.P.G., Feb. 3, 1708, S.P.G. Mss., A 4, no. 19.

[63] Vestry of St. James Goose Creek Parish to Bishop of London, Oct. 29, 1717, Fulham Palace Manuscripts, VI: South Carolina, 1706–1769, no. 116, Fulham Palace, London (transcripts in Lib. Cong.); Vestry of St. Paul's Parish to S.P.G., Aug. 22, 1711, S.P.G. Mss., A 7, Carolina Papers, no. 1; see also Bryan Hunt to Bishop of London, Dec. 18, 1727, Fulham Palace Mss., VI, no. 158; other known dissenters who served on vestries included Joseph Blake, Jr., William Bellinger, and John Stanyarne.

[64] LeJau to Sec. S.P.G., July 10, 1711, Klingberg, ed., LeJau Chronicle, 93; see also "Instructions of the Clergy of South Carolina to Mr. Johnston . . . Explained by the said Mr. Johnston," [1713], Klingberg, ed., Johnston Chronicle, 119–31.

[65] Johnston to Sec. S.P.G., July 5, 1710, Klingberg, ed., Johnston Chronicle, 37.

presents, while in the parish of St. James Goose Creek gifts never amounted to more than £10 a year. Ministers who had been sent to South Carolina by the S.P.G. were more fortunate than their brothers, for the Society paid them an additional £50 sterling a year.[66]

The Society for the Propagation of the Gospel supplied most of the Anglican ministers in South Carolina. The letters they sent back to the S.P.G. reveal the first missionaries as dedicated and pious men. Particularly impressive were Dr. Francis LeJau, Robert Maule, and Thomas Hasell. After the first decade of the century, however, the quality and effectiveness of the missionaries declined, and finding acceptable ministers became a problem. The S.P.G. also supplied South Carolina with its commissaries, beginning with Gideon Johnston. Johnston was a rather sickly but able man, who soon learned the secret of dealing with Carolinians, which was to suggest rather than to command and to avoid any appearance of outside interference in the colony.[67]

The S.P.G. pursued a program based on three points: conversion of Negroes, conversion of Indians, and care of the Anglican community.[68] Despite the efforts of Thomas Nairne and others, no S.P.G. missionary was found who was willing to work steadily among the Indians, and this objective was largely ignored. As for conversion of Negroes, this became a matter of serious conflict between the clergy and the colonists, who still believed conversion would automatically free their slaves. No other topic occupied so much space in the letters from the missionaries to the Society. It became a common practice for a rector to require a potential slave convert to swear that he did not expect to gain his freedom by becoming a Christian, and the clergy persuaded the assembly to pass a law in 1712 stating that baptism would not free a slave. Such devices failed to convince the slaveowners, however, and they stubbornly refused to permit the conversion of their Negroes. It was not until 1715 that a planter agreed to widespread conversions among his slaves. S.P.G. missionary Ebenezer Taylor convinced Alexander Skene, a wealthy landowner from Barbados, that conversion of his slaves would do no harm. Skene was the exception, however, and no other master was willing to follow his example.[69]

[66] Vestry of St. Andrew's Parish to Sec. S.P.G., Jan. 17, 1716, Vestry of St. Paul's to Sec. S.P.G., Dec. 24, 1716, Vestry of St. James Goose Creek Parish to Sec. S.P.G., Nov. 26, 1716, S.P.G. Mss., B 4, nos. 43, 82, 83.

[67] Hewatt, *Historical Account*, in Carroll, ed., *Hist. Collections of S. C.*, I, 145; Johnston to Sec. S.P.G., Jan. 27, 1711, Klingberg, ed., *Johnston Chronicle*, 82.

[68] See Frank J. Klingberg's introduction to *LeJau Chronicle*, 5–7.

[69] Klingberg, *The Negro in Col. S. C.*, 13, 39–40; Cooper and McCord, eds., *Statutes*, VII, 364–65.

The S.P.G. scored its greatest triumphs in meeting the spiritual needs of the Anglicans in South Carolina and in preserving the colony as a predominantly Anglican settlement. Grudging testimony to the Society's triumph was given by no less a person than Cotton Mather, a man who had no love for either the Society or the Church of England. In 1716 Mather wrote to a member of the S.P.G., "The colony of *Carolina,* was in a fair Way to have been filled with a religious people; until your *Society for the Propagation of Religion in foreign Parts,* unhappily sent over some of their Missionaries thither." [70]

VI

When Governor Craven arrived in South Carolina in 1712, the old political factions were beginning to fade away. During his administration they disappeared completely, and the political history of South Carolina was no longer merely the history of the struggle between the Goose Creek men and the dissenters. New issues appeared and new factions formed without any relation to old issues and old factions. The chief reason for the change in South Carolina's politics seems to have been the end of religious antagonism. Although religion had played only a minor part in the original formation of parties, it had always been an issue and after 1700 it had become the major issue. By 1712, however, the religious quarrels had ended. The Anglicans had obtained a law establishing the Church of England, but they had been forced to tone down their first plans. Dissenters had won readmission to political office, they had defeated Governor Johnson in the battle over the Indian trade, and they began to accept the Anglican parish as an important institution of local government open to men of all religions. Therefore, dissenters as well as Anglicans seemed satisfied, if not pleased, with South Carolina's laws on religion, so much so that the Commons House at its session in November 1712 adopted a message to Governor Craven congratulating him on the political harmony in the colony, the first time it had passed such a resolution since Archdale's departure. [71]

[70] Mather to Anthony William Boehm, Aug. 6, 1716, Massachusetts Historical Society, *Collections,* 7th Ser., 8 (1912), 412.
[71] Nov. 20, 1712, Commons Journal, IV, 110, S. C. Archives.

Part II

BREAKDOWN AND RECOVERY

1712–1743

Beginning in 1712 South Carolina entered one of the most unsettled periods in its history. First, the colony suffered heavy losses in the Yamasee War of 1715, and the Indians continued to threaten the existence of the colony for five years after the war had supposedly ended. Then, when the proprietors, who were misinformed about the gravity of the Indian danger, refused to send any substantial aid to South Carolina, the colonists rebelled, overthrew the proprietary government in 1719, and persuaded the Crown to send over a royal governor. Although Francis Nicholson, the first royal governor, restored order for a few years, the establishment of royal government failed to solve South Carolina's problem. The provincial government was undermined first by economic troubles and then by riots over paper money. Finally, the colonial government collapsed in 1728 and did not function at all for more than two years.

It took South Carolina over a decade to recover from the combined effects of the Revolution of 1719 and the breakdown of the provincial government. Governor Robert Johnson laid the foundations for a restoration of political harmony with his "township scheme" in 1730, but his administration was plagued by disputes arising out of the land system. His successor, Lieutenant Governor Thomas Broughton, ruined most of Johnson's accomplishments by provoking unnecessary quarrels. South Carolina did not recover fully until the administration of Lieutenant Governor William Bull, who followed the patterns set by Governor Johnson to restore order and harmony to the government.

Although many problems contributed to South Carolina's political disorder, there was one issue—the dispute over local currency—that lasted throughout the whole period of breakdown and recovery. A minor issue before 1720, paper money became the central issue in the mid-twenties and underlay much of the antagonism after 1730. Irreconcilable factions grew out of the dispute, with a few merchants opposing local currency in any form and small farmers demanding increasingly large emissions of bills of credit. There could be no enduring political peace in South Carolina until the issue was settled. Fortunately for the colony, there was also a moderate group, which was made up of wealthy planters and merchants who favored a limited use of local currency. They were the men who ultimately worked out an acceptable solution to the currency problem.

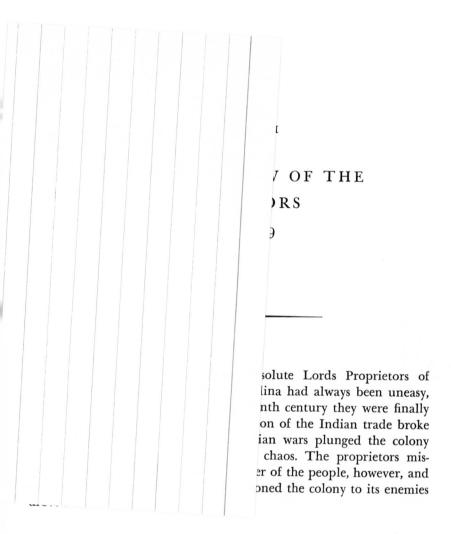

solute Lords Proprietors of
lina had always been uneasy,
nth century they were finally
on of the Indian trade broke
ian wars plunged the colony
chaos. The proprietors mis-
er of the people, however, and
oned the colony to its enemies

I

When the South Carolina assembly convened for its annual meeting
on February 29, 1716, Governor Charles Craven made a special point
of praising the abilities of the members of the Commons House of
Assembly. "I must own a particular satisfaction," he said, "to see the
body of the people represented by such Gentlemen, from whose
interests in the country and known zeal for the publick welfare I
cannot but expect all the assistance that is necessary on this important
and pressing occasion." [1] The governor was not just flattering the
assembly. The men who met with him in 1716 were the most

[1] Feb. 29, 1716, Commons Journal, V, 6, S. C. Archives.

experienced politicians in the colony, if not its ablest men. The South Carolina Commons House had built up a tradition of continuity in assembly membership. Not more than two or three men in either house lacked political experience, and in most cases the members of the assembly belonged to the families that had dominated provincial politics for thirty years or more. For example, the rolls of the Commons House in 1716 included such names as Izard, Middleton, Broughton, Howes, Bull, Moore, Schenkingh, Stanyarne, Godfrey, Morton, Waring, Elliott, and Beresford.[2] Their fathers had run the government of South Carolina in the 1680's and 1690's, and the sons were carrying on in the same tradition. These families were probably not established well enough to be called a political aristocracy, but certainly the nucleus of such an aristocracy was present in the assembly between 1712 and 1719.

Just as the general membership of the assembly reflected a tradition of continuity, the leadership of the Commons House reflected a similar tradition. The party battles of the first decade of the eighteenth century had disrupted the continuity of leadership in the house, but after 1712 the leadership reflected the same trends as before, with one exception. Thirteen men were especially active in the affairs of the Commons House from 1712 to 1719. The largest group among them were the Berkeley County planters, several of whom had a secondary interest in the Indian trade. The leadership again included a couple of lawyers. As in the 1690's, all old political factions were represented among the leaders. Such stalwarts of the Church party as Thomas Broughton and William Rhett cheerfully worked in the Commons House alongside Thomas Nairne and John Barnwell, dissenting opponents.

Despite the basic continuity of membership and leadership in the assembly, a new group of men—the merchants of Charles Town—was beginning to exert an influence in politics. After the introduction of a profitable rice culture in South Carolina, a number of London and Bristol mercantile firms had sent representatives to Charles Town to buy rice from the planters. Unlike the Indian traders and most of the older merchants, these men were economic specialists whose primary concern was trade. Perhaps the most prominent of the newcomers were Samuel Eveleigh, Samuel Wragg, and John Fenwicke. At the same time that these men were immigrating to the colony, several old residents also turned to trade as their sole or primary economic interest. Among them were the Huguenots Benjamin Godin and

2 Feb. 28, 1716, *ibid.*, 1–3.

Benjamin de la Conseillere. Whether recent immigrants or established residents, the merchants constituted a new force in South Carolina politics. Samuel Wragg and John Fenwicke served in the Commons House, Samuel Eveleigh was appointed to the council, and five of the thirteen leaders in the lower house were merchants. Two of them, William Rhett and George Logan, were elected speakers.[3]

Although powerful in the assembly, neither the older families nor the merchants had much influence in patronage appointments. Both royal and proprietary offices in South Carolina were controlled by two men, Nicholas Trott and his brother-in-law William Rhett. Trott was chief justice and judge of the court of vice-admiralty, while Rhett was surveyor general of customs, naval officer, and receiver general of quit rents. Their attitude toward their many offices was almost entirely venal. According to the colony's lawyers, Trott charged exorbitant fees in his courts, while Rhett treated with the utmost disrespect the very men who appointed him to office. When Rhett received his commission as receiver general of quit rents from Governor Craven in 1712, he remarked, according to Craven, "This is but a Lords proprietors Government and I wou'd wipe my Arse with the Commission." Craven suspended Rhett from office for this outburst of obscenity, but the proprietors promptly ordered his reinstatement.[4] Rhett held the proprietary government in such contempt that he did not bother to discharge his responsibilities as receiver general, and he never settled his quit rent accounts.[5] Despite Rhett's inefficiency and scornful attitude toward his employers, he and Trott continued to hold office, which suggests strongly that they must have had influence with someone in authority. That person appears to have been Richard Shelton, the secretary to the proprietors. The proprietors had lost interest in South Carolina almost entirely and paid little attention to what was happening there. Shelton was responsible for screening their

[3] In addition to those named in the text, the following men were leaders in the Commons House: planters Robert Fenwicke, Ralph Izard, and Arthur Middleton; merchants Benjamin de la Conseillere, Benjamin Godin, and Benjamin Quelch; and lawyers George Evans and Henry Wiggington; see Greene, *Quest for Power*, 475–88.

[4] Proprietors to Rhett, Jan. 31, 1713, S. C. Pub. Recs., VI, 50, S. C. Archives; on the lawyers' charge against Trott, see Francis Yonge, *A Narrative of the Proceedings of the People of South Carolina in the Year 1719* (London, 1721), in Carroll, ed., *Hist. Collections of S. C.*, II, 151–52.

[5] The proprietors said in 1728 that they had not settled quit rent accounts for about 20 years; see "An Estimate of the Arrears due to the Proprietors of Carolina," 1728, S. C. Pub. Recs., XIII, 10–11, S. C. Archives. Governor Robert Johnson said that Rhett's "Neglect and Obstinacy" was partly responsible for this situation; see Memorial of Johnson, Nov. 7, 1727, *ibid.*, XII, 262.

correspondence with the colony and for recommending policy to them; in fact, he seems almost to have dictated proprietary policy in the decade before 1719. Thus, with Shelton as their friend and patron, Trott and Rhett were secure in their offices.[6]

It was not unusual in South Carolina politics for a more or less rapacious clique to control patronage, but in the past the governors had organized such cliques. During the period of Trott and Rhett's dominance, however, the governors had little control over patronage, if any. In fact, Trott apparently tried to undermine the governor's power by urging the proprietors to strip the governor of many of his perquisites of office.[7] The chief justice succeeded in 1714 when he visited England and so charmed the proprietors, who were pleased with his codification of the provincial laws, that they granted him extraordinary powers, stipulating that no law could become valid without his approval and vesting control of the office of provost marshal in him.[8] At the time the proprietors vested Trott with these vast powers, his and Rhett's influence in South Carolina was at its peak. Not only did they control patronage, but they also exerted influence in the assembly. From 1711 to 1715, when Rhett was speaker of the Commons House, he and Trott held "great Sway" with the voters of Charles Town, where twenty of the thirty representatives in the lower house were elected. With this advantage they were often able to secure the election of their followers to the assembly.[9]

Other political leaders in the colony resented the influence of Trott and Rhett, especially after the proprietors gave Trott his unusual powers. The assembly petitioned the proprietors in 1715, asking them to rescind their grant. The governor vetoed a bill to limit Trott's authority, but in 1716 the proprietors accepted the assembly's protest and revoked Trott's extraordinary powers.[10] The opponents of Trott and Rhett also managed to nullify their influence in the Commons House of Assembly. Rhett failed to win re-election to the assembly in 1716, probably because the voters, like the Commons House, resented

[6] Shelton's role in South Carolina politics is suggested by Yonge, *Narrative,* in Carroll, ed., *Hist. Collections of S. C.,* II, 162; on Shelton's influence with the proprietors, see Memorial of Robert Johnson, Nov. 7, 1727, S. C. Pub. Recs., XII, 259–60, S. C. Archives. See also Herbert L. Osgood, *The American Colonies in the Eighteenth Century,* 4 vols. (N. Y., 1924), II, 356–57.

[7] Unidentified letter of July 19, 1715, S. C. Pub. Recs., VI, 105–6, S. C. Archives.

[8] Salley, ed., *Commissions and Instructions,* 264–66.

[9] Yonge, *Narrative,* in Carroll, ed., *Hist. Collections of S. C.,* II, 149.

[10] Feb. 25, 1715, Apr. 17, 1716, Commons Journal, IV, 376–78, 382, V, 63, S. C. Archives.

his brother-in-law's expanded powers. In Rhett's absence the assembly passed a new elections act designed to prevent Rhett and Trott from regaining their influence. In the first place, the law prohibited persons who held offices of profit from sitting in the Commons House, a provision which would keep both Trott and Rhett out of the assembly. The law also transferred elections from the counties to the parishes and assigned a specified number of seats to each parish. The influence of Trott and Rhett was confined to Charles Town, and after the passage of the new law only four representatives were elected in town, while twenty-six assemblymen were chosen by rural parishes. The law was a popular one, not only because it reduced the influence of Trott and Rhett, but also because voting by parish was more convenient for the electorate.[11]

Aside from the campaign to reduce the influence of Trott and Rhett, the political issues current in 1712 and immediately after originated in the colony's economic troubles. The basic problem was that many planters had gone into debt to buy slaves, but they had failed to increase their exports of rice and naval stores. The colony more than doubled its importation of slaves between 1711 and 1715. Prior to 1711 planters had rarely purchased more than 100 slaves a year, but in 1711 they bought 170 Negroes and three years later the figure rose to 419. The Negro population of South Carolina jumped from 4,100 in 1708 to about 10,000 in 1715.[12] In order to offset debts incurred by buying slaves on credit, the assembly tried to expand the market for South Carolina's rice with a petition to the House of Commons in 1714. The petition pointed out that the existing Navigation Acts required South Carolina to ship its rice to England before sending it elsewhere. The best markets for rice were in Spain and Portugal, but by the time South Carolina rice reached those markets they had been fairly well supplied and prices had fallen to almost nothing. The assembly's petition therefore requested permission for South Carolina to ship rice directly to the continent of

[11] Cooper and McCord, eds., *Statutes*, II, 683–91; Yonge, *Narrative*, in Carroll, ed., *Hist. Collections of S. C.*, II, 149; Commons Journal, Apr. 12, 1717, V, 252, S. C. Archives.
[12] Donnan, ed., *Documents Illustrative of Slave Trade*, IV, 255; *The Report of the Committee of the Commons House . . . on the State of the Paper-Currency . . .* (London, 1737), in J. H. Easterby and Ruth S. Green, eds., *The Colonial Records of South Carolina: The Journal of the Commons House of Assembly, 1736–1750*, 9 vols. (Columbia, 1951–62), *1736–39*, 305–6; Evarts B. Greene and Virginia D. Harrington, *American Population before the Federal Census of 1790* (N. Y., 1932), 173.

Europe.[13] Unfortunately, Parliament took no action at that time.

The increased number of Negro slaves in South Carolina created a social problem, too. The danger of a slave insurrection existed, and twice, in 1711 and again in 1714, groups of Negroes tried to start rebellions without any success.[14] Governors Gibbes and Craven both urged the assembly to amend the slave laws, but it refused to act until after the abortive revolt of 1714. In that year the assembly enacted a law that strengthened disciplinary control over slaves. The act also tried to discourage the further importation of Negroes by levying a prohibitive import duty of £2 per slave. The duty was successful, for the number of Negroes imported annually dropped from 419 in 1714 to 81 in 1715 and 67 in 1716.[15]

The economic issue that generated the greatest amount of heat concerned the bills of credit printed by the colony and issued by the provincial government to its creditors. Such certificates stated that the government owed the bearer a certain amount of money, which it would pay at a specified future date. The emission of bills of credit in this way enabled the colony to embark on expensive projects, such as military campaigns, and to pay for them over a period of time. In addition, bills of credit served another and more controversial function as a local medium of exchange. As in other colonies, South Carolina's supply of specie was drained away to England to pay for slaves and English goods. With no gold or silver available, the colonists found it hard to transact local business. South Carolina had tried to attract foreign coins by giving them an excessive value. The legal rate of exchange between sterling and colonial money in South Carolina was 161 to 100, the highest in colonial America. The British government disapproved of the practice of overvaluing coin, which was common in most colonies, and Queen Anne issued a proclamation in 1704 that attempted to set an official rate of exchange of four to three, or 133 1/3 to 100. Parliament passed a law establishing the same ratio in 1708, but South Carolina and other colonies ignored both proclamation and law by continuing to set liberal rates for foreign coins. By 1708, however, South Carolina had discovered that bills of

[13] June 12, 1714, Commons Journal, IV, 287–88, S. C. Archives.

[14] June 20, 1711, ibid., III, 563; Francis LeJau to Sec. S.P.G., Jan. 22, 1714, Klingberg, ed., LeJau Chronicle, 136–37.

[15] May 15, 1711, Nov. 19, 1713, Nov. 10, 1714, Commons Journal, III, 552, IV, 180–81, 295, S. C. Archives; "An Additional Act to an Act . . . for the better Ordering . . . of Negroes," 1714, South Carolina Session Laws, S. C. Archives; Donnan, ed., Documents Illustrative of Slave Trade, IV, 255.

credit made a better medium of exchange than foreign coins for local business.[16]

South Carolina was the second colony in America, after Massachusetts, to experiment with bills of credit, and it printed more bills than any other colony in the early years of the eighteenth century. It emitted its first issue of bills of credit in 1703 to pay for James Moore's expedition against St. Augustine. The bills were issued to the colony's creditors, who were paid an annual interest of 12 per cent. The law provided for the retirement of the bills in two years through a tax on real and personal estates, but South Carolina failed to retire the bills on schedule because it needed money for its other military campaigns. By 1711 it had emitted seven issues of bills of credit, usually to finance campaigns against the Indians, and there was a total of £20,000 in paper bills circulating in the colony. After 1707 the colony had abandoned interest payments, and it had made bills of credit legal tender, which meant that everyone had to accept the bills in payment for goods or services. South Carolina continued to include provisions for the early retirement of the bills, however, and for this reason they did not depreciate but circulated at par value.[17]

In 1712 South Carolina launched a new experiment with paper currency by founding a land bank, the first of its kind in America. The bank act emitted £52,000 in new colonial currency—£32,000 to establish the bank's fund for loans to individuals at 12½ per cent annual interest, with land as security, £4,000 for current expenses of the government, and £16,000 to retire old bills of credit. The law made no provision for retirement of the £4,000 emission of November 1711 for an expedition against the Tuscarora Indians, but it did provide for the retirement of the new bank bills at the rate of £4,000 a year. Although the bank act was administered faithfully and bills retired on schedule, South Carolina's bills of credit depreciated in value for the first time. By 1716 bills of credit were worth only half

---

[16] Nettels, *Money Supply*, 208, 241–44, 247–48. On the history of paper currency in South Carolina, see Richard M. Jellison, "Paper Currency in Colonial South Carolina: A Reappraisal," *S. C. Hist. Mag.*, 62 (1961), 134–47; Leslie Van Horn Brock, The Currency of the American Colonies, 1700–1764 (unpubl. Ph.D. diss., University of Michigan, 1941), 115–22. Contemporary accounts include the following: *Currency Report*, in Easterby, ed., *Commons Journal, 1736–39*, 291–320; [William Bull, Sr.], "An Account of the Rise and Progress of the Paper Bills of Credit in South Carolina," [1739], Cooper and McCord, eds., *Statutes*, IX, 766–80; and *An Essay on Currency, Written in August 1732* (Charles Town, 1734).

[17] Nettels, *Money Supply*, 253, 261 n, 264; Brock, Currency of Colonies, 118–20; [Bull], "Account of Paper Bills," Cooper and McCord, eds., *Statutes*, IX, 766–69.

their face value and were exchanged for specie at the rate of two to one. The reason for the depreciation of bills of credit after passage of the bank act seems to lie in the stated aims of the law. Previous acts of emission had treated bills of credit as temporary, but the bank act stated flatly that South Carolina could not pay its debts "in any tolerable time." Furthermore, earlier bills of credit had been issued in order to delay payment for specific projects. The bank act, however, was supposed to stimulate the provincial economy by pumping more money into circulation, and the law admitted that the bills of credit would be a local currency. Finally, the bank act nearly trebled the amount of bills of credit in circulation, from £20,000 to £56,000.[18]

The bank act created a new division in South Carolina politics, one which basically pitted merchants against planters. Paper currency was favored by the men whose business was confined to South Carolina —planters and shopkeepers. It was opposed by the import-export merchants of Charles Town, who could not pay their English creditors with South Carolina bills of credit, and by men who lived on fixed incomes, especially Anglican clergy and placemen.[19] Few men opposed paper currency more than did Nicholas Trott and William Rhett. They depended on fees for a living, and when bills of credit depreciated to half their face value, the incomes of Trott and Rhett were cut in half.

The merchants were not entirely united in their opposition to paper money, for there were gradations of opinion in the mercantile community. At one extreme stood Benjamin de la Conseillere of the Huguenot firm of Godin and Conseillere. No one fought paper currency longer or more loudly than he. For two decades he refused to compromise on the issue of bills of credit, even when his beliefs cost him his political influence. At the other end of the mercantile spectrum were several merchants who were willing to accept a local currency, provided the amount in circulation was not too large. In this group were some of the more active merchant politicians, such as Samuel Wragg, John Fenwicke, James Kinloch, Samuel Eveleigh, Thomas Hepworth, and Alexander Parris. Perhaps the difference between the two groups of merchants arose from their non-mercantile economic interests. The moderate merchants were beginning to buy land and to set themselves up as country squires. Although trade

[18] Cooper and McCord, eds., *Statutes*, IX, 759–65; [Bull], "Account of Paper Bills," *ibid.*, IX, 768–70; Brock, Currency of Colonies, 118–20.

[19] Francis LeJau to Sec. S.P.G., Apr. 20, 1714, Aug. 22, 1715, Klingberg, ed., *LeJau Chronicle*, 138, 140, 162.

remained their primary concern, their landholdings gave them a bond with the planters. Thus, Samuel Wragg bought the 12,000-acre Shaftesbury barony in 1717, while Alexander Parris and Thomas Hepworth each owned more than 3,000 acres of land. In contrast, neither William Rhett nor Benjamin de la Conseillere ever owned an acre of land outside Charles Town.[20]

II

In spite of South Carolina's economic difficulties and the resentment against Trott and Rhett, the anti-proprietary movement was born of other grievances. The colony's hard-won law regulating the Indian trade failed to produce the results Thomas Nairne and other reformers had hoped for. The worst abuses in the trade, notably fraud and coercion, continued until the Indians revolted against the trade system and came close to destroying the colony. The campaign to make South Carolina a royal colony originated as an aftereffect of Indian wars when the proprietors ignored the colony's needs.

The first Indian war to concern South Carolina was an uprising of the Tuscarora Indians in North Carolina. Although all the fighting took place in North Carolina, that area was too poor and too thinly populated to defend itself, and Virginia's politicians were too busy quarreling among themselves. Forced by circumstances to assume the financial and military burdens of the Tuscarora War, South Carolina sent out one expedition under John Barnwell in 1712 and another under James Moore, Jr., in 1713, inflicting heavy casualties on the Tuscaroras and breaking their power. Most of the surviving Tuscaroras migrated northward to join their kinsmen in the Iroquois league. Although Indian auxiliaries did most of the fighting under Barnwell and Moore, the financial burden was not light, and South Carolina late in 1711 issued £4,000 in new bills of credit, called Tuscarora bills, in order to finance the expeditions.[21]

Less than two years after the Tuscarora War, another and more devastating Indian conflict burst with terrible swiftness upon South Carolina. The Yamasee War, the longest and perhaps the costliest Indian war in Carolina history, involved nearly every Indian nation

[20] On Conseillere, see Hirsch, *Huguenots*, 145–46; on Wragg, Henry A. M. Smith, "The Baronies of South Carolina," *S. C. Hist. Mag.*, 11 (1910), 86; on Parris, Mabel L. Webber, "Colonel Alexander Parris, and Parris Island," *ibid.*, 26 (1925), 138; on Hepworth, Salley, ed., *Land Warrants*, III, 173, 222, 224, 228.

[21] Crane, *Southern Frontier*, 158–61; [Bull], "Account of Paper Bills," Cooper and McCord, eds., *Statutes*, IX, 768.

that traded with South Carolina—Creeks, Choctaws, and Catawbas as well as Yamasees—and the Lower Creeks took the lead in some phases of the war. Unlike most colonial Indian wars, the expansion of white settlement was not a primary cause of the Yamasee War. Nor was there any evidence that Spain or France instigated the revolt, although some Carolinians tried to blame them. The sole cause of the Yamasee War was South Carolina's failure to regulate the Indian trade, and the Indians were driven to revolt by their resentment of the abuses practiced by the traders, "notoriously infamous for their wicked and evil actions." [22]

Regulation of the Indian trade under the act of 1707 had never worked well. At first Governor Nathaniel Johnson had impeded the work of the trade commission and of Thomas Nairne, the agent. The commission consistently had trouble with traders who refused to obtain licenses. Landgrave Thomas Smith, for example, declined to buy licenses for his traders on the grounds that they traded beyond the boundaries of South Carolina. The commissioners themselves were not sure they had the power to prosecute unlicensed traders like Smith and his men.[23] John Wright, who had succeeded Thomas Nairne as agent, was inefficient, and Nairne charged him in 1712 with maladministration. The assembly then dismissed Wright and re-appointed Nairne. Even Nairne's return to the agency failed to improve regulation, however, and by 1714 the licensing system had broken down completely. Nairne and the commissioners began to make plans for further legislation, but before they could do anything Wright tried to vindicate himself by accusing Nairne of malfeasance in office. Although the assembly cleared Nairne in November 1714 of all charges except that of issuing irregular warrants, Wright had delayed needed reforms for half a year. Before the commissioners and Nairne could take effective action, the Yamasee War had started.[24]

The war began on Good Friday, April 15, 1715, when the Yamasees fell upon the frontier settlements near Port Royal with sickening suddenness and murdered about a hundred whites. One of the first victims was Thomas Nairne, who was captured and slowly tortured to death. Ironically, his painful death was shared by his rival for the Indian agency, John Wright, who happened to be with him at the

[22] Crane, *Southern Frontier*, 165–67.

[23] *Ibid.*, 152–53; William L. McDowell, ed., *The Colonial Records of South Carolina: Journals of the Commissioners of the Indian Trade, September 20, 1710–August 29, 1718* (Columbia, 1955), 47–48, 56.

[24] Nov. 21, 27, 1712, June 8, Nov. 17–19, 23, 1714, Commons Journal, IV, 115, 124, 272, 302–9, S. C. Archives; Crane, *Southern Frontier*, 153.

time. The attack on Port Royal was the signal for a massive uprising among the southern Indians. Led by the Lower Creeks, they butchered the traders who had abused them so long. Even the coastal and northern Indians joined the massacre, and only the Cherokees and Chickasaws spared their traders. Governor Charles Craven called out the militia, attacked the Yamasees in their villages, and forced them to retreat beyond the Savannah River. In the fall an expedition under the command of Robert Daniel pushed the Yamasees into Florida. Meanwhile, frightened settlers from all over South Carolina abandoned their homes and fled to Charles Town. For half a year the town resembled a fortress, and it was not until October 1715 that the men felt safe enough to go home. Even then most of the women and many settlers from the southwest stayed in town.[25]

South Carolina's situation was still desperate in the fall of 1715. Craven's counterattack had reduced the menace of the Yamasees, but the Creeks were still on the warpath. The colony needed help, and its best hope was the Cherokees, the traditional enemies of the Creeks and the largest Indian nation on the southern frontier with nearly 3,000 warriors and a total population of more than 10,000. Moreover, the Cherokees had taken no part in the uprising. Governor Craven negotiated a treaty with the Cherokees in August 1715, and planned a campaign against the Creeks with them in November. When November came, however, the Cherokees stayed at home.[26]

In order to bind the Cherokee nation more closely to South Carolina, Governor Craven and the assembly hit upon the idea of an unusual show of force combined with skillful Indian diplomacy. Under the command of Maurice Moore, a son of the late governor, an expeditionary force of 300 marched deep into the mountainous Cherokee country to persuade the Cherokees to honor the treaty of alliance. Moore and his men discovered the Cherokee nation was split into two camps, a peace party centered in the middle and lower towns and a pro-English war party centered in the overhill towns. Negotiations dragged on for a month. During this time a delegation of Creek chiefs tried to talk the overhill Cherokees into a joint massacre of the English force. Unknown to the whites, a band of 200 to 500 Creeks was secretly camped near the lower towns waiting to execute the planned ambush.

[25] Crane, *Southern Frontier*, 167–79; George Rodd to ?, May 8, 1716, S. C. Pub. Recs., VI, 74–85, S. C. Archives; William Tredwell Bull to Sec. S.P.G., Oct. 31, 1715, S.P.G. Mss., A 11, 96.

[26] Crane, *Southern Frontier*, 179–80; on Cherokee population, see Swanton, *Indians of Southeastern U. S.*, 110, 114; "Numbers and Names of all Towns belonging to the Cherokees," 1721, S.P.G. Mss., A 17, 155–58.

Before they could act, however, friendly Cherokees from the lower towns killed the Creek chiefs, thus committing the Cherokee nation to an English alliance. The Cherokees signed a treaty on January 31, 1716, and joined Moore and most of his men in a fruitless pursuit of the Creeks.[27]

The signing of the Cherokee treaty turned the tide of the Yamasee War in South Carolina's favor. The lesser tribes along the coast, including the Catawbas, also signed treaties, and since the remaining Yamasees had been chased to Florida, South Carolina's borders were no longer seriously threatened. The Yamasee War was not over, however, for the Creeks, Yamasees, and Choctaws had signed no treaties and their raiding parties continued to attack frontier settlements throughout 1716. To meet this threat the assembly built forts at four key points in the colony: Fort Moore at Savannah Town, near present-day Augusta, Georgia; Congaree Fort, near the site of modern Columbia; Palachacolas Fort, on the Savannah River; and Beaufort Fort, on Port Royal Sound. The forts alone proved inadequate, however, because war parties were able to slip past them and attack isolated settlements. The assembly solved this problem by hiring troops of rangers to patrol the frontier between the forts, and the combination of forts and rangers gave the colony's frontiers a fair degree of protection. South Carolinians were fortunate in having such protection, for the colony did not make peace with the Creeks until near the end of 1717 and then the peace was an uneasy one.[28]

For South Carolina the cost of survival was high. Many colonists went hungry, because planters had fled to Charles Town for safety and left their fields untended. According to one estimate, nearly half the land under cultivation was abandoned in 1716.[29] As a result, the colony suffered a drastic food shortage in 1717, and one colonist reported that the people of Charles Town were "ready to Eat up one another for Want of provisions."[30] Suffering and hunger cannot be calculated mathematically, but population and financial losses can. Governor Robert Johnson later figured that 400 Carolinians had been killed during the Yamasee War, and he did not attempt to calculate

[27] Crane, *Southern Frontier,* 180–82; Langdon Cheves, ed., "A Letter from Carolina in 1715, and Journal of the March of the Carolinians into the Cherokee Mountains, 1715–1716," City of Charleston, *Year Book,* 1894 (Charleston, 1895), 313–54.

[28] Crane, *Southern Frontier,* 183–90.

[29] Memorial of Joseph Boone and Richard Beresford, Feb. 22, 1717, S. C. Pub. Recs., VII, 7, S. C. Archives.

[30] Letter to Richard Beresford, Apr. 27, 1717, *ibid.,* VII, 19.

the number who had fled the colony in terror. As for financial losses, the assembly estimated in 1717 that the first two years of the war had cost South Carolina £116,000 sterling.[31] To the assembly's estimate of financial losses should be added the burden of higher taxes. In 1710 the government of South Carolina had spent £4,500 sterling; in 1717 it spent twice as much.[32]

While South Carolina was just beginning to get back on its feet during 1716, the assembly took up the painful task of reconstruction. Turning first to the Indian trade, the Commons House of Assembly drew up a plan it hoped would eliminate the abuses of the trade and thereby forestall future wars. Convinced that the people of the colony wanted a trade law that would "prevent for the future the practices of evil minded persons to bring upon us an Indian war, by putting entirely in the power of the Representatives of the Colony the management of all affairs with the Indians," [33] the Commons proposed nothing less than the abolition of private trading for profit, substituting instead a monopoly under the exclusive direction of the Commons House of Assembly "for the sole use, benefit and behoof of the publick." The council grumbled a little about letting the Commons House have complete control, but it gave in and passed the bill in June 1716.[34] A minor problem growing out of the Indian conflict involved the Yamasee lands, a large area in southeastern South Carolina formerly reserved for the Yamasees but abandoned by them when they fled to Florida. The assembly passed a law reserving the Yamasee lands for immigrants, offering grants of 300 to 400 acres each and suspending payment for four years, provided the immigrants settled on the land immediately.[35]

The problem of financing the Indian war was even more complex. In 1715 the assembly had issued £30,000 in new bills of credit, and wartime expenses threatened to make further emissions necessary. The assembly of 1716 flirted briefly with the idea of an income tax, but in the end it decided to stick to more conventional methods of public finance, printing an additional £20,000 in bills of credit and providing for their retirement with a property tax. The emission of 1716 raised the total amount of paper bills of credit in circulation to £90,000,

[31] Robert Johnson to Bd. of Trade, Jan. 12, 1720, "The Case of the Colony of South Carolina," [1717], *ibid.*, VII, 234, 45.

[32] [Nairne], *Letter from S. C.*, 39; June 13, 1717, Commons Journal, V, 316, S. C. Archives.

[33] Apr. 13, 1717, Commons Journal, V, 254, S. C. Archives.

[34] June 29, 1716, *ibid.*, 146; Cooper and McCord, eds., *Statutes*, II, 677–80.

[35] Cooper and McCord, eds., *Statutes*, II, 641–46.

which was more than the colony's credit could bear in view of South Carolina's precarious situation. The value of the bills of credit depreciated still further from an exchange ratio of two to one in 1716 to a ratio of four to one by the end of 1717.[36]

By far the most important product of the Yamasee War was a rapidly growing popular disgust with proprietary government. As early as 1715 the political leaders in the South Carolina Commons House began to fear that "the Lords Proprietors are not capable of supporting us in a Warr of this nature."[37] During the war the proprietors contributed practically nothing to the defense of the colony; by their own admission they had sent over less than £1,000 sterling.[38] To many colonists the answer to proprietary weakness seemed obvious: South Carolina should get rid of the proprietors in some way and become a royal colony. The earliest recorded expression of this sentiment is a letter written in 1715 by Dr. Francis LeJau, who said, "Our Wisest Men wish Earnestly this Country were in His Majesty's Hands, who is best able to Defend us."[39] LeJau's letter may indicate that the anti-proprietary movement originated among the old Goose Creek faction, for he was rector of St. James Goose Creek Parish and a former adherent of the Church party. Whatever the origins of anti-proprietary sentiment, however, the feeling was soon shared by nearly all the older political leaders, dissenters as well as Anglicans.

Though widespread, anti-proprietary resentment was not universal, for the merchants of Charles Town generally favored proprietary government. Many merchants later changed sides, but until 1719 the anti-proprietary movement was basically confined to the planters. Even as late as November 1719 an anonymous proprietary man identified his opposition as "the Landed Men" and "the Country Gentlemen."[40] The cause of the split between merchants and planters, on this issue as on so many others, was paper money. Acting on the advice of Trott and Rhett, the proprietors opposed the emission of bills of credit, a policy which won the approval of a large segment of the merchant population. The proprietors did not go so far as to veto

[36] *Ibid.*, 627–33, 662–76; Brock, Currency of Colonies, 120; Mar. 23, Apr. 28, 1716, Commons Journal, V, 57, 88, S. C. Archives; on the exchange ratio of 1717, see Oct. 30, 1717, *ibid.*, 340.

[37] Petition of Commons House, Aug. 1715, *ibid.*, VI, 116–17.

[38] Proprietors to Governor and Council, Mar. 3, 1716, S. C. Pub. Recs., VI, 151, S. C. Archives.

[39] To Sec. S.P.G., May 14, 1715, Klingberg, ed., *LeJau Chronicle*, 156.

[40] "Extract of a Letter dated from Charles Town," Nov. 14, 1719, S. C. Pub. Recs., VII, 218–19, S. C. Archives.

the bank act of 1712, but they ordered Governor Craven to call a special session of the assembly in 1714 to reconsider the act. Craven did as he was told, but when the assembly met in February 1715, it refused to repeal or amend the bank act.[41] Although the law remained in force, the proprietors had made their position clear and the merchants appreciated it.

The Commons House of Assembly took the lead in articulating the colony's resentment against the proprietors. During the special session of February 1715, the assembly appointed two agents, Joseph Boone and Richard Beresford, and sent them to London to appeal for royal assistance in the Indian wars.[42] The Indian depradations of 1715 and 1716 forced the assembly into more drastic action. It sent an anti-proprietary petition to the Crown in November 1716, and a year later it drew up another petition that was signed by the members of the Commons House and 568 other residents of the colony.[43]

The petitions of 1716 and 1717 indicate that although resentment against the proprietors was common, the majority of the colonists had not yet made up their minds on the vital question of becoming a royal colony. Both petitions, which were nearly identical in wording, complained of proprietary neglect and requested royal aid, but neither petition asked unequivocally for the Crown to make South Carolina a royal colony. The key sentence in each petition asked that "this once flourishing Province, may be added to those under your [Majesty's] happy protection." The sentence is ambigious, for it can be interpreted either as a request for the Crown to make South Carolina a royal colony or simply as an appeal for royal military assistance. In fact, the assembly later took advantage of the ambiguity of the petitions and denied that they did more than ask for military assistance. The Commons House said in October 1717 that the petitions had intended no disrespect for the proprietors and were merely an "expedient." [44] The authors of the petitions probably made them ambiguous in order to attract as much support as possible. Whatever the motives of the authors, however, the petitions signified no more than a general resentment against the proprietors, not a clear demand for royal government.

[41] Feb. 9, 11, 1715, Commons Journal, IV, 345–48, 350–51, S. C. Archives.
[42] Feb. 24, 1715, ibid., 373–74.
[43] The petitions are in S. C. Pub. Recs., VI, 258–60, VII, 88–96, S. C. Archives; on the number of signers of the petition of Nov. 1717, see Memorial of Joseph Boone, May 13, 1718, ibid., VII, 126.
[44] Oct. 31, 1717, Commons Journal, V, 343, S. C. Archives.

III

It was still possible in late 1717 for the proprietors to restore normal relations with their colony. Instead, they dismissed the sentiment against their government as the "Business of a Faction and Party" and alienated the people of the colony by making one blunder after another in 1718 and 1719.[45] The proprietors took the view that the Yamasee War had ended with the signing of the Cherokee peace treaty in January 1716. They ignored equally the Indian raids of the next two years and the threat of new outbreaks after 1717. They also failed to realize that conditions in the colony were anything but normal. Consequently, the proprietors would neither send aid to South Carolina nor permit the colony to work out its own solutions to its problems. The basic trouble, of course, was that the proprietors had lost interest in their colonies. The original proprietors were dead, and their successors knew they would never make any money out of their American possessions. They therefore took only the most casual interest in South Carolina and believed whatever they were told by Richard Shelton and his friends, Nicholas Trott and William Rhett.[46]

The already strained relations between proprietors and colonists began to deteriorate further when Governor Charles Craven decided to go home in the spring of 1716. Though unable to cope with the intrigues of Trott and Rhett, Craven had handled his job capably; he had smoothed over the religious controversy of the previous decade, and he had defended the colony well during the Yamasee War. Before leaving the colony, however, he made two serious errors in judgment. First, he thought the Indian wars were over. Hearing this opinion from a man who should have known better staggered the assembly. It resolved unanimously that "those Clouds of danger and destruction are Still hanging over us," but it could not change the governor's mind.[47]

Craven's second mistake was his choice of a successor. For some unfathomable reason he picked Robert Daniel and appointed him deputy governor. Daniel was an old man who had been active in local politics for upwards of forty years and was beginning to exhibit a few signs of senility. The Commons House of Assembly objected because

[45] The quotation is from Address of the Commons House, [1716], S. C. Pub. Recs., VII, 10, S. C. Archives.

[46] Proprietors to Bd. of Trade, June 4, 1717, Memorial of Robert Johnson, Nov. 7, 1727, ibid., VII, 53–55, XII, 259–60; Yonge, Narrative, in Carroll, ed., Hist. Collections of S. C., II, 162.

[47] Address of Commons House, [1716], S. C. Pub. Recs., VI, 211, S. C. Archives.

Craven had not consulted it on Daniel's selection, but the governor embarked for England on April 25, 1716, and left South Carolina in Daniel's care.[48] Daniel was never able to get along with the lower house, partly because of its initial hostility to the method of his appointment, partly because of its dislike of his political tactics; he refused to approve the Indian trade bill of 1716 until the assembly granted him an additional £100 a year in lieu of presents.[49] Another source of trouble was the assembly's custom of appointing commissions to administer specific laws. Daniel thought such powers should be vested solely in the governor and council. He objected to the Indian trade bill and to a bill to regulate local navigation, because both acts named commissioners to execute the laws. In both cases, however, Daniel bowed to the wishes of the assembly.[50]

Daniel also quarreled with the proprietary faction in one of the most ludicrous incidents ever to involve a provincial governor. A sloop named the *Betty* had been seized for trading with pirates, and William Rhett, in his office of surveyor general of customs, went on board to claim the Crown's share of the cargo. He took with him a detachment of sailors from a royal ship anchored at Charles Town. Daniel insisted that Rhett could not carry off any of the cargo until the court of vice-admiralty had condemned the ship and sent Attorney General George Rodd with an order for Rhett and his sailors to leave the *Betty*. When Rhett refused, Daniel called out the Charles Town militia and ordered it to fire on the *Betty* while the royal sailors were still aboard. Rhett's party then left the ship, but the outraged Rhett attacked the attorney general with a shovel, and that gentleman was forced to defend himself with his sword. Rhett was restrained before he could hurt anyone, but he turned his anger on Daniel. According to the governor, Rhett screamed, "I will kill the old Rogue let me goe God damn me I will kill the Dogg." Although Daniel wanted to prosecute Rhett and the captain of the naval ship for treason, the Commons House and the council forced him to drop the charges.[51]

Robert Daniel's administration fortunately did not last long, and he was replaced by Robert Johnson, the son of Sir Nathaniel Johnson, in

---

[48] *Ibid.*, 213.

[49] James Fellows to ?, Aug. 3, 1716, *ibid.*, VI, 234; June 7, 1717, Commons Journal, V, 306, S. C. Archives.

[50] June 29, Dec. 29, 1716, Commons Journal, V, 146, 215–16, S. C. Archives.

[51] Depositions of George Rodd and others, July 12–16, 1716, James Fellows to ?, July 19, Aug. 3, 1716, S. C. Pub. Recs., VI, 190–210, 217–22, 223–26, 233, S. C. Archives; the quotation is from Governor Daniel's deposition, July 14, 1716, *ibid.*, VI, 221.

the fall of 1717. Johnson was one of the proprietors' wisest appointments. He possessed his father's political insight but relied more on persuasion than the cruder political tactics of Sir Nathaniel. He had none of his father's bigotry or his low cunning and therefore quickly won the respect of even the most bitter anti-proprietary men; when he took office he owned every talent necessary for a successful career except experience.

For all of his natural ability, Johnson's lack of experience betrayed him at first and he handled himself poorly during his first session with the assembly. His difficulty began with a change in proprietary land policy. The proprietors were upset by William Rhett's failure to collect quit rents efficiently, but they blamed the failure on the quit rent law instead of Rhett. They directed Johnson to work for the enactment of a new law governing rent collections, and as an inducement to the assembly they offered to remit quit rent arrears for two years if the law were passed. The loss of revenue resulting from the depreciation of South Carolina's paper currency also upset the proprietors. The price of land was £3 currency per 100 acres; with bills of credit valued at four to one, this meant the proprietors received only 15s. sterling per 100 acres. They therefore ordered Johnson to raise the price to £3 sterling, or £12 currency. At the same time the proprietors announced that they did not approve of the assembly's plan for settlement of the Yamasee lands. They recommended a similar plan, which would also reserve the land for immigrants but would restrict grants to 200 acres. After the assembly convened on October 30, 1717, Johnson announced the proprietors' changes and proposals in land policy, but the Commons House objected to every part of their plans. Raising the price of land would discourage immigration, the house argued, and it regarded the existing laws on rent collection and the Yamasee lands as adequate. It therefore refused even to consider new legislation. Nevertheless, William Rhett, acting as receiver general of quit rents, announced he would raise the price of land to £12 currency per 100 acres.[52]

The assembly's rejection of the proprietors' offer angered Governor Johnson, who decided that the Commons House needed to be put in its place. In November 1717 he picked the occasion. When Matthew Porter, the colony's powder receiver, died, the lower house immediately nominated a successor, claiming the exclusive right to nominate officials who handled public funds and citing a law of 1707 as

---

[52] Oct. 30, Nov. 1, 5–6, 1717, Commons Journal, V, 339–41, 351–52, S. C. Archives.

confirmation of that right. Johnson promptly challenged the house's prerogative and nominated his own candidate. The act of 1707 applied only to the public receiver; since 1703 the duties of powder receiver had been assigned to the captain of the battery, who had always been appointed by the governor. As commander of the military forces, therefore, Johnson claimed the right to choose the powder receiver. The Commons House refused to abandon its claim, and Johnson withdrew his nomination but did not yield entirely. On December 11 he directed the powder receiver to obey the orders of the commander of the colony's powder magazine, an officer who reported directly to the governor.[53]

While this dispute was still in progress, the Commons House raised a new issue on December 6. On the day before Johnson had casually referred to the proprietors as "our masters" in a message to the house. The members of the house took this opportunity to let Johnson know that they did not recognize the proprietors or anyone else as their masters, although they conceded that "we cannot but approve of your Honor's care of their Lordships interest, who are as you say your masters." Johnson lectured the Commons that the proprietors were "your masters likewise," but the house did not bother to answer him. It had made its position clear.[54]

In spite of their bickering, Governor Johnson and the assembly managed to cooperate on the important question of financial stability. They agreed on two laws in December 1717 that were designed to restore order to the colony's chaotic fiscal affairs. The first law increased provincial revenues by raising the import duty on Negro slaves to £30 currency per head. The second and more important law attempted to restore the colony's credit. It called in all the old bills of credit, except the bank bills and Tuscarora bills, and issued new ones, levying a heavy property tax to sink them within two years.[55] If the law had worked successfully, it would have withdrawn over three-fourths of South Carolina's paper money from circulation. It did not succeed, but its passage represented a serious effort by the provincial government to meet its fiscal obligations.

Governor Johnson's position was difficult at best, but it became untenable because of a few dissatisfied individuals who were pursuing

[53] Nov. 28–29, Dec. 7, 11, 1717, *ibid.*, 380–81, 384, 399, 407–10. When Johnson submitted to the proprietors the law vesting appointment of the powder receiver in the house, they disallowed it in 1718. But after the overthrow of the proprietors in 1719, the house declared the act still in force.

[54] Dec. 5–6, 9, 1717, *ibid.*, 394–95, 401.

[55] Cooper and McCord, eds., *Statutes*, III, 32–38.

their own selfish ends. William Rhett was one of them. Although the merchants generally accepted the import duties and currency act passed in 1717, Rhett took it upon himself to protest these acts in the name of the mercantile community. In a letter to the English commissioners of customs, he attacked the laws, alleging that the planters were too cheap to tax their own estates. Instead, he wrote, the planters were trying to evade their debts by forcing the burden of taxation on merchants and discriminating against English merchants.[56]

Another source of discord was the public monopoly of the Indian trade. The old traders resented the monopoly, and one of them, Landgrave Thomas Smith, a council member, was so put out that he boycotted council meetings as a means of protest. The traders and the import merchants of Charles Town lined up together in opposition to the monopoly and petitioned the proprietors for repeal of the trade law. By witholding credit and trade goods, they hampered the work of the trade commissioners, effectively crippling the public monopoly.[57]

Although Governor Johnson tried to persuade the proprietors that South Carolina was still in deep trouble, they were never able to comprehend the extent of destruction caused by the Yamasee War. Consequently, they failed to realize that bills of credit were necessary to finance military expenditures or that the public monopoly of the Indian trade was an attempt to prevent further Indian wars. Instead of listening to Governor Johnson, they heeded the complaints of William Rhett, Nicholas Trott, and the merchants and Indian traders. The proprietors interpreted paper currency as an attempt by the planters to evade their debts; they believed that the planter-dominated assembly had levied high import duties in order to shift the burden of taxation to merchants; and they saw the Indian trade law as another example of discrimination against merchants. The Commons House of Assembly had also become an object of proprietary displeasure. It had rejected the proprietors' suggestions for a compromise on land policy and quarreled with the governor over the right to nominate public officials.

In order to reform the abuses they believed to exist in the government of South Carolina, the proprietors settled upon a disastrous course of action in the summer of 1718, launching a wholesale attack on some of South Carolina's most popular laws. On July 22,

<hr>

[56] Rhett to Commissioners of Customs, Dec. 31, 1717, S. C. Pub. Recs., VII, 104–6, S. C. Archives.

[57] Crane, *Southern Frontier*, 193–98; "Some Short Remarks on the Indian Trade," n. d., S.P.G. Mss., Miscellaneous Unbound Manuscripts, South Carolina, pp. 2–26; on Smith, see June 26, 1717, Commons Journal, V, 326–27, S. C. Archives.

1718, they disallowed the import duty on British goods, the Indian trade law of 1716, and the act of 1707 that had established the right of the Commons House to nominate the public receiver and other officers. They also vetoed the election law of 1716, which had undermined the influence of Trott and Rhett by transferring assembly elections to the parishes. The proprietors ordered Governor Johnson to dissolve the present assembly and issue writs for elections in the counties. For good measure they disallowed the assembly's plan for settlement of the Yamasee lands and ordered the governor to put their own plan into operation. In September the proprietors went still further. They demanded that Governor Johnson work for the immediate retirement of all bills of credit and ordered him and the council not to assent to any more emissions of bills of credit. Then, disgusted with the breakdown in quit rent collection, the proprietors closed the land office and directed that no more land grants be issued without their specific consent. In February 1719 the proprietors vetoed the 1717 import duty of £30 currency on each Negro, and they advised the assembly to repeal the duty of £2 sterling per Negro, which had been levied in 1714. Finally, in April 1719, the proprietors decided to abandon all plans for settlement of the Yamasee lands and to claim that land for themselves and their secretary, Richard Shelton. They directed the surveyor general to lay out fifteen 12,000-acre baronies in the Yamasee lands, two baronies for each proprietor and one for Shelton.[58]

The heavy-handed policy of the proprietors only aggravated the crisis in South Carolina. The veto of the public Indian trade seemed to herald the return of a private trade, complete with all the abuses that had caused the Yamasee War. No one in South Carolina was hurt more by the proprietors than a group of about 500 Irish Protestants who had settled on the Yamasee lands. They lost the title to their land, and they could not even recover the money they had paid for the land.[59] For the colony as a whole, however, the most harmful aspect of the proprietors' policy was their opposition to import duties and paper currency. The assembly could neither levy import duties nor issue more bills of credit. It had no major source of revenue left but the tax on estates, a tax which was already twice its prewar size. Yet if the

[58] Proprietors to Governor and Council, July 22, Sept. 4, 12, 1718, Feb. 27, 1719, Proprietors to Francis Yonge, Apr. 17, 1719, S. C. Pub. Recs., VII, 143–48, 156–57, 159–60, 175, 183, S. C. Archives.

[59] Petition of Council and Assembly, Feb. 3, 1720, "A True State of the Case between the Inhabitants of South Carolina, and the Lords Proprietors," 1720, ibid., VII, 292–93, VIII, 21–22.

assembly obeyed the proprietors, it would be forced to raise the property tax again, not only in order to meet current expenses but also to retire bills of credit. The new policy resulted in the alienation of many men who had previously supported the proprietors. In particular, most Charles Town merchants turned against the proprietors in 1718 and 1719. Only a few hard money advocates, led by Benjamin de la Conseillere, continued to favor proprietary rule.

Governor Johnson and the assembly tried to cope with the situation as best they could. Johnson was convinced the proprietors had acted hastily, so he ignored some of their orders. He permitted the existing assembly to remain in session, refusing to announce officially that the proprietors had vetoed the election laws. The assembly then passed a new and more effective quit rent law, probably in the hope of persuading the proprietors to re-open the land office. Next it established a new system for the Indian trade, half public and half private. The law set up a public trade at three forts, and it forbade private trading within twenty miles of any fort. As for finances, the assembly levied a property tax to raise £70,000 currency and drew up a new schedule for retiring bills of credit. Realizing the colony's revenues were inadequate, the assembly ignored the proprietors and re-enacted the old import duties. Governor Johnson also recognized the need for more revenue, and he again defied the proprietors by assenting to the import duties.[60]

While the assembly was struggling with provincial finances and the Indian trade, a new grievance against the proprietors developed. Pirates still roamed the Atlantic Ocean, and several bands established a base of operations on the Cape Fear River in North Carolina in 1718. From there they began a series of raids along the coasts of South Carolina and Virginia. With its rich cargoes of rice and its weakened defensive condition, South Carolina became a favorite target. Edward Teach, better known as Blackbeard, anchored outside Charles Town harbor in June 1718, blockaded the port, and terrorized the colony and its shipping for a week, seizing passengers from merchant ships and holding them for ransom, before slipping away to the safety of the Cape Fear. Other pirates followed him to Charles Town, and a wave of terror gripped the colony for five months. The colonists appealed to the proprietors for help, but they did nothing. The people of South Carolina then took matters into their own hands, and with Virginia's assistance they launched a series of naval expeditions against the pirate

[60] Yonge, *Narrative*, in Carroll, ed., *Hist. Collections of S. C.*, II, 148; Cooper and McCord, eds., *Statutes*, III, 44–49, 56–84, 86–96.

base on the Cape Fear in the early fall of 1718. A Virginia fleet killed Blackbeard and most of his crew, while a South Carolina force led by William Rhett captured another well-known buccaneer, Stede Bonnet, and his crew. Another South Carolina fleet, under the personal command of Governor Johnson, broke up a second attempt to blockade the port of Charles Town. The captured pirates were tried before the court of vice-admiralty in Charles Town, and Stede Bonnet and forty-eight other pirates were hanged. By November South Carolina and Virginia had driven the pirates from the mainland, but the people of South Carolina remembered only too well that once again the colony had been in danger and once again the proprietors had done nothing about it.[61]

IV

By the summer of 1719 anti-proprietary sentiment had crystallized in favor of royal government. The proprietors had lost all their friends in the colony except for the faithful few headed by Nicholas Trott and William Rhett. The proprietors had given the colonists many grievances, and the situation wanted only a catalytic agent for a rebellion against proprietary government.

Before such a catalyst appeared, the proprietors gave the colonists still more grounds for complaint. The first was the re-organization of the council in June. The proprietors appointed twelve men to the council and dropped three former council members who had been active in the anti-proprietary movement. A fourth anti-proprietary councilor, Francis Yonge, remained on the council only because one of the proprietors, Lord Carteret, was his patron.[62] It was a common occurrence for the proprietors to replace councilors who opposed their policy, but the re-organization of the council in 1719 bothered many South Carolinians because the proprietors also basically changed the nature of the council. The council had originally consisted of the governor, who represented the palatine, and seven deputies, each of whom represented a specific proprietor. The proprietors had stopped appointing deputies around 1700, and every councilor had begun to represent the proprietors as a group. The re-organization of 1719

[61] Hughson, *Carolina Pirates*, 69–128; South Carolina Admiralty Records, 1716–1763, A (1716–1732), 250–99, Federal Records Center, East Point, Ga.

[62] Proprietors to Robert Johnson, June 19, 1719, S. C. Pub. Recs., VII, 193, S. C. Archives; Yonge, *Narrative*, in Carroll, ed., *Hist. Collections of S. C.*, 160. The anti-proprietary councilors who were excluded were Alexander Skene, Thomas Broughton, and James Kinloch.

abandoned the concept of deputies completely and raised the number of councilors from seven to twelve. The colonists found this change disturbing. If the proprietors could alter the nature of the council by executive order, there was nothing to prevent them from similarly changing other governmental institutions, including the Commons House of Assembly.[63]

In re-organizing the council the proprietors tried to win the support of the Charles Town business community by giving merchants control of the council. They appointed seven merchants to the council and gave the other five seats to placemen and sympathetic planters. The proprietors' plans miscarried, however. Two merchants had gone to England, and three others refused to accept their appointments. The seven active members included Nicholas Trott and another placeman, Benjamin de la Conseillere and one of his business associates, and three planters, one of whom supported Conseillere's hard money views. This left the council under the control of Trott and Conseillere's hard money faction, and it failed to attract any additional followers to the proprietary party.[64]

The proprietors pushed South Carolina to the brink of rebellion in July 1719 with new grievances. They vetoed the new import duties and the new quit rent law, and they repeated their disallowance of the election law. They had learned of Johnson's refusal to dissolve the old assembly, so they again ordered him to announce their vetoes and call new elections. This time Johnson dared not disobey. He carried out his instructions and issued writs for elections in the counties. In September the proprietors reiterated their refusal to re-open the land office.[65] In effect, the proprietors had rejected both the assembly's attempt to please them and the governor's advice. South Carolina was now ripe for rebellion.

The catalyst came in November 1719 in the form of a rumor that Spain would soon invade the colony. The reports seemed to be well verified; they said the Spanish were outfitting a fleet at Vera Cruz, which would attack the French fort at Mobile and then sail for Charles Town. Fearful that the proprietors would once again fail to help the

[63] Petition of Council and Assembly, Feb. 3, 1720, S. C. Pub. Recs., VII, 281, S. C. Archives.

[64] The other active councilors were placeman Charles Hart, merchant Jacob Satur, and planters Ralph Izard (the hard money advocate), William Bull, and Hugh Butler. Samuel Wragg and Francis Yonge were in England; William Gibbon, Peter St. Julian, and Jonathan Skrine refused to serve.

[65] Proprietors to Governor and Council, July 24, Sept. 4, 1719, S. C. Pub. Recs., VII, 199, 205-6, S. C. Archives; Yonge, Narrative, in Carroll, ed., Hist. Collections of S. C., II, 158-60.

colony, the panic-stricken council dispatched a plea to the Crown for at least 500 soldiers and a couple of frigates.[66]

The rumors convinced the anti-proprietary party that it was time to act. Governor Johnson had set November 26 as the date for assembly elections, and a meeting of the rebel leaders decided to form an association pledged to support the new assembly and to reserve allegiance solely to the king.[67] On November 28 Governor Johnson received a letter from the rebels asking him to take over the government and hold it for the king. The rebels appointed a committee to discuss their grievances with the governor. Johnson immediately issued a call for his seven active councilors to meet in emergency session and proposed vigorous suppression of the revolt. By the time the council met, the members of the rebel committee had changed their minds and gone home. The council took this as a sign of retreat and persuaded Johnson to do nothing until the assembly met.[68]

When the assembly convened on December 10, the Commons House declared itself to be "a Convention, delegated by the People, to prevent the utter Ruin of this Government, if not the Loss of the Province, until His Majesty's Pleasure be known." The convention then refused to recognize the council on the grounds that the proprietors had acted unconstitutionally in changing the nature of its membership. They next offered the governorship to Johnson again, but he refused because of "my honor as being Intrusted by their Lordships." [69] The convention then elected James Moore, Jr., as provisional governor.

Johnson had previously set December 21 for a muster of the militia, and the rebels selected that day to proclaim Moore governor. Johnson issued an order for the militia to stay at home, but he was ignored. When the militia assembled on December 21 Johnson tried to dismiss them, but the convention formally proclaimed Moore governor. At some point during these proceedings William Rhett was wounded by gunfire, the only casualty of the revolution. The convention petitioned the Board of Trade and asked unequivocally for South Carolina to be made a royal colony. The core of the petition was a recitation of the

[66] Governor and Council to Bd. of Trade, with enclosures, Nov. 6, 1719, S. C. Pub. Recs., VII, 208–17, S. C. Archives.

[67] "Extract of a Letter dated from Charles Town," Nov. 14, 1719, ibid., VII, 218–21.

[68] Except where otherwise noted, this account of the events of Nov.–Dec. 1719 is taken from Yonge, Narrative, in Carroll, ed., Hist. Collections of S. C., II, 165–82.

[69] Johnson to Proprietors, Dec. 27, 1719, S. C. Pub. Recs., VII, 227, S. C. Archives.

colony's woes, chief among which were continued warfare and proprietary neglect.[70]

V

The rebellion of 1719 that ended proprietary government in South
Carolina was not a revolt against tyranny, for questions of political
rights played almost no part in the overthrow of the proprietors; it was
more a rebellion against neglect and maladministration. Uninterested
in South Carolina and unable to comprehend the truly desperate
circumstances of the colony, the proprietors let themselves be misled
by the likes of Nicholas Trott and William Rhett. After the proprietors had failed repeatedly to help South Carolina during and after its
Indian wars, the colonists finally decided there was no alternative to
destruction but rebellion. As a resident of the colony said half a
century later, the basic cause of the revolution was "the Inability of
the Lords Proprietors to protect their Colony . . . , and their Reluctance to advance any Money out of their Estates in *England*." [71]

Throughout their dispute with the proprietors, the people of South
Carolina, in proper English fashion, had confined themselves to
specific grievances and ignored theoretical implications. Seven years
after the rebellion, in 1726, South Carolinian John Norris took up the
question of theory in a short treatise called *The Liberty and Property
of British Subjects*.[72] Relying on the political writings of John Locke,
Norris said that the proprietors had a contract with the colonists, the
charter of 1665. He argued that the proprietors had broken their
contract by endangering their subjects' property, which dissolved the
old government and permitted the people to create a new government.
Ironically, Norris thus used the ideas of John Locke to justify the
overthrow of a government Locke himself had helped to create.

[70] Petition of Council and Assembly, Dec. 24, 1719, *ibid.*, VII, 223–26; on Rhett,
see Joseph Redlington, ed., *Calendar of Treasury Papers, 1557–1728*, 6 vols. (London,
1868–89) , *1714–19*, 487–88.

[71] George Milligen, *A Short Description of the Province of South Carolina*
(London, 1770) , in Chapman J. Milling, ed., *Colonial South Carolina: Two
Contemporary Descriptions . . .* (Columbia, 1951) , 116 n.

[72] The full title is *The Liberty and Property of British Subjects Asserted in a
Letter from An Assembly-man in Carolina to His Friend in London* (London,
1726) .

CHAPTER VII

THE COLLAPSE OF THE PROVINCIAL
GOVERNMENT
1720–1730

The Revolution of 1719 caught the British government by surprise. The Board of Trade opposed proprietary colonies as a matter of policy, and thanks to the work of South Carolina's agents in England the Board was well aware of the colony's exposed position. Immediate action was necessary, but to make South Carolina a royal colony was to countenance rebellion. The Board of Trade postponed a final answer and advised the Privy Council to take over the administration of South Carolina on a temporary basis. The Privy Council accepted the Board's proposal on the grounds that the Crown should protect England's position on the southern frontier. On August 11, 1720, the Privy Council assumed responsibility for the government of South Carolina and appointed Francis Nicholson as the colony's first royal governor.[1]

I

In South Carolina, meanwhile, the rebels were trying to carry on under the governorship of James Moore, Jr. They elected their own assembly and selected a twelve-man council. Generally speaking, the

[1] Christopher C. Crittenden, "The Surrender of the Charter of Carolina," *North Carolina Historical Review*, 1 (1924), 390–93; W. L. Grant and James Munro, eds., *Acts of the Privy Council of England, Colonial Series, 1613–1783*, 6 vols. (Hereford and London, 1908–12), II, 779.

rebels took care of the housekeeping chores of government and avoided all long-range policy decisions, concerning themselves mostly with such routine matters as collecting taxes, keeping the courts open, providing an ample supply of arms and ammunition, and building roads. They made two exceptions to this rule, however. The interim assembly decided that the laws governing judicial procedure needed revision, and it passed a law regulating the provincial courts, a law which remained in force until the American Revolution. The assembly also decided that South Carolina needed additional currency. It made rice legal tender in the payment of debts, and it emitted £25,000 in new bills of credit. The new bills became known as rice bills, because the assembly planned to retire them with a tax on rice.[2]

The major threat to the interim government emanated from William Rhett and the deposed proprietary governor, Robert Johnson. Neither Rhett nor Johnson presumed at first to try to restore the proprietary government; they were more concerned about their personal incomes. Johnson had hoped to become the first royal governor of South Carolina, and he had written a letter to the Board of Trade seeking a commission as such. In the meantime he was concerned about his loss of the governor's salary and fees, and he hoped to persuade the rebels to recognize him as interim governor until the Privy Council decided what to do with South Carolina. Rhett at first played a double game, in which he sympathized with the rebels in public while supporting the proprietors in private. But after the assembly accused Rhett and Captain Hildesley, the commander of H.M.S. *Flamborough,* of selling arms and ammunition to Florida and the council had instructed the provincial agent in London to press for Rhett's dismissal from his various offices, Rhett openly opposed the rebel government.[3]

In the spring of 1721, Johnson and Rhett made an abortive bid for control of the rebel government. Governor Moore had ordered the Anglican clergy to perform no marriage without a license from him. Johnson, in an attempt to reassert his authority, responded by ordering the clergy not to obey Moore. The Anglican rectors, who

---

[2] Cooper and McCord, eds., *Statutes,* III, 97–121; Brock, Currency of Colonies, 120–21; on the court act, see Edward McCrady, *The History of South Carolina under the Royal Government, 1719–1776* (N. Y., 1899) , 7.

[3] Hewatt, *Historical Account,* in Carroll, ed., *Hist. Collections of S. C.,* I, 244, 246; Johnson to Bd. of Trade, Dec. 27, 1719, William Dry to John Barnwell, Aug. 19, 1720, Governor and Council to Joseph Boone, Jan. 19, 1721, S. C. Pub. Recs., VII, 227–29, VIII, 241, IX, 4–5, S. C. Archives.

sympathized with Johnson, hoped to stay out of politics, but Moore and Johnson forced them to make a choice and they chose to obey Johnson. While this issue was still in dispute, Captain Hildesley sailed into Charles Town harbor with five ships, and Johnson appointed Hildesley commander of the Berkeley County militia. After issuing a call to the militia, Johnson armed the forty militiamen who responded and added eighty sailors from Hildesley's ships; he then called his old council into session, and told Moore that he would resume the governorship until Nicholson arrived. Moore called Johnson's bluff simply by refusing to yield, and Johnson disbanded his troops rather than risk a fight.[4]

Francis Nicholson, the first royal governor of South Carolina, landed at Charles Town late in May 1721 and was greeted with a petition of welcome signed by more than 500 South Carolinians. Sixty-six years old and the most experienced colonial administrator in the British empire, Nicholson was a professional soldier whose career in America had begun in New England in 1686. He had served as governor or acting governor of New York, Virginia, Maryland, and Nova Scotia and as commander of the British expedition that had seized the last named of these from the French during Queen Anne's War. Nicholson was best known, perhaps, for his fiery temper and his blind devotion to the Church of England, but he had other, less-publicized traits as well. The lack of colonial schools disturbed him, and he had helped to found the College of William and Mary in Virginia and a public grammar school in Maryland. Science interested him, too, and while governor of South Carolina he helped to finance Mark Catesby's expeditions into the American wilderness. Nicholson had long advocated English expansion in America on both the northern and southern frontiers, and it was probably his interest in expansion, along with his military and administrative experience, that prompted the Board of Trade to offer him the governorship of South Carolina.[5]

After Nicholson's arrival, the proprietary faction soon fell apart. Johnson and Hildesley quieted down at once, because neither of them wanted to antagonize a Crown appointee. Hildesley was a career naval officer, and Johnson still hoped for a commission as royal governor. William Rhett continued to cause trouble, however, and he was joined

4 Richard P. Sherman, Robert Johnson: Proprietary and Royal Governor of South Carolina (unpubl. Ph.D. diss., University of Southern California, 1957), 69–75; William Tredwell Bull to Sec. S.P.G., May 12, 1720, S.P.G. Mss., A 14, 74–75.

5 See Leonard W. Labaree in DAB s.v. "Nicholson, Francis."

by a small coterie of followers that included his son and two sons-in-law, Nicholas Trott, and proprietor Joseph Blake.[6] Trott's grievance was a simple one. Governor Nicholson and the new royal council re-appointed every other proprietary officeholder, but they appointed a new chief justice in Trott's place. Trott denied Nicholson's authority to dismiss him and tried in vain to persuade the Board of Trade to recognize him as chief justice.[7] Rhett's actions were more serious. He claimed the governorship by virtue of a proprietary appointment that the proprietors themselves knew nothing about. Nicholson later accused Rhett of illegal trading with the French in partnership with the collector of customs at Nassau in the Bahama Islands. Rhett countered Nicholson's accusations by charging that the governor himself had been smuggling goods into South Carolina and that he had acted illegally in trying to find evidence of Rhett's smuggling. Rhett died of apoplexy on January 11, 1723, but his charges were picked up by men in London who had an interest in the Bahamas, including several Carolina proprietors who were members of the Bahama Company. These accusations plagued Nicholson throughout his administration, although the most reliable evidence in the case indicates that the governor was guilty of nothing more than an attempt to enforce the Navigation Acts.[8]

II

When Nicholson landed in South Carolina he found the colonists especially worried about economic and military problems. The provincial economy looked sound on the surface, but a close examination revealed a number of potential soft spots. South Carolina in 1721 had a population of about 19,600 persons, of whom 7,800 were whites and 11,800 were Negro slaves.[9] That same year the colony exported 25,000 barrels of rice, 14,000 pounds of pitch, and 7,000 pounds of tar. Total

[6] Wallace, *Hist. of S. C.*, I, 289–90; the petition of welcome is in Alexander S. Salley, Jr., ed., *Journal of His Majesty's Council for South Carolina, May 29, 1721–June 10, 1721* (Atlanta, 1930), 5–8.

[7] June 2, 1721, Salley, ed., *Council Journal, 1721,* 17; Trott to [Lord Carteret?], Jan. 18, 1722, S. C. Pub. Recs., IX, 103–7, S. C. Archives.

[8] Nicholson to Charles de la Faye, Oct. 16, 1722, Nicholson to Lord Carteret, Jan. 14, [1723], S. C. Pub. Recs., IX, 148, 101, S. C. Archives; *An Apology or Vindication of Francis Nicholson, Esq. . . . from the Unjust Aspersions Cast on Him by Some of the Members of the Bahama-Company* (London, 1724).

[9] James Moore to ?, Mar. 21, 1721, S. C. Pub. Recs., IX, 22–23, S. C. Archives; Governor Moore's statistics were based on the tax returns of 1721 and were therefore more reliable than other estimates.

production increased over the next three years; the exportation of rice stayed at about the same level, while the production of pitch and tar had risen by 1724 to 26,000 and 13,400 pounds, respectively. Statistics on the Indian trade are not available, but Governor Nicholson reported in 1723 that it was prospering more than ever before. Most important of all, South Carolina seems to have consistently enjoyed a

ιgland, exporting more than it
ɔny, anticipating that prosperity
s at an ever-growing rate. While
antially unchanged, slave traders
ι 1721 and 1725.[11]
to the economic picture of South
·kets for rice were Spain and
orbade the colonies to ship rice
ducers of naval stores in South
ιger. They depended on Parlia-
, and Parliament was thinking
ꞓ bounties. South Carolina com-
ι of naval stores, but the colony
of production. South Carolinians
ɔm trees that had been cut down
s followed the more tedious and
ʒh and tar from green trees. The
other Englishmen, believed the
ιnd the Board had recommended
ꞓs on naval stores produced by

eas in South Carolina's economy,
ly launched a promotional cam-
most of it to Francis Yonge, the

ꞓ, May 23, 1723, enclosure in Nicholson
ιerton to Nicholson, Aug. 3, 1724, *ibid.*,
ιlance of trade in the 1720's are not
ːn South Carolina exported goods worth
ꞓ3,000, see "Representation of the State
t of America," Sept. 8, 1721, Hardwicke
Γapers, Additional Manuscripts, 35907, ɪoll. 30–32, British Museum, London (transcripts in Lib. Cong.) ; see also Fayrer Hall's estimate that in the 1720's South Carolina annually exported goods worth £200,000 and imported goods worth £120,000, *Importance of British Plantations*, 66.

[11] Letter to Joseph Boone, June 24, 1720, List of Negroes Imported, 1721–26, S. C. Pub. Recs., VIII, 26, XII, 180, S. C. Archives.

[12] Francis Yonge, *A View of the Trade of South Carolina* (London, 1722), 6–11, 12–15; Gray, *Hist. of Agriculture*, I, 155–56, 284–85.

provincial agent in London after 1721. Yonge tried to persuade Parliament to take rice off the enumerated list, which would permit the direct shipment of rice to Spain and Portugal. He also tried to convince the Board of Trade that South Carolina's naval stores were just as good as Sweden's and that the bounties should not be reduced. Yonge worked hard at his job. He bombarded the various agencies in London with petitions and memorials, and in 1722 he published a tract called *A View of the Trade of South Carolina*. Despite Yonge's best efforts, the campaign failed. Rice remained on the enumerated list, and Parliament discontinued all bounties on naval stores except those produced by Swedish methods.[13]

Governor Nicholson and many others in the colony were even more concerned about the military and diplomatic situation on the southern frontier than they were about their economic troubles. South Carolina had been protected from foreign encroachment during the Revolution of 1719 by a Franco-Spanish war over control of Pensacola, but Spain and France settled their differences in 1721. The danger in a renewed collaboration of these two powers against the English became greater because of the attitude of the Creek nation. Under the leadership of their sagacious Emperor Brims, the Creeks adopted a policy of strict neutrality. The Creeks expected that they would benefit from a continuation of the three-way European competition; all three powers would try to woo them with gifts and favorable trade agreements. If one European nation should dominate the southern frontier, however, then it would no longer need the friendship of the Creeks and there would be no more presents or trade bargains. The victorious European power might even drive the Creeks from their land. Therefore, the Creeks tried to maintain the existing international competition, and they would do nothing that might eliminate any of the competitors. They would help a European colony only if it became weak; in this way they would keep the balance of power. Although there were pro-English and pro-French factions among the Creeks, Emperor Brims and most of the leading chiefs favored neutrality. In dealing with the Creeks, South Carolina suffered two handicaps. The French had built Fort Toulouse on the Alabama River in 1717, and the fort gave Louisiana control of the southwestern Creek towns. Futhermore, South Carolina was allied with the Cherokees, the traditional blood enemies of the Creeks.[14]

[13] Gray, *Hist. of Agriculture*, I, 156, 285.
[14] Crane, *Southern Frontier*, 185, 259–63; Swanton, *Indians of Southeastern U. S.*, 154; James Adair, *Adair's History of the American Indians*, ed. Samuel Coles Williams (Johnson City, Tenn., 1930), 276–77.

The most hopeful plan for safeguarding England's interest on the southern frontier was worked out by John Barnwell, who was occasionally called "Tuscarora Jack" because he had commanded the first Tuscarora expedition in 1712. A Dubliner by birth, Barnwell had been closely associated with Thomas Nairne in the early part of the century. He had later distinguished himself as South Carolina's best Indian fighter in campaigns that ranged from the Pamlico to the Chattahoochee. The South Carolina assembly had sent him to London in 1720 as its agent, and there he presented his plan of defense to the Board of Trade. He proposed that the Crown build and garrison a ring of forts beginning at the mouth of the Altamaha River and ending in Cherokee country on the Tennessee River. He later added to this plan by suggesting that the Crown and South Carolina jointly sponsor settlement of the English frontier along the Savannah and Altamaha rivers. He thought the English could most easily settle the area by establishing townships and by starting a promotional campaign among Protestant refugees from the continent of Europe.[15]

Barnwell's plans were never implemented, because he failed to win the necessary support in England. The Board of Trade liked the idea of the forts, but the Privy Council refused to go along. It approved only one fort, the one at the mouth of the Altamaha River. Barnwell returned to South Carolina on the ship which brought Governor Nicholson, and he personally supervised the construction of the fort. In 1721 he finished the job and turned the fort over to an independent company of royal troops. The fort was no more than a blockhouse, but Barnwell optimistically called it Fort King George and planned to replace it with a better structure as soon as possible. The Crown refused to do anything about the second phase of Barnwell's plan—frontier settlement—but the South Carolina assembly approved the idea with enthusiasm and ordered the colony's Indian commissioners to lay out a township near Fort Moore on the Savannah River. Then, in an attempt to attract settlers to the new township, the assembly passed a law that granted immigrants a seven-year immunity from law suits for debts and an indefinite exemption from taxation. The project attracted the attention of Jean Pierre Purry, a Swiss who hoped to start a colony of Swiss Protestants there, but the Carolina proprietors, who still owned the land, raised so many objections to Purry's plans that the whole project collapsed. Nothing remained of Barnwell's plans after that but the makeshift Fort King George, and it lost even its

[15] Crane, *Southern Frontier,* 163, 229–31, 282–83; Alexander S. Salley, Jr., "Barnwell of South Carolina," *S. C. Hist. Mag.,* 2 (1901), 47–50 and notes.

symbolic value when the assembly transferred its garrison to Port Royal in 1727 as a protection against Creek war parties.[16]

Governor Nicholson shared Barnwell's frustrations. The governor tried to strengthen English influence among the Creeks by obtaining the election of a pro-English emperor to succeed Brims. He hoped eventually to persuade the Creeks to attack the Yamasee towns in Florida, but his scheme failed when his candidate for emperor was killed in 1724. Brims was succeeded instead by Chipacasi—whom the English called Seepeycoffee—a Creek chieftain with French sympathies. Even under Seepeycoffee, however, the Creek nation adhered to its basic policy of neutrality and continued to uphold a balance of power on the southern frontier.[17]

Although Nicholson made no progress in diplomacy, he was much more successful in the regulation of the Indian trade. After years of trial and error, the government of South Carolina finally worked out a satisfactory regulatory system during his administration. When Nicholson arrived in South Carolina the colony was still struggling along under the law adopted in 1716, which combined a public and a private trade under the supervision of a single commissioner. No one liked the existing law, and on September 1, 1721, the Commons House of Assembly voluntarily surrendered its control over the trade by asking the governor and council to take over trade regulation. Nicholson was reluctant to assume such a responsibility and persuaded the assembly to try a different plan. A new Indian trade law abolished the public trade and turned everything over to private merchants. This part of the new law satisfied both the government and the traders, but the question of who should enforce trade regulations remained unsolved. A three-man commission lasted only a year, and the assembly then entrusted regulation to the governor and any three councilors. This plan failed, too, largely because the council was forced to spend too much time on the minutiae of enforcement. Finally, in 1725, the assembly returned to the original idea of appointing a single trade commissioner. This time the system worked, because Commissioner George Chicken found a solution to one of the basic problems of trade regulation. No one before Chicken had been able to enforce trade laws in the Indian villages that were far from Charles Town, but Chicken spent a lot of time traveling among the various tribes. More important, he appointed special agents who lived with the major

[16] Crane, *Southern Frontier*, 233–47, 282–87; Cooper and McCord, eds., *Statutes*, III, 122–24.

[17] Crane, *Southern Frontier*, 264–68.

Indian tribes and assumed responsibility for trade regulation in their areas. With the introduction of this regulatory structure, South Carolina had found an answer to an old and vexing problem, and it had gone as far as a colony could go in regulating Indian trade without the help of the British government.[18]

With the exception of trade regulation, Nicholson failed to make progress in his attempts to solve the problems of the frontier. Nevertheless, Nicholson managed to prevent any real crisis from developing there, and in doing so he gave the colony four years of relative peace, years it needed badly to recuperate from the Yamasee War and the Revolution of 1719. In fact, Nicholson's lack of positive accomplishment in external affairs counted far less in the long run than South Carolina's failure to eliminate the weak spots in its economy. The colony's troubles in the late 1720's were economic, not military or diplomatic.

III

In directing the internal affairs of South Carolina, Nicholson obeyed a precept that he quoted on every appropriate occasion. The governor explained that his duty demanded that he serve "those two inseparables, That of his Majestys Interest and Service and that of this his Province." [19] Nicholson interpreted this duty to mean that he should try, above everything else, to heal the factional wounds in the provincial government, and he thought the best way to do so was to unite all parties behind the royal government. He therefore deliberately set out to win over the proprietary men in the colony, even if it occasionally meant catering to what he must have regarded as their whims.

Nicholson applied the principle of reconciliation most clearly in his relations with his council. The Board of Trade had empowered Nicholson to select the members of the council himself, but it made it clear to the governor that it expected him to consult with the provincial agents in London, Joseph Boone and John Barnwell, and with the Board itself. Before Nicholson sailed for South Carolina the agents and the Board drew up separate lists of nominations for the council in October 1720, but neither slate satisfied Nicholson, possibly because the rebels of 1719 monopolized both lists. Nicholson met with

[18] Sept. 1, 1721, Nov. 8, 1722, Journal of the Upper House, 1721–1774, I, 82, II, Pt. i, 89, S. C. Archives; Cooper and McCord, eds., Statutes, III, 141–46, 184–86, 229–32; Crane, Southern Frontier, 200–203.

[19] See, e.g., Nov. 8, 1722, Commons Journal, VI, 62, S. C. Archives.

the agents and the Board of Trade on October 18, and they agreed on a council that represented every major political and economic group in South Carolina. Eight of the twelve councilors were rebels and four were proprietary men; eight were planters, three were merchants, and one was the provincial secretary. The inclusion of two leading religious dissenters gave the council an even better balance. The Privy Council later added the surveyor general of customs in the southern colonies to the councils of South Carolina, Virginia, and Jamaica, but he never sat with the South Carolina body.[20]

Governor Nicholson carried his efforts to win the support of his council even to the extent of ignoring his instructions. These said clearly that the oldest member of the council should become its president, but the governor permitted the council to elect a president. The council chose Arthur Middleton. The governor's instructions further implied that the seniority of councilors should be determined by their ages, but Nicholson allowed the council members to establish seniority among themselves by ballot. Nicholson was empowered to appoint councilors himself, but when Hugh Butler refused to serve he let the council elect a new member. The councilors voted for Benjamin de la Conseillere, South Carolina's leading hard money advocate. Finally, the governor's instructions directed him to draw up a list of twelve men he thought would be qualified to fill vacancies in the council, but he again ignored his instructions and turned this job over to the council in 1724.[21] Nicholson's courtship of the council succeeded. Nine of the twelve councilors supported his policies without reservation, and he was opposed only by the two dissenters, who objected to his high Anglicanism, and by Benjamin de la Conseillere, who thought Nicholson was soft on the paper money issue.[22]

During Nicholson's administration the council came to enjoy more prestige and influence than it had ever known before. Nicholson's policy of deference to the council accounted for much of its increased

[20] M. Eugene Sirmans, "The South Carolina Royal Council, 1720–1763," *William and Mary Quarterly*, 3d Ser., 18 (1961), 381–82, 389–90. The rebels on the council were planters Arthur Middleton, Joseph Morton (dissenter), Benjamin Schenkingh, Alexander Skene, and Landgrave Thomas Smith (dissenter), and merchants William Gibbon, James Kinloch, and Francis Yonge; the proprietary men were planters William Bull, Hugh Butler, and Ralph Izard, and provincial secretary Charles Hart.

[21] Leonard W. Labaree, ed., *Royal Instructions to British Colonial Governors, 1670–1776*, 2 vols. (N. Y. and London, 1935), I, 30, 50, 78–79; May 31, June 3, 1721, Salley, ed., *Council Journal, 1721*, 10, 18; enclosure in Nicholson to Bd. of Trade, July 26, 1724, CO 5/359, fol. 207, PRO.

[22] Council to Bd. of Trade, Oct. 28, 1721, Address of Council, Jan. 14, 1725, S. C. Pub. Recs., IX, 80–81, XI, 290–91, S. C. Archives.

prestige, but a change in the tenure of council appointments may have carried even more weight. The proprietors had appointed councilors during pleasure, and they had always been prompt to replace any councilor who opposed proprietary policy. The Crown, however, appointed councilors during good behavior, which meant that neither the governor nor the Crown could suspend a councilor unless he had abused his position or neglected his duties. This change freed councilors from arbitrary supervision and enabled the royal council to act with a high degree of independence. John Lloyd, a leading member of the Commons House, testified to the prestige of the council when he wrote to the assistant secretary of state in 1725: "As the next and most Honourable Stepp in these parts is that of a Councellour I hope you will favour me with your Recomendation to be one of his Majesties Councill in this Province." [23] The councilors themselves fully appreciated their improved status, so much so that they laid claim to all the rights and privileges of the House of Lords in 1725. The claim is an unusually interesting one, if only because it seems not to have been common in colonial America, and it illuminates the comment of Alexander Hewatt, the historian of South Carolina writing half a century later: "The council, though differing in many respects from the house of peers, are intended to represent that house." [24]

In his relations with the other branch of the legislature, Governor Nicholson had to tread even more carefully, for the Commons House was dominated by the rebels of 1719. They had placed their hope for improvement of conditions in royal government, but for that very reason they could be troublesome.[25] Thirty-two men sat in Nicholson's first assembly; fourteen of them had also served in either the rebel assembly or the rebel council. Seven others had definitely favored the revolution, while only one representative was a known proprietary man. A significant change had taken place in the Commons House since the preceding decade. Most leaders of the proprietary assemblies had been planters and Indian traders, with a sprinkling of merchants and lawyers. Now the situation was reversed. Of the ten outstanding leaders in the Commons House between 1720 and 1725, four were merchants and two were lawyers. Only three assembly leaders were

[23] To Temple Stanyan, May 28, 1725, *ibid.*, XI, 318; see also Sirmans, "S. C. Royal Council," *Wm. and Mary Qtly.*, 3d Ser., 18 (1961), 382.

[24] Mar. 5, 1725, Upper House Journal, II, Pt. ii, 244, S. C. Archives; Hewatt, *Historical Account*, in Carroll, ed., *Hist. Collections of S. C.*, I, 277.

[25] Richard Splatt to Samuel Barons, July 20, 1720, S. C. Pub. Recs., VIII, 34, S. C. Archives.

planters, while one man combined the Indian trade with the practice of law.[26]

Governor Nicholson's handling of the assembly emulated his handling of the council. He tried to keep the Commons House on the side of royal government by bowing to its wishes except in unusual circumstances. Nicholson began by allowing the laws passed by the rebel government to stand. Among them were the emission of £25,000 in the so-called rice bills and the act regulating judicial procedure. The governor continued to defer to the Commons House by approving almost every bill it passed. One such act confirmed the assembly's right to nominate and appoint the public treasurer and every other official whose salary was paid by the public. The act hurt later governors, because it gave the assembly the power to control officials who handled public funds and the Commons House used that power to encroach upon the governor's prerogatives. Nicholson approved still another statute that brought complaints from his successors. This was the election act of 1721, which remained in force until the American Revolution. Almost a verbatim re-enactment of the election act of 1716 which the proprietors had disallowed, the new law apportioned assembly seats among the parishes, limited the duration of a single assembly to three years, and forbade the lapse of more than six months between the dissolution of one assembly and the first meeting of its successor. The law also required that all candidates for the assembly must own 500 acres of land and ten slaves or personal property worth £1,000 currency, and it set franchise requirements at a fifty-acre freehold or the payment of 20s. currency in taxes. Later governors complained that the suffrage requirements were too liberal and permitted every adult freeman to vote.[27]

The broad franchise of the election act of 1721 made the Commons House of Assembly extremely responsive to public opinion. Politicians, at least on the paper money issue, found it necessary to adopt the ideas of the electorate. Governor Nicholson complained in 1725 that candidates for the assembly were advocating an increase in the local currency "because they think that will prevail with the People to

[26] The leaders were merchants John Fenwicke, Thomas Hepworth, Charles Hill, and John Lloyd; lawyers Richard Allein and Benjamin Whitaker; planters John Barnwell, James Moore, Jr., and Percival Pawley; and Indian trader-lawyer William Blakeway; see Greene, *Quest for Power*, 475–88.

[27] Cooper and McCord, eds., *Statutes*, III, 135–40, 148–49; on the election law, see, e.g., James Glen to Bd. of Trade, Dec. 23, 1749, S. C. Pub. Recs., XXIII, 438, S. C. Archives.

Choose them." [28] The same point may be illustrated by the political career of John Lloyd, an ambitious Charles Town merchant. As a merchant, Lloyd habitually signed anti-paper money petitions throughout the 1720's, but in order to serve in the Commons House he was forced to adopt a completely different position. He was a member of the house when it made some of its most radical currency proposals, and after his election as speaker of the house in 1730 he became an official spokesman for the paper money faction.

Conflicts between the Commons House and the governor were rare during Nicholson's administration. The only one of any significance was caused by the governor's religious views. Nicholson was a High Church Anglican who despised and distrusted religious dissenters. He said once, "I think it no very Difficult thing to Prove that all the Dissenters here, in New England and other his Majestys Collonys and Provinces are of Common Wealth Principles both in Church and State and would be Independent to the Crown of Great Brittain if it were in their Power." [29] When Nicholson met his first assembly in July 1721 he requested that all assembly members must take their oaths of office by swearing on the Bible. Several dissenters refused to do so, and Nicholson did not want to let them take their seats. Both the Common House and the council urged Nicholson to change his mind, and he let the dissenters simply make an affirmation saying that they were loyal to the Crown and would perform their duties. When the new election bill came before the assembly in September, Nicholson persuaded the council to insert a clause that required all assemblymen to be sworn in by a formal oath. The Commons House agreed reluctantly, and thereafter dissenters either took the oaths or refused their assembly seats.[30] Nicholson continued to harass the dissenters of South Carolina. He tried to stop dissenting ministers from performing marriages, but the assembly rebuffed him and allowed them to continue. The colony's dissenters remained apprehensive about Nicholson, fearing more persecution, until the governor returned to England.[31]

Although the governor did not resort to persecution, he did help the colony's Anglicans strengthen the established church. The Yamasee

[28] To Bd. of Trade, Jan. 1725, S. C. Pub. Recs., XI, 365, S. C. Archives.
[29] To Bishop of London, Aug. 5, 1724, Fulham Palace Mss., S. C., no. 112.
[30] July 28, Sept. 14–15, 1721, Upper House Journal, I, 30, 105, 113, S. C. Archives; Wallace, *Hist. of S. C.*, I, 258.
[31] Petition of Archibald Stobo, 1722, Francis Varnod to Sec. S.P.G., Jan. 15, 1723, Clergy of S. C. to Sec. S.P.G., Feb. 25, 1725, S.P.G. Mss., A 16, 107–10, A 17, 121, A 19, Carolina Letters for 1725, no. 2.

War had greatly weakened the Church of England in South Carolina; many parishes had lost their rectors, and the ministers who remained suffered when the provincial currency depreciated. With the help of a new Anglican commissary, Alexander Garden, Nicholson set out to revitalize the church in South Carolina. In 1721 he persuaded the assembly to raise ministerial salaries to £100 proclamation money per year and to build churches and chapels where they were needed.[32] The Society for the Propagation of the Gospel assisted by sending missionaries to fill the vacant parishes. Commissary Garden eliminated the worst disciplinary problems in the ministry through the establishment of an ecclesiastical court. The S.P.G. also founded a free grammar school in Charles Town, and its missionaries began to report a limited, but promising, degree of success in Negro slave conversions. The S.P.G. fell down only in its program of converting Indians, probably because most rectors shared the opinion of one who called the Indians "a headstrong, idle Stupid People [who] seem incapable of instruction in the Christian religion." [33] With this exception, the Church of England in South Carolina prospered during Nicholson's administration, and the clergy was able to report in 1724 that the religious establishment was in a "flourishing condition." [34]

Governor Nicholson even won the assembly's support for the establishment of local institutions of government comparable to those found in other English colonies. South Carolina had not developed any political institutions below the provincial level, and Nicholson considered this a serious defect in the colony's government. The most important of his innovations sought to establish courts outside Charles Town. Many South Carolinians, especially the planters, had wanted local courts for some time, and Nicholson suggested in 1721 that the assembly erect local courts modeled after those in Virginia. The merchants of Charles Town opposed the governor's plan, because they feared that local courts would make it harder for them to collect debts from planters. The assembly nevertheless passed a law that set up three county courts in Craven, Colleton, and Granville counties and two precinct courts in Berkeley County outside Charles Town. Five justices of the peace, three of whom were a quorum, were to preside over each

[32] Cooper and McCord, eds., *Statutes,* III, 174–76; Clergy of S. C. to Sec. S.P.G., July 12, 1722, S.P.G. Mss., A 16, 76–78.

[33] Brian Hunt to Sec. S.P.G., May 25, 1724, S.P.G. Mss., A 18, 82; see also Edgar L. Pennington, "The Reverend Alexander Garden," *Protestant Episcopal Church History Magazine,* 3 (1934), 52–53; Helen E. Livingston, "Thomas Morritt, Schoolmaster at the Charleston Free School, 1723–1728," *ibid.,* 14 (1945), 151–67; Klingberg, *The Negro in Col. S. C.,* 31–32, 50–58.

[34] Clergy of S. C. to Sec. S.P.G., Mar. 10, 1724, S.P.G. Mss., B 4, no. 141.

court. The primary functions of the new courts were to hear debt cases and to serve as courts of record in business transactions; they heard civil cases involving less than £100 sterling and criminal cases that did not involve imprisonment or death. All other cases went to the Courts of Common Pleas and Assizes in Charles Town.[35]

Nicholson's ideas extended beyond expansion of the court system, and again at his suggestion the assembly passed two other imporatnt laws on local government. The first, also adopted in 1721, reorganized the colony's road system. Before then the assembly had passed a separate law for every road or bridge that was built or repaired, appointed a separate commission to supervise each job, and paid the cost of construction from the public treasury. The new law divided the colony into districts and established a permanent road commission for each district. The act directed the commissioners to meet semi-annually to decide what road work was necessary and to let contracts, and it empowered them to levy necessary taxes. The other important law relating to local government provided for the incorporation of Charles Town. The act, passed by the assembly in 1722, followed the general outlines of the laws governing Philadelphia and New York. It placed Charles Town under the control of a closed corporation, granted in perpetuity the right to govern the town to nineteen men named in the statute, and gave them the sole right to elect their successors. The law also gave Charles Town a new name—Charles City and Port.[36]

The introduction of political innovations did not stop with local government but extended even into the legislature. Both houses appointed standing conference committees, which met to resolve differences whenever the two houses failed to agree. The standing conference committees superseded the old custom of appointing a different committee each time a conference was needed. The council also replaced several former standing committees, and appointed an executive committee to draft laws, handle correspondence, read petitions, and perform other basic chores.[37] Finally, the assembly changed its procedure for passing bills. Previously, both houses had

[35] Aug. 30, Sept. 14, 18, 1721, Upper House Journal, I, 78, 104, 119, S. C. Archives; Cooper and McCord, eds., Statutes, VII, 166–76; on earlier demands for local courts, see Petition of Council and Assembly, Feb. 3, 1720, S. C. Pub. Recs., VII, 285, S. C. Archives.

[36] Cooper and McCord, eds., Statutes, IX, 49–57; on the act of incorporation, see Bridenbaugh, Cities in the Wilderness, 145–46; Wallace, Hist. of S. C., I, 286–87.

[37] Aug. 3, 1721, Commons Journal, V, 506, S. C. Archives; Aug. 3, 1721, Upper House Journal, I, 35, S. C. Archives; on the council's executive committee, see Aug. 16, 18, 1721, ibid., 58, 62.

read every bill three times, but bills had been sent from house to house after each reading. The house that introduced a bill now began to read and pass it three times before sending it to the other house, which was the procedure followed by Parliament.

Almost none of these political innovations lasted very long, and the first to disappear was the incorporation of Charles Town. Many townsmen opposed the act, because it discriminated against them. Everyone had to pay taxes and serve on juries, but only the nineteen men named in the act of incorporation had any political power. Seventeen members of the corporation were merchants connected with the London trade; the other two were the Huguenots Benjamin de la Conseillere and Benjamin Godin. Some of the excluded merchants petitioned the Crown for disallowance of the act on the grounds of discrimination and hired Richard Shelton, the influential secretary to the proprietors, to represent them in London. Shelton persuaded the Privy Council to disallow the act. Nicholson was indignant, but there was nothing he could do.[38]

The other political reforms did not fare much better. As early as March 1722, the council complained about the inconvenience of the new method of passing laws. It proposed a return to the old procedure of alternate readings in each house, and the lower house concurred.[39] The standing conference committees and the council's executive committee disappeared soon after, and the two houses reverted to their earlier practices. The county and precinct courts did not last a decade. They became involved in the paper money controversy of the middle 1720's and closed during the state of near anarchy in the late twenties. The law creating the courts remained on the statute books, but the courts failed to reopen when order was restored. Only the road commissions survived the 1720's. They continued to meet throughout the colonial period, but the assembly later found them inadequate and had to pass supplementary laws on roads and bridges at nearly every assembly session.

IV

The first year and a half of Nicholson's administration was peaceful. The governor encountered little opposition except from the religious

[38] Petition of "the Major part of the Inhabitants of Charles Town," May 30, 1723, Nicholson to Bd. of Trade, Oct. 14, 1723, S. C. Pub. Recs., X, 93–95, 173–74, S. C. Archives. Bridenbaugh says the act of incorporation was opposed mostly by the planters, because they dominated the assembly and wanted to keep Charles Town under its control; see *Cities in the Wilderness*, 304.

[39] Mar. 1, 1722, Upper House Journal, I, 201, S. C. Archives.

dissenters and the opponents of the incorporation act. Late in 1722, however, the paper money controversy of the preceding decade reappeared and split the colony into uncompromising factions. As before, the debate contained some elements of a division between merchants and planters, but the conflict may be more accurately called a contest between debtors and creditors. Even this description requires modification, however, especially in view of the work of a middle-of-the-road group. Governor Nicholson appreciated South Carolina's need for a local currency and agreed to demands for a new emission of bills of credit. By doing so he antagonized the hard money faction, and his reputation suffered because of its criticism.[40]

The basic cause of internal divisions over paper currency was the unequal distribution of wealth in South Carolina. Two Anglican ministers—one writing in 1723 and the other in 1728—reported that only Charles Town and five nearby parishes were prosperous. The other five parishes were poor, especially those on the northern and southern frontiers.[41] Even within the wealthy parishes, there was great economic disparity. Reliable economic indices exist only in the form of an S.P.G. missionary's report on slave ownership in St. George's Parish, one of the wealthy low country parishes. Slaveholdings were a reliable indicator of wealth, however, and there is no reason to suppose that St. George's differed from the rest of the prosperous central area of the colony. The great majority of the white men in St. George's were small farmers who owned few slaves, if any. Of the 107 families in the parish nearly one out of five owned no slaves, while 56 per cent owned five slaves or less; two-thirds owned ten slaves or less. At the other end of the economic structure were the large planters. Of the 1,347 slaves in St. George's, the nine largest slaveholders owned 572, or 42.5 per cent. The disparity is likely to have been even greater than these figures indicate, because it is quite possible that some of the nine large planters owned land and slaves in other parishes.[42]

The demand for an increased local currency came primarily from

[40] The best accounts of the paper money disputes in South Carolina in the 1720's are Jellison, "Paper Currency," *S. C. Hist. Mag.*, 62 (1961), 138–47; W. Roy Smith, *South Carolina as a Royal Province, 1719–1776* (N. Y., 1903), 234–68. The following account differs somewhat from those by Jellison and Smith, especially on the role of the council, the work of the moderate party, and the importance of the collapse of the market for naval stores.

[41] William Tredwell Bull to Bishop of London, Aug. 23, 1723, Fulham Palace Mss., S. C., nos. 277–78; Brian Hunt to Sec. S.P.G., Oct. 5, 1728, S.P.G. Mss., A 21, Carolina Letters, no. 14. The prosperous parishes were St. Philip (Charles Town), St. Andrew, St. George, St. James Goose Creek, St. John, and St. Paul.

[42] Klingberg, *The Negro in Col. S. C.*, 58–60; this reprints a report made by Francis Varnod in 1726.

the men at the bottom of the economic scale, the small farmers. A few merchants like John Lloyd and William Dry agreed with them publicly, but they apparently did so only in order to advance their own political careers. Most merchants opposed large emissions of paper bills. A few large planters, such as Landgrave Thomas Smith, favored additional currency, but most large planters preferred the middle of the road. The most revealing evidence on the composition of the easy money party comes from six petitions for an increased currency, which the assembly received in 1727 at the height of the paper money dispute. All the petitions came from rural parishes, thus indicating the agrarian origins of the agitation. A total of 274 men signed the petitions. Only one of them, James Colleton, was definitely a large planter. Furthermore, no more than fifteen of the petitioners ever served in the assembly, which may mean that many of them could not satisfy the minimum requirements for a seat in the Commons House. Finally, the council said a year later that "most" of the signers were "of the meaner sort." [43] The presumption must be, therefore, that the great majority of the paper money advocates were small farmers.

The first decade of royal government was a difficult time for small farmers because of South Carolina's stagnant economy. They depended largely on naval stores because they did not own enough slaves to grow rice. When Parliament allowed the bounty on naval stores to lapse, the market for pitch and tar collapsed and the small farmers found themselves so deeply in debt that they faced bankruptcy. Percival Pawley, one of the outspoken advocates of a paper currency, may have typified the plight of the small farmer; he went so far into debt that he finally ran away to North Carolina to escape his creditors.[44] Men like Pawley rarely had enough cash on hand to pay their debts, and they blamed their troubles on the shortage of currency. They hoped that an expanded currency would not only make it easier for them to obtain the money to pay their debts, but that it would also stimulate a period of growth and prosperity in the provincial economy. The paper money advocates never indicated in any way that they wanted to force a depreciation of the local currency in order to pay their debts at a more favorable rate of exchange. At most they hoped to delay debt payments by temporarily closing the courts.[45]

[43] Representation of the Council, Dec. 19, 1728, S. C. Pub. Recs., XIII, 302, S. C. Archives; the petitions are in ibid., XII, 19–32.

[44] William Guy to Sec. S.P.G., Apr. 24, 1729, S.P.G. Mss., A 22, 236.

[45] See, e.g., "Representation of the Inhabitants of South Carolina," [May 1727], Representation from the Parishes of St. Paul and St. Bartholomew, [Aug. 1727], S. C. Pub. Recs., XII, 211–14, XIII, 19–25, S. C. Archives.

At the other extreme stood those who flatly opposed a local currency under any circumstances. Nearly all its members were merchants who had loaned money to the farmers and feared that the paper money would depreciate still further. A few large planters like Ralph Izard agreed with them, but the hard money faction had little support outside Charles Town. As in the previous decade, this group was led by the mercantile firm of Godin and Conseillere, with Benjamin de la Conseillere as its spokesman in South Carolina and Stephen Godin as its representative in England. Also as before, Godin and Conseillere cooperated with Richard Shelton, the influential secretary of the Carolina proprietors. Personal grievances complicated the political attitudes of the faction's leaders. Conseillere and the Godins disliked Governor Nicholson because he had accused them of smuggling, while Shelton was disappointed by the governor's refusal to appoint him as agent for South Carolina.[46]

There was still a third group involved in South Carolina's currency disputes. More amorphous than either of the extreme factions, its members still managed to agree on two key points. First, they thought South Carolina needed a local medium of exchange. At the same time, however, they feared that too large a local currency would result in depreciation of the paper bills and hurt South Carolina's credit. They therefore wanted to limit the amount of paper currency in circulation and demanded adequate provisions against its depreciation. Most of them thought South Carolina already had an adequate supply of currency and opposed further emissions except in emergencies. Many of South Carolina's most influential politicians belonged to the moderate group, including a majority of the council. Many of the wealthiest merchants in Charles Town favored the moderate position, among them Joseph and Samuel Wragg, John Fenwicke, William Gibbon, Paul Jenys, and Othniel Beale. The middle of the road was also favored by nearly all the large planters, who were neither debtors nor creditors. They were led by councilors Arthur Middleton, William Bull, and Alexander Skene.

The first emission of bills of credit in the 1720's had come at the very beginning of the decade, when the rebel assembly had emitted £34,000 in rice bills. Governor Nicholson approved a law in 1721 that emitted an additional £15,000 in rice bills and provided for the retirement of all bills at the rate of £4,000 a year. The two issues gave South Carolina a total of £80,000 in bills of credit in circulation. Despite the fact that the value of the bills dropped from an exchange rate of £4 currency to £1 sterling to a ratio of £6 to £1, no one

[46] Nicholson to Bd. of Trade, Oct. 14, 1723, Jan. 20, 1724, *ibid.*, X, 74, XI, 18.

objected to either of the new emissions.[47] The provincial economy took a turn for the worse the next year, however, when heavy rains and floods destroyed a third of South Carolina's crops, including nearly half its rice. The Commons House promptly introduced a bill that would make produce legal tender, but the council refused to consider it.[48]

The currency dispute reached the first stage in a series of crises in December 1722, when the Commons House took up a bill to emit £43,000 in new bills of credit. Twenty-eight merchants submitted a petition to the Commons House that asked the assembly to defeat the law on the ground that the continued emission of paper bills was destroying the public credit. The petitioners represented almost the entire mercantile community, for the signers included moderates as well as hard money men. The lower house interpreted the petition as an accusation that the assembly was committing a breach of faith by considering the bill and ordered its messenger to arrest all twenty-eight petitioners on December 8. The merchants appealed to the council but it refused to intervene, and the lower house kept the merchants in jail until each one made a public apology to the house.[49]

The two houses of the legislature then began serious bargaining on a new currency issue. The Commons House wanted to print enough bills to cover provincial debts until the following September, an amount it calculated at £43,000. The council thought that the existing currency was sufficient for South Carolina's needs, but it said it would agree to emit £30,000 because of the damage caused by the previous summer's flood. The two houses failed to compromise their differences before the Christmas holidays and did nothing until February 1723. Then the council gave way, possibly as a result of Nicholson's

[47] [Bull], "Account of Paper Bills," Cooper and McCord, eds., *Statutes*, IX, 773–74; on the value of bills of credit, see Memorial of the Merchants of Charles Town, Dec. 1722, S. C. Pub. Recs., IX, 182–83, S. C. Archives. In its *Currency Report* of 1737, the Commons House of Assembly consistently estimated the amount of bills of credit in circulation at £4,000 below the figures given by Bull; see *Currency Report*, in Easterby, ed., *Commons Journal, 1736–39*, 293. Reports made by the assembly for 1727 and 1728, however, support Bull's figures exactly; see Aug. 31, 1727, Commons Journal, VII, 590, S. C. Archives; Feb. 15, 1728, *ibid.*, Public Records of South Carolina, I, 379; the Commons Journals for 1728–34 in the S. C. Archives are bound in two volumes labeled "Public Records of South Carolina," which should not be confused with S. C. Pub. Recs.

[48] *Currency Report*, in Easterby, ed., *Commons Journal, 1736–39*, 308; Francis Yonge to Allured Popple, Dec. 10, 1722, S. C. Pub. Recs., IX, 170–71, S. C. Archives; June 23, 1722, Upper House Journal, II, Pt. i, 51, S. C. Archives.

[49] Memorial of the Merchants of Charles Town, Dec. 1722, S. C. Pub. Recs., IX, 179–901, S. C. Archives; Dec. 8, 13–14, 1722, Commons Journal, VI, 113–14, 122–26, S. C. Archives; Dec. 12, 1722, Upper House Journal, II, Pt. i, 129–30, S. C. Archives.

intercession, and agreed to an emission of £40,000 by a vote of six to two.[50] The assembly also decided to call in and reprint all old bills of credit, except the last £8,000 of the bank bills issued in 1712, and it set up a plan to retire all paper currency within the next twenty-two years. The act of 1723 gave South Carolina a total of £120,000 in paper money, and its bills of credit depreciated to an exchange value of seven to one.[51]

The currency act of 1723 went too far for nearly every merchant in South Carolina. Only a handful of merchants, such as John Fenwicke and William Gibbon, failed to support the rest of the mercantile community. Led by Samuel and Joseph Wragg, the moderates joined the hard money faction in a campaign to repeal the law. The merchants petitioned the Board of Trade for disallowance of the act and engaged Richard Shelton as their agent. Hiring Shelton was a mistake. He belonged to the extreme hard money faction, and he showed no hesitancy in exceeding his instructions. In August 1723 he obtained the disallowance not only of the act of 1723 but also of the act of 1721, which had emitted £15,000.[52] Shelton's meddling offended everyone but the hard money faction. Moderates thought he had gone too far and that disallowance of both laws would reduce the local currency too much. Again led by the Wragg brothers, the moderates broke away from the anti-currency party.[53]

The currency acts of 1721 and 1723 had already gone into operation, so the Board of Trade instructed Governor Nicholson to secure passage of a law to retire the bills. The people of South Carolina were nearly unanimous in the belief that immediate sinking of the bills would deprive the colony of an adequate medium of exchange and ruin the economy. The assembly was flooded with petitions from every sector of the colony asking for gradual retirement. Petitions came from the chief justice and assistant judges, the justices of the county and precinct courts, the grand and petit juries, the inhabitants of Granville County, and even the Anglican clergy.[54] Both houses of the assembly

---

[50] Dec. 14–15, 1722, Commons Journal, VI, 126–27, S. C. Archives; Dec. 13, 1722, Feb. 21, 1723, Upper House Journal, II, Pt. i, 134, 220, S. C. Archives.

[51] Cooper and McCord, eds., Statutes, III, 188–93; [Bull], "Account of Paper Bills," ibid., IX, 775; Currency Report, in Easterby, ed., Commons Journal, 1736–39, 307.

[52] Memorials of Merchants Trading to South Carolina, May 22, June 5, 1723, Nicholson to Bd. of Trade, Nov. 12, 1723, S. C. Pub. Recs., X, 87–91, 111–12, 195–96, S. C. Archives.

[53] Compare the signatures to the petitions cited in n. 52 with the signatures on an anti-currency petition of 1724; see Petition of Merchants and Traders to South Carolina, Oct. 16, 1724, ibid., XI, 231–35.

[54] The petitions are in ibid., XI, 221–28, 369–82; the clergy's petition is in Fulham Palace Mss., S. C., no. 229.

sent joint petitions to the Board of Trade and the Privy Council protesting disallowance of the laws. They argued that South Carolina would never have enough specie to carry on its local trade unless its exports exceeded its imports, a situation which would contravene the doctrines of English mercantilism. The provincial council made its position clear in a separate petition to the Privy Council. It said that £120,000 in local currency, the amount in circulation before the Privy Council's veto, was both necessary and sufficient; it thought the paper bills should neither be reduced nor increased.[55] With public opinion solidly behind it, the assembly passed an act in February 1724 that provided for very slow retirement of the bills of credit. The act set no time limit for sinking the bills issued in 1721 and 1723; instead it said that such bills would be retired as they were received in payment of import duties or debts incurred under the bank act of 1712. No other bills could be used to pay import duties and bank act debts, and the bills of 1721 and 1723 were not legal tender in any other transaction. The act thus provided for sinking £55,000. The remaining £65,000 in paper bills would continue to circulate until they were retired according to the original acts of emission.[56]

Governor Nicholson's backing of the currency laws won him the support of nearly every person in South Carolina, but it damaged his reputation in London. Merchants who traded to South Carolina accused him of disobeying his instructions, and Richard Shelton used his influence to make sure their accusations reached the Board of Trade and the Privy Council. Nicholson was also still under fire from the Bahama interests because of his quarrel with William Rhett. The governor had previously asked the Privy Council for a leave of absence, so that he could return to England to take care of some private affairs and recover from various physical ailments. The Privy Council granted him the leave on August 7, 1724, but it did so on the grounds that he needed to answer the charges that had been brought against him.[57] The governor left South Carolina in May 1725, intending to return within a year, but he never came back. When he sailed home, however, he carried with him the good wishes of most of the colony. For example, the council presented him with an address

[55] Petitions of the Council and Assembly, Nov. 15, 1723, Feb. 15, 1724, Petition of Council, Nov. 14, 1724, S. C. Pub. Recs., X, 206-9, XI, 19, 254-55, S. C. Archives.

[56] Cooper and McCord, eds., *Statutes*, III, 219-21; [Bull], "Account of Paper Bills," *ibid.*, IX, 775-76.

[57] Grant and Munro, eds., *Acts of Privy Council, Col. Ser.*, III, 81-82; for Nicholson's defense against the Bahama Company, see *An Apology or Vindication of Francis Nicholson.*

that praised his administration in enthusiastic terms. Even the three proprietary men on the council signed the address, and only Benjamin de la Conseillere, the hard money leader, and Landgrave Thomas Smith, a religious dissenter, refused to sign.[58] The hard money faction could not forgive Nicholson, and after he had gone its members circulated a petition that criticized the governor. The petition was signed by a number of merchants, but it attracted few signatures outside Charles Town.[59]

V

Governor Nicholson was succeeded by the president of the council, Arthur Middleton, a wealthy planter and a leader in the overthrow of the proprietors. Middleton was not particularly well qualified for the governorship, for he possessed little of the tact a governor needed. Moreover, he approached the major political issue of his administration with an unfortunate timidity. Nicholson's instructions severely limited Middleton's authority. They forbade him to approve any laws except "such as shall be immediately necessary for the peace and welfare" of South Carolina.[60] Middleton interpreted the instruction literally and was reluctant to act decisively on controversial questions. The council shared Middleton's timidity, and together they permitted South Carolina's government to drift. Since both Middleton and the council favored a limited currency and opposed change in either direction, they exhibited a special reluctance to tamper with the existing currency laws.

By way of contrast, the Commons House of Assembly was not the least bit timid. When the provincial economy declined in the late 1720's, the lower house grew increasingly zealous on the currency issue. It finally became so radical that most of the merchants of Charles Town did not want to have anything to do with it, and many declined to sit in the Commons House after they were elected.[61] Their refusal to serve in the assembly, however, did not greatly change the leadership of the house. Some merchants, such as John Fenwicke and John Lloyd, continued to sit in the Commons, and the house continued to trust them with positions of responsibility. Nine men emerged as leaders in

<hr/>

[58] Address of Council, Jan. 14, 1725, S. C. Pub. Recs., XI, 290–91, S. C. Archives.
[59] William Guy to Nicholson, June 28, 1725, S.P.G. Mss., B 4, no. 193.
[60] Labaree, ed., *Royal Instructions*, I, 78.
[61] See, e.g., the refusals of Joseph Wragg, Charles Hill, and Jonathan Skrine, Commons Journal, July 12, 1728, Public Records of S. C., I, 536, S. C. Archives.

the Commons House. Four were planters, three were merchants, one was a lawyer, and one combined trade and agriculture. The influence of the merchants in the house thus declined slightly after 1725, but the change was not at all significant.[62]

Immediately upon Governor Nicholson's embarkation for England the Commons House began to agitate for a larger currency. On May 27, 1725, at the very first session after Nicholson's departure, the Commons House introduced a bill that would suspend the sinking act, re-issue all the old bills of credit, and add £40,000 to the currency. Middleton rejected the scheme on the grounds that he lacked the power to approve such a law, and the council voted the bill down. The council pointed out that a petition asking for permission to continue the existing currency was already on its way to England, and the upper house repeated its belief that the existing currency would be sufficient. The Commons House tried again in November by passing a resolution to suspend the sinking act, but the council once again refused to concur.[63] A month later the lower house decided to punish the council for its obstinacy. The upper house amended the annual tax bill after it had passed its third reading in the lower house, and the Commons protested. At first it objected to the amendments only on the ground that neither house should amend a bill on its third reading. When the conference committee from both houses failed to work out a compromise, the Commons House refused to take further action on the bill. Middleton prorogued the assembly overnight to permit reintroduction of the tax bill, but the Commons House then broadened the scope of the argument. Beginning with the premise that the House of Lords did not have the right to amend English money bills, it reasoned that the South Carolina council should not exercise more power than the Lords. The Commons House therefore resolved on December 14 that the upper house did not have the right to amend tax bills. The council defended its prerogatives and pointed out that Governor Nicholson's instructions specifically gave it the power to alter money bills. In order to avoid further trouble, however, the council withdrew its amendments to the tax bill and approved the version passed by the lower house. It added that it intended to petition the Crown for a decision

---

[62] The leaders were planters Thomas Broughton, Tobias Fitch, George Smith, Jr., and Benjamin Waring; merchants John Fenwicke, John Lloyd, and William Rhett, Jr.; lawyer Benjamin Whitaker; and merchant-planter William Dry; see Greene, *Quest for Power*, 475–88.

[63] May 27, June 1, 1725, Salley, ed., *Commons Journal, Feb.–June 1725*, 123–24, 128, 141; Nov. 24, 1725, *ibid., 1725–26*, 35.

on its right to amend tax bills.[64] The argument settled nothing, but it raised for the first time the fundamental constitutional question of the council's legislative rights and marked the beginning of the lower house's fight for exclusive control of money bills.

Both houses of the assembly abandoned their disputes over currency and constitutional rights in 1726 because of two distractions. The first was the sale of public offices by Arthur Middleton, who openly sold the offices of clerk of the Crown, vendue master, and provost marshal. When Benjamin Whitaker of the Commons House criticized Middleton for venality, the acting governor defended himself by saying that his predecessors had always regarded the three offices in question as part of their perquisites of office. He admitted that Nicholson had never sold an office, but he insisted that proprietary governors had always done so. The Commons House supported Whitaker and adopted a resolution protesting that the sale of offices was "of the utmost ill Consequence to his Majesties Subjects in this Province." Middleton believed the Commons was merely trying to embarrass him because he had supported the council in December, and he disregarded the assembly's censure.[65]

The provincial government was again distracted later in 1726, this time by the threat of the restoration of proprietary government. Alleging that the provisional royal governor had served his purpose by restoring order, the proprietors informed the Privy Council on February 26, 1726, that they were ready to resume control of South Carolina and nominated Colonel Samuel Horsey as the new proprietary governor. As soon as Arthur Middleton heard the news, he called the assembly into special session on May 17. He and the lower house composed their differences long enough to draft a memorial to the Privy Council opposing the proprietors. Meanwhile, the provincial agent, Francis Yonge, convinced the Privy Council that restoration of the proprietors would revive the disorders of the preceding decade, and the Council voted against restoration of the proprietors on June 26. The proprietors, who were really more interested in money than political control, then changed their tactics and asked the Privy Council to instruct Middleton to help them collect quit rents and other duties, as well as recognize all proprietary appointments.

---

[64] Dec. 4, 7–9, 14, 16, 1725, *ibid., 1725–26*, 55, 57–61, 66–67, 71–73; see also Labaree, ed., *Royal Instructions*, I, 112–13.

[65] Wallace, *Hist. of S. C.*, I, 307–9; the quotation is from Salley, ed., *Commons Journal, 1725–26*, Feb. 3, 1726, 80.

Middleton called another special session of the assembly in November 1726 in order to counter the latest proprietary gambit. The assembly again cooperated in drafting a new petition. The Privy Council took its time about making a decision, and uncertainty disturbed many South Carolinians throughout most of 1727.[66]

During the assembly session in November 1726 the Commons House decided to revive the currency debate. It proposed a series of laws to increase the local currency, and for the next four months the lower house battled the president and the council without making any headway. The Commons House first tried to appease the council by including a saving clause which would prevent the law from going into effect until the Crown had approved it. The council, however, rejected the bill and told the lower house it would be more proper to petition the Crown for prior approval of such a law. The Commons thought the council's suggestion would take too long; to stress the need for speed it asked the council in January 1727 to suspend the sinking act. The council refused again. The lower house tried to force the council to act by delaying the tax bill, but this time the council held out longer. The Commons House gave up in March, passed the tax bill, and agreed to petition the Crown for prior approval of a new currency law.[67]

Meanwhile the assembly had also been debating a related secondary issue, that of the county and precinct courts. The assembly received complaints in December and January that various groups were trying to undermine the local courts. A committee of the house reported that the Charles Town court, with the help of the town's lawyers, had attempted to extend its jurisdiction at the expense of other courts. If successful, such a move would benefit the merchant-creditors of the port, because more debt cases would be tried in Charles Town. The Commons House drafted a bill to strengthen the local courts and limit the jurisdiction of the Charles Town court. Despite opposition by the merchants of Charles Town and the council, the Commons House had its way and the law passed.[68]

Not long after the assembly adjourned in March 1727, South Carolina plunged suddenly and unexpectedly into a devastating

[66] Crittenden, "Surrender of Charter," N. C. Hist. Rev., 1 (1924), 395–96; Nov. 22, Dec. 3, 1726, Salley, ed., Commons Journal, 1726–27, 10–12, 25.

[67] Nov. 23, Dec. 10, 15, 1726, Jan. 26, 28, Mar. 4, 8, 1727, Salley, ed., Commons Journal, 1726–27, 13, 32–33, 38, 85–87, 157, 163.

[68] Dec. 22, 1726, Jan. 13, Mar. 7, 9, 11, 1727, ibid., 46–47, 67–70, 161, 167, 172–73; Acts Passed at Various Times, South Carolina, 1721–1727, CO 5/412, no. 81, PRO.

economic depression. The roots of the economic crisis went back to Parliament's decision to allow its bounties on naval stores to lapse in 1724. Parliament's action did not affect South Carolina immediately, for the market for naval stores continued to be good for another two years. The colony's planters had greatly increased their purchases of Negro slaves in 1726, perhaps because pitch and tar still brought good prices without the stimulus of a bounty. From 1721 through 1725 South Carolina had imported a total of 1,881 slaves, but in 1726 alone the colony imported 1,751 Negroes, buying most of them on credit. Then in the spring of 1727, before the farmers could pay off their debts, the market for naval stores collapsed suddenly and the price of pitch and tar dropped to almost nothing.[69] At the same time the rice market improved, and South Carolina nearly doubled its rice production between 1725 and 1728.[70] Consequently, the collapse of the naval stores industry had an uneven effect on the provincial economy. Men who concentrated on rice planting were able to pay their debts by increasing their production of rice, while those who concentrated on naval stores faced bankruptcy. Since rice required a large labor force and naval stores did not, the decline in naval stores hunt small farmers much more than large planters.

The farmers of South Carolina did not wait long before taking action to alleviate their distress. In April 1727 they organized an anti-tax association in the northern parishes, which had been especially hard hit by the collapse of the naval stores market. They drew up a remonstrance that demanded a suspension of tax collections, an increase in paper currency, more power for the local courts, and an official port of entry in the northern parishes. Members of the association circulated the remonstrance throughout the colony, but while it was still circulating they began to take the law into their own hands. They forcibly prevented the provost marshal from serving writs in debt cases, and they stopped the collection of taxes everywhere but Charles Town and two nearby parishes. Arthur Middleton tried to block the remonstrance, first by issuing a proclamation for the association to disband and then by attempting to make a deal with the association's leaders, but a mob of some two hundred men forced him

[69] List of Negroes Imported, 1721–26, Middleton to Nicholson, May 4, 1727, S. C. Pub. Recs., XII, 180, 202–5, S. C. Archives; William Guy to Sec. S.P.G., Mar. 23, 1727, S.P.G. Mss., B 4, no. 198.

[70] Charles J. Gayle, "The Nature and Volume of Exports from Charleston, 1724–1774," South Carolina Historical Association, *Proceedings, 1937* (1940), 30–31.

to receive the petition in May.[71] Middleton ignored the remonstrance, however, and the association began to sponsor mass protest meetings. Then Landgrave Thomas Smith placed himself at the head of the incipient rebellion, arguing that the presidency of the council and thus the acting governorship were rightfully his. He had a persuasive argument, for Nicholson's instructions had said that in the governor's absence the administration should devolve upon the eldest councilor and Smith was older than Middleton. At first the council ignored Smith, but when it intercepted some of the landgrave's letters, which indicated he was plotting a rebellion, it arrested Smith on charges of treason. The arrest infuriated Smith's followers, and several hundred marched on Charles Town in June. Middleton called out a militia company only to see the entire company, with its captain, join the mob. Acting on the advice of the town's merchants, the frightened Middleton promised the mob's leaders that he would call the assembly into session to consider their demands. Satisfied, the mob dispersed without further trouble.[72]

The assembly met on August 1, sat only four days, and ended without accomplishing anything. The Commons House received and read petitions from six parishes signed by 274 men. The petitions were similar to the remonstrance of May, with an additional demand which called for a guarantee of the rights of petition and habeas corpus. After the arrest of Landgrave Smith, Chief Justice Richard Allein had ordered him held without bail and had refused to grant him a writ of habeas corpus. The Commons House found Allein's action so offensive that it ignored its other business and concentrated on an attack on the chief justice. Rather than permit the attack to continue, Middleton prorogued the assembly to August 23.[73]

When the assembly reconvened as scheduled, the situation in South Carolina had changed. Chief Justice Allein had released Landgrave Smith on a bond of £10,000. More important, the Yamasee Indians had attacked English traders again, and the Lower Creeks appeared ready to join them. The Creeks were angry with South Carolina, because a Creek town had been attacked by a band of Cherokees and

[71] Middleton to Nicholson, May 4, 1727, Middleton to Bd. of Trade, May 6, 1727, Representation of the "Inhabitants of South Carolina," [May 1727], Representation of the Council, Dec. 19, 1728, S. C. Pub. Recs., XII, 202–5, 208–10, 211–14, XIII, 292–93, S. C. Archives; William Guy to Sec. S.P.G., June 19, 1727, S.P.G. Mss., A 20, 84–87.

[72] Representation of the Council, Dec. 19, 1728, S. C. Pub. Recs., XIII, 294–301, S. C. Archives.

[73] Aug. 2, 4, 1727, Commons Journal, VII, 556, 564–65, S. C. Archives; the petitions are in S. C. Pub. Recs., XIII, 19–32, S. C. Archives.

Chickasaws who carried a flag and drum given them by President Middleton. When a Yamasee war party killed and scalped five South Carolina traders in July 1727, a number of Lower Creeks joined them. Many South Carolinians believed another uprising was imminent.[74] Both houses of the assembly agreed that an immediate expedition against the Yamasees was vital, and the council was willing even to expand the local currency to pay for the operation. The assembly figured the expedition would cost £25,000 currency; by suspending the sinking act of 1724 it hoped to pay half that amount, and it agreed to levy taxes for the rest. No one but Benjamin de la Conseillere opposed the act. The sinking act had already retired £13,500 in bills of credit, which left South Carolina with a local currency of £106,500.[75]

The assembly's decision to suspend the sinking act paid a handsome dividend. President Middleton ignored party lines and appointed a political opponent, Colonel John Palmer, to command a force of about 100 whites and 100 Indians in an attack on the Yamasee settlements near St. Augustine. In February 1728 the small army killed thirty Yamasees, captured fifteen men, and burned the chief Yamasee village. The Indians retreated into the fort at St. Augustine, and Colonel Palmer kept both Indians and Spanish penned up in the fort for three days while he sought a chance to attack the Yamasees again. Yamasee casualties were not heavy, but Colonel Palmer had scored an impressive victory. By failing to protect their allies, the Spaniards lost the respect of all southern Indians and never regained it. The Lower Creeks were so impressed by Palmer's victory that they immediately made peace with South Carolina on English terms. As a result, South Carolina enjoyed a greater security than it had known for a decade and a half.[76]

Peace returned to the southern frontier, but within South Carolina peace was only a word. Between September 1727 and May 1728 the business of government settled into a dreary routine that resolved nothing and served only to exacerbate the colony's internal strife. The Commons House proposed a series of bills to expand the currency, usually in the form of attempts to attract foreign coins by juggling the

[74] Representation of the Council, Dec. 19, 1728, S. C. Pub. Recs., XIII, 307, S. C. Archives; Crane, *Southern Frontier*, 248–49, 268–70.
[75] Aug. 31, Sept. 2, 22, 1727, Commons Journal, VII, 590, 601–2, 620, S. C. Archives; Acts Passed at Various Times, 1721–27, CO 5/412, no. 83, PRO; Representation of the Council, Dec. 19, 1728, S. C. Pub. Recs., XIII, 308, S. C. Archives; [Bull], "Account of Paper Bills," Cooper and McCord, eds., *Statutes*, IX, 776; Brock, Currency of Colonies, 121–22.
[76] Crane, *Southern Frontier*, 249–51, 271–72.

official rate of exchange. Each time the council agreed to the bill but added a saving clause, which was later struck out by the lower house. Each time the council rejected the bill rather than pass it without a saving clause. The Commons House then refused to pass a tax bill until its currency act passed, and President Middleton was forced to keep the assembly in session. By May 1728 both sides were exhausted and short-tempered.[77]

In May 1728 the government of South Carolina broke down. Once again Landgrave Thomas Smith was the catalytic agent. He demanded that Chief Justice Allein either bring him to trial or release him from bail, and the Commons House ordered Allein to appear before it to explain his position. Allein refused, and the house sent its messenger to take the chief justice into custody. Allein was with the council, and when the messenger tried to enter the council room President Middleton threw him out. With the council's consent, Middleton then dissolved the assembly. When a new assembly met in July, the council rejected another currency bill, and a majority of the Commons House decided to boycott the assembly's sessions. The assembly had to adjourn, and when it was supposed to meet again in September the Commons House again failed to muster a quorum. The same thing happened in November 1728 and in January 1729. The assembly sat briefly later in 1729, but since it accomplished nothing Middleton did not even try to convene the legislature during his last year in office.[78]

After 1728 South Carolina's government fell into a state of near anarchy. Not only did the assembly stop meeting, but no taxes were collected and the judicial system almost ceased to function. Court officers were able to execute only one writ in five, and the only courts that met regularly were the court of vice-admiralty and the chancery court, both of which could act without a jury.[79] According to one witness, only the presence of a warship and an independent company of English soldiers prevented further riots and violence.[80]

One result was a hardening of the council's attitude toward popu-

[77] Representation of the Council, Dec. 19, 1728, S. C. Pub. Recs., XIII, 308–25, S. C. Archives.

[78] May 10, 11, July 19, 20, 22–24, 1728, Jan. 18, 1729, Commons Journal, Public Records of S. C., I, 519–22, 551, 554, 556, 561–62, S. C. Archives.

[79] William Bull to Thomas Lowndes, Dec. 24, 1729, S. C. Pub. Recs., XIV, 111, S. C. Archives; S. C. Admiralty Records, A (1716–32), 596–762, Fed. Records Center, East Point, Ga.; Anne King Gregorie, ed., *Records of the Court of Chancery of South Carolina, 1671–1779*, in *American Legal Records*, VI (Washington, 1950), 346–51.

[80] Sir Alexander Cuming to the Duke of Newcastle, July 11, 1730, S. C. Pub. Recs., XIV, 220, S. C. Archives.

lar demands. It appointed Stephen Godin, an adamant opponent of any local currency, as its agent in London. It attacked the county and precinct courts, which it had earlier been willing to tolerate, by asking the Privy Council to repeal all laws relating to local courts.[81] Most important, the council drafted a long, detailed report to the Board of Trade on South Carolina's currency problems; it seems likely that Conseillere wrote it, since it followed a hard money line. The report reviewed the events of the 1720's in a prejudicial manner that reflected upon the integrity of Governor Nicholson and all other advocates of a local currency. As a result, the report contained a number of factual errors; the most important of these said the council had consistently opposed all currency emissions, whereas the council had actually favored a local currency of about £100,000 until 1728. The signatures of all active councilors at the end of the report attested to the council's wholehearted conversion to the anti-currency faction.[82]

VI

By the late 1720's South Carolina had arrived at the most serious political crisis in its sixty-year history. The breakdown of the provincial machinery created greater disorder in the government than at any previous time, worse even than at the time of the overthrow of Governor James Colleton in 1690 or the rebellion against the proprietors in 1719. It seemed to prove that the colonists were not able to solve their own problems, and it looked at first as though they would get no help from London. Governor Nicholson died on March 5, 1728, but neither the Board of Trade nor the Privy Council did anything about the government of South Carolina for another year and a half. When the Privy Council finally took up the crisis in South Carolina on October 31, 1729, it decided to do nothing until a new governor was appointed.[83]

South Carolina was fortunate enough, however, to have two able men in London who were working quietly to find a solution to the colony's dilemma. One was former Governor Robert Johnson, who had been in London since 1724 trying to obtain a commission as royal

[81] Middleton to Bd. of Trade, Jan. 23, 1728, Memorial of Council, [1729], *ibid.*, XIII, 239, 343–49.

[82] Representation of the Council, Dec. 19, 1728, *ibid.*, 270–335.

[83] William A. Shaw, ed., *Calendar of Treasury Books and Papers, 1729–1745*, 5 vols. (London, 1897–1903), *1729–30*, 136; Grant and Munro, eds., *Acts of Privy Council, Col. Ser.*, III, 229–30.

governor. Assisting him was Samuel Wragg, who had been the London agent for the Commons House of Assembly since 1727. Wragg had generally taken a moderate position on paper currency in the 1720's and had supported all emissions of bills of credit except the one passed in 1723. In South Carolina his brother and partner, Joseph Wragg, had joined with sixteen other merchants and a few planters to organize a private bank in order to alleviate the colony's shortage of currency on a temporary basis. The owners of the bank had printed and loaned £50,000 in private bills. The bank owners regarded their venture as an expedient, however, and their bank notes carried the picture of a drowning man, who was supposed to symbolize South Carolina's plight. Like many other people, the bank owners looked to Johnson and Samuel Wragg for a permanent solution.[84] The chief obstacle for Johnson and Wragg was their fellow Carolinian, Stephen Godin, the London agent of the council. Godin not only fought every attempt to establish a permanent local currency, but he proposed in 1729 that the Privy Council disallow the county court act and the election act of 1721.[85] Both the Board of Trade and the Privy Council had allowed themselves to be guided by Godin and his hard money faction ever since South Carolina had become a royal colony. Johnson and Wragg therefore had to negate Godin's influence before they could do anything else.

The work of Johnson and Wragg was simplified by the sale of the Carolinas to the Crown and by the further relaxation of tension on the southern frontier. In May 1727 the Carolina proprietors had changed tactics again and asked the Crown to buy the two colonies. The proposal had aroused the interest of several Crown officials, largely because of South Carolina's value to the rest of the British empire as a barrier against French and Spanish aggression. With Robert Johnson taking a leading role as mediator, the Crown entered into negotiations with the proprietors and the two parties agreed in 1729 on a price of £2,500 for each proprietorship, plus a lump sum of £5,000 as compensation for quit rent arrears. One proprietor, Lord Carteret, decided to keep his title to one-eighth of the land in the Carolinas, but he relinquished all his political rights to the Crown.[86]

[84] Currency Report, in Easterby, ed., Commons Journal, 1736–39, 309–10; [Benjamin Whitaker], The Chief Justice's Charge to the Grand Jury for the Body of this Province (Charles Town, 1741), 25 n; on Johnson, see Shaw, ed., Cal. of Treas. Books and Papers, 1729–30, 432–33.

[85] Memorandum, July 23, 1729, S. C. Pub. Recs., XIII, 338, S. C. Archives.

[86] Crittenden, "Surrender of Charter," N. C. Hist. Rev., 1 (1924), 397–401; "Reasons for the Crown to Purchase the Carolinas," [1729], Sydney Family Papers, William L. Clements Library, Ann Arbor, Mich.; Shaw, ed., Cal. of Treas. Books and Papers, 1729–30, 432–33.

While the negotiations were in progress, South Carolina's position in international affairs had improved still further as a result of the improbable activity of an idealistic Scot named Sir Alexander Cuming. After Colonel Palmer's expedition against the Yamasees in 1727, the Creeks had come to terms with the English, but the Cherokees had begun to talk of war. At that point Cuming landed in Charles Town, and although he had no experience in Indian affairs, he announced he would go to the Cherokees in person and make peace with them. For some inexplicable reason, his scheme worked. The Cherokees took a liking to the Scottish visionary, and the nation sent seven chiefs back to England with Cuming. There they became the social hit of the season and even had an audience with the King. More important, they signed a treaty in which they recognized the sovereignty of England and promised not to trade with any white men but the English. The treaty, along with Palmer's victory, made South Carolina the temporary master of the southern frontier.[87]

Johnson and Wragg won their first major victory on December 11, 1729, when the Privy Council approved Johnson's appointment as governor of South Carolina. The appointment was a defeat for Stephen Godin and his friends, and it marked the end of their influence at Whitehall. After 1729 the Board of Trade and the Privy Council turned to Robert Johnson and Samuel Wragg for advice on South Carolina; Conseillere, the Godins, and Richard Shelton were ignored. Wragg began to round up support for a compromise policy on paper money, and he presented to the Board of Trade in February 1730 a petition signed by twenty-one merchants in South Carolina who asked that "a paper Currency might be continued there under proper Limitations." [88] Johnson performed an even more important service by submitting his "township scheam" in March and April of 1730.

Johnson's plan, which drew heavily on the earlier ideas of Thomas Nairne and John Barnwell, was designed to cope with all the colony's difficulties at once. Johnson proposed that South Carolina establish ten townships on its frontiers and settle them with poor Protestant refugees from Europe; he also suggested that the provincial government give land and tools to the refugees. In addition he argued that South Carolina should suspend the sinking act of 1724 for seven years and use the income from customs duties to pay for township settlement; at the end of the period the sinking act would resume

[87] Crane, *Southern Frontier*, 249–50, 270–80, 294–302; a copy of the treaty is in CO 5/4, foll. 211–14, PRO.

[88] Petition of Merchants Trading to S. C., Feb. 4, 1730, S. C. Pub. Recs., XIV, 32–33, S. C. Archives; on Johnson's appointment, see Grant and Munro, eds., *Acts of Privy Council, Col. Ser.*, III, 266.

operation and continue until all bills of credit were retired. Johnson hoped his scheme would solve three different problems at the same time: it would give South Carolina greater military protection; it would guarantee an adequate local currency for at least seven years; and it might provide a more desirable balance between the free and slave segments of the colony's population. Johnson's plan impressed the Board of Trade, which incorporated the scheme in his instructions in June 1730. The Privy Council added its approval in September.[89]

Johnson's township scheme pointed the way to better government in South Carolina. No less successful were the efforts of Samuel Wragg, who had influence among London merchants and used it to persuade Parliament to restore its bounties on South Carolina's naval stores and to allow South Carolinians to ship their rice directly to the markets of Spain and Portugal. The new laws started a boom in the colony's rice production, but they came too late to save the naval stores industry. The producers of pitch and tar never recovered from the depression of the 1720's, and the center of naval stores production shifted to North Carolina.[90]

Finally, Johnson and Wragg also used their newly won influence with the Crown to obtain appointments for their friends and relatives. On Johnson's recommendation, the Crown appointed his brother-in-law, Thomas Broughton, as lieutenant governor. Wragg persuaded the Crown to appoint his brother, Joseph Wragg, and a business associate, John Fenwicke, to the royal council; both were moderates on the currency issue, and they replaced the extremists, Benjamin de la Conseillere and Landgrave Thomas Smith.[91] The triumph of Johnson and Wragg was complete, and Conseillere's hard money faction had lost all its power.

VII

South Carolina's government had indeed reached its nadir in 1728 because of the inflamed paper money controversy. The assembly, the council, and most of the courts had ceased to function, and the

[89] Crane, Southern Frontier, 292–94; Robert L. Meriwether, The Expansion of South Carolina, 1729–1765 (Kingsport, Tenn., 1940), 17–21.

[90] Feb. 19, 1743, Easterby, ed., Commons Journal, 1742–44, 225; Gray, Hist. of Agriculture, I, 156–57, 285.

[91] Johnson to [Duke of Newcastle], Apr. 28, 1730, Bd. of Trade to Privy Council, June 16, 1730, Order in Council, Oct. 1, 1730, S. C. Pub. Recs., XIV, 88, 142, XV, 282, S. C. Archives.

colony's prospects for the future could not have appeared less promising. Despite the odds against them, however, former governor Robert Johnson and merchant Samuel Wragg had found a way to guide South Carolina through its crisis. They had displaced the hard money faction both in London and in Charles Town, they had secured Johnson's appointment as governor and the Crown's approval of a moderate currency policy, and most important, they had obtained the Crown's assent to Johnson's township scheme. At the same time the Crown had bought out the Carolina proprietors, and through a combination of skill and good luck, South Carolina had become the dominant force on the southern frontier. When Robert Johnson sailed from England in the fall of 1730, there remained only one unsolved problem that might yet prevent the fulfillment of South Carolina's promise—the need to restore internal tranquility.

CHAPTER VIII

THE EXPANSION OF
SOUTH CAROLINA
1731–1737

Governor Robert Johnson was the most remarkable politician in the colonial history of South Carolina. As governor throughout the Revolution of 1719 he had managed to keep the good will and respect of the people of the colony, even when he had tried to restore the proprietary government. He had next shown himself to be a man of vision by drawing up his township scheme, a plan which sketched a blueprint for settling the crisis of the 1720's. When Johnson resumed the governorship in 1730, he again proved his practical ability by making his scheme work. Using his township plan as a starting point, he restored political harmony to the provincial government and gave South Carolina one of the happiest administrations of the colonial period.

I

When Johnson disembarked from his ship he found the politicians of South Carolina eager to compromise their differences. The excesses of the preceding decade had exhausted the province's capacity for disputation, and men had also come to recognize the futility of extremism. Perhaps most important, they had come to realize that political disorder would only hinder economic growth. An S.P.G. missionary accurately reported the prevailing mood of South Carolina in 1730 when he said, "I think the People have done with their former animosities, and have been in an indifferent easy quiet condition." [1]

Johnson also found, however, that South Carolina was in a state of financial crisis. His instructions had anticipated some of his difficulties, but not nearly all of them. Most notably, the Crown had permitted him to assent to a seven-year suspension of the sinking act of 1724, which would permit a total of £106,500 in bills of credit to remain in circulation, and it had directed him to divert customs duties to the establishment of a fund for township settlement.[2] The Crown and the governor, however, had underestimated the magnitude of South Carolina's financial trouble. The assembly had raised no taxes for four years, and the colony owed its creditors more than £100,000 currency. To compound the fiscal crisis, the provincial treasurer, Alexander Parris, had bankrupted the public treasury. Like other colonial treasurers, Parris failed to distinguish between public funds and his own money. He had continued to collect import duties and license fees from 1727 to 1731 according to law, but no one had inspected his books since 1727 and he had apparently used this money to pay his personal creditors. By 1731 he owed the colony £40,000 and was not able to pay any of it.[3]

Governor Johnson had to make a difficult decision. If he followed his instructions to the letter, the taxes needed to pay the public debt would cripple the economy, while the colony would simultaneously siphon off funds for township settlement at a time when there were no immediate prospects for settlers. Johnson elected to put the colony's welfare first and interpreted his instructions liberally. In November 1731 he signed a so-called "appropriations act," which went far beyond the limits of his instructions. The law suspended the sinking act for seven years, but it gave first priority to payment of the colony's debts instead of township settlement. The assembly, which calculated the annual income from customs duties at £13,500, set aside £8,500 a year to pay debts and only £5,000 a year to establish a township fund. The assembly estimated the public debt at £104,775 currency, and the appropriations act provided for the emission of that amount in "public orders" to cover the debt. Public orders were paper money,

---

[1] Daniel Dwight to Sec. S.P.G., Dec. 21, 1730, S.P.G. Mss., A 23, Carolina Letters for 1730, no. 17.

[2] Labaree, ed., *Royal Instructions,* I, 231; on the economic crisis, see Samuel Eveleigh to James Oglethorpe, Nov. 7, 1734, Egmont Manuscripts, 1732–1743, vol. 14200, 292–93, University of Georgia Library, Athens, Ga.

[3] Treasurer's Books: Ledgers and Journals, 1725–1773, A (1725–29), esp. foll. 69, 99, 122, S. C. Archives.

but they differed from bills of credit in several ways: they were issued only to public creditors; they bore an annual interest rate of 5 per cent; they were receivable only in payment of taxes and were not legal tender, but they circulated unofficially as a local currency. The appropriations act provided for the repayment of £59,500 of the public debts in seven years; the remaining £40,000 would be paid off as Alexander Parris repaid his debts to the public treasury.[4]

The appropriations act generally favored the old paper money faction, so Governor Johnson immediately settled another old issue, that of the local courts, in favor of the other side. He persuaded the assembly to enact a law that allowed the plaintiff in a civil suit to choose the site of the trial, an act which brought all debt suits into the Charles Town court. Moreover, the Privy Council, probably with Johnson's consent, disallowed the court act of 1726, which had been opposed by the merchants of Charles Town.[5] As a result, the county and precinct courts disappeared quickly and completely.

Johnson's compromise policy won the approval of nearly every political leader in South Carolina. Only two groups of dissidents opposed him at the beginning of his administration, and neither of them was very large. The first group consisted of a few royal placemen who were dissatisfied with their fees and blamed Johnson. The second was the remnant of the hard money faction, which continued to fight a paper currency of any kind. One member of the faction, Ralph Izard, withdrew from the council rather than compromise his principles.[6] Men like Izard were exceptional, however, and the governor's mastery of local politics was complete in every other respect. Although the same assemblymen who had caused so much trouble for Arthur Middleton still sat in the Commons House, Johnson quarreled with the house only twice. In the first dispute he insisted that the house give up the privilege of appointing its clerk, and the Commons reluctantly surrendered that power to the governor. The second quarrel began

[4] The act provided for the retirement of only £99,500 of the total debt of £104,775; perhaps the remainder was to be paid by Parris as interest on his debt. Cooper and McCord, eds., Statutes, III, 334–41; Brock, Currency of Colonies, 122–23. The appropriations act did not state specifically that Parris owed the treasury £40,000, only that there was £40,000 unapplied in the treasury; the assembly was probably trying to protect Parris's reputation; see Cooper and McCord, eds., Statutes, III, 501.

[5] Robert Johnson to Bd. of Trade, Nov. 14, 1731, Order in Council, July 21, 1732, S. C. Pub. Recs., XV, 36–37, 139–40, S. C. Archives.

[6] Samuel Eveleigh to Oglethorpe, Apr. 3, 1735, Egmont Mss., 14200, 536–37, Univ. of Ga. Lib.; Copy of a Letter from a Carolina Merchant to Sir Alexander Cuming, May 25, 1730, S. C. Pub. Recs., XIV, 117, S. C. Archives.

when Johnson proposed that the assembly set up a perpetual revenue to pay the salaries of Crown officials; the Commons House rejected the proposal but came within one vote of granting a permanent salary to Johnson himself.[7] The governor managed even to prevent a renewal of the conflict between the upper and lower houses. His instructions stated clearly that the council should have the right to frame and amend money bills, and the governor insisted that the council be allowed to do so. The Commons House resented its loss of power, but it challenged the council's right to amend money bills only once between 1731 and 1735 and then it did not press the issue.[8]

II

Johnson's administration would have been a success if he had done no more than restore political harmony to the colony. But with harmony came prosperity and rapid colonial expansion, and for both Johnson could claim major credit. Some of the credit belonged also to Samuel Wragg, who had won the Parliamentary concession which allowed South Carolinians to ship their rice directly to European ports south of Cape Finisterre, thus reopening the valuable Spanish and Portuguese markets. As a result South Carolina entered into an economic boom that started in 1732 and lasted until the outbreak of the War of Jenkins' Ear in 1739. Production and prices rose together. The market value of rice increased from 6s. currency per hundred-weight in 1732 to 10s. 6d. per hundredweight in 1738, while the colony's exportation of rice rose from 37,000 to 67,000 barrels per year in the same period. Planters continued to borrow large sums of money to buy slaves, often more than they needed. A writer in the *South-Carolina Gazette* in 1738 remarked, "*Negroes* may be said to be the Bait proper for catching a *Carolina* Planter, as certain as Beef to catch a Shark."[9] So long as the rice boom lasted, however, the planters did not have much trouble repaying their debts.

Governor Johnson's most important personal contribution to the expansion of South Carolina was his township scheme. It began to produce results in 1732, when the Swiss colonizer, Jean Pierre Purry,

[7] Greene, *Quest for Power*, 135–36, 208–10.

[8] Labaree, ed., *Royal Instructions*, I, 112–13; Feb. 12, 1732, Commons Journal, Public Records of S. C., I, 848, S. C. Archives.

[9] *South-Carolina Gazette* (Charles Town), Mar. 9, 1738; see also Gayle, "Exports from Charleston," S. C. Hist. Assn., *Proceedings*, 1937 (1938), 30; George Rogers Taylor, "Wholesale Commodity Prices at Charleston, South Carolina, 1732–1791," *Journal of Economic and Business History*, 4 (1932), 372.

sailed into Charles Town harbor with sixty-one Swiss immigrants. Purry had been trying to start a Swiss colony in South Carolina for more than ten years, but under the proprietors his hopes had been frustrated. Once the Crown had approved the township plan, however, Purry was free to begin recruiting Swiss Protestants. After his arrival he arranged for the council to furnish supplies for his followers, and he settled his people on a bluff overlooking the Savannah River, christening the new township Purrysburg. Within another three years Purry had persuaded more than seven hundred of his countrymen to join him, and the township was flourishing. By the time of Johnson's death in 1735, South Carolina had surveyed the sites for nine townships, and settlers had moved into six of them. None prospered so well as Purrysburg, but a floodtide of immigration had begun, as the townships attracted German, Irish, and Welsh Protestants as well as Swiss.

Purrysburg set the pattern for the first townships. The primary reason for founding townships in the early 1730's was defense against the Indians, and the pattern of township settlement reflected that need. The surveyors selected township sites with defense in mind, and settlers often occupied land that was easy to defend but hard to cultivate. The need for defense was greatest in the western part of South Carolina, so the provincial government gave more assistance to immigrants who would settle there. Consequently, four of the first six townships were in the west, and no more than sixty people settled in the two eastern townships. As a further defensive measure Johnson and his council usually located the western townships near older garrisons. Purrysburg was near the Palachacola garrison, Saxe Gotha near the Congarees garrison, New Windsor near Fort Moore, and Amelia on the Cherokee trading path. As the townships grew the colony abandoned the Palachacola and Congarees garrisons. South Carolina's military preoccupation in selecting township sites may have made life harder for the immigrants, but it enhanced the value of the townships to the colony.[10]

Governor Johnson and his colony were no less pleased by another phase of English expansion, the settlement of Georgia in 1733. The founding of Georgia proceeded from the confluence of two interests in England, the government's concern for the southern frontier and the humanitarian ideals of several interrelated philanthropic organizations. The leading humanitarians were Dr. Thomas Bray, founder of the S.P.G., and Colonel James Oglethorpe, chairman of the Parlia-

[10] Meriwether, *Expansion*, 34–35, 42–44, 53–54, 66–67, 79–80, 89.

mentary committee on prisons. Oglethorpe's committee had called public attention to the deplorable conditions in English jails, with emphasis on the treatment of debtors, and Dr. Bray had conceived the idea of a colony for debtors in America. After Dr. Bray died in 1730, several of his friends had formed a philanthropic organization called the Associates of Dr. Bray. Oglethorpe and other members of his committee on prisons joined the new group. The Associates developed Dr. Bray's idea of a charitable colony into concrete form and secured a royal charter in 1732 that incorporated many of the Associates as the Trustees of Georgia. The charter directed the Trust to establish a colony to the south of South Carolina and to settle it with debtors and other deserving indigents. With the financial support of Parliament, the Trustees sent out the first boatload of settlers under Oglethorpe's command in 1732.[11]

The prospect of a buffer colony between South Carolina and its enemies delighted the people of the older colony. When Oglethorpe's ship, the *Anne,* anchored outside Charles Town harbor on January 13, 1733, the people of Charles Town gave the passengers an enthusiastic welcome. When the ship anchored again at Beaufort the planters there repeated the welcome. More important, South Carolina supplied Oglethorpe with the money and advice he needed to make the settlement successful. Johnson sent William Bull, one of the ablest members of his council, to accompany Oglethorpe to Georgia.[12] Bull spent most of the next year at Savannah, where he assisted Oglethorpe in such tasks as surveying, carpentry, and militia organization. Bull also helped Oglethorpe negotiate a treaty with the Yamacraw Indians, a tribe of Lower Creeks who lived near Savannah, and the Yamacraw chief, Tomochichi, became one of Oglethorpe's closest friends in America. Other Carolinians were almost as helpful in both their public and private capacities. The assembly appropriated £8,000 currency, the parishioners of St. Andrew's Parish took up a special collection, merchants Samuel Eveleigh and Gabriel Manigault took up another collection in Charles Town, planters loaned Oglethorpe their

[11] Crane, *Southern Frontier,* 303–25; Verner W. Crane, "Dr. Thomas Bray and the Charitable Colony Project, 1730," *Wm. and Mary Qtly.,* 3d Ser., 19 (1962), 49–63.

[12] Governor and Council to Oglethorpe, Jan. 26, 1733, Egmont Mss., 14200, 9, Univ. of Ga. Lib.; E. Merton Coulter, ed., *The Journal of Peter Gordon, 1732–1735* (Wormsloe Foundation, *Publications,* 6 [1963]), 31, 33, 37. Contrary to the legend, as related in Hewatt, *Historical Account,* in Carroll, ed., *Hist. Collections of S. C.,* I, 290, Bull did not select the site of Savannah; Oglethorpe himself selected it, although he may have been advised by Bull and others; see Gordon, *Journal,* ed. Coulter, 35.

tools and slaves, and individuals, including Governor Johnson himself, made gifts of horses, cattle, and money. It was due in large part to South Carolina's help that Georgia thrived without having to endure a "starving time." Oglethorpe, pleased with his colony's progress, returned to England in 1734.[13]

The phase of South Carolina's expansion that caused the most trouble for Governor Johnson was the land boom. The increasingly prosperous rice market created a demand for land, and rice planters all along the coast tried to put as much land as possible into rice cultivation. The colony's land system, however, was in a mess. The land office had been closed since 1719, and the proprietors had not maintained an accurate rent roll. The confusion was compounded by the variety of proprietary quit rents. The proprietors had issued most grants at an annual rent of 1s. per 100 acres, according to Archdale's law of 1696, but they had also granted land with at least four other rent rates. Moreover, there was still another complicating factor in the land system. Because the land office had been closed during the 1720's, colonists who had wanted new land at that time had been compelled to revive old proprietary claims of questionable legality. By using such devices, the colonists had added 210,000 acres of land to their holdings in the 1720's.[14] The most common of the old claims were baronial patents—directives from the proprietors to the governor and council which ordered them to issue land warrants to a landgrave or cassique. Such patents stated the number of acres the nobleman was entitled to but did not specify a location. The South Carolina Chancery Court had ruled in 1726 that baronial patents were valid, but the English attorney general and solicitor general had advised the Privy Council in 1730 that patents were invalid because they failed to specify the location of the grants.[15] Despite the legal uncertainties, several holders

[13] *Report of the Committee Appointed to Examine into the Proceedings of the People of Georgia* . . . (Charles Town, 1736), in Easterby, ed., *Commons Journal, 1736–39*, 154–57; Gordon, *Journal*, ed. Coulter, 37–40, 42–45; John Pitts Corry, *Indian Affairs in Georgia, 1732–1756* (Phila., 1936), 69–70; Amos A. Ettinger, *James Edward Oglethorpe, Imperial Idealist* (Oxford, 1936), 134.

[14] These figures are based on statistics compiled by Benjamin Whitaker in "Observations on . . . an Act to remedy some defects in his Majestys Rent Roll," 1744, S. C. Pub. Recs., XXI, 346–47, S. C. Archives. I have used Whitaker's statistics in preference to others, because he compiled them from the tax lists and because he was a member of an assembly committee in 1742 that investigated the whole question of land ownership. Whitaker's statistics must be used with caution, however, because of his partiality and because his arithmetic was occasionally inaccurate.

[15] Gregorie, ed., *Chancery Court Recs.*, 324–25; Report of Attorney General and Solicitor General, July 28, 1730, Shelburne Papers, 1663–1797, LVI, 479–80, Clements Lib.

of old patents had dusted them off and sold their land rights to the settlers. Most notably, Landgrave John Bayley of Ireland had appointed an agent who sold 20,500 acres of land to twenty-nine men in South Carolina. Other baronial patentees had done the same thing, and their sales had accounted for about 120,000 of the 210,000 acres of land taken up during the 1720's.[16]

Johnson's instructions offered a partial solution to South Carolina's land problems. The Crown promised to remit quit rent arrears if the assembly would pass a new law for rent collections and repeal Archdale's law of 1696. The governor's instructions said the new quit rent act should require all persons with proprietary land claims to record them on a rent roll within a reasonable length of time. The Crown authorized the governor and council to issue new land grants with a quit rent of 4s. per 100 acres, provided that no man should own more than 50 acres for each member of his family, including his servants and slaves. Finally, in order to protect the new townships, the Crown directed that no one could own land inside a township unless he lived there.[17] As in the case of Johnson's financial instructions, however, his instructions on land did not cover every contingency. For example, the instructions failed to mention baronial patents, and Johnson again was free to make many key decisions himself.

When Governor Johnson proposed a new quit rent act to the South Carolina assembly in 1731, baronial patents became a major point of contention between the Commons House and the governor. The house wanted to recognize such patents, while Johnson and the council were opposed. The Commons finally persuaded the governor and council to recognize all proprietary land claims on the theory that many people had purchased the claims in good faith. Proprietary quit rents became another point of contention. The council proposed that if a land claimant had lost his original grant he should pay the "most probable rent." The lower house argued that 1s. per 100 acres had been the standard proprietary rent since the passage of Archdale's law and insisted that the new law establish this rate as the rent on all proprietary land grants. Once again the Commons House persuaded the council to give way.[18] As approved by the assembly and governor in

[16] These statistics were compiled from the index to Mesne Conveyances, 1719–1800, Office of Register of Mesne Conveyances, Charleston County Courthouse, Charleston, S. C.; on Bayley, see also Smith, "Baronies of S. C.," *S. C. Hist. Mag.,* 15 (1914), 3–5, 10–11.

[17] Labaree, ed., *Royal Instructions,* II, 542–44, 549–51, 564–65.

[18] Johnson to Bd. of Trade, Nov. 14, 1731, S. C. Pub. Recs., XV, 34–35, S. C. Archives; May 6, 1731, Commons Journal, Public Records of S. C., I, 670–75, S. C. Archives.

August 1731, the new land law required all holders of proprietary grants to register them within eighteen months. Men who claimed land under proprietary warrants or patents were required to take out grants and register them within two years. The law validated all proprietary land claims. Landholders had to pay their rents in proclamation money by March 25 of every year. If a landholder was more than three months late in paying his rent, Crown officials could seize his property and sell it. If he did not pay his rent for five years, his grant became void. Finally, the new law remitted all rent arrears and repealed Archdale's law.[19]

Once the assembly had passed the new quit rent act, Governor Johnson reopened the provincial land office on November 27, 1731. He reported that the people were so pleased with the law that they called it the "Magna Carta of Carolina." [20] The colony's landowners obeyed the most important sections of the law by promptly registering their proprietary land claims, and Johnson was able to report within two years that the rent roll was substantially complete. He and the council confirmed proprietary claims amounting to about 1,450,000 acres of land.[21] Johnson did not enforce the entire law, however. He refused to recognize the validity of baronial patents and insisted that he must wait for the Privy Council to approve them. The Duke of Newcastle, the secretary of state for the southern department, advised Johnson unofficially to recognize the patents, and the South Carolina council suggested that it permit surveys without grants. Johnson still refused to act without official approval. His decision was a wise one, because the Privy Council never acted formally on the quit rent act, and the Board of Trade did not accept it as valid until 1755. In the meantime, Johnson refused to recognize the patents, and the Privy Council refused to act whenever a patentee appealed the governor's decision.[22]

The quit rent act of 1731 was a successful and efficient law as far as it went, but it did not go far enough. The law covered only proprietary land claims and said nothing whatsoever about new royal land grants. This omission meant, for one thing, that the townships had no protection except that which the governor and council could give them. Johnson recognized, however, that the land boom might

[19] Cooper and McCord, eds., *Statutes*, III, 289–304.

[20] To Bd. of Trade, June 26, 1732, S. C. Pub. Recs., XV, 136, S. C. Archives.

[21] Johnson to Bd. of Trade, Apr. 6, 1733, Whitaker, "Observations," *ibid.*, XVI, 79, XXI, 347.

[22] Johnson to Bd. of Trade, Dec. 16, 1731, Johnson to Mr. Hutcheson, Dec. 21, 1732, Bd. of Trade to Lords Justices, Apr. 22, 1755, *ibid.*, XV, 68, 268, XXVI, 164; Grant and Munro, eds., *Acts of Privy Council, Col. Ser.*, III, 380–91, 480, 427–28.

undermine the township plan if he permitted older settlers to claim land inside the townships. He and the council therefore set aside a square six miles long and six miles wide for each township, reserving this land for immigrants and prohibiting grants to South Carolinians.[23] Generally, the governor and council had little trouble with planters trying to claim township lands, but Purrysburg was an exception. Purry himself had selected the site of Purrysburg in 1731, and councilor William Bull surveyed the township limits in 1732. Bull discovered that several South Carolinians already claimed land inside the southern boundaries of the township, and among the claimants were Governor Johnson, Lieutenant Governor Thomas Broughton, and Stephen Bull, the councilor's son. Bull proposed that the governor and council let the claimants keep their land and give Purrysburg an equivalent amount of land north of the township. The proposal seemed fair to all concerned, and Purry accepted the compromise. The council approved Bull's survey of Purrysburg on September 6, 1733.[24]

The failure of the quit rent law to mention royal land grants exposed South Carolina to a second and more extensive abuse in the land system. This was the danger that speculators would control the land boom. But Governor Johnson and his council perceived the dangers inherent in speculation and took steps to prevent it. Most notably, they refused to approve land grants until the grantee had sworn the land was for his own use and not for speculation.[25] In addition, the governor and council tried to set up a court of exchequer to settle land disputes and prevent abuses. They especially hoped that such a court might provide relief for a large number of squatters who had settled on land near Port Royal in the previous decade and now faced eviction. The council issued a commission for a court of exchequer in 1732, but the court was sabotaged by the Commons House of Assembly. The members of the assembly opposed the court because they believed no court could be legally established without their consent. The court of exchequer was to be a common law court that could not function without a jury, so the Commons House simply

[23] S.-C. Gaz. (Charles Town), Nov. 11, 1732; Feb. 27, 1735, Journal of His Majesty's Honourable Council, 1734–1774, CO 5/437, PRO.

[24] Francis Varnod to Sec. S.P.G., Dec. 2, 1731, S.P.G. Mss., B 4, no. 258; Johnson to Bd. of Trade, Nov. 9, 1734, S. C. Pub. Recs., XVII, 185–87, S. C. Archives; James St. John, "List of several Tracts of Land taken up within the township of Purrysburg," June 23, 1734, ibid., XVI, 343–44; Sept. 6, 1733, Upper House Journal, V, 514, S. C. Archives; Henry A. M. Smith, "Purrysburgh," S. C. Hist. Mag., 10 (1909), 196–200.

[25] Feb. 9, 1733, Upper House Journal (executive records), V, 272, S. C. Archives; S.-C. Gaz. (Charles Town), Feb. 3, 1733.

refused to pass a law requiring jury duty in the new court. Consequently, the court was never able to function.[26]

Despite the failure of plans for the court of exchequer, Governor Johnson kept the land boom from falling into the hands of speculators. His refusal to recognize baronial patents prevented speculation by the nobility. Landgrave Thomas Smith tried to claim land under his patents and advertised 27,000 acres of land for sale, but he found no buyers. Altogether the nobility sold less than 2,000 acres during the 1730's.[27] Other would-be speculators were less ambitious than Landgrave Smith but no more successful. Three men tried to found private townships on the road between Charles Town and Port Royal, but not one of the towns attracted enough settlers to make the venture pay.[28] As a result, the land boom of the 1730's belonged to the small farmers. The governor and council issued royal land grants for a total of about 900,000 acres during the 1730's; most of the land was granted in tracts of 400 to 1,000 acres, the size South Carolinians deemed suitable for a plantation.[29] The grants signed by the council on August 7, 1735, one of its busiest days, were typical. The council issued eighty-two grants for a little more that 42,000 acres of land to seventy-six men and women. The average size of the grants was 500 acres, and the council approved only three grants of 1,000 acres or more.[30]

Although Governor Robert Johnson's overall administration of the land system was creditable, his handling of the royal land claims left a lot to be desired. Once again, the quit rent act of 1731 was at fault. The law's failure to mention royal claims left the government without a legal guide other than the governor's instructions, which were susceptible to misinterpretation and evasion. Johnson appears to have misunderstood part of his instructions; at least he did not obey them

[26] "Observations on the Revenues of South Carolina," Shelburne Papers, XLIX, 170–71, Clements Lib.; Nov. 10, 21, 1732, Upper House Journal (executive records), V, 218, 224, S. C. Archives.

[27] See the index to Mesne Conveyances, Charleston Co. Courthouse; on Landgrave Smith, see S.-C. Gaz. (Charles Town), Oct. 7, 1732.

[28] Henry A. M. Smith, "Radnor, Edmundsbury, and Jacksonborough," S. C. Hist. Mag., 11 (1910), 38–49; on the failure of the speculators, see George Hunter to Bd. of Trade, Oct. 23, 1743, S. C. Pub. Recs., XXI, 174–75, S. C. Archives.

[29] Meriwether, Expansion, 24; Grants, [1670]–1775, vol. I, passim, S. C. Archives; Plats, 1731–1775, vol. I, passim, S. C. Archives; the estimate of 900,000 acres in royal land claims is based on figures compiled in Horace Walpole, "An Account of the Quit Rents . . . of South Carolina. . . ," Feb. 23, 1731, and Whitaker, "Observations," S. C. Pub. Recs., XX, 348–51, XXI, 347–48, S. C. Archives; Mar. 3, 1742, Easterby, ed., Commons Journal, 1741–42, 460.

[30] Aug. 7, 1735, Council Journal, CO 5/437, PRO; see also, e.g., Apr. 29, May 12–13, June 6, Aug. 6, 1735, ibid.

carefully. His instructions said that no man should own more than fifty acres of land for each member of his family, but Johnson applied the rule only to new grants. He thus ignored the amount of land a man already owned and allowed a few men to accumulate more than their fair share.[31] Governor Johnson also let some men claim land without paying quit rents on it by allowing them to secure warrants and plats for specific tracts, but he did not force them to take out grants. This procedure enabled the landholders to establish their claims without paying quit rents. Some 175,000 acres of land was claimed in this way, a figure which represented about one-fifth of all land held under royal claims.[32] Both practices hurt the colony, for they permitted a few men to engross more land than they needed, and those men often managed to avoid paying both local taxes and quit rents on their excess land.[33]

The deficiencies of the quit rent law caused trouble for other officials besides the governor. The Crown simply did not collect as much money in quit rents as it should have. South Carolina recognized proprietary land claims amounting to 1,450,000 acres and royal claims amounting to 900,000 acres for a total of 2,350,000 acres. Quit rents should have yielded an annual income of £2,400 proclamation money, £600 on proprietary claims and £1,800 on royal claims.[34] Crown officials, however, never collected more than £1,585 in any one year, and the average yearly income during the 1730's amounted to only £1,200, just half what it should have been. The trouble was not caused by proprietary land claims, which were covered by the quit rent act; the income from proprietary land grants never fell below £400 and once reached the maximum of £600.[35] The trouble was in the royal land claims. The royal rent roll was deficient by at least 175,000 acres

---

[31] For example, according to the slaveholdings of Arthur Middleton and Joseph Wragg, they each owned at least 1,500 acres more than they were entitled to; William Bull owned at least 12,500 acres above his headrights; all three were members of Johnson's council. See Sirmans, "S. C. Royal Council," *Wm. and Mary Qtly.*, 3d Ser., 18 (1961) , 392.

[32] Memorial of George Hunter, Apr. 29, 1743, S. C. Pub. Recs., XXI, 184–203, S. C. Archives.

[33] Mar. 30, Apr. 2, 1743, Easterby, ed., *Commons Journal, 1742–44*, 345, 355.

[34] For reliable, similar estimates on royal rents, see Walpole, "Account of Quit Rents," Whitaker, "Observations," S. C. Pub. Recs., XX, 348–51, XXI, 347–49, S. C. Archives. The estimate on proprietary rents is my own; it is based on Whitaker's statistics on proprietary grants, but I have estimated that baronial grants bearing only nominal rents accounted for about 250,000 acres of land; neither Walpole nor Whitaker made an allowance for such grants.

[35] Quit Rent Books, 1733–1774, vols. I-II, *passim*, S. C. Archives; Walpole, "Account of Quit Rents," S. C. Pub. Recs., XX, 352–59, S. C. Archives.

of land. The rent roll became even more deficient when land was sold, because the buyers often did not register the sales. There was no law that compelled them to do so. In addition, the receiver general of quit rents was not able to collect all the rents due on land that was properly registered. Every royal grant contained a clause that required the grantee to pay his rents on time or forfeit his grant, but the receiver general and other officials were reluctant to enforce such a condition without the support of a provincial law.[36] The deputy receiver general calculated in 1740 that the Crown lost one-sixth of the quit rents it should have collected. His estimate was on the low side, for Crown officials did well to collect half the royal rents due at any time. Royal rents never yielded more than £1,092 in any year, and they usually fluctuated between £800 and £1,000.[37]

In spite of the difficulty in collecting quit rents, the Crown still received a steady income from them. The Lords of the Treasury in England used the rents to pay the salaries of royal officeholders. The chief justice, attorney general, provincial secretary, auditor general, provost marshal, and clerk of the Crown all received their salaries from quit rent payments. Their salaries amounted to about £700 proclamation money a year, and in addition the receiver general was paid a 10 per cent commission and the auditor general a 5 per cent commission on all rents collected.[38]

Thus, Governor Johnson's handling of the land boom produced mixed results. Passage of the quit rent law of 1731 led to the prompt registration of proprietary land claims and the efficient collection of quit rents on such claims. Furthermore, the governor kept land speculators from taking over the boom, partly by refusing to recognize baronial patents, and he saved the new townships from land-hungry older settlers. On the other hand, Johnson allowed a few wealthy landowners to engross more land than they were entitled to, and he permitted some men to claim land without taking out grants or paying quit rents on it. Moreover, royal officials were able to collect only about half the rents due on royal land claims, although they did much better on proprietary land claims. In short, the abuses of South Carolina's land system derived almost entirely from the failure of the

[36] S.-C. Gaz. (Charles Town), July 13, 1734, Aug. 2, 1735, Aug. 23, 1742; James Abercromby to James West, June 25, 1750, Clark, ed., N. C. Col. Recs., IV, 1097.

[37] For the deputy receiver's estimate, see Shaw, ed., Cal. Treas. Books and Papers, 1739–41, 319; on rent collections, see the sources cited above in n. 35.

[38] Shaw, ed., Cal. Treas. Books and Papers, 1735–38, 38, 575, 1739–41, 168; Quit Rent Books, 1760–68, Pt. i, 23, S. C. Archives.

quit rent act of 1731 to mention royal land claims. This omission was Governor Johnson's only real failure in administering the land system, but this failure was a serious one that caused trouble for Johnson's successors.

III

South Carolina's land system became the major political issue of Johnson's administration when a motley collection of would-be speculators and professional placemen tried to upset the quit rent law of 1731. The group's leaders were James St. John, appointed surveyor general by the Crown in 1731, and Benjamin Whitaker, his deputy. St. John was interested in his royal office solely for its perquisites, which he thought were too small, while Whitaker was a political opportunist. In the 1720's, for example, Whitaker, who served as attorney general of the colony, had switched from side to side in the local currency disputes as it suited his purposes, but he had been dismissed from office in 1731. He needed to find a way to ingratiate himself with Crown officials at Whitehall and had accepted an appointment as deputy surveyor general and inspector and collector of quit rents. Whitaker and St. John were joined by a number of land speculators who hoped to profit from the confusion that might follow disallowance of the quit rent act. Among them were Dr. Thomas Cooper, merchant Job Rothmahler, and lawyer Robert Hume.[39]

The first sign of trouble appeared in March 1732 when the council quarreled with St. John over township surveys. The council asked St. John to make preliminary surveys of the first six townships at £500 currency per township, a job which involved nothing more than selecting township sites and marking their outside boundaries. Detailed surveys of individual tracts would come later. The quit rent act had set the surveyor general's fees at 4d. proclamation money for every acre surveyed, and so St. John insisted that the council pay him at that rate for preliminary surveys, too. If the council had accepted his demands, the surveyor general would have netted a fee of £2,300 proclamation money—more than £16,000 currency—for the preliminary surveys, plus another £2,300 in fees for surveying individual tracts later. The council wisely decided the colony could not bear the expense of St. John's fees, and it entrusted the preliminary surveys to

---

[39] Wallace, *S. C.: Short History*, 143. For the complete membership of this group, see Petition of Robert Hume and others, 1734, S. C. Pub. Recs., XVII, 110, S. C. Archives.

five of its members at the rate of £500 currency per township.[40] Despite this disagreement, however, the council hesitated to criticize a royal official and remained on good terms with St. John for another two months.

Meanwhile, the Commons House of Assembly had uncovered irregularities in St. John's administration of his office. It found that his surveys favored his friends and that he and his deputies were charging exorbitant fees. Johnson and the council, who were still reluctant to break with St. John, dismissed the charges on the grounds that they were too vague. The governor and council learned in May 1732, however, that St. John had claimed another royal office under false pretenses; St. John had announced he held a commission as auditor general for South Carolina, but an examination of his commission showed that he was only a deputy to the auditor general in England. The council then investigated the lower house's charges against St. John in detail and found that the Commons had erred only in underestimating the extent of malfeasance. It discovered that St. John and his deputies had increased surveying fees by 50 per cent; the surveyor general had formerly split his fee of 4d. an acre with the deputy surveyor who actually made the survey, but St. John claimed 4d. an acre for himself and let his deputies charge an additional 2d. an acre. The council also found that St. John had approved improper surveys and that he had dismissed two deputy surveyors to make room for two of his cronies, one of whom was Benjamin Whitaker. When the council confronted St. John with its findings, he flew into a rage, insulted the council, and called Governor Johnson a Jacobite. This was too much. The council asked Johnson to seek St. John's dismissal, and the governor soon laid formal charges before the Lords of the Treasury, in which he asked them to dismiss the surveyor general.[41]

With Benjamin Whitaker's aid, St. John retaliated by attacking the validity of the quit rent law in a series of letters to the Board of Trade. Focusing on the obvious point of baronial patents, St. John and Whitaker insisted that recognition of these patents would give more than 800,000 acres of land to less than thirty men. Not only did the two critics thus ignore Johnson's refusal to recognize patents, but they

[40] Johnson to Bd. of Trade, June 26, 1732, *ibid.*, XV, 136–38, S. C. Archives; Sherman, *Robert Johnson,* 278–80; Mar. 10, 1732, Upper House Journal (executive records), V, 192–93, S. C. Archives.

[41] Mar. 2–3, May 31–June 2, June 26, 1732, Upper House Journal, V, 178–80, 195–200, 202, S. C. Archives; Representation of the Council, Dec. 15, 1732, S. C. Pub. Recs., XVI, 43–48, S. C. Archives; Articles of Complaint against Mr. St. John, 1732, Treasury Office Papers, 1/375, fol. 32, PRO (transcripts in Lib. Cong.).

also greatly exaggerated the amount of land involved. In addition, they championed the cause of the displaced squatters in the Port Royal area, whom they depicted as victims of ruthless speculators, without bothering to mention Johnson's attempt to erect a court of exchequer to handle this problem. St. John and Whitaker also called attention to the practice of holding land without grants, the only complaint they made which had any real substance. More pertinently, perhaps, St. John also petitioned the Board of Trade for the right to make preliminary township surveys at the rate of 4d. an acre.[42]

St. John and Whitaker knew they could help themselves best by discrediting Governor Johnson, and they found the issue they needed in the compromise on the township limits of Purrysburg. Johnson's approval of the compromise had been rather unwise because his own land had been involved; he owned a 12,000-acre barony, 4,000 acres of which were located inside the original limits of the township. Jean Pierre Purry had approved the compromise at first, but St. John and Whitaker managed to enlist his aid because he was temporarily at odds with Johnson; the provincial government had promised Purry 48,000 acres of land for Purrysburg if he would bring over 600 settlers, and he was angry because the council had rejected his request for the entire amount after he had delivered only the first 152 immigrants. Purry now denounced the compromise as a fraud and insisted that the council restore the township's original limits as surveyed. Johnson and the council agreed to Purry's demands at once; they restored the original township limits and nullified all grants to South Carolinians inside the township. Johnson himself relinquished the 4,000 acres of his barony inside Purrysburg without seeking compensation elsewhere. St. John and Robert Hume tried to take advantage of the ensuing confusion by claiming land for themselves and their associates on the 8,000 acres of Johnson's barony outside Purrysburg, but the council rejected their claims.[43] Nevertheless, Whitaker and St. John succeeded in their primary objective of embarrassing Johnson. The Board of

[42] St. John's and Whitaker's attacks on the quit rent law are in S. C. Pub. Recs., XV, 149–58, 161–85, 189–97, 206–13, S. C. Archives. Some historians have accepted their criticism at face value and have therefore misunderstood the land boom in South Carolina; see Wallace, *Hist. of S. C.*, I, 325–29; Smith, *S. C. as Royal Province*, 34–48; Osgood, *18th Century*, IV, 116–23; Beverly W. Bond, Jr., *The Quit-Rent System in the American Colonies* (New Haven, 1919), 318–26; Thomas Jefferson Wertenbaker, *The Old South: The Founding of American Civilization* (N. Y., 1942), 240–42.

[43] Johnson to Bd. of Trade, Nov. 9, 1734, S. C. Pub. Recs., XVII, 185–89, S. C. Archives; Feb. 9, Mar. 22, 1733, Upper House Journal, V, 296, 369–70, S. C. Archives; Grants, I, 91, III, 60, 191, S. C. Archives.

Trade believed Purry's version of the story and ordered Johnson to restore Purrysburg's original limits. The fact that Johnson had already done so did not save him from the Board's censure. The incident hurt Johnson further by creating antagonism between him and the foreign colonizers who were interested in South Carolina.[44]

St. John and Whitaker won the first round of the fight when the Board of Trade recommended disallowance of the quit rent law on November 11, 1732. The decision caught South Carolina by surprise, for only two weeks earlier the *South-Carolina Gazette* had reported, "there is no doubt but the Act will be passed." [45] The Privy Council had not yet acted on the recommendation, however, so the colony launched a campaign for reversal of the Board of Trade's action. South Carolina enjoyed an advantage in dealing with the Privy Council, for Johnson had a powerful friend on it in the person of the Duke of Newcastle. In England the campaign was run by Peregrine Fury, the provincial agent and a protégé of Newcastle, and by Francis Yonge, an influential councilor who happened to be in London. They bombarded the Privy Council with petitions and letters supporting the law, while Johnson wrote from South Carolina to say that Benjamin Whitaker had engineered the attack on the law for personal reasons. Johnson added that repeal would throw the colony into anarchy again. Fury and Yonge also emphasized the threat of renewed disorder and reminded the Privy Council of the colony's strategic position on the southern frontier.[46] Belated though it was, the campaign succeeded, as the Privy Council chose to make no ruling on the law; Newcastle's influence was probably decisive. Although the Crown continued to regard the South Carolina land system as unsettled for several years, it allowed the quit rent law of 1731 to remain in force but did not explicitly accept it for another twenty years.[47]

Although the ultimate victory thus belonged to Governor Johnson, the initial success of his opponents started another political controversy in South Carolina. As soon as the Board of Trade's recommendation for repeal was known in the colony, the opponents of the quit

[44] Petitions of Sebastian Zouberbuhler and Charles Purry, Mar. 14, May 18, 1738, S. C. Pub. Recs., XIX, 53, 171–75, S. C. Archives; for a different view of this incident, see Meriwether, *Expansion*, 35.

[45] Bd. of Trade to Privy Council, Nov. 11, 1732, S. C. Pub. Recs., XV, 240–46, S. C. Archives; *S.-C. Gaz.* (Charles Town) , Oct. 28, 1732.

[46] Johnson to Bd. of Trade, Sept. 28, 1732, S. C. Pub. Recs., XV, 230–31, S. C. Archives; the petitions and memorials of Fury and Yonge are in *ibid.*, XVI, 328–29, XVII, 286–96, 299–302.

[47] Bd. of Trade to Newcastle, May 30, 1738, Bd. of Trade to Lords Justices, Apr. 22, 1755, *ibid.*, XIX, 71, XXVI, 164.

rent act formed a land company called Cooper, Rothmahler, and Company, with Benjamin Whitaker and Robert Hume as silent partners. With St. John's cooperation the company began to resurvey land near Port Royal and to resell it to the displaced squatters in that area.[48] Some thirty-nine landowners from the Port Royal area petitioned the assembly in February 1733, alleging that Cooper, Rothmahler, and Company had surveyed land illegally, and the Commons House responded by taking Cooper and St. John into custody. When Cooper's lawyers applied for a writ of habeas corpus the house took them into custody, too, on the grounds that they were trying to abridge the rights and privileges of the house. The house resolved that no one had the right to question its proceedings and that habeas corpus did not apply to men taken into custody by the assembly. When the prisoners applied to the council for relief, the council supported the lower house, resolving on April 20, 1733, that "it is the Opinion of this House, that his Majesty does allow . . . the Commons House of Assembly, the same Privileges as the House of Commons doth enjoy in *England*," a resolution the council came to regret later.[49] The assembly then passed a bill, introduced by the council, that suspended habeas corpus when either house took a person into custody and offered protection to judges who refused to issue a writ in such a case. The prisoners found only one friend on the council, Chief Justice Robert Wright, whose son-in-law, James Graeme, was one of the imprisoned lawyers. The Commons House regarded Wright's support of the prisoners as an attempt to abridge its rights and privileges, and since it could not arrest a member of the council, it stopped payment of Wright's salary.[50]

The feud between Chief Justice Wright and the Commons House touched off the first newspaper debate in South Carolina. Timothy Whitmarsh had founded the *South-Carolina Gazette* in 1732, and he opened the columns of his paper to both sides. Councilor Francis Yonge and former Commons Speaker John Lloyd defended the assembly by repeating the assertion that the lower house had the same rights as the House of Commons, including the right to arrest anyone

---

[48] Johnson to Bd. of Trade, Apr. 6, 1733, Francis Yonge to Allured Popple, Feb. 18, 1735, *ibid.*, XVI, 79–80, XVII, 287–88; Sherman, Robert Johnson, 317–18.

[49] *S-C. Gaz.* (Charles Town), Apr. 28, 1733.

[50] Feb. 9, Apr. 7, 1733, Commons Journal, Public Records of S. C., I, 920–21, 1001–2, S. C. Archives; Apr. 20, 26, 1733, Upper House Journal, V, 427–29, 433, S. C. Archives; Cooper and McCord, eds., *Statutes*, III, 347–48; Samuel Eveleigh to Oglethorpe, Apr. 3, 1735, Egmont Mss., 14200, 536–37, Univ. of Ga. Lib.; McCrady, *Royal Gov't.*, 151–59.

without being subject to habeas corpus. Lloyd even demanded Wright's suspension from office. Wright took to the newspaper to defend himself and accused the Commons House of encroaching upon the royal prerogative. The newspaper dispute continued well into the summer of 1733, until it ended inconclusively with an anonymous essay written "to divert the Auditory with new Matter" on the subject of "the properest Method of absterging the Posteriors." [51]

The controversy ended in victory for the assembly. Cooper and his attorneys remained in custody until they made the proper apologies to the Commons House. St. John also remained in custody until he apologized to the house in order to gain his release; the assembly then passed a new law to regulate his fees more precisely. The lower house continued to refuse to grant Wright's salary for the remainder of his term. The only setback for the assembly was the Crown's disallowance of the act to suspend habeas corpus.[52] Most important, the colony never again heard from the critics of the quit rent law. St. John thereafter tended to his surveying and stayed out of politics. Whitaker had managed to stay in the background and was able eventually to re-enter politics as a member of the Commons House, but he, too, chose to keep quiet about the quit rent law.

IV

The generally successful administration of Robert Johnson ended when the governor died on May 3, 1735, and was succeeded by his brother-in-law, Lieutenant Governor Thomas Broughton. Alexander Hewatt, South Carolina's first historian, later described Broughton as "a plain honest man, but little distinguished either for his knowledge or valour." [53] Hewatt may have been too kind, for Broughton's record indicates he was something of an adventurer with little regard for moral niceties. Broughton had been one of the more unscrupulous Indian traders in the days before effective trade regulation, and he had helped his father-in-law, Sir Nathaniel Johnson, frame Thomas Nairne on a charge of treason in 1708. In 1735, however, South Carolina was more interested in Broughton's political ability than his morals, and it soon became apparent that he was deficient in this respect, too.

[51] S-C. Gaz. (Charles Town) , Apr. 21, 28, May 12, 19, June 2, 16, 23, 30, July 7, 14, 1733; the author of the essay on "absterging the Posteriors" decided in favor of corncobs.

[52] Cooper and McCord, eds., Statutes, III, 343–47, 349; Grant and Munro, eds., Acts of Privy Council, Col. Ser., III, 397.

[53] Hewatt, Historical Account, in Carroll, ed., Hist. Collections of S. C., I, 311.

Broughton was confronted by the same basic issues that had plagued Nicholson and Middleton as well as Johnson; few men accepted Johnson's solution of the currency dispute as permanent, and the Commons House of Assembly still wanted to reduce the legislative powers of the upper house. Johnson had suppressed controversy over these and other issues through persuasion and compromise, but his weaker successor was unable to do the same. In fact, Broughton actually seemed to go out of his way at times to aggravate the revival of political conflict, and he poisoned the political atmosphere still further with his maladministration of the land system.

Signs of strain in Johnson's political settlement began to appear during the last months of the governor's life. The Commons House had never reconciled itself to the restoration of the council's right to amend money bills, and it challenged that right in March 1735. The council tried to persuade the lower house to vote a salary for Chief Justice Wright, and when persuasion failed the upper house amended the annual tax bill to include an appropriation for him. The lower house rejected the bill and passed resolutions accusing the council of encroaching on its rights. The council cited the Crown's instructions giving it an equal power in framing money bills, but the Commons insisted that royal instructions could not abridge its rights as the representatives of the people. Both houses adhered to their convictions for a month, and even a prorogation failed to heal the breach between them. The council finally surrendered rather than face the consequences of not passing a tax bill. It conceded nothing in principle, but it approved the tax bill without a provision for Wright's salary on April 25.[54]

After Thomas Broughton assumed the governorship he tried to settle the dispute through personal intervention but succeeded only in making things worse. The Lords of the Treasury solved the problem of Chief Justice Wright's salary for the future by ordering it to be paid out of quit rent receipts. The Treasury did nothing about Wright's back salary, however, and the Board of Trade recommended that the South Carolina assembly pay his arrears. When the assembly met in 1736, Lieutenant Governor Broughton warned the Commons House that it must pay Wright's arrears, and he persisted in his warnings until the lower house agreed to appropriate £700 currency for the chief justice.[55] Broughton's interference angered the Commons, be-

[54] Feb. 7, Mar. 27–29, Apr. 16–17, 23, 25, 1735, Commons Journal, IX, 58–59, 183, 187–88, 190–91, 199–200, 209, 217–18, 235, S. C. Archives.

[55] Jan. 30, 1736, *ibid.*, IX, 391; Smith, *S. C. as Royal Province,* 299–301.

cause it believed that the governor had only the right to accept or reject its laws. It regarded any effort by a governor to influence a law before its final passage as an encroachment on its right of freedom of debate. The Commons House in 1737 started another quarrel with the council. The lower house refused to appoint a committee to discuss the tax bill with representatives from the council, because it thought the mere existence of such a committee would compromise its authority over money bills. The council passed the tax bill anyway, but only because rumors of an impending invasion were sweeping the colony.[56]

The whole series of conflicts among the lieutenant governor, the council, and the Commons House came to a head in March 1737. Although the fundamental issues were entirely serious, the dispute began on a note of comedy. It all started when the clerk of the Commons House scribbled in the margin of the tax bill some "very absurd and ludicrous Lines" about John Hammerton, the provincial secretary and a member of the council. When the upper house protested mildly, the Commons House pretended it did not know what the council was talking about. The council denounced the reply as a "Continuance of the former ill Treatment complained of by this House," and Lieutenant Governor Broughton sent a message to the Commons House demanding that it reprimand its clerk. The Commons House promptly seized upon Broughton's intervention as an excuse to air its grievances about executive interference. First, however, the house received the report of a committee that had uncovered evidence of Broughton's maladministration. The committee reported that the township fund was nearly exhausted, because Broughton had allowed a few merchants to delay the payment of their import duties and the merchants now owed the township fund more than £12,000 currency. Having thus embarrassed the lieutenant governor, the house adopted a series of resolutions relating to freedom of debate on March 4. One resolution restated the house's belief that the governor could not take official notice of its proceedings until it presented them in proper parliamentary fashion, while another resolution denounced Broughton's intervention as a breach of the assembly's freedom of debate. Finally, the house resolved to do no more business until it received satisfaction. In addition it slapped at Broughton indirectly by ordering the public treasurer to collect the arrears of import duties for the township fund and to charge interest on arrears in the future.[57]

[56] Feb. 24–25, 1737, Easterby, ed., *Commons Journal, 1736–39*, 249–52, 254–55.
[57] Mar. 2–4, 1737, *ibid.*, 269–71, 276, 278–83.

The assembly had defeated Broughton so decisively that the lieutenant governor never again dared to interfere with the legislature's business. Although the council still conceded nothing in theory, it retreated, too, by dropping its demands for an apology to Hammerton.

At the same time the two houses of the assembly were reviving their dispute over legislative rights, other men were disinterring the paper money debate. The old extreme factions did not reappear, for most men now accepted the need for a local currency of some kind. There was, however, room for disagreement about the amount of such a currency. Many merchants, along with a few large planters, thought South Carolina had gone too far. They had objected to the appropriations act of 1731, because it had emitted £104,775 in public orders. They protested again in 1735, when the assembly permanently suspended the sinking act in order to establish a permanent township fund. The merchants appealed to the Privy Council, but it merely recommended that South Carolina change its laws.[58] Other men thought the colony's currency supply was still deficient, and several essayists published plans to expand the currency in the *South-Carolina Gazette* between 1734 and 1736.

In the latter year the Commons House of Assembly entered the discussion by publishing a long committee report on the history of paper bills in South Carolina, a report which favored further expansion of the currency.[59] Responding to the demand for more paper bills, the assembly in 1736 passed an act to establish a permanent local currency of £210,000. In an effort to avoid the mistakes of earlier currency acts, the assembly drafted the new bill with great care. The act provided for calling in and reprinting the existing currency and for the emission of enough new bills of credit to bring the total to £210,000. The assembly tried to establish adequate support for the currency by setting up a bank, which would put the new bills of credit into circulation through loans at 8 per cent interest on good security. The act also made the bills of credit legal tender in all transactions, and it included a suspending clause.[60] Despite the care with which the assembly wrote the act, many South Carolina merchants objected to it, even merchants who had taken a moderate position on paper currency

[58] Grant and Munro, eds., *Acts of Privy Council, Col. Ser.*, III, 394–95; Cooper and McCord, eds., *Statutes*, III, 409–11; June 6, 1735, Upper House Journal, VI, 144–45, S. C. Archives.

[59] Richard M. Jellison, "Antecedents of the South Carolina Currency Acts of 1736 and 1746," *Wm. and Mary Qtly.*, 3d Ser., 16 (1959), 556–61; *Currency Report*, in Easterby, ed., *Commons Journal, 1736–39*, 291–320.

[60] Cooper and McCord, eds., *Statutes*, III, 423–30.

in the 1720's. Fearing that the new law would cause a sharp depreciation in the currency's value and ruin the public credit, they appealed to the Board of Trade, only to find that the Board sympathized with the colony's desire for more currency. The Board approved the law in principle, but it found two technical flaws in the act: The assembly had neglected to require borrowers to repay the principal of their bank loans, and the act permitted a 10 per cent discount on duties paid in foreign coins, which violated Queen Anne's proclamation of 1704. The Board of Trade therefore recommended disallowance of the act and the passage of a new law, and the Privy Council accepted its recommendation.[61]

It was not the fault of Lieutenant Governor Broughton that currency disputes reappeared in South Carolina, nor could he be blamed for the revival of legislative conflict, although he had certainly made it worse. Nevertheless, Broughton could be blamed for other troubles that developed during his term of office, most notably his administration of the land system. Broughton continued many of Johnson's policies. Although he sympathized with baronial patentees, he refused to validate these patents. He tried to prevent some irregularities in the system, and he once forced seventy-two landholders to correct errors in their plats. Like Johnson, however, he did nothing to expedite the collection of royal quit rents, and he allowed some men to claim land without grants.[62] Broughton also completed the resurvey of Purrysburg, forcing all South Carolinians to take up land elsewhere, but he administered the townships poorly in every other respect. He violated the integrity of the townships by allowing native Carolinians to settle in the new townships east of the Santee River, he allowed merchants to fall behind in the payment of their import duties, and he misappropriated money in the township fund by using it to pay the salaries of royal officials. By 1737 he had almost entirely dissipated the township fund, and it was saved only when the Commons House of Assembly intervened and called the lieutenant governor to order.[63]

[61] Protest of Arthur Middleton, James Kinloch, and Joseph Wragg, May 29, 1736, Bd. of Trade to Privy Council, July 6, 1738, S. C. Pub. Recs., XIX, 39–42, 214–16, S. C. Archives; Grant and Munro, eds., Acts of Privy Council, Col. Ser., III, 552–53.

[62] S-C. Gaz. (Charles Town), Aug. 16, 1735, Mar. 27, Apr. 10, 1736, Mar. 26, Aug. 20, 1737; for Broughton's attitude toward baronial patents, see his treatment of Landgrave Thomas Smith, in Wills, Inventories, and Misc. Recs., IV, 147, Charleston Co. Courthouse.

[63] Grants, III, 60, 191, S. C. Archives; May 24, June 6, 1735, Council Journal, CO 5/437, Pt. ii, 14, 16, PRO; Meriwether, Expansion, 80–81, 86–87.

V

Thomas Broughton erred frequently as governor, but his worst blunder came when he reversed Johnson's policy toward Georgia and embroiled South Carolina in a quarrel with the younger colony. Other men shared the blame for starting the dispute, but Broughton adopted a belligerent attitude that precluded compromise and prolonged the argument unnecessarily. The central issue in the dispute was control of the Indian trade, and Broughton placed the authority of his office at the disposal of South Carolina's Indian traders, the only group of men in the colony who opposed the Georgia project. In the early years, the trade in South Carolina had been controlled by men who devoted themselves exclusively to commerce with the Indians or combined that trade with farming. By 1735, however, control of the trade had shifted to the leading merchants of Charles Town, for whom the Indian trade was only one among a variety of mercantile interests.[64] At the same time, the profits of the trade were steadily diminishing, partly because of South Carolina's strict regulation and high export duties. The Cherokee trade suffered most and had become almost profitless. These changes made the Creek trade more valuable than ever, but South Carolina had to compete with Georgia for the Creek trade and Georgia's merchants enjoyed a definite competitive edge. They lived closer to the Creeks, and they could undersell Charles Town merchants by as much as 25 per cent because Georgia did not have high export duties. The South Carolina traders wanted to drive their competitors out of business and tried every expedient they could think of, even to selling their goods in Savannah at half price. Nothing worked, however, and the Charles Town merchants grew desperate as their profits continued to fall.[65]

So long as Robert Johnson had been governor of South Carolina,

---

[64] For a reasonably complete list of the South Carolina Indian traders, see Memorial of Benjamin Godin and others, July 4, 1735, S. C. Pub. Recs., XVII, 421, S. C. Archives; at least 23 of the 31 men who signed the memorial were general merchants rather than just Indian traders.

[65] Samuel Eveleigh to Oglethorpe, Nov. 20, 1734, Egmont Mss., 14200, 295-99, Univ. of Ga. Lib.; Eveleigh to William Jeffries, July 4, 1735, *ibid.*, 14201, 71-72; Robert G. McPherson, ed., *The Journal of the Earl of Egmont, 1732-1738* (Wormsloe Foundation, *Publications*, 5 [1962]) , 215, 319; Patrick Mackay to Trustees, Nov. 20, 1734, Allen D. Candler and Lucien L. Knight, eds., The Colonial Records of Georgia, XX, 55-57; vols. XX, XXVII-XXXIX of the Colonial Records of Georgia have not been published and are available in typescript at the Georgia Department of History and Archives, Atlanta, and the Georgia Historical Society, Savannah.

the merchants of Charles Town could do nothing but wait. Johnson wanted to help Georgia and had little sympathy for the Indian traders. He regarded unified trade regulation as a necessity, and when the Georgia Trustees appointed Patrick Mackay as their Creek agent, Johnson appointed Mackay as South Carolina's agent, too. He ordered all South Carolina traders to obey Mackay, and when South Carolina's Indian commissioner refused to cooperate with Mackay, Johnson suspended him from office. Johnson's death changed everything, however. The South Carolina traders knew Broughton for a friend, and after Johnson's death they acted with almost indecent haste. In July 1735 several of the leading merchants—including John Fenwicke, George Austin, and Othniel Beale—met privately to consider plans for eliminating their competition.[66]

On the Georgia side of the dispute, much of the trouble began in 1734 when the Trustees passed an Indian trade law. The act closely followed South Carolina's trade laws and set up an identical system of control. It required traders to obtain licenses and entrusted trade supervision to a commissioner and resident agents in each major tribe. The Trust appointed Oglethorpe as its first Indian commissioner, but while he stayed in England Indian affairs were directed by Patrick Mackay, the Creek agent. The Trust enacted two other laws at the same time that increased the importance of the Indian trade to Georgia's economy. The first outlawed Negro slavery, which made it impossible for Georgia to develop a plantation economy. The second prohibited the importation of rum, which kept Georgia from starting a trade in foodstuffs to the West Indies as South Carolina and other colonies had done when they were young.[67] Both laws reflected the humanitarian desire of the Trust to save the people of Georgia from evil influences, but they left Georgians with almost nothing but the Indian trade as a source of income, and the colonists had no choice except to fight their South Carolina competitors as best they could.

The quarrel between the two colonies started in the early summer of 1735, when Patrick Mackay, the Creek agent, began to enforce the Georgia Indian trade law. He expelled South Carolina traders from Georgia and seized their goods unless they had licenses from Georgia as well as South Carolina. Thomas Broughton was out of town when news of Mackay's expulsions reached Charles Town, and the council

[66] Robert Johnson to Oglethorpe, Jan. 28, 1735, Samuel Eveleigh to Oglethorpe, July 7, 1735, Candler and Knight, eds., Ga. Col. Recs., XX, 178–79, 653, Ga. Dept. of Hist. and Archives.

[67] Corry, *Indian Affairs*, 41–45; By-Laws and Laws, Allen D. Candler and Lucien L. Knight, eds., *The Colonial Records of Georgia*, 25 vols. (Atlanta, 1904–16), **I,** 32–52.

simply wrote to Mackay and asked if the reports were true. Broughton came to town about the first of July and immediately assumed the belligerent pose that characterized his behavior throughout the rest of the dispute. He ordered Mackay not to bother South Carolina traders and told him that no colony had the right to interfere with duly licensed traders from another colony. The magistrates of Georgia, who governed the colony in Oglethorpe's absence, sent back a conciliatory reply, but Broughton was adamant. He accused the magistrates of evading the issue, insulted them, and threatened to cut off South Carolina's financial assistance to Georgia unless they obeyed him.[68] Then the chief magistrate of Georgia, Thomas Causton, impounded a few South Carolina ships on the Savannah River and accused their captains of smuggling rum into Georgia. Broughton promptly demanded free navigation of the river for all South Carolina shipping. Neither the magistrates nor the Trustees of Georgia knew how to cope with Broughton's demands. Colonel Oglethorpe was planning to return to Georgia in 1736, so the Trustees directed him to investigate the controversy, and they discharged agent Mackay as a conciliatory gesture.[69]

Even a man of Oglethorpe's stature could not restore peace between South Carolina and Georgia. He arrived in America in February 1736, but he put off negotiations on the trade dispute for five months. Oglethorpe was an English imperialist who wanted to expand the British empire into Spanish Florida, and he spent all his time from February to June on imperial concerns. He built two new forts, one on St. Simon's Island and the other at the mouth of the St. John's River.[70] It was not until Oglethorpe had completed the forts that he turned to the Indian trade dispute. Oglethorpe believed that Mackay and the other Georgia officials had acted properly, but he sent Broughton a friendly letter, in which he blamed the quarrel on "the Artifices of a few designing men." [71] The way seemed clear for a compromise, and the Carolina assembly began to plan a conference to discuss a settlement. Without warning, however, Lieutenant Governor Broughton intervened and once again made compromise impossible. He de-

[68] John Fenwicke to Mackay, June 12, 1735, Broughton to Mackay, July 4, 1735, Magistrates of Ga. to Broughton, July 21, 1735, Broughton to Magistrates, July 29, 1735, Egmont Mss., 14201, 17–18, 77–79, 133–35, 157–60, Univ. of Ga. Lib.

[69] Benjamin Martyn to Broughton, Jan. 2, [1736], ibid., 14208, 225–27; Corry, Indian Affairs, 51–52.

[70] Trevor R. Reese, Colonial Georgia: A Study in British Imperial Policy in the Eighteenth Century (Athens, 1963), 55–58; Ettinger, Oglethorpe, 156–57, 169, 173; Corry, Indian Affairs, 86–87, 117.

[71] Oglethorpe to Broughton, June 5, 1736, Egmont Mss., 14201, 529–32, Univ. of Ga. Lib.; see also Oglethorpe to Paul Jenys, June 5, 1736, ibid., 14201, 533–35.

manded that the assembly pass an ordinance to pay indemnity up to £2,000 currency to traders whose goods were seized by Georgia. A majority of the Commons House, including Speaker Paul Jenys, disliked the bill, but Broughton refused to let the assembly adjourn without passing his bill. The lower house finally adopted the ordinance, but only by a vote of ten to nine. Next, Broughton demanded that the assembly appeal the whole conflict to the Board of Trade. In such an atmosphere there was no hope for compromise. An assembly committee met Oglethorpe in August, but the delegates could agree on only one point; they decided to go along with Broughton's plan to refer the whole dispute to the Board of Trade.[72]

There can be little doubt that the negotiations failed because Lieutenant Governor Broughton wanted them to fail. Neither the ordinance of indemnity nor the appeal to the Board of Trade was necessary, at least not until after the two colonies had tried to compromise their differences, and Broughton's actions must be regarded as a deliberate attempt to sabotage the negotiations with Oglethorpe. The reasons for his behavior are puzzling, but it seems possible that he and the merchants were afraid of compromise. Oglethorpe had many friends in the South Carolina assembly, and it might well have approved a settlement that would have been unacceptable to the merchants. On the other hand, the merchants had always been able to exert influence on the Board of Trade, and they may therefore have felt more confident in appealing the quarrel to London.

Once negotiations had failed, attitudes hardened in both colonies. The Georgia Trust told Oglethorpe to enforce the Indian trade law and the prohibition on rum. He forced South Carolina traders to buy Georgia licenses, and he began to halt and search South Carolina ships on the Savannah.[73] Meanwhile, Broughton strengthened his control over the government of South Carolina in the assembly elections in the fall of 1736. The anti-Georgia merchants and their allies carried the elections with ease, and Oglethorpe reported that "those in the interest of Georgia are either browbeat or turned out of the Assembly." [74] The

[72] Petition of Assembly and Council, July 17, 1735, S. C. Pub. Recs., XVIII, 83–101, S. C. Archives; McPherson, ed., *Egmont Journal*, 186–88; on the ordinance of indemnity, see Paul Jenys to Oglethorpe, June 28, 1736, Egmont Mss., 14202, 33–35, Univ. of Ga. Lib.; Cooper and McCord, eds., *Statutes*, III, 448–49.

[73] [Harmon Verelst] to Oglethorpe, Sept. 13, 1735, Egmont Mss., 14208, 365–66, Univ. of Ga. Lib.; Oglethorpe to [Newcastle], Apr. 1737, Candler and Knight, eds., Ga. Col. Recs., XXXV, 99–101, Ga. Dept. of Hist. and Archives.

[74] *Manuscripts of the Earl of Egmont: Diary of Viscount Percival, Afterwards First Earl of Egmont, 1730–1747* (Historical Manuscripts Commission, *Sixteenth Report*, 3 vols. [London, 1920–23]) , II, 448; see also *ibid.*, III, 201.

most conspicuous victim of the election was the speaker of the Commons House, Paul Jenys, who failed to carry his district.

After a final spat with Broughton, Oglethorpe went home in November 1736 and both colonies maintained an uneasy peace. Broughton tried to claim the right to command the Georgia militia in Oglethorpe's absence, but Oglethorpe silenced him by giving the militia command to William Bull, one of Oglethorpe's best friends in South Carolina. Broughton must have resented Bull's appointment, but Bull was a South Carolinian and the lieutenant governor could find no legitimate cause for complaint.[75] In December the South Carolina assembly adopted a long report, which reiterated the argument that no colony had the right to interfere with the Indian trade of another colony. The assembly sent the report to the Board of Trade, which opened hearings on the dispute in the spring of 1737.[76]

The conflict between the two colonies disappeared temporarily in 1737 because of rumors of an imminent Spanish invasion. Both South Carolina and Georgia lived in fear of an invasion from January to September, and both governments were too busy preparing their defenses to take the time for further argument. Even Thomas Broughton was moved to swear that "the People of this Province will exert their utmost Strength and Ability to Defend the Colony of Georgia." [77]

Lieutenant Governor Broughton died on November 22, 1737, not long after the invasion scare ended, and the two colonies did not renew their quarrel. Broughton was succeeded by William Bull, the president of the council and a friend of Oglethorpe who was unlikely to start trouble. Like most people in both colonies, the new acting governor was content to let the Board of Trade decide the issues.

VI

Governor Robert Johnson had worked hard to rebuild the foundations of a stable government in South Carolina, but within two years of his death his political settlement had fallen apart. Ironically, Johnson's brother-in-law, Lieutenant Governor Thomas Broughton, bore the chief responsibility for upsetting the government. Broughton

---

[75] Sainsbury *et al.*, eds., *Cal. St. Papers., Col., Amer. and W. Indies, 1735–36*, 102; *Egmont Diary*, II, 393.

[76] Corry, *Indian Affairs*, 54–56; *Georgia Report*, in Easterby, ed., *Commons Journal, 1736–39*, 72–157.

[77] Broughton to Bd. of Trade, Feb. 6, 1737, S. C. Pub. Recs., XVIII, 197, S. C. Archives; see also Broughton to Thomas Causton, Mar. 2, 1737, Candler and Knight, eds., *Ga. Col. Recs.*, XXI, 371.

alone could not be blamed for what happened, because Johnson's compromise had not satisfied everyone. Specifically, the Commons House of Assembly had been dissatisfied because the council had regained the right to amend money bills, and the currency problem also had remained unsettled. It would be pointless to speculate on the possibility that Johnson might have been able to cope with such disputes, but it is certain that Broughton only made things worse than they needed to be by antagonizing the Commons House and deliberately sabotaging the attempt to compromise the dispute with Georgia. His conduct in office hastened the disintegration of Governor Johnson's political armistice, and the politicians of South Carolina inherited the difficult chore of restoring political order one more time.

CHAPTER IX

WARS AND RUMORS OF WARS

1737–1743

After the death of Lieutenant Governor Thomas Broughton in 1737, South Carolina politics cooled off again under a new acting governor, Colonel William Bull. The colony's politicians adjusted most of their disputes between 1737 and 1740, but their compromises did not represent a new departure in provincial politics. Instead, Colonel Bull and other leaders reconstructed the political settlement that Governor Robert Johnson had negotiated in the early part of the decade. Although the compromises of Bull's administration opened the way to a period of internal stability, South Carolina's time of troubles was not yet over. In 1738 the colony became involved in another Indian crisis that was complicated by increasing diplomatic tension between England and Spain. In 1739 a large number of Negro slaves rebelled against their masters, and a month later England declared war on Spain. The southern frontier became a major battlefield in the War of Jenkins' Ear that followed, with English regulars invading Florida in 1740 and Spanish troops invading Georgia in 1742. Such unrelenting external pressure undoubtedly encouraged internal compromise, but the cure for internal discord was, in this case, worse than the disease.

I

Despite Lieutenant Governor Broughton's death, the dispute with Georgia dominated South Carolina politics throughout 1738 and into 1739. The Board of Trade heard arguments from both colonies in the spring and summer of 1737 and finally approved a report favoring South Carolina in September 1737. The Georgia Trust appealed to the Privy Council, which referred the problem to a special committee, and the committee submitted a report in March 1738 that dodged most of the issues. It merely suggested that the Privy Council instruct both colonies to settle the quarrel to their mutual advantage by passing new Indian trade laws and that the Crown disallow the South Carolina ordinance of indemnity. The committee also proposed that each colony recognize the licensed Indian traders of the other, at least until new trade laws were enacted. The Trustees objected to this provision, because they feared South Carolina traders would overrun Georgia and ruin the Georgia trade. The Privy Council approved the report, however, and issued the appropriate instructions on July 21, 1738.[1]

In the meantime the Georgia Trustees had decided to settle the dispute another way: by obtaining the appointment of a new governor of South Carolina who would be sympathetic to the Georgia venture. Oglethorpe was the obvious choice, and Sir Robert Walpole, the king's chief minister, had offered him the appointment immediately after Johnson's death. Oglethorpe had rejected the offer, however, because he would have had to resign his seat in the House of Commons if he had accepted it. Oglethorpe found another suitable candidate for the post in the person of Colonel Samuel Horsey, a man who knew something about South Carolina because he had helped negotiate the Crown's purchase of Carolina a decade earlier. After Oglethorpe personally endorsed Horsey's candidacy to Walpole, Horsey received his commission as governor and took the oaths of office on August 1, 1738. At the same time Oglethorpe persuaded the Walpole ministry to appoint William Bull lieutenant governor. Since Bull was one of Oglethorpe's closest friends in South Carolina and was already acting as governor, his and Horsey's appointments meant that the Georgia Trust would be able to rely on the governor of South Carolina in the future. Oglethorpe placed Bull even further in his debt by paying the fees for the lieutenant governor's commission himself.[2]

The carefully executed plans of the Georgia Trust were frustrated, however, when Colonel Horsey died of apoplexy on August 19, 1738, less than three weeks after receiving his commission. The Crown quickly replaced him with James Glen, an impecunious young Scot. According to the gossipy Earl of Egmont, Glen obtained the appoint-

[1] Corry, *Indian Affairs*, 60–62; *Egmont Diary*, II, 490–91, 500.
[2] *Egmont Diary*, II, 185, 368, 503; Oglethorpe to Newcastle, Apr. 22, 1743, Georgia Historical Society, *Collections*, 3 (1873), 153.

ment because his sister was Sir Robert Walpole's mistress and his wife was the illegitimate daughter of the Earl of Wilmington, the president of the Privy Council. In spite of such impressive credentials, Glen needed the help of the Georgia Trust. English merchants trading to South Carolina opposed his appointment, because they distrusted his youth and his views on paper money. But the Earl of Egmont invoked the influence of the Georgia Trust in a personal letter to the Duke of Newcastle, the final authority on colonial appointments, and Glen received his commission.[3] Egmont's solicitation should have placed Glen in debt to the Georgia Trustees, but a salary dispute between Glen and Oglethorpe nullified any sense of gratitude the young governor might have felt. Every previous royal governor of South Carolina had received an annual salary of £1,000 sterling as commander-in-chief of the military forces stationed in the colony. This was the only regular salary the governors had received, because the assembly had refused to establish a permanent civil list. The Crown had unified the military command of the southern frontier in 1737 by giving Oglethorpe a commission as general in command of all forces in both South Carolina and Georgia, and it had transferred the salary of £1,000 to him at the same time. Oglethorpe and Horsey had agreed to split the salary, but Glen did not have a private income of any kind and wanted the whole £1,000 for himself. Glen spent the next three years in England, petitioning for his salary and quibbling over minor points in his instructions. It was not until 1741 that the Lords of the Treasury agreed to let him have £800 a year.[4] Even after that Glen preferred to remain in England for reasons known only to himself, and he did not reach South Carolina until the end of 1743, more than five years after he received his commission.

As a result of the machinations of the Georgia Trustees and the procrastination of Governor Glen, the government of South Carolina remained in the hands of Oglethorpe's friend, William Bull. The outcome not only satisfied the Trust, but it also opened the way to an amicable settlement of the dispute between the two colonies.

Even if Oglethorpe and Bull had not been close friends, a reconciliation between Georgia and South Carolina would have become

---

[3] *Egmont Diary*, II, 506–7, III, 49; The Traders to South Carolina to Newcastle, [1738], S. C. Pub. Recs., XX, 201–2, S. C. Archives; Egmont to Newcastle, Sept. 19, 1738, Newcastle Papers, 1697–1768, Additional Manuscripts, 32691, fol. 362, Brit. Mus. (transcripts in Lib. Cong.).

[4] *Egmont Diary*, II, 417–18; Journal of the Earl of Egmont, Candler and Knight, eds., *Ga. Col. Recs.*, V, 66; Shaw, ed., *Cal. of Treas. Books and Papers, 1739–41*, 463.

imperative after 1737. England and Spain were rapidly drifting into war, with the southern frontier becoming a major area of conflict. At the beginning of the Anglo-Spanish crisis neither country had paid much attention to the southern frontier. The issues at first were the trade agreements in the Treaty of Utrecht of 1713 and Spain's harshness in trying to stop English smuggling. Later, however, the boundary between Georgia and Florida became an increasingly important issue between England and Spain. England maintained that the St. John's River was the boundary, and Oglethorpe had built a fort there in 1736. Spain insisted that the Altamaha River was the true boundary and wanted to demolish Oglethorpe's fort. The Walpole ministry in England followed a cautious policy at first and was reluctant to insist on the St. John's. The ministry changed its mind as tensions increased, however, and it entrusted the military command of the southern frontier to the aggressive Oglethorpe in 1737. By doing so it committed England to a policy of no retreat in the south and increased the likelihood of war there.[5]

The crisis in Anglo-Spanish relations prompted Lieutenant Governor Bull to concentrate on military preparations, often to the exclusion of other problems. He had little time for Indian affairs, much less for a dispute over who should control them. Bull ordered a survey of South Carolina's fortifications and military supplies within a month of taking office, and the survey showed that South Carolina was not able to defend itself. Bull set out at once to prepare the colony to repel an invasion. He persuaded the Crown to give muskets and cannon to South Carolina, and the royal navy promised to send warships in the event of an attack. With the assistance of the speaker of the assembly, Charles Pinckney, he reorganized the provincial militia. He persuaded the assembly to increase the military budget, to build a new armory, and to increase the number of lookouts and scouts. He could not, however, induce the assembly to provide adequately for the colony's ports, and Charles Town, Beaufort, and George Town remained somewhat vulnerable to attack. Despite this failure, South Carolina was ready to defend itself by the end of 1739.[6]

---

[5] Reese, *Colonial Ga.,* 53–61; John Tate Lanning, *The Diplomatic History of Georgia: A Study of the Epoch of Jenkins' Ear* (Chapel Hill, 1936), 85–123.

[6] Bull to Newcastle, with enclosures, Dec. 23, 1737, S. C. Pub. Recs., XIX, 86–93, S. C. Archives; Newcastle to Oglethorpe, June 15, 1739, *ibid.,* XX, 48–50; Bull to Charles Pinckney, June 14, 1740, Wills, Inventories, and Misc. Recs., LXIX–B, 714–16, Charlestown Co. Courthouse; Nov. 8, 9, Dec. 12, 17, 1739, Easterby, ed., *Commons Journal, 1739–41,* 12–13, 17, 21–22, 112, 129–30; Oct. 29, Dec. 3, 1741, *ibid., 1741–42,* 266–67, 284.

While South Carolina was preoccupied with its military defenses, a new crisis was building up in Indian affairs. The Creeks were angry with the English, because they were being cheated by unscrupulous traders; the dispute over control of the trade had undermined trade regulations, and neither South Carolina nor Georgia was able to protect the Indians. The Chickasaws on the Mississippi River were under attack from the French and were demanding English protection. The Cherokees were the most upset of all. South Carolina traders had brought in a smallpox epidemic that threatened to destroy the Cherokees. To make matters worse, the Cherokees were also being disturbed by the preaching of Christian Gottlieb Priber, a German immigrant. Priber was a utopian mystic who wanted to found a Christian communal republic among the Cherokees based on the principles of liberty and equality. Few men understood Priber—the English thought he was a French spy—but everyone agreed that he was upsetting the Cherokees. The only hopeful sign for the English among all the tribes concerned the Choctaws, who had been faithful French allies for forty years. They sent a delegation to Charles Town in 1738 to discuss a trade agreement with South Carolina and possibly even a treaty of alliance.[7]

General Oglethorpe returned to Georgia in 1738 and found Lieutenant Governor Bull eager to cooperate with him in Indian affairs. Bull was much too deeply indebted to Oglethorpe to risk offending him, and besides, he was busy with defensive preparations at home. Bull therefore turned Indian affairs completely over to Oglethorpe and let the general do as he pleased. He even admitted, according to the Earl of Egmont, that Oglethorpe was "best able to manage the Indians."[8]

Oglethorpe's handling of the Indian crisis justified Bull's confidence in him generally, although not in every particular. Oglethorpe pacified the Cherokees by supplying them with corn until the smallpox epidemic ended. He tried to arrest Christian Gottlieb Priber, and although Priber eluded capture for several years, he eventually died in prison at Frederica. In order to expedite diplomatic negotiations with the Cherokees in the future, both Georgia and South Carolina took an unprecedented step, recognizing one of the tribal chiefs, Moytoy of

[7] Jan. 19, 1739, Easterby, ed., *Commons Journal, 1736–39*, 595; Oglethorpe to [Harmon Verelst], June 15, 1739, Egmont Mss., 14204, 9, Univ. of Ga. Lib.; Swanton, *Indians of Southeastern U. S.*, 117; Oglethorpe to Verelst, Oct. 19, 1739, Ga. Hist. Soc., *Collections*, 3 (1873), 87–88; Bull to Newcastle, July 20, 1738, S. C. Pub. Recs., XIX, 243–48, S. C. Archives. On Priber, see Verner W. Crane, "A Lost Utopia of the First American Frontier," *Sewanee Review*, 27 (1919), 48–61.

[8] Egmont Journal, Candler and Knight, eds., *Ga. Col. Recs.*, V, 233; see also Oglethorpe to Trustees, Oct. 11, 1739, Ga. Hist. Soc., *Collections*, 3 (1873), 84.

Great Tellico, as Cherokee emperor. Previously, the English colonies had recognized only village and regional chiefs. The new procedure made it easier to negotiate with the entire Cherokee nation, but it stirred up jealousies among the Indians. The traditional capital of the Cherokee nation was the overhill town of Chota, and the warriors of Chota regarded Moytoy and the warriors of Great Tellico as usurpers and upstarts.[9] Oglethorpe thus preserved the Cherokee alliance, but he could do little with the Creeks. For twenty years the Creeks had followed a policy of neutrality, and they had no intention of changing course. As a Creek chief explained it, "The land belonged to the English as well as the French and indeed to neither of them. But both had liberty to Come there to Trade." [10] The Creeks remained neutral, rejecting French and Spanish alliances as well as English. As for the Chickasaws and the Choctaws, the English actually lost ground during the late 1730's. Neither Georgia nor South Carolina was able to help the Chickasaws, except to move a few of them to the Savannah River. France remained on the attack in the Mississippi region and stopped the new trade between the Choctaws and South Carolina.[11]

With Oglethorpe and Bull working together in harmony, the dispute between South Carolina and Georgia had finally ended. The two men were not entirely successful in handling the Indian crisis of the late 1730's, but at least their colonies were at peace. Perhaps more important, their cooperation made it possible for South Carolina and Georgia to prepare for an Anglo-Spanish war united and in good order.

II

The key figure in the internal politics of South Carolina from 1737 to 1743 was Lieutenant Governor William Bull. In his private life he was a wealthy rice planter, an amateur historian and musician, and an avid though untrained gardener and botanist. Like so many South Carolinians he liked to entertain and kept a well-stocked wine cellar, which included 230 gallons of rum at the time of his death. At Ashley

[9] Oglethorpe to Trustees, July 4, 1739, Candler and Knight, eds., *Ga. Col. Recs.*, XXII, Pt. ii, 166; Crane, "Lost Utopia," *Sewanee Review*, 27 (1919), 60–61; David H. Corkran, *The Cherokee Frontier: Conflict and Survival, 1740–62* (Norman, Okla., 1962), 15–16.

[10] A. Willy to Capt. Croft, May 10, 1740, S. C. Pub. Recs., XX, 259–60, S. C. Archives.

[11] Feb. 25, 1738, Upper House Journal, VII, 75–77, S. C. Archives; Bull to Newcastle, Feb. 11, 1740, S. C. Pub. Recs., XX, 252, S. C. Archives.

Hall, the family estate near Charles Town, he entertained such distinguished guests as Mark Catesby, John Wesley, and James Oglethorpe. In his public life Bull was an ambitious politician. His father, Stephen Bull, had been an influential political leader in the late seventeenth century, but he had always remained in the shadow of his better known contemporaries. William Bull's ambition was nothing less than to make his family the outstanding political family in the colony. Therefore he accepted Oglethorpe's patronage eagerly and used his office to increase his family's power and prestige. The measure of his success may be seen in many ways. The Bulls, with their in-laws and allies, became a definite force in provincial politics, although they never dominated the government entirely. Three men connected with the family were elected speakers of the assembly in the 1730's and 1740's, six were appointed to the council, and William Bull, Jr., succeeded his father as lieutenant governor. For two years, from 1740 to 1742, all laws passed by the provincial assembly were signed by William Bull, Sr., as lieutenant governor, and William Bull, Jr., as speaker of the assembly.

An important aspect of the lieutenant governor's bid for power was his relationship with the Commons House of Assembly. Bull realized that the Commons House was becoming the center of power in the provincial government, so he made it his policy to cultivate a close association with the house. He adopted its speaker, Charles Pinckney, as his special protégé, and when Pinckney resigned the speakership, he was succeeded by William Bull, Jr. More important, the lieutenant governor supported the Commons House in its drive to expand its political powers. Frequently this meant that Bull sided with the Commons in its disputes with the council, and occasionally it meant that he tolerated an invasion of the royal prerogative. Nevertheless, Bull generally allied himself with the Commons House in order to keep its friendship. This alliance at first cost him the support of the council, which turned against him in 1739. Within another two or three years, however, Bull had regained the council's friendship by partially yielding to it on a critical issue. He was so successful in handling the council that in later years its members looked back wistfully to his administration as a time when all branches of the government were properly balanced. In this way Bull built up a broad base of political support in the colony by cultivating the friendship of both houses, even when it involved giving in to their demands.[12]

[12] M. Eugene Sirmans, "Politicians and Planters: The Bull Family of Colonial South Carolina," S. C. Hist. Assn., *Proceedings,* 1962 (1963) , 32–41.

When Bull took office in 1737 South Carolina was still split into two major factions, one dominated by merchants and the other by planters. Each faction was well represented in both the council and the Commons House of Assembly, but during Bull's administration the merchants gained control of the council. Members of the council were appointed by the Privy Council upon recommendation of the Board of Trade, and council appointments were determined by influence with the Board of Trade. The leading merchants of Charles Town usually had relatives or business partners in England, and as a result they wielded more influence with the Board of Trade than any other group in South Carolina. The Crown appointed seven new councilors during Bull's administration, and five of them were merchants. Every time a vacancy occurred the same thing happened. Bull recommended either lawyer Charles Pinckney or planter Joseph Blake to fill the vacancy, but the Board of Trade ignored them and selected a merchant. Pinckney and Blake did not become councilors until after 1740, and by that time the Charles Town merchants controlled seven or eight of the twelve seats in the council. Furthermore, the planters lived in the country and could not attend council meetings regularly. The merchants therefore composed an even larger majority of council members present and voting.[13]

The major issue dividing merchants and planters at the beginning of Bull's administration concerned the township fund. Prior to 1731 South Carolina had used the import duty on slaves to retire bills of credit, but the assembly in that year had diverted that income to settlement of the townships. The merchants, of course, added the cost of the duty to the price of the slaves, but the responsibility for paying it still rested on the merchants. Planters liked the system, but the merchants wanted to shift the responsibility to someone else and many of them would also have liked to return to the old practice of using the slave duty to retire the local currency. The merchants were not opposed to Governor Johnson's township plan; they merely wanted to finance it in a different way.

Late in 1737 the township fund became a political issue, because the act that had set it up was due to expire in 1738. Furthermore, Lieutenant Governor Broughton's misuse of the fund had nearly bankrupted it, and when a large number of Irish immigrants landed in 1737 there was no money to help them. The council proposed on December 15, 1737, that the assembly solve the problem by including

[13] Sirmans, "S. C. Royal Council," *Wm. and Mary Qtly.*, 3d Ser., 18 (1961), 384, 392.

an appropriation for township settlement in the annual tax bill, a suggestion which would have eliminated the need for a slave duty. After the Christmas recess, in February 1738, the Commons House countered with a bill to continue the slave duty for ten years. The council then sidetracked the argument by injecting a new issue; it directed the public treasurer not to pay any money out of the township fund without its permission. The directive was an obvious attempt to reduce the lower house's control over finances, and the Commons responded promptly. It insisted on a conference, and the two houses agreed that in the future the governor, council, and lower house, whether acting jointly or independently, could appropriate money from the township fund.[14] This dispute amounted to very little, but it enabled the council to postpone action on the township fund and slave duty for a year. The leading merchants took advantage of the delay by appealing to the Board of Trade for help. Their agent asked the Board to prohibit a re-enactment of the slave duty, but for once the Board of Trade rejected a merchant petition. It refused to issue further instructions and even refused to let the merchants' agent submit additional arguments against the slave duty.[15]

When the assembly reconvened in February 1739, the council and Commons House not only resumed their debate over the duty bill but also expanded the controversy to include the basic parliamentary rights of both houses. The two houses opened the argument with a dispute over the minor issue of whether petitions and accounts should be examined by a joint committee of both houses or by a separate committee in each house; the council favored the customary joint committee, while the Commons House thought separate committees would be better parliamentary practice. Before this question was settled the Commons House on February 8 asked the upper house for prompt action on the slave duty bill. The council promised to consider the bill at once, but it managed to postpone action for six weeks and gave the lower house nothing but evasive promises. In the interim another minor issue arose when the council amended a bill to maintain a watch in Charles Town. The Commons House interpreted the bill as a money bill and protested the council's amendments on the grounds that the upper house did not have the right to amend money bills of any kind. Finally, on April 6, when it no longer had a

<hr/>

[14] Dec. 15, 1737, Feb. 4, 1738, Upper House Journal, VII, 16, 65, S. C. Archives; Feb. 1, Mar. 6, 11, 1738, Easterby, ed., Commons Journal, 1736–39, 439–40, 513, 537.

[15] William Wood to [Bd. of Trade], Feb. 7, 1738, Wood to Thomas Hill, July 11, 1738, S. C. Pub. Recs., XIX, 36–38, 217–19.

legitimate excuse for stalling, the council passed the slave duty bill but amended it to remove the features the merchants did not like. The lower house thought the duty bill was a money bill, too, and adopted resolutions charging that the council had encroached upon its parliamentary rights.[16]

On April 11 the council decided that the time had come to assert its rights and sent to the lower house a short message that was nonetheless one of the sharpest it had ever written. It flatly denied the validity of all previous agreements on money bills and asserted that it had the right to amend any bill by virtue of local custom and royal instructions: "We are determined to suffer no Law to pass this House that is not submitted to such Alterations and Amendments as we think necessary for his Majesty's Service and the good of this Province." [17] Having challenged the lower house, the council turned on the lieutenant governor. Like other colonial councils it had long resented the presence of the governor in the council when it was acting as the upper house of assembly, because it thought his presence an executive intrusion upon the legislature. So long as Bull was only president of the council, the other councilors did not object to his presence because the president was only the first in rank among equals. Then Bull's commission as lieutenant governor arrived on April 3, which meant that he was now an official representative of the Crown. The council therefore resolved, "The Governor or Commander in chief being Present during the Debates of this House is of an unparliamentary nature." It refused to transact any legislative business until Bull withdrew.[18]

The council continued to press its case, but it overreached itself and suffered a humiliating setback. When the lower house made its predictable claim to exclusive control of money bills, the council advised Bull to adjourn the assembly. This was an error. South Carolina custom followed English practice and recognized the governor's right to call, prorogue, and dissolve the assembly but not the right to adjourn it; the assembly had the privilege of adjourning itself, and the governor could only grant permission for it to adjourn. Bull followed custom, and probably his own wishes as well, by rejecting the council's advice and granting the assembly permission to adjourn.

[16] Feb. 8–9, 21, 23, Apr. 5–6, 10, 1739, Easterby, ed., *Commons Journal, 1736–39,* 622–24, 629, 633, 689, 691–96.

[17] Apr. 11, 1739, *ibid.,* 696.

[18] Apr. 3, 1739, Council Journal, CO 5/440, Pt. ii, 10, PRO; Apr. 11, 1739, Upper House Journal, VII, 218, S. C. Archives.

Before adjourning on April 13 the lower house sent the council a stinging, sarcastic message, in which it gloated over Bull's refusal to follow "that mistaken Advice you have just now officiously offered." [19]

The assembly adjourned for six weeks in order to let both sides cool off, but after it reconvened on May 30 it soon became obvious that the two houses were hopelessly deadlocked. Although the assembly had not passed the annual tax bill, neither house was ready to concede an inch. The upper house opened the session with an offensive reply to the Commons' message of April 13, in which it said, "If you are capable of Joy on so slender an Occasion, we think you have a Right to enjoy it." It then advised the lower house to get down to business, to "shew a greater Regard to Decency and good Manners," and "to restrain the little Affection you have discovered, on this Occasion of being witty." [20] The Commons House's response was equally childish: It pretended the council did not exist, and when communication was unavoidable it sent messages to the lieutenant governor. The council appealed to Bull for assistance, but since the upper house had excluded him he had no desire to help. Bull blamed the council for the deadlock and said he was upset because neither the tax bill nor the slave duty had been enacted. Both houses realized there was little point in sitting longer; the lower house asked permission to adjourn and the council asked Bull to prorogue or dissolve the assembly. Bull again followed the wishes of the Commons and granted permission for the assembly to adjourn until September. As the assembly had been in existence for nearly three years, the limit prescribed by law, the effect of Bull's action was to dissolve the assembly without passage of a tax bill or a slave duty. [21]

Before adjourning, the Commons House of Assembly adopted the most complete and most radical statement of its rights that it had ever considered. The author of the resolution, attorney Maurice Lewis, addressed himself to the house's claim to the exclusive privilege of framing money bills. In previous resolutions the house had always relied on its interpretation of royal instructions and on local custom for support for its privileges, but Lewis recognized that instructions and custom could be uncertain constitutional foundations. He therefore based the case of the Commons House on the rights of the house

[19] Apr. 12–13, 1739, Easterby, ed., *Commons Journal, 1736–39*, 699–701, 704.
[20] May 30, 1739, *ibid.*, 707.
[21] June 7, 1739, *ibid.*, 725, 727; June 5–7, 1739, Upper House Journal, VII, 238–46, S. C. Archives.

as representatives of Englishmen. "The Common Law and the Principles of our Constitution immediately take Place upon the forming of a new Colony of British Subjects," he said, "and . . . no Usage or Royal Instructions can take away the Force of it in America." Lewis maintained that the privileges of the House of Commons extended to colonial assemblies, including the sole right to frame and amend money bills. Extension of parliamentary privilege was an old argument, but the denial of the power of custom or royal instructions to change the rights of Englishmen marked a change in the theoretical basis of South Carolina politics.[22]

The voters of South Carolina elected a new Commons House in August, but there was no change in its leadership or its convictions. When it met in November it again elected Charles Pinckney as its speaker, and although Maurice Lewis had died, other leaders, like Benjamin Whitaker and Andrew Rutledge, were back again, too. The house informed the council that it hoped to "cultivate a good Harmony" in the legislature, but it added that its first duty was to "maintain that Freedom and Independence by which the Constitution of our Mother Country is to be preserved to each Branch of the Legislature."[23] It was not long before the cultivation of a good harmony again seemed impossible. The houses again disagreed on whether there should be a joint committee or separate committees to inspect petitions and accounts, and the upper house again amended the Charles Town watch bill. These were the same issues that had touched off the earlier deadlock. Now, however, neither house wanted another prolonged stalemate, because the colony had too many pressing problems: South Carolina needed a tax bill, slaves had revolted three times that fall, the War of Jenkins' Ear had begun, and General Oglethorpe wanted South Carolina to join him in an expedition against Florida. The assembly therefore ended its disputes with remarkable alacrity. Both houses appointed a conference committee to discuss control of money bills, and both adopted the committee's proposals without further argument, except to say that the compromise should not be considered a binding precedent. In effect, the compromise called for the council to surrender on every major constitutional point. It agreed to allow the Commons House to frame and initiate all money bills, and it relinquished its right to amend them. It kept only the right to accept or reject money bills and the right to suggest amendments to them. The council then passed the tax bill and suggested twenty-two

[22] June 5, 1739, Easterby, ed., *Commons Journal, 1736–39*, 717–24.
[23] Nov. 28, 1739, *ibid., 1739–41*, 60–61.

amendments, of which the Commons accepted nineteen and rejected three.[24]

The legislative settlement of December 1739 began a new period of political harmony in South Carolina, and there were no more serious disputes between the two houses of assembly for the rest of Bull's administration. Both houses respected the agreement of 1739 and stayed within its limits. The only flare-up that occasioned any animosity at all came in the spring of 1740 when Andrew Rutledge and councilor Edmund Atkin exchanged heated words during a conference committee meeting. Rutledge criticized remarks that Atkin had allegedly made in a debate in the upper house, and the council interpreted Rutledge's criticism as a breach of its freedom of debate. The council refused to proceed with business until Rutledge and the Commons House apologized.[25] With the legislative controversy laid to rest, Lieutenant Governor Bull and the upper house were able to compose their differences, too. The council admitted Bull to its legislative sessions as an observer, a compromise which satisfied both parties.[26]

The political settlement of 1739 endured largely because the colony's leaders were finally working out a permanent solution to the local currency problem. Governor Johnson, of course, had started South Carolina on the way to a currency settlement, but the paper money agitation during Broughton's administration had undermined his success. Once again, in currency as in the Georgia dispute and other issues, Lieutenant Governor Bull's administration resolved the controversies of Broughton's term of office. After the Privy Council disallowed the currency act of 1736, South Carolina had abandoned bills of credit and turned instead to public orders and tax certificates. Both were short-term notes issued by authority of the assembly, and the only difference between them was that public orders remained in circulation longer than tax certificates. Although public orders and tax certificates were not legal tender and were legally valid only for payment of taxes, in practice they were widely accepted as legal tender. The notes were not really an innovation, because the assembly had issued public orders in 1731 to pay the debts of the Middleton administration, but the first extensive use of public orders and tax certificates came during the War of Jenkins' Ear when South Carolina

[24] Nov. 22, 27, Dec. 8, 11, 14–15, 17–18, 1739, *ibid.*, 41–42, 52, 90–93, 97–98, 120–22, 127–28, 131–33, 137–38.
[25] Mar. 27, May 2, 1740, *ibid.*, 263–65, 324, 327.
[26] "Report of the Committee appointed to enquire into the Constitution," Upper House Journal, May 7, 1745, XIII, 147, S. C. Archives.

emitted £119,500 for military purposes. Private citizens added to the amount of currency in circulation for a while by organizing unincorporated banks that issued their own notes, but Parliament outlawed such banks in 1740.[27]

Widespread acceptance of the paper currency, even by creditors, marked the final step in the solution of the colony's currency shortage. Creditors accepted paper money more readily than before for several reasons. In the first place, the assembly always retired public orders and tax certificates on schedule. Furthermore, the currency demonstrated a remarkable resiliency during a brief wartime recession in 1739 and 1740; when the market value of rice fell 50 per cent, local currency declined to an exchange ratio of 8 to 1 during the recession, but as the economy began to recover in 1741 the exchange ratio climbed again to 7 to 1. The currency's quick recovery proved to many former doubters that the value of local paper money could be stabilized.[28] A third reason for accepting the currency was a decision that the Court of Common Pleas in Charles Town handed down in 1741. Chief Justice Benjamin Whitaker ruled that if a debt were contracted in sterling and if the local currency depreciated after the debt was made, then the debtor had to repay the creditor at the higher rate of exchange. In other words, the debtor would have to bear the loss if the currency depreciated.[29] The ruling enabled creditors to protect themselves against fluctuations in the value of the currency by contracting loans in sterling.

One result of resolving the paper money question was a compromise on the township fund. The dispute over the fund had originated in a conflict between merchants and farmers, a division which was similar to the division over local currency. Then, when the major issue of paper money was settled, it became possible to settle the minor issue of the township fund, too. The assembly passed a new law in May 1740 that both merchants and planters were willing to accept. The key provision in the act said the slave duty would be paid by the purchaser of the Negro instead of the importer, a solution which the Crown had suggested ten years earlier. The law also set aside all income from the slave duty to pay for township settlement. The township fund therefore gained an adequate income, while the financial responsi-

[27] Brock, Currency of Colonies, 123–27; Dec. 9, 1749, Easterby, ed., Commons Journal, 1749–50, 333–36; [Whitaker], Chief Justice's Charge, 18–31.

[28] Taylor, "Wholesale Commodity Prices," Jour. Econ. and Bus. Hist., 4 (1932), 360, 372; David D. Wallace, The Life of Henry Laurens . . . (N. Y., 1915), 53.

[29] Hext v. Executors of Jenys, Proceedings of the Court of Common Pleas: Judgment Books, 1740–41, 265–73, S. C. Archives.

bility was transferred from the importing merchant to the slaveowning planter.[30]

Thus, in 1739 and 1740 under the governorship of William Bull, the internal politics of South Carolina returned to a state of unity. The two houses of the assembly settled their disputes, the colony developed an adequate and generally acceptable currency supply, and the old political factions began to disappear. The remaining years of Bull's term as governor were certainly not tranquil, but his administration was never again troubled by any kind of internal political division. Every political crisis of the next three years found South Carolina's leaders united against some opponent from outside the colony.

III

The return of political stability also cleared the way for legislative action on still another matter of importance to South Carolina: the institution of slavery. The assembly had not changed the colony's basic slave laws since 1696, although it had re-enacted the slave code of 1696 three times and amended it twice. The old law was becoming obsolete and needed drastic revision, but the assembly disputes of the 1730's prevented effective legislative action.

South Carolina was haunted by the fear of a slave insurrection throughout the 1730's, because the Negro population was growing much more rapidly than the white. By 1740 Negroes outnumbered whites 39,000 to 20,000, and merchants were importing more slaves at the rate of 2,500 a year. South Carolinians could also remember that slaves had risen in rebellion on at least three previous occasions, and although the earlier revolts had failed, the next one might not. Whites had often treated their slaves indulgently without trying to enforce all provisions of the slave code, and white control of the slaves became even more uncertain in the 1730's. As many as two hundred Negroes sometimes engaged in drinking parties in Charles Town, while many slaves openly defied the law by buying and selling goods in the Charles Town market.[31] Then, in an attempt to forestall English aggression on the southern frontier by stirring up South Carolina's slaves, the governor of Spanish Florida published a royal edict in 1738 that promised freedom to all English slaves who made good their escape to

[30] Cooper and McCord, eds., *Statutes*, III, 556–68.
[31] Sirmans, "Legal Status of Slave," *Jour. of So. Hist.*, 28 (1962), 468–70; William Bull, Jr., to the Earl of Hillsborough, Nov. 30, 1770, S. C. Pub. Recs., XXXII, 382, S. C. Archives.

St. Augustine. General Oglethorpe heard a report that the Spanish had even sent agents into South Carolina to spread the news of the edict. The report was probably an unfounded rumor, but even so, publication of the edict was followed by several successful escapes and an unknown number of abortive attempts. News of the runaways, combined with the lax enforcement of slave laws, convinced many whites that a general slave insurrection might break out at any moment.[32]

Preoccupied with the struggle between the upper and lower houses over control of money bills, the assembly ignored all the signs of warning, however, and every effort to relieve the approaching crisis fell a victim to that struggle. Blind to the dangers of a slave insurrection, the assembly clung to the old laws and passed no corrective legislation, except for an ineffective patrol law which failed to meet the challenge of the Spanish edict.[33]

The insurrection that had been brewing finally broke out on Sunday, September 9, 1739, although in fact it was less an insurrection than an attempt by the slaves to fight their way to St. Augustine. The trouble started on Saturday night when about twenty slaves, led by a Negro named Jemmy, broke into a warehouse near the Stono River and armed themselves with guns, ammunition, and other military supplies. The armed slaves killed ten whites and burned several houses on Sunday morning. Then, with flags flying, drums beating, and shouts of "liberty," about sixty Negroes set out to march to St. Augustine. Lieutenant Governor William Bull, who had escaped the initial outburst only by fast riding, called out the militia, which caught up with the slaves at four o'clock that afternoon. The Negroes fought desperately, but the militia outnumbered them and many of the slaves were drunk on rum. By sunset the insurrection had ended, with forty Negroes and twenty whites dead.[34]

Two other abortive uprisings followed the Stono insurrection, but new legislation was postponed until the political settlement of December 1739. Even then reform of the slave laws was held up by the dispute in the spring of 1740 between councilor Edmund Atkin and

[32] Jan. 19, 1739, Upper House Journal, VII, 142–43, S. C. Archives; Bull to Newcastle, May 9, 1739, S. C. Pub. Recs., XX, 40–41, S. C. Archives; June 18, 1742, Council Journal, no. 8, 81, S. C. Archives.

[33] See, e.g., Dec. 13, 1737, Mar. 22, 1738, Jan. 24, Mar. 16, 1739, Easterby, ed., Commons Journal, 1736–39, 362–64, 547, 604, 673; see also Cooper and McCord, eds., Statutes, III, 395–99, 456–61.

[34] "An Account of the Negroe Insurrection in South Carolina," Candler and Knight, eds., Ga. Col. Recs., XXII, Pt. ii, 232–36; see also Bull to Bd. of Trade, Oct. 5, 1739, S. C. Pub. Recs., XX, 179–80, S. C. Archives.

assemblyman Andrew Rutledge.[35] Not until May 1740 did the Commons House and council agree on a new slave code, one which represented a new departure in South Carolina's slave laws. Defining slaves as personal chattels, that is, the personal property of the master, the law gave the first precise definition of slavery since the disallowed act of 1690; slavery no longer rested upon custom but upon law. Furthermore, in adopting a precise legal definition of a slave, South Carolina definitely and finally abandoned its Barbadian traditions of slavery and set the institution upon the legal foundation developed in other English mainland colonies.

In other respects, the slave code of 1740 was consistent with previous practices in South Carolina. The assembly sought to maintain a tradition of lenient treatment of slaves by enacting provisions designed to keep "owners and other persons having the care and government of slaves" from "exercizing too great rigour and cruelty over them." The law forbade masters to work their slaves on Sunday or more than fourteen or fifteen hours a day during the week. Owners were required to provide sufficient food and clothing. If any white were accused of killing or maiming a slave, he was to face a jury trial, and he could be fined up to £100 sterling if he were found guilty. The assembly re-enacted all the old provisions designed to keep slaves "in due subjection and obediance" and added new ones, outlawing all assemblies of slaves, forbidding the sale of alcohol to them, and prohibiting them from learning to write. At the same time it passed the new slave code the assembly strengthened the patrol system by vesting responsibility for it in the militia, and it tried to reduce the number of Negroes being shipped to the colony by raising the import duty.[36]

The new slave code was permitted to go into effect despite some opposition in England, where the Crown's legal advisors seemed suddenly aware of chattel slavery. The Board of Trade's legal counsel, Mathew Lamb, recommended disallowance of the South Carolina code in 1748 on the grounds that the colonial law conflicted with an act of Parliament of 1732 designed to help English merchants recover debts in the colonies. One of the provisions of this act directed that slaves be treated as real estate in the recovery of colonial debts. Lamb argued that the Parliamentary act sanctioned freehold slavery but not chattel slavery. The Board of Trade took no action on the South Carolina

[35] Petition of Assembly, July 26, 1740, S. C. Pub. Recs., XX, 300–301, S. C. Archives; Apr. 29, May 2, 1739, Easterby, ed., *Commons Journal, 1739-41*, 307, 324, 327.

[36] The slave code of 1740 is in Cooper and McCord, eds., *Statutes*, VII, 397–417; see also *ibid.*, III, 556–73.

slave code, however, and the code remained in force, although three years later the Board secured the disallowance of a Virginia law because it defined slaves as chattels. The Crown's permissive treatment of the code of 1740 may well have been due to the intercession of the Charles Town merchants, who often owned slaves and probably favored the new slave code.[37]

The slave code of 1740 seems to have served its purpose well enough, for there were no more major rebellions in the colonial period. A few changes in the law became necessary, but they were minor; the assembly amended the patrol law, and by 1750 the patrols functioned effectively.[38] In some other cases the assembly found provisions of the 1740 law too severe on the slaves and either amended the law or permitted it to be ignored. Most notably, it allowed the Society for the Propagation of the Gospel to operate a grammar school for fifty to sixty Negro boys in Charles Town.[39]

IV

The War of Jenkins' Ear began officially with England's declaration of war on Spain on October 19, 1739, and for the next three years the southern frontier became the center of land warfare in America. No battles were fought on South Carolina soil and the war created no internal crises for the colony, but the war produced two developments of major importance for the provincial government. The first was a new dispute with Georgia, which began after the failure of General Oglethorpe's invasion of Florida in 1740. The second saw South Carolina re-emerge as the chief spokesman for English interests among the southern Indians at a time when English officials were making fundamental changes in their Indian policy.

In the opinion of General James Oglethorpe, the War of Jenkins' Ear provided a first-rate opportunity to eliminate Spain as a competitor on the southern frontier. The English government was really more interested in naval warfare in the Caribbean than land warfare on the southern frontier, but it instructed Oglethorpe in October 1739 to attack St. Augustine if such a plan seemed feasible. The Crown's rather cautious instructions gave Oglethorpe the excuse he needed. He

[37] Sirmans, "Legal Status of Slave," *Jour. of So. Hist.*, 28 (1962), 472.
[38] Cooper and McCord, eds., *Statutes*, III, 681–85; Klaus G. Loewald *et al.*, trans. and eds., "Johann Martin Bolzius Answers a Questionnaire on Carolina and Georgia," *Wm. and Mary Qtly.*, 3d Ser., 14 (1957), 234.
[39] James Glen to Bd. of Trade, Jan. 29, 1752, S. C. Pub. Recs., XXV, 7–8, S. C. Archives; Robert Smith to Sec. S.P.G., July 25, 1759, S.P.G. Mss., B 5, no. 252.

sent a small military force into Florida in December 1739 to test the Spanish defenses, and when his troops met little resistance he began to plan a full-scale invasion. He could not expect much help from England, so he went to Charles Town in January 1740 to solicit the aid of South Carolina. After two months of haggling, the assembly agreed to contribute 429 infantrymen, 40 rangers, 10 small boats, and supplies for the South Carolinians and 500 Indians. The assembly also promised to appropriate over £40,000 currency for the expedition and enlisted the support of five British warships that were stationed at Charles Town. Oglethorpe returned to Georgia and told the provincial secretary, William Stephens, that he was "well satisfied with his Reception in Carolina, and the Aid he was assured of from thence." [40]

Oglethorpe's invasion of Florida was a fiasco from beginning to end. He landed his troops south of the St. John's River on May 9, 1740, but instead of advancing toward St. Augustine he spent the next month wandering around Florida capturing small outposts. Oglethorpe did not begin the siege of St. Augustine until June 12, and even then he positioned his troops poorly. Spanish soldiers wiped out a South Carolina detachment on June 15, and Oglethorpe seemed to lose his spirit. The commandant of the South Carolina militia, Colonel Alexander Vander Dussen, pleaded with Oglethorpe to continue the siege, but the commander of the British warships insisted that the navy must withdraw by July 5 in order to avoid the hurricane season. Then the navy blundered by letting Spanish ships slip through the English blockade and land supplies at St. Augustine. Oglethorpe gave up and ordered a general retreat on July 4. His handling of the invasion amazed the Spanish governor, Don Manuel de Montiano, who said, "I cannot arrive at a comprehension of the conduct, or rules of this General." [41]

The failure of the St. Augustine expedition started a new dispute between South Carolina and Georgia when Oglethorpe tried to blame South Carolina for his own mistakes. He charged that the English failure was due entirely to the South Carolina assembly's tardiness and

[40] Reese, *Colonial Ga.*, 78–79; Mar. 29, Apr. 4–5, 1740, Easterby, ed., *Commons Journal, 1739–41*, 273–74, 298–99, 301; the quotation is from Journal of William Stephens, Candler and Knight, eds., *Ga. Col. Recs.*, IV, 548.

[41] The best account of this campaign is John Tate Lanning's introduction to J. H. Easterby, ed., *The St. Augustine Expedition of 1740: A Report to the South Carolina Assembly* (Columbia, 1954), reprinted from Easterby, ed., *Commons Journal, 1741–42*, 78–247. See also Ettinger, *Oglethorpe*, 233–35; *Letters of Montiano, Siege of St. Augustine* (Ga. Hist. Soc., Collections, 7 [1909], Pt. i). The quotation is from Montiano to [Don Juan Francisco de Guemes y Horcasitas], July 28, 1740, *ibid.*, 60.

parsimony in supporting his campaign, forgetting his earlier remark that he was well satisfied with the assembly's assistance. With much more justification the people of South Carolina blamed Oglethorpe for the expedition's failure, and according to one witness they were so angry that "they cannot hear the name of Col. Oglethorpe, but they fall into such a rage as sets the very dogs a barking." [42]

Both houses of the South Carolina assembly, realizing the need for a careful study of the debacle in Florida, appointed a joint investigating committee. After hearing testimony from both sides and weighing the evidence, the committee found that Oglethorpe was primarily responsible for the failure of the invasion. The assembly approved the committee's report on July 2, 1741, and ordered it printed in both South Carolina and England.[43] Peter Timothy, the editor of the *South-Carolina Gazette,* printed the report in Charles Town in 1742, but the colony's agent in England, Peregrine Fury, failed to publish it there. Fury was in an unenviable position, because he was also agent for Oglethorpe's regiment and risked losing one agency no matter what he did. He decided at first to obey the South Carolina assembly, but Anne Oglethorpe, the general's sister, persuaded him to turn the report over to Governor James Glen and the Georgia Trustees induced Glen to suppress it. Glen kept quiet about his own role in the affair and led the South Carolina assembly to believe that Fury alone was responsible for suppressing the report. As a result, the assembly lost its trust in Fury and dismissed him from the agency a few years later.[44]

A curious lethargy settled down upon South Carolina after the failure of Oglethorpe's expedition. The assembly seemed to believe that it had done its share in the war, and despite the very real danger of Spanish retaliation it would do no more. It paid off South Carolina's share of the expenses of the Florida campaign, which amounted to about £70,000 currency, but after that it refused to spend any more money for defense. The outports of Beaufort and George Town needed protection, and a fire swept Charles Town on November 18, 1740, destroying some of its defenses as well as many homes and shops. The assembly concentrated on rebuilding the city, which had

[42] Egmont Journal, Candler and Knight, eds., *Ga. Col. Recs.,* V, 499; see also *Egmont Diary,* III, 214; Oglethorpe to James Vernon, Jan. 26, 1741, Egmont Mss., 14205, 248, Univ. of Ga. Lib.; Ettinger, *Oglethorpe,* 235–37.

[43] July 18, 24, 1740, Easterby, ed., *Commons Journal, 1739–41,* 358–59, 369; July 2–3, 1741, *ibid., 1741–42,* 248, 259. The report has been reprinted in *ibid., 1741–42,* 78–247, and separately as cited above in n. 41.

[44] Egmont Journal, Candler and Knight, eds., *Ga. Col. Recs.,* V, 572, 580; *Egmont Diary,* III, 238; Apr. 21, 1744, Easterby, ed., *Commons Journal, 1744–45,* 133.

suffered losses estimated at £250,000 sterling, and ignored South Carolina's military needs despite the pleas of Lieutenant Governor Bull.[45] It petitioned the Crown for reimbursement of the colony's expenses in the Florida expedition, for relief after the Charles Town fire, and for three independent companies to be stationed in South Carolina. All the petitions recited the calamities that had befallen South Carolina and entered the plea that the colony could no longer defend itself. The petitions had some effect, for Parliament voted £20,000 sterling for the relief of Charles Town.[46]

South Carolina was abruptly jolted out of its lethargy by the Spanish invasion of Georgia in July 1742. The Spanish force, a large expedition from Havana commanded by Governor Montiano, landed on St. Simon's Island and drove Oglethorpe up the Altamaha River to Frederica. The invaders outnumbered Oglethorpe's troops, and as Bull reported to the Duke of Newcastle, " 'Tis not expected he [Oglethorpe] can long hold out against so great a force." [47] But then the fortunes of war shifted. Oglethorpe's rearguard defeated the Spanish vanguard in a skirmish that became known as the Battle of Bloody Marsh, which was not much of a battle and not especially bloody, although it was fought in a marsh. Spain lost only fifty men in the fight, but Governor Montiano did the same thing Oglethorpe had done in Florida: He panicked after a minor setback. When a rumor reached Montiano that a fleet of British warships was on its way to Georgia, he re-embarked his army and sailed home. Spain's last hope of eliminating the colony of Georgia sailed with him, and the Spanish were never again able to threaten the southern English colonies.[48]

The dispute betweeen Oglethorpe and South Carolina went on in spite of the English victory, because the general again chose to display his penchant for invective. Oglethorpe claimed that he could have destroyed the Spanish force if reinforcements had arrived from South Carolina in time, and he blamed Lieutenant Governor Bull for the delay. There was some justification for Oglethorpe's charges, because as late as June 16 Bull had refused to pay any attention to

[45] Sept. 11, Nov. 20, 1740, Feb. 26, 1741, Easterby, ed., *Commons Journal, 1739–41,* 389, 408, 508.
[46] May 25, 1742, *ibid., 1741–42,* 552–55; Petitions of the Assembly, July 26, Nov. 21, 1740, [Peregrine Fury to Bd. of Trade], July 2, 1741, S. C. Pub. Recs., XX, 300–308, 327–30, 369, S. C. Archives.
[47] Letter of July 7, 1742, S. C. Pub. Recs., XX, 585, S. C. Archives.
[48] Ettinger, *Oglethorpe,* 243–45; Patrick Sutherland, "An Account of the late Invasion of Georgia," 1742, Egmont Mss., 14206, 220–30, Univ. of Ga. Lib.; *The Spanish Official Account of the Attack on the Colony of Georgia* (Ga. Hist. Soc., *Collections,* 7 [1913], Pt. iii) , esp. 72–81, 88–96.

Oglethorpe's prediction of an invasion.[49] Once news of the Spanish fleet had reached Charles Town, however, Bull had acted quickly. He had raised a fleet of twelve ships with a supporting force of more than a thousand men, and he had obtained additional men and supplies from Jamaica and Virginia. All Bull's work had been in vain, however, because Captain Charles Hardy, commander of the British fleet in South Carolina, had delayed his sailing for a week after the fleet was ready, and then, without making contact with the enemy and in direct disobedience to Bull's orders, he had sailed back to Charles Town.[50] Oglethorpe paid little attention to this explanation and continued to disparage Bull's efforts. Perhaps what disturbed Oglethorpe most was the fact that, as Oglethorpe put it, Bull had "strangely changed" and "will neither take my advice or obey my orders." Fortunately for Bull, Oglethorpe's charges no longer carried much weight with the British government, and the Board of Trade commended Bull for the "Zeal and Expedition" he had shown in assisting Georgia.[51]

Bull had a more serious problem to deal with than Oglethorpe. South Carolina's defenses were still inadequate, and the Commons House of Assembly still obstinately opposed military expenditures. The lieutenant governor and his council feared that Spain might launch another invasion, and they daily expected news that France had entered the war on Spain's side. Foreign threats failed to impress the lower house, however, and it tried repeatedly to adjourn in 1742 and 1743 without providing for defense. Bull responded by insisting that the assembly remain in session until it had finished its work. He had the support of the council, but the key figures in obtaining military appropriations were Benjamin Whitaker, the speaker of the house, and William Bull, Jr., who acted as his father's floor leader in the Commons. Whenever the house considered the lieutenant governor's requests for defensive expenditures, Whitaker appointed a sympathetic committee to consider the request with William Bull, Jr., as chairman. Bull then reported in favor of his father's plans, and the house gave its reluctant approval, too. The lieutenant governor and his allies were successful, for by 1744 the assembly had completed Charles Town's defensive works and had established batteries and

[49] Ettinger, *Oglethorpe*, 242–43; Oglethorpe to Newcastle, Jan. 22, 1743, Candler and Knight, eds., Ga. Col. Recs., XXXVI, 16, Ga. Dept. of Hist. and Archives; Aug. 13, 1742, Council Journal, no. 8, 196–97, S. C. Archives.

[50] July 3–13, 24, 30–31, 1742, Council Journal, no. 8, 86–109, 156–57, 161–65, S. C. Archives.

[51] Oglethorpe to Newcastle, Feb. 22, 1743, Ga. Hist. Soc., *Collections*, 3 (1873), 147; Bd. of Trade to Bull, Feb. 18. 1743, S. C. Pub. Recs., XXI, 15, S. C. Archives.

garrisons at the outports.[52] While Bull was coaxing appropriations from the assembly, he also continued to urge the Crown to grant South Carolina's earlier petitions for military assistance, and once again he succeeded. The Crown replaced the cannon lost on Oglethorpe's expedition and assigned three independent companies of infantry and a forty-gun ship to the colony.[53]

The dispute between Georgia and South Carolina that began in 1740 spread immediately to include the old issue of Indian affairs. Before 1740 prospects for a permanent, formal settlement had appeared to be excellent. The South Carolina assembly was prepared to compromise, and the Georgia Trust and Governor Glen had reached a tentative agreement. The failure of the St. Augustine expedition, however, had caused South Carolina to lose its faith in Oglethorpe, and the assembly would not even discuss Indian affairs with him in 1741.[54] The issue became an active one that same year when another Indian crisis arose. The Cherokees went to war against the Creeks, and French agents began to harass the Cherokees. Lieutenant Governor Bull and his assembly ignored Oglethorpe and handled the crisis themselves. South Carolina sent agents with presents to both the Cherokees and Creeks and reassured the Cherokees of English protection in the event of a Franco-Cherokee war. The warring nations agreed to a truce, and by the fall of 1741 the crisis was over for a while.[55] Oglethorpe did not interfere because he was busy preparing Georgia's defenses, and in settling the crisis South Carolina had regained its old position as chief arbiter of Indian affairs for the southern English colonies.

At the same time that South Carolina was reasserting its control over the southern Indians, the English colonies were adopting a new Indian policy that depended upon intercolonial cooperation. There had been no coordinated English Indian policy before the 1740's, and each colony had normally worked alone. The new policy was devised by Lieutenant Governor George Clarke of New York, who first applied it

[52] Sept. 15–17, Dec. 4, 1742, Feb. 16, 23, Mar. 12, 1743, Easterby, ed., *Commons Journal, 1742–44,* 15, 22, 24–25, 98–102, 215–16, 234–40, 300–303; James Glen to Newcastle, July 2, 1744, S. C. Pub. Recs., XXI, 378–82, S. C. Archives.

[53] Orders in Council, Dec. 16, 1742, July 19, 1744, S. C. Pub. Recs., XX, 394–98, 653–55, S. C. Archives; Oct. 6, 1743, Easterby, ed., *Commons Journal, 1742–44,* 466.

[54] Mar. 26, 1740, Easterby, ed., *Commons Journal, 1739–41,* 260–61; Egmont Journal, Candler and Knight, eds., *Ga. Col. Recs.,* V, 546–48; Oglethorpe to James Vernon, Jan. 26, 1741, Egmont Mss., 14205, 248–49, Univ. of Ga. Lib.

[55] Journal of William Stephens, Candler and Knight, eds., *Ga. Col. Recs.,* IV, Supplement, 55, 81–82, 126, 154; Bull to Newcastle, Oct. 14, 1741, S. C. Pub. Recs., XX, 394, S. C. Archives.

to the Iroquois and other northern Indians. Clarke wanted to unite all pro-English Indians in a "Covenant Chain" of alliances, in which all English allies would also become each other's allies.[56] The primary obstacle to Clarke's policy was the traditional enmity among some of the English Indians; most notably, the Iroquois were raiding Cherokee and Catawba villages. Under Clarke's plan it would be the job of the English governors to end such wars by negotiating a series of peace treaties.

Clarke wrote to Bull and Oglethorpe in 1741 outlining his plans and asking for their assistance; specifically, he proposed that the Cherokees and Catawbas sign a treaty with the Iroquois. Oglethorpe enthusiastically endorsed the proposal as "one of the noblest designs and most advantageous for all the British Subjects on the Continent of America." [57] Bull wasted no superlatives praising the policy, but he put it into effect immediately by persuading the Cherokees and Catawbas to accept a treaty with the Iroquois in 1742.[58] The treaty was broken within a few years, but Bull's action had committed South Carolina to the implementation of Clarke's plan.

South Carolina kept its dominant role in Indian affairs after 1742, in part because General Oglethorpe left Georgia for the last time in 1743 and returned to England. After he left, the dispute between South Carolina and Georgia withered away, and James Glen said a few years later that it was "buried in oblivion." [59] The two colonies worked out an informal division of authority, with Georgia assuming responsibility for the Upper Creeks and South Carolina the other tribes. Nevertheless, the two disputes had left a very real scar. Neither colony could regulate the Indian trade adequately, because many traders took advantage of the jurisdictional confusion and traded without a license from either colony. There was thus no way to prevent trade abuses, and the Indian trade remained a source of trouble.[60] The ultimate solution was direct Crown regulation of Indian affairs, but neither Georgia nor South Carolina was prepared to surrender any portion of its authority in the 1740's.

[56] Clarke to Georgia Trust, May 19, 1742, Candler and Knight, eds., Ga. Col. Recs., XXIII, 330.

[57] Oglethorpe to Trustees, Mar. 3, 1742, Ga. Hist. Soc., Collections, 3 (1873), 118.

[58] Bull to Bd. of Trade, June 15, 1742, S. C. Pub. Recs., XX, 570, S. C. Archives; June 20, 1748, Easterby, ed., Commons Journal, 1748, 333.

[59] To President and Assistants of Ga., Oct. 1750, Candler and Knight, eds., Ga. Col. Recs., XXVI, 61.

[60] Reese, Colonial Ga., 111–12; Wilbur R. Jacobs, ed., Indians of the Southern Colonial Frontier: The Edmond Atkin Report and Plan of 1755 (Columbia, 1954), 34–35, hereafter cited as Jacobs. ed., Atkin Report.

V

Throughout the 1730's most political issues in South Carolina had arisen out of English expansion on the southern frontier. By the early 1740's, all the problems of expansion had been settled with one exception—the land boom. The boom itself ended by 1741. There was no further demand for land, and many landowners were willing to give away their surplus land in order to avoid quit rents and taxes.[61] Nevertheless, South Carolina's land system had not recovered from the boom, and the provincial government still tolerated irregular and even fraudulent practices. Governor Johnson had granted land to individuals in excess of their headrights, and Lieutenant Governor Broughton had granted land inside the townships to natives of South Carolina. The defects of the land law were even more serious. The quit rent act of 1731 regulated proprietary land claims effectively, but it did not cover royal land claims. As a result, landholders claimed land by virtue of royal warrants or plats without grants, they failed to register conveyances of royal land claims, and they avoided paying royal quit rents.

Such abuses invited criticism, and a new critic of the land system appeared in 1741 who tried to overthrow the entire system. He was Henry McCulloh, the king's special commissioner of quit rents in North and South Carolina. McCulloh was a prosperous land speculator and London merchant with good connections at Whitehall, especially at the Board of Trade where he enjoyed the friendship of Board member Martin Bladen. McCulloh's major interest was land speculation in North Carolina, and his activities in South Carolina were never more than a sideline to him. McCulloh had first become involved in the affairs of North Carolina after the Crown had completed the purchase of the Carolinas in 1727. After he had used his influence to obtain the appointment of Gabriel Johnston as governor of North Carolina, Johnston had reciprocated by issuing warrants for 1,200,000 acres of land to McCulloh and his associates. In the late 1730's, however, Johnston double-crossed McCulloh and worked with a competitive group of speculators. McCulloh, worried about the prospect of holding on to his claims, proposed that the Crown appoint him commissioner of quit rents with the authority to reform the land system and increase quit rent collections. McCulloh included South

---

[61] George Hunter to Bd. of Trade, Oct. 23, 1743, Aug. 12, 1749, S. C. Pub. Recs., XXI, 174–75, XXIII, 393–94, S. C. Archives.

Carolina in his proposal—probably as window dressing to make the need for land reform appear more urgent—and on May 16, 1739, the Crown appointed him commissioner of quit rents for both Carolinas.[62]

In spite of McCulloh's political influence, he failed to obtain a satisfactory commission and set of instructions. The commission granted him an annual salary of £600 sterling, but it stipulated that he would receive his salary only if quit rent collections increased. In the second place, his commission and instructions gave him a broad investigative power but nothing more. He could not give orders to any other royal official; he could only make recommendations to the governors and assemblies. For example, the fifteenth and sixteenth articles of the instructions suggested that every land claimant should take an oath on the validity of his headrights before the governor and council, that the claimant should return a plat or survey within a year of receiving his warrant, and that he should obtain a grant within another six months. Such a procedure would have eliminated many frauds, but McCulloh had no power to enforce it.[63] Immediately upon receiving his commission and instructions, McCulloh petitioned the Crown for an appointment to the council in both provinces and for additional instructions from the Crown binding both governors to obey his fifteenth and sixteenth instructions. He also petitioned for the repeal of South Carolina's quit rent law of 1731 on the ground that it was "plainly calculated to defraud His Majesty." [64] McCulloh's petitions had little effect, however. The Privy Council issued an order in council directing the two governors to obey the fifteenth and sixteenth articles of McCulloh's instructions, but such an order carried less authority than did other forms of instructions. More important, Governor James Glen used his influence to block McCulloh's appointment to the councils and to prevent the repeal of the quit rent act.[65]

Somewhat frustrated by his failures in London, McCulloh sailed to the Carolinas and landed at Charles Town in March 1741. He immediately antagonized almost everyone in the colony with a presumptuous attempt to usurp authority that was not rightfully his. He posted a public notice that ordered all land claimants to obtain

[62] Charles G. Sellers, Jr., "Private Profits and British Colonial Policy: The Speculations of Henry McCulloh," *Wm. and Mary Qtly.*, 3d Ser., 8 (1951), 535–42.

[63] Commission and Instructions for McCulloh, May 16, 1739, Walter Clark, ed., *The State Records of North Carolina*, 16 vols. (Winston and Goldsboro, N. C., 1895–1905), XI, 31–41.

[64] Petition of McCulloh, May 30, 1739, S. C. Pub. Recs., XX, 22, S. C. Archives; see also Petition of McCulloh, 1739, *ibid.*, XX, 145–47.

[65] Order in Council, Aug. 14, 1740, Petition of McCulloh, Nov. 8, 1741, *ibid.*, XX, 313–18, 431–32.

grants, commanded the immediate registration of deeds of conveyance, and threatened to prosecute landowners who claimed more than their headrights permitted. Next he ordered the public officials responsible for the collection of quit rents to put his fifteenth and sixteenth instructions into operation. The surveyor general complained to the council, which compared McCulloh's commission and instructions with the orders he had promulgated since arriving in the colony. Finding that McCulloh had far exceeded his authority, it reprimanded him and countermanded his orders. Thus McCulloh's first attempt to reform the land system, by issuing illegal promulgations, ended in failure.[66]

McCulloh next turned to the assembly. He submitted proposals for a new quit rent law, which were cordially received by both houses and Lieutenant Governor Bull. The key provisions of his proposed bill extended the quit rent law of 1731 to cover royal land claims and required prompt registration of all deeds of conveyance. Both houses passed the first reading of the bill with minor amendments before adjourning for the summer.[67] During the summer recess, however, opposition to the bill developed outside the assembly. The grand jury in Charles Town condemned the bill as prejudicial to the property rights of South Carolinians. There must have been other popular objections to the bill, too, for the Commons House changed its opinion completely. Using the weak excuse that Governor Glen might arrive soon with new instructions, the Commons refused to give the bill a second reading despite the council's pleas for its passage.[68]

Henry McCulloh moved on to North Carolina in the summer of 1741 and stayed there a year and a half. During his absence the South Carolina assembly ignored the land system, but Lieutenant Governor Bull initiated several minor reforms on his own. Bull stopped the practice of granting township land to natives of the colony, although he made no attempt to interfere with deeds already issued by Broughton. Bull also began to require land claimants to take an oath as to their headright claims before the council, and he required everyone who received a warrant to return a plat within twelve months. Bull may have wanted to institute other reforms, but he was handicapped by the incompetence of other royal officials. For example, he discovered in 1742 that both the surveyor general, James St. John,

[66] Public Notice [1741], Council Minutes, Apr. 3, 1741, *ibid.*, XX, 445–54, 464–69; Memorial of McCulloh, [1748], Treas. 1/330, fol. 142, PRO.
[67] May 21, 23, 26–27, June 30, July 1, 1741, Easterby, ed., *Commons Journal, 1741–42,* 27–29, 33–34, 40–44, 47, 75, 248.
[68] Dec. 3, 1741, Mar. 1–2, 1742, *ibid.,* 284, 450, 452.

and the provincial secretary, John Hammerton, were nearly a year and a half behind with their work.[69]

McCulloh returned to South Carolina in February 1743 and, in his usual manner, made everyone mad at him. He celebrated his return by charging Bull and other officials with obstructing the king's commands. Although he acknowledged that Bull had made some reforms, he belittled their importance and argued that more reforms were necessary. Next he asked the assembly to reconsider his quit rent bill, but the Commons House buried the bill in a committee.[70] Finally, he outraged both houses of the assembly by proposing that the offices of public treasurer, a provincial post, and receiver general of quit rents, a royal office, be combined. He argued that his plan would increase rent collections, because the treasurer had access to the tax lists, which included landed property. The incumbent public treasurer had just resigned, and McCulloh asked Bull to fill the vacancy by appointing the receiver general. Unfortunately for McCulloh, the public treasurer was appointed by the assembly, not the governor, and both houses regarded his proposal as an infringement of their rights. The council reprimanded McCulloh once again, this time for "assuming and unbecoming" conduct.[71]

When Henry McCulloh sailed for London, never to return to the Carolinas, he had accomplished very little in the way of land reform in South Carolina and even less in North Carolina, but he had achieved his primary goal in coming to America. He had secured a clear title to his land claims in North Carolina, and in the next thirty years, he sold enough land to make a considerable fortune.[72]

Although McCulloh himself had failed to reform the South Carolina land system, his visits to the colony had a salutary effect. Immediately after his departure, Lieutenant Governor Bull found a way to introduce further reforms. When the old and incompetent surveyor general, James St. John, died, Bull replaced him on April 29, 1743, with George Hunter, a former law partner of councilor Charles Pinckney who probably owed his appointment to Pinckney.[73] Hunter turned out to be the ablest surveyor general in the history of the

[69] McCulloh to Bull, Feb. 16, 1743, S. C. Pub. Recs., XXI, 110–23, S. C. Archives; Sept. 16, 1742, Council Journal, no. 8, 254–56, S. C. Archives.

[70] McCulloh to Bull, Feb. 16, 1743, S. C. Pub. Recs., XXI, 110–23, S. C. Archives; Mar. 2, 8–9, 1743, Easterby, ed., Commons Journal, 1742–44, 262–63, 282–86.

[71] Mar. 23, 1743, Council Journal, no. 10, 74–75, S. C. Archives.

[72] Sellers, "Private Profits and Colonial Policy," Wm. and Mary Qtly., 3d Ser., 8 (1951), 545–48.

[73] Gregorie, ed., Chancery Court Recs., 281n; Apr. 29, 1743, Council Journal, no. 10, 181, S. C. Archives.

colony. With the support of Bull and the council, he launched a drive against the practice of claiming land without a formal grant. He published in the *Gazette* a list of all claims for which there were no grants, and the lieutenant governor and council promised to withdraw recognition of the claims unless warrants were secured within six months. Bull's earlier reform had eliminated claiming land by warrant, and by 1745 Hunter seems to have eliminated most cases in which land was claimed by plat. In effect, Bull and Hunter had put into practice the method of granting land set forth in McCulloh's fifteenth and sixteenth instructions.[74]

Governor James Glen finally sailed from England in 1743 and disembarked at Charles Town on December 17. He found a colony that was more at peace with itself and its neighbors than it had been at any time during the preceding forty years. Since 1712 one controversy after another had disrupted the political harmony of South Carolina. First had come the Indian wars with the Tuscaroras and Yamasees, then the rebellion against the proprietors, followed by the currency disputes. Then, in rapid succession, there had been conflicts over the land system and arguments with Georgia. Throughout the whole period political factions arising out of the currency shortage had split the government internally. By December 1743, however, all those issues had been resolved, except for the land system and the assembly was ready for action on it. Even paper money was no longer a major issue, and the hard and easy money factions had disappeared. In short, by the time Governor Glen landed at Charles Town South Carolina's time of troubles had ended.

Shortly after Governor Glen's arrival in December, the assembly settled the whole land question without dissension or delay. The new quit rent act of 1744 was essentially the same as the bill McCulloh had proposed in 1741; it extended the provisions of the act of 1731 to cover royal land claims, and it required the immediate registration of deeds of conveyance. McCulloh predicted the act would "open a door for New Frauds," but his estimate was entirely wrong. After its passage quit rent collections rose by a third, although the colony was in a depression and there were few new grants. Prior to 1744 rent collections had averaged £1,200 proclamation money a year and had never risen above £1,585 in any one year. Between 1745 and 1751, by

[74] See George Hunter's reports to Bd. of Trade, with enclosures, May 1, 1745, Sept. 1, 1746, June 25, 1748, S. C. Pub. Recs., XXII, 57–66, 164–92, XXIII, 132–47, S. C. Archives; see also Aug. 24, 1743, Council Journal, no. 10, 297–99, S. C. Archives; *S-C. Gaz.* (Charles Town), Aug. 29, 1743, Supplement.

contrast, annual collections averaged £1,600 and in 1748 rose to £2,167.[75]

The speed with which the provincial government adopted land reforms after Henry McCulloh left the colony indicates the major reason for McCulloh's failure. McCulloh himself tried to blame all his defeats on the council, even though it was the Commons House that had defeated his quit rent bill in 1741. His analysis of his opposition, like his estimate of the quit rent act of 1744, was entirely wrong. McCulloh himself should bear the blame for the failure to reform the land system sooner. His arbitrary and often illegal manner of proceeding alienated both houses of the assembly, and as long as McCulloh remained on the scene no one was willing to cooperate with him except Lieutenant Governor Bull. Once McCulloh had left the colonies, however, the provincial government reformed the land system without delay. South Carolinians did not oppose land reform; they merely opposed Henry McCulloh.

VI

Two men—Governor Robert Johnson and Lieutenant Governor William Bull—were chiefly responsible for ending the colony's period of disorder. Johnson had laid the foundations of political stability in 1731, but Johnson had neglected some issues and his successor, Thomas Broughton, had raised new ones. William Bull's task had been the reconstruction of Johnson's political settlement, and during his administration the provincial government had found solutions to all the problems that Johnson and Broughton had left unsolved. The Indian trade dispute with Georgia had ended, even though General Oglethorpe had later started a second quarrel with South Carolina; both the local currency and the township fund had been placed on more secure foundations; the assembly had resolved its internal conflicts; a new slave code had been adopted; and reform of the land system had begun. At the same time Bull had improved the colony's military defenses and had regained for South Carolina its former role as leading English spokesman among the southern Indians. The accomplishments of Bull's administration had been impressive, but he should not receive all the credit. The other political leaders of South Carolina had also been eager to put an end to the long years of controversy, and the political harmony of South Carolina at the end of 1743 was as much the work of such men as Charles Pinckney and Benjamin Whitaker as it was the work of William Bull.

[75] Cooper and McCord, eds., *Statutes*, III, 633–37; Account of Quit Rents in South Carolina, 1745–1751, Treas. 1/347, fol. 79, PRO; the quotation is from McCulloh to Thomas Hill, Jan. 16, 1745, S. C. Pub. Recs., XXII, 8, S. C. Archives.

Part III

THE RISE OF THE COMMONS HOUSE
OF ASSEMBLY
1743–1763

Governor James Glen's long-delayed arrival in South Carolina in 1743 marked the end of an old era in the colony's political history and the beginning of a new one. Prior to the 1740's provincial politics had followed a roughly rhythmical pattern of chaotic disputes and compromise settlements. The normal political cycle had seen a period of violent internal dispute resulting in near anarchy followed by a period of adjustment and relaxation of tensions. Thus, the controversy over the establishment of the Church of England had been followed by Charles Craven's peaceful administration, and the currency disputes of the 1720's had been followed by Robert Johnson's sponsorship of compromise. From 1743 to 1763 the pattern of politics was quite different. The old cycle of conflict and compromise disappeared and was replaced by an enduring internal harmony. There were political disputes, to be sure, but after 1743 they concerned only the assembly and did not divide the general public into opposing factions. Anglicans and dissenters, merchants and planters lived together in peace; the old controversies were dead, never to be revived.

The outstanding feature of South Carolina from 1743 to 1763 was the threefold struggle for power among the governor, council, and Commons House of Assembly, with the victory going to the Commons House. In 1743 the three contenders shared political power in a more or less equal fashion, but none of them was satisfied with its position in the government. Each of them tried to expand its authority at the expense of the other two, and the resulting conflict dictated the course of local politics for the next twenty years. In the long run the governor and the council were the losers. By 1763 the Commons House had become the dominant branch of the government of South Carolina, while the council had degenerated into little more than a cipher and the governor had suffered a similar, but less drastic, reduction in his authority.

The rise of the Commons House was certainly not a new development in South Carolina history, for in a broad sense the house had been steadily encroaching upon the prerogatives of the governor and council ever since its establishment as a separate branch of the legislature in 1693. Nevertheless, there was a distinct difference in the nature of the house's rise to power before and after 1743. Prior to that time the rise of the Commons House had been subordinate to other political developments, but afterwards the demands of the house itself tended to dominate provincial politics. Before 1743 constitutional issues relating to the rights and privileges of the house appeared only as by-products of social and economic conflicts involving the entire population. For example, the house's acquisition of the sole right to frame and amend money bills originated as an incident in the conflict over local currency. But after 1743, the frequently violent constitutional struggles in the assembly stood in marked contrast to the general political calm that prevailed outside the legislature.

Thus, the political history of the years between 1743 and 1763 showed two major characteristics. A lasting political peace existed in the colony at large, and there were no major internal divisions. At the same time, however, the governor, council, and Commons House were fighting constitutional battles over their respective rights and privileges, and the Commons House was gradually emerging as the dominant force in the provincial government.

CHAPTER X

THE COLONY AT MID-CENTURY

By the middle of the eighteenth century South Carolina had grown up as a colony. The frontier outpost of 1670 or even of 1700 had long since disappeared and been replaced by a more sophisticated and more complex society. Indeed, South Carolina's society and economy had reached an advanced stage of maturity that did not change markedly again until after the American Revolution. The colony had built up a prosperous economy based on a variety of staple products. In turn, economic prosperity had given many white Carolinians the opportunity to improve their social positions and the time to enlarge the scope of their social activities. A few critics grumbled at the ways in which leisure was used, but Charles Town became a social capital as well as a major port.

South Carolina's political institutions had likewise matured, although they continued to change more rapidly than either economic or social customs. The governor was still the central figure in politics, and his office had changed little since the establishment of royal government. Change was more evident in the council and Commons House. Each house had developed its own set of traditions, notably a tradition of freedom from outside interference, and its own methods of procedure, especially the elaborate network of committees in the Commons House. Other parts of the government, such as the court system and local administration, had matured less fully and remained in a rather primitive state. The governor, council, and lower house continued to be the most important elements in the provincial government, and as such they deserve more careful consideration than other political institutions.

I

The increasing maturity of political institutions in eighteenth-century South Carolina coincided with a remarkable economic expansion which created the most affluent society among the English settlements on the American mainland. Life in South Carolina at mid-century rested upon a bedrock of economic prosperity, and widespread prosperity generally kept economic issues out of politics. The colony reaped profits from a varied economy that drew returns from the Indian trade, livestock, and timber as well as rice, and the introduction of indigo in the 1740's gave the economy even greater variety and stability. Consequently, South Carolina enjoyed a prosperity that could be matched by few other colonies, if any, and the good times lasted without interruption until the Revolution, except for a recession in the middle and late 1740's. Individual Carolinians amassed some of the largest private fortunes in the colonies and the Carolina low country gloried in the highest per capita income in America.[1] The assembly in 1742 calculated the total value of property in South Carolina at £15,000,000 currency, or about £2,000,000 sterling. With a white population of about 20,000, the assembly's estimate indicates that the average value of the property belonging to white families would have been about £4,500 currency (£600 sterling) per family.[2]

Not every colonist, of course, struck it rich in South Carolina. Men often extended their credit too far, especially in order to buy slaves, and went bankrupt. Creditor's auctions were all too common during the recession of the 1740's, but the bankruptcy of a few men should not obscure the basic prosperity of the colony. The debts of South Carolinians never approached the size of those of Virginia planters, and the health of the South Carolina economy made it possible for a good businessman to amass a fortune quickly. According to some of the colonists, an intelligent planter could often regain his initial investment in land and slaves within three or four years.[3]

A key figure in the provincial economy was the lowcountry planter,

[1] Carl Bridenbaugh, *Myths and Realities: Societies of the Colonial South* (Baton Rouge, 1952), 55–57, 67.

[2] Mar. 3, 1742, Easterby, ed., *Commons Journal, 1741–42*, 460; Greene and Harrington, *American Population*, 174; this estimate is based on the Greene and Harrington average of 5.7 to 6 members per family; see *ibid.*, xxiii. Even at the highest reasonable estimate of South Carolina's population in the early 1740's—25,000 whites—the average wealth per family would have been about £3,500 currency, or over £450 sterling. A few free Negroes owned property, but there were certainly not enough of them to affect these estimates.

[3] Loewald *et al.*, eds., "Bolzius Questionnaire," *Wm. and Mary Qtly.*, 3d Ser., 14 (1957), 244, 252; Bridenbaugh, *Myths and Realities*, 56–57.

who might own as many as a dozen plantations and five hundred slaves. Wealthy planters preferred to buy several small plantations, rather than a single large one, because rice was most profitably grown in comparatively small units. Consequently, the planters of South Carolina, unlike those of Virginia, could not supervise their plantations in person and made a practice of hiring overseers. They usually placed about thirty slaves and a white overseer on each of their plantations. Nor did the consignment system, so familiar in Virginia, develop in South Carolina. After harvesting his crop the rice planter either sold it to a Charles Town merchant or made his own arrangements for shipment.[4] The poorer lowcountry planters could not afford overseers and directed their farms themselves, but even the poorest of them owned two or three slaves. They sold their produce to middlemen called "country factors," who resold it in Charles Town and then brought goods from the city to the outlying plantations. Farmers who lived in the townships led a harder life than any of the lowcountry planters. They owned few slaves or none at all, tilled the land themselves, raised livestock, and grew wheat, corn, and vegetables. The township farmers lived on the edge of poverty for years, but in the 1740's they began to enjoy a modest prosperity by selling foodstuffs to the lowcountry.[5]

The second key figure in the provincial economy was the merchant, the prototype of the individual entrepreneur who sat in a small countinghouse and carried on a world-wide correspondence. Most mercantile offices were in Charles Town, but there was enough trade at Beaufort and George Town to support a few businesses there, too. Whatever his location, the merchant was a jack of all trades. He imported slaves, English goods, rum, wine, and other wares and exported rice, deerskins from the Indian trade, lumber, and, beginning in the 1740's, indigo. He often accepted commissions from London or Bristol merchants, but he was never a factor in the sense of being a permanent representative of a single British firm. If he were one of the wealthier merchants, however, he might have a partner in England, most likely a relative. He owned few ships, if any, and usually rented space for his cargoes from English and northern sea captains. Two of

---

[4] James Glen, *A Description of South Carolina* (London, 1761), in Milling, ed., *Colonial S. C.,* 16; Henry Laurens to William Thompson, Mar. 15, 1763, Henry Laurens Letterbook, 1762–66, 28, Laurens Papers, Historical Society of Pennsylvania, Philadelphia, Pa.

[5] Charles Pinckney to Alexander Vander Dussen, Feb. 28, 1742, Newcastle Papers, Add. Mss., 32700, fol. 342, Brit. Mus.; Bridenbaugh, *Cities in the Wilderness,* 344; Glen, *Description,* in Milling, ed., *Colonial S. C.,* 44–45.

the busiest merchants in the 1730's and 1740's were Joseph Wragg and Gabriel Manigault, and their business typified the trade of Charles Town. During the fiscal year 1735–1736, according to records kept by the public treasurer, Wragg imported 6,230 gallons of rum from Antigua and Barbados, 341 slaves from Africa, and paid duties amounting to £296 currency on sundries imported from Philadelphia and Barbados. He exported 6,095 deerskins to Bristol and London. Manigault eschewed the slave trade, but in the same year he imported 11,333 gallons of rum from Barbados and Antigua and paid £640 in duties on goods from Barbados, New York, Philadelphia, Jamaica, and Madeira. He exported 6,600 pounds of leather to Barbados. Both men also exported rice and imported English goods, but the provincial treasurer did not keep records of these goods because there were no duties on them.[6]

Economic differences divided South Carolina's white population into social classes, whose existence was generally recognized although men disagreed on the number and composition of classes. Governor James Glen divided the whites into four groups. He said there were five thousand people "who have plenty of the good things of Life," another five thousand "who have some of the Conveniencys of Life," ten thousand "who have the Necessarys of Life," and five to six thousand "who have a bare subsistance." [7] Other writers simply divided the white population into the rich and the poor; there was no middle class except for a few artisans in Charles Town. When contemporaries referred to the upper class by name, they most often called it the gentry, and because of South Carolina's wealth, an unusually large number of people had the money necessary to claim membership in that class. According to a reliable observer, Dr. George Milligen, "The Men and Women who have a Right to the Class of Gentry . . . are more numerous here than in any other Colony in North-America." [8] Differences between classes were well understood. For example, Lieutenant Governor William Bull, Sr., often invited the congregation of Prince William's Parish to Sheldon plantation after Sunday services. He received the gentry himself inside his house, while the rest of the parishioners remained outside and were entertained by

[6] Treasurer's Books: Journal A (1735–1748), 1–13, S. C. Archives. See also Joseph W. Barnwell and Mabel L. Webber, eds., "Correspondence of Henry Laurens," *S. C. Hist. Mag.*, 28–31 (1927–30); Wallace, *Laurens*, 44–56; for a different interpretation of the merchant, see Leila Sellers, *Charleston Business on the Eve of the Revolution* (Chapel Hill, 1934), 49–78.

[7] "An Attempt towards an Estimate of the value of South Carolina," Mar. 1751, S. C. Pub. Recs., XXIV, 318–19, S. C. Archives.

[8] *Short Description,* in Milling, ed., *Colonial S. C.,* 134.

his overseer.[9] Although class distinctions were recognized, class lines were not rigid, because economic prosperity enabled many men to accumulate fortunes and to rise into the gentry in the middle of the eighteenth century. Among them were such well-known South Carolinians as Gabriel Manigault, Charles Pinckney, Andrew Rutledge, and Henry Laurens.

Social life in South Carolina was dominated by the gentry, the five thousand or so whites who had "plenty of the good things of Life." Like most colonists who had money the South Carolina gentry tried to reproduce the life of the English gentry. They imitated English fashions and amusements, and they bought English goods whenever possible. There were still traces of a Barbadian influence in South Carolina, as the people retained some West Indian customs and blended them with English imitation. Such blending was most obvious in architecture, for South Carolinians usually added West Indian piazzas to their Georgian houses.[10] Visitors to the colony often found the people to be irresponsible pleasure-seekers; for example, Josiah Quincy, Jr., a native of Massachusetts who visited South Carolina in 1773, said, "State, magnificence and ostentation, the natural attendants of riches, are conspicuous among this people. . . . Cards, dice, the bottle and horses engross prodigious portions of time and attention: the gentlemen (planters and merchants) are mostly men of the turf and gamesters."[11] Wealth and the employment of overseers freed South Carolinians from constant attention to work, and unlike many people in the northern colonies, they lacked a strong puritanical sense of moral duty. Pleasure became the goal of social life, and as Eliza Lucas complained, "It is become so much the fashion now to say everybody that is greave [grave] is religiously mad."[12] The high style of living and the quest for pleasure shocked native conservatives as well as visitors; Chief Justice Benjamin Whitaker once used his annual address to the grand jury as the occasion to deliver an exhortation to the people of the colony "to return to our former Frugality, Temperance and moderate Enjoyments."[13]

If a South Carolinian was looking for pleasure, Charles Town was

[9] Frederick Dalcho, *An Historical Account of the Protestant Episcopal Church in South-Carolina* . . . (Charleston, 1820) , 383.

[10] Thomas Jefferson Wertenbaker, *The Golden Age of Colonial Culture,* 2d rev. ed. (N. Y., 1949) , 127–28, 130–31.

[11] Mark A. DeWolfe Howe, ed., "Journal of Josiah Quincy, Junior, 1773," Massachusetts Historical Society, *Proceedings,* 49 (1916) , 455.

[12] Eliza Lucas to Mrs. Charles Pinckney, n. d., Eliza Lucas Pinckney Letterbook, 8, Pinckney Papers, South Carolina Historical Society, Charleston.

[13] [Whitaker], *Chief Justice's Charge,* 10.

the place to find it. An excellent system of roads made it easy for planters to travel to the city, and in the 1750's they began to build town houses there. Every winter the roads were crowded with planters and their families on their way to town for the annual social season, which began in January and lasted into the spring. When they arrived they were soon caught up in a social whirl that was hectic, fast-paced, and exuberant. South Carolinians were the most socially minded people in colonial America. They delighted in the theater and in music. Professional actors appeared more often in Charles Town than anywhere else in the colonies, and the best musicians in America were more likely to perform there than elsewhere. The St. Cecilia Society was the first musical society organized in America. Moreover, Carolinians were not content merely to listen to music. They danced better and more often than any other colonists; too often, perhaps, for Henry Laurens once complained that the Commons House was planning to adjourn early so that its members could attend a ball. It was often said that during the social season a South Carolina gentleman could be found anywhere except at home. He was most likely to be found at his club, or rather, at *one* of his clubs, for another Charles Town superlative was its incredible number of clubs. There was a club devoted to smoking, another to beefsteak, and a third to laughing. Other clubs were known simply as the Monday Night and Friday Night Clubs. If a gentleman could not be found at his club, the next place to look for him was the race track. The sport of kings was popular in Charles Town throughout the middle decades of the eighteenth century. The purse for a race occasionally amounted to £1,000 sterling, horses often sold for £300, and as much as £2,000 might be bet on a single race. Henry Laurens, who could be a kill-joy when he wanted, once lamented the fact that he could not get a ship unloaded because his workmen had gone to the races.[14]

Life on the plantations moved at a more leisurely pace. Planters who lived near the colony's borders suffered from the same kind of isolation that plagued Virginia planters. Most of the lowcountry was more thickly settled, however, and isolation was not a problem for the majority of planters. Eliza Lucas Pinckney has left us a charming picture of the normal pattern of life on a lowcountry plantation. A half-dozen families lived near the Pinckneys, and there was frequent visiting back and forth. When they were alone the Pinckneys enjoyed

[14] Bridenbaugh, *Myths and Realities*, 77–94; Wertenbaker, *Golden Age*, 146–49; Wallace, *Laurens*, 29–33; M. Eugene Sirmans, "Charleston Two Hundred Years Ago," *Emory University Quarterly*, 19 (1963), 129–36.

playing musical instruments, tending their formal garden, and reading from the works of such authors as Virgil, John Milton, John Locke, Joseph Addison, Alexander Pope, and Samuel Richardson.[15]

In a pleasure-seeking society like South Carolina, it is not surprising that the people neglected religion. Josiah Quincy, Jr., said, "The state of religion here is repugnant not only to the ordinances and institutions of Jesus Christ, but to every law of sound policy." [16] Quincy undoubtedly exaggerated, but many clergymen echoed his criticism. One Anglican rector inveighed against the "fashionable principles of Libertinism and infidelity"; a second was upset because the "People are not much given to marriage"; and a third reported that in all the marriages he had performed during the last year only two or three of the brides had not been pregnant.[17]

Symptomatic of South Carolina's religious indifference was the failure of the Great Awakening to have any lasting impact on the colony. Despite three visits from George Whitefield the religious revival affected South Carolina less than any other mainland colony. Whitefield's failure was not due entirely to religious indifference, however, for he also faced two other insuperable obstacles. The first was the opposition of Anglican Commissary Alexander Garden. Whitefield's official position was that of rector to the Anglican church at Savannah, a circumstance which placed him under Garden's jurisdiction. When Whitefield's sermons in Charles Town antagonized Garden, the commissary simply hauled Whitefield before an ecclesiastical court and had him suspended from his office.[18] The second obstacle was ridiculous, but perhaps even more decisive. Whitefield's chief disciple in South Carolina was a planter named Hugh Bryan, a religious mystic who let his evangelical fervor get the better of him. He preached to Negro slaves and predicted that they would revolt against their masters and win their freedom. For this he was forced to appear before the assembly, where he promised to mend his ways. Instead, Bryan convinced himself that he was endowed with supernatural powers. He tried, like Moses, to divide the waters of a river with a wand, and when that failed he tried to walk across the river on top of

[15] Eliza Lucas Pinckney Letterbook, Pinckney Papers, S. C. Hist. Soc.

[16] Howe, ed., "Journal of Josiah Quincy, Jr.," Mass. Hist. Soc., *Proceedings*, 49 (1916), 455.

[17] Francis Varnod to Sec. S.P.G., June 29, 1736, Timothy Millechamp to Sec. S.P.G., May 20, 1736, S.P.G. Mss., B. 4, nos. 272, 269; Charles Boschi to Sec. S.P.G, Apr. 7, 1746, Florence G. Geiger, ed., "St. Bartholomew's Parish as Seen by Its Rectors," *S. C. Hist. Mag.*, 50 (1949), 191.

[18] Garden to Bishop of London, Jan. 28, [1742], Feb. 1, 1750, Fulham Palace Mss., S. C., nos. 254, 290.

the water. When news of Bryan's misadventures spread throughout the colony, he became the laughingstock of South Carolina and thereafter few people were able to take evangelism seriously.[19]

The religious indifference of South Carolina was matched by a pervasive intellectual indifference. The colony's active social life left little time for intellectual pursuits, and few Carolinians made the effort necessary to fit such activities into their crowded schedules. There were, however, two groups that stood out as notable exceptions to this generalization. The first were the colony's physicians, who took an active interest in science, especially botany and zoology. The doctors often collected specimens of South Carolina's flora and fauna and sent them to scientists in Europe, and one South Carolina physician, Dr. Alexander Garden, won an international reputation for himself as a biologist. The second group consisted of the merchants, artisans, and professional men who belonged to the Charles Town Library Society. Organized in 1748, the society loaned books to the general public and sponsored scientific experiments. Such men were exceptional, however, and it was more typical of South Carolina that the colony neglected education even by the low standards of the eighteenth century. There were free grammar schools in Charles Town and a few of the rural parishes, but the assembly was notoriously unwilling to spend money on schools and repeatedly turned down petitions to establish them. Rich planters and merchants hired tutors and sent their children to England, but the children of the poor could only attend an inadequate grammar school at best. At worst, in most of the rural parishes, they could not even learn to read and write.[20]

Thus the society of South Carolina was characterized by a whole-hearted devotion to amusement and the neglect of religion and intellectual pursuits. Economic affluence certainly contributed to the formation of such a society, but an even more basic reason for the development of the Carolina society can be found in the colony's religious tradition. The New England and middle colonies had been founded by Calvinistic or pietistic religious dissenters, who took a stern view of earthly pleasures but at the same time believed in the

[19] Garden to Bishop of London, Jan. 28, 1741, *ibid.*, N. C., S. C. and Ga., no. 3; Eliza Lucas to George Lucas, Mar. 11, [1742], Letterbook, 40, Pinckney Papers, S. C. Hist. Soc.; Mar. 3, 1742, Easterby, ed., *Commons Journal, 1741–42*, 461–62.

[20] Bridenbaugh, *Myths and Realities*, 100–108; Wertenbaker, *Golden Age*, 136–41, 145–46; Frederick P. Bowes, *The Culture of Early Charleston* (Chapel Hill, 1942), 34–53; Brooke Hindle, *The Pursuit of Science in Revolutionary America, 1735–1789* (Chapel Hill, 1956), 50–56. On the assembly's attitude, see, e.g., Apr. 13, 1744, Upper House Journal, XII, 47, S. C. Archives; Feb. 1, Mar. 10, 1750, Easterby, ed., *Commons Journal, 1749–50*, 378–79, 448–49.

need for an educated clergy and laity. By contrast, South Carolina at mid-century was predominantly Anglican, and the Church of England made little effort either to regulate the lives of its communicants or to promote intellectual pursuits. Consequently, while colonies like Massachusetts and Pennsylvania had produced socially dull but mentally stimulating societies, South Carolina had developed in just the opposite direction.

II

Charles Town was the political capital of South Carolina as well as its social and economic center, for the provincial government transacted all its business there with only a very few exceptions. Despite its political importance, however, Charles Town did not look like a capital city. There were no public buildings of any kind in the town until the assembly built a state house in 1756. The assembly met in private homes, the governor rented a house, and as the council complained once, "The Courts are kept in Taverns and the Prisons in private Houses." [21]

The arrival of a new governor always created a stir in Charles Town, for the townspeople turned the event into a ceremonial and festive occasion. As the governor's ship sailed into the harbor he was greeted by a barrage of fifteen-, eleven-, and seven-gun salutes from the various forts and batteries. The entire militia regiment of the town turned out in full-dress uniform and lined the streets along which the governor proceeded to the council chamber. The governor then produced his commission, which was read to the people from Granville's Bastion, and the members of the council administered the oaths of office to him. Finally, the governor—along with councilors, assembly members, militia officers, public officials, and "other Gentlemen"— adjourned to one of the better taverns for an informal celebration. By mid-century the welcome had solidified into a formal routine, which did not change even when Governor James Glen was so inconsiderate as to disembark at three o'clock in the morning. [22]

Once the governor had recuperated from his welcome, he began to turn his thoughts to the serious business of government. His position in the provincial government was somewhat ambiguous. He was the chief executive of South Carolina, yet at the same time he was the leading representative of the Crown in the colony. Because of the dual

[21] Nov. 22, 1750, Upper House Journal, CO 5/461, 178–79, PRO.
[22] Dec. 17, 1743, Council Journal, no. 11, 1–2, S. C. Archives.

nature of his position, the governor was often caught in the political crossfire between the conflicting interests of the provincial assembly and the Board of Trade. Moreover, it was his responsibility to reconcile these two forces and to maintain a balance between them. He could best perform this function through compromise when times were normal, but compromise became impossible when either the assembly or the Board of Trade dogmatically insisted on its own point of view. No governor could act effectively under such circumstances.

It was a difficult job at best. The governor held commissions as governor in chief, captain general, and vice-admiral of South Carolina, but as James Glen complained, "Alas! these high-sounding Titles convey very little Power." The governor had almost no power over other public officials. Many were appointed and controlled by the assembly, while many others were commissioned by the Crown and owed their appointments to their patrons in England. During James Glen's term, for example, most of the royal placemen were protégés of the Duke of Newcastle and remained loyal to him. The governor controlled only justices of the peace and militia commissions, which Glen described as "Offices of no Profit and some Trouble, and therefore few will accept of them unless they are much courted." [23] Similarly, the governor had little control over finances. The assembly allowed him to spend money only from a small contingency fund without its consent. It also refused to grant him a permanent salary, although it usually gave him £3,500 currency annually plus house rent on a year-to-year basis.[24]

Although both the assembly and the Crown thus circumscribed the governor's powers, he still enjoyed a high degree of independence. The assembly's control of his salary did not seriously affect him, because he received an additional annual salary of £800 sterling from the Crown plus fees that amounted to about £300 sterling a year. This was more than twice the allowance he received from the assembly.[25] More important, the governor of South Carolina benefited from a tradition of freedom from close supervision by the Crown. The first royal governors had interpreted their instructions as recommendations, not as orders to be obeyed literally. Governors Nicholson and Johnson had ignored or even disobeyed their instructions on several occasions, and

[23] Glen, *Description*, in Milling, ed., *Colonial S. C.*, 40–42; see also Arthur B. Keith, *Constitutional History of the First British Empire* (Oxford, 1930), 199, 201.

[24] Smith, *S. C. as Royal Province*, 75–77, 80–81.

[25] *Ibid.*, 77; Clarence J. Attig, William Henry Lyttelton: A Study in Colonial Administration (unpubl. Ph.D. diss., University of Nebraska, 1958), 63.

the Board of Trade had made no attempt to reprimand them. The Board had accepted a passive role in the government of South Carolina and allowed the governors to act as independent executives. It had questioned a governor's decisions only if international or intercolonial affairs were involved, as in the Georgia disputes, or if the governor antagonized a powerful clique, as in the currency disputes. In short, the Board of Trade had consistently exercised only a minimum of supervision over the governors of South Carolina.

Most of South Carolina's royal governors left the imprints of their personalities on the governorship, and no governor did so more completely than James Glen. Glen held the office of governor for twelve and a half critical years, longer than any other man in the history of South Carolina. Forty-two years old when he disembarked at Charles Town in 1743, he was a Scottish lawyer who had attended the University of Leyden.[26] To the historian, Glen's most obvious trait was a compulsive urge to explain himself, an urge which expressed itself in long, rambling letters to the authorities at home. The letters laid bare Glen's personality and showed that he was a man with a pathetically eager desire to please. Although he was not wealthy he often spent his own money on public projects in the hope that his obvious concern for the public good would please both the people and the Crown. Glen's desire to please made him try to present himself in the best possible light even at the cost of the truth. Once, when the assembly presented him with a routine resolution of appreciation, he grossly misrepresented the importance of the resolution in his report to the Board of Trade. He wrote, "No Governour has hitherto had cause to Glory in the Complaisance of their Addresses to him." [27] There were more attractive sides to Glen's personality, however, particularly the zeal with which he performed his duties. He spent most of his first months in South Carolina reading the assembly journals so that he could be "master of their Affairs," and as soon as he could break away from Charles Town he toured the entire colony, visiting parts of it that no previous governor had ever seen.[28]

As a lawyer Glen prided himself on his knowledge of the British constitution, and he found much in the South Carolina constitution

[26] Mary F. Carter, Governor James Glen of Colonial South Carolina: A Study in British Administrative Policies (unpubl. Ph.D. diss., University of California, Los Angeles, 1951) , 1.

[27] Glen to Bd. of Trade, July 15, 1751, S. C. Pub. Recs., XXIV, 347, S. C. Archives; see also Carter, James Glen, 170.

[28] Glen to Newcastle, Feb. 6, 1744, Feb. 11, 1746, S. C. Pub. Recs., XXI, 242, XXII, 133–38, S. C. Archives.

that was contrary to English practice. In fact, he complained that on his arrival in the colony he "found the whole frame of Government unhinged." [29] Among the many customs Glen objected to were voting by secret ballot, the property tax, the length of assembly sessions, and the practice of basing assembly representation on population. Most of all Glen objected to the governor's lack of power. He thought the assembly had encroached too far on the royal prerogative, he wanted to control lesser public officials, and he insisted that the upper house did not have the right to exclude him from its legislative sessions.[30] It is not surprising that Glen spent a good portion of his term in office agitating for a return to what he regarded as sound constitutional practice.

The governor shared his executive authority with the council, which sat also as the upper house of assembly and the court of chancery.[31] The council consisted of twelve men appointed by the Privy Council upon nomination by the Board of Trade. The Board had long ago established the criteria that councilors should be "men of good life and well affected to our government and of good estates and abilities and not necessitous persons or much in debt." Three thousand miles of ocean made it hard for the Board to apply its criteria, however, and it once mistakenly appointed a French citizen, Hector Beringer de Beaufain, a Huguenot immigrant who had neglected to take the oaths of naturalization. The Board tried to handle the problem of distance by keeping a list of men who would be qualified to fill vacancies on the council. It solicited recommendations from the governor and other men acquainted with South Carolina, but in practice it usually had only two or three names on hand when a vacancy occurred. Even then the Board often ignored its list of formal nominations and chose someone else, most likely someone who knew a member of the Board. In fact, it selected almost one-third of South Carolina's royal councilors in this informal way.

The politicians who sat on the council represented a cross-section of the wealthiest families in the gentry. Forty-nine men were appointed

[29] Glen to Bd. of Trade, Feb. 6, 1744, ibid., XXI, 235.

[30] Ibid., 236–40; Glen to Duke of Bedford, Oct. 10, 1748, Glen, "An Attempt towards an Estimate of the value of South Carolina," Mar. 1751, ibid., XXIII, 241, XXIV, 321–22; May 29, 1744, Easterby, ed., Commons Journal, 1744–45, 203; Glen, Description, in Milling, ed., Colonial S. C., 40–41; Osgood, 18th Century, IV, 142–43.

[31] Except where otherwise noted, the following discussion of the council is based upon Sirmans, "S. C. Royal Council," Wm. and Mary Qtly., 3d Ser., 18 (1961), 373–84.

to the South Carolina council between 1720 and 1763, and an indication of their wealth may be gained from the remaining records of their landholdings and slave ownership and from inventories of the estates of seventeen councilors. The average value of the seventeen estates for which there are inventories was £9,022 sterling, and a majority of the estates were worth between £5,000 and £12,000 sterling. The average slaveholding for eighteen councilors was 172 slaves, and the average landholding for all councilors was 7,750 acres. It should be pointed out, however, that estate inventories estimated only the value of the decedent's personal property and ignored his real estate. Therefore, if a man had invested a large portion of his capital in land, the inventory would cover only a fraction of his total worth. It is quite possible that the total value of a large landowner's estate would be twice the amount given in the inventory.[32] As for occupational groups, the council membership from 1720 to 1763 included eighteen planters, sixteen merchants, nine placemen, four lawyers, one professional soldier, and one man whose occupation is not known. As might be expected, the planters owned more land than other councilors but less personal property. The average value of the personal estates of seven planters was about £6,500 sterling, which included some 150 slaves, and the average landholding of all the planters was 12,000 acres. With such large investments in land, however, the total average value of the planters' estates was certainly much more than £6,500. The merchants owned more personal property than the planters, for the average value of the personal estates of six merchants was £7,500 sterling. The lawyers may have been the wealthiest group of all, for two of them left personal estates worth about £12,000 sterling and the other two lawyers were even more prominent in the South Carolina bar. Merchants and lawyers followed no set pattern in investing in land and slaves; some invested heavily and others not at all. Nothing is known about the wealth of the placemen, except that they rarely invested in slaves or land. In the 1730's and 1740's there were never more than two placemen on the council at one time, usually the chief justice and the provincial secretary.

Council membership was not simply a question of wealth, however. Political influence in England counted for more, and two groups of South Carolinians displayed a special talent for obtaining council

[32] For example, William Bull, Jr., who owned nearly 14,000 acres of land, plus other real estate in Charles Town and Beaufort, estimated the value of his personal property in 1784 at £27,440 sterling and the value of his real property at £24,100 sterling; see Henry D. Bull, *The Family of Stephen Bull . . . , 1600–1960* (Georgetown, S. C., 1961), 56–58.

appointments. The first was an inter-related, intermarried clan of six native planter families that filled more than a third of the seats on the council, a total of nineteen between 1720 and 1763. The six families were the Blakes, Bulls, Draytons, Fenwickes, Izards, and Middletons. Most members of these families were related to each other in one way or another; for example, William Bull, Sr., had three daughters and two nieces who married, respectively, two Draytons, two Middletons, and an Izard. These families acquired their influence by controlling the governorship; both Robert Johnson and William Bull, Sr., belonged to the clan and helped their kinsmen to obtain seats on the council. The second bloc was the mercantile elite of Charles Town, which supplied about one-fifth of the councilors appointed between 1720 and 1763. Business partnerships, rather than family ties, bound the members of this group together. A few merchants constituted almost an interlocking directorate of Charles Town business in the mid-eighteenth century, and although they often formed new partnerships they always elected other merchants in the business elite as their partners. Seventeen merchants can be identified as members of this group, and ten of them became councilors. Most of them had immigrated from England, and they cultivated influence with the Board of Trade through their relatives and partners in England.

Men who did not belong to either bloc had a difficult time obtaining council appointments, especially after 1730. Only placemen and lawyers managed consistently to secure council seats without such connections. Of the fourteen outsiders appointed between 1730 and 1763, eight were placemen, four were lawyers, two were merchants, and none were planters. Placemen could obtain appointments through their contacts in England, while lawyers depended upon winning the favor of the governor and always had to prove their political ability by serving apprenticeships in the Commons House. By contrast, merchant John Fenwicke secured his son's appointment to the council simply by asking the Board of Trade for it.

Whatever their backgrounds the South Carolina councilors had built up a strong tradition of independence for the council, a tradition which owed much of its vigor to the events of the 1720's. The mere transfer from proprietary to royal government had strengthened the council, because royal councilors served during good behavior while proprietary councilors had served during pleasure and had often lost their positions for disagreeing with the proprietors. Francis Nicholson had further enhanced the council's prestige by his constant deference to it. Even the paper money riots had helped the council, because it had acted as the bastion of conservative government, which appealed to the wealthier colonists. Since the 1720's the council had been challenged only by the Commons House. It had lost the power to amend money bills, but it still retained the right to propose amendments and it had excluded the governor from its legislative sessions. Thus, in the 1740's the council still enjoyed its autonomy, and as a result it was respected by the people of the colony. Men valued a council appointment above any other political office, even though councilors were not paid. For example, councilor Edmund Atkin turned down a nomination for the very lucrative post of public treasurer, because he would have had to resign his council seat in order to accept it.[33] Members of the council were generally satisfied with their prestige and independence, and they were less likely to demand political change than either Governor Glen or the Commons House. When they were challenged, however, they defended the council and even counter-attacked with spirit and ability.

III

While the council was satisfied with the status quo and Governor Glen hoped for a return to a more constitutional past, the Commons House of Assembly looked to the future. Like Glen, the lower house disliked the existing distribution of power, but unlike him, it showed little interest in the past. Instead it looked forward to the continued expansion of its powers at the expense of both governor and council. It is not surprising, therefore, that the driving ambition of the Commons House made it the most volatile element in the provincial government.

The governor and council represented the interests of the Crown in varying degrees, but the Commons House truly represented the interests of the people of South Carolina. Elections to the house were governed by the election act of 1721, which was the absolute authority on elections and took precedence even over the governor's writs and proclamations.[34] There are no useful election statistics for the colonial period in South Carolina, but the act of 1721 apparently established, in practice, universal suffrage for white freemen. Any freeman could vote if he owned fifty acres of land or paid 20s. currency in taxes. The Crown continued the old practice of granting a fifty-acre headright to anyone who applied for it until the Revolution, while the provincial

---

[33] Mar. 24, 1743, Upper House Journal, X, 57, S. C. Archives.

[34] See, e.g., Nov. 18–19, 1742, Easterby, ed., Commons Journal, 1742–44, 30, 35–39; the act of 1721 is in Cooper and McCord, eds., Statutes, III, 135–40.

government levied a capitation tax of 20s. currency on every free adult male. Thus, any white freeman over the age of twenty-one could vote if he wanted to.[35] In addition, representation in the assembly was apportioned roughly according to population. The act of 1721 had set the number of representatives for each parish according to its estimated population, and the assembly followed the same principle whenever it created new parishes. In the early 1740's forty assemblymen represented fourteen parishes, and after the creation of two new parishes in 1745 and 1747 there were forty-four representatives in the Commons House. The least democratic feature of the act of 1721 was the requirement for assembly membership. A man had to own 500 acres of land and ten slaves or real estate worth £1,000 currency to be eligible for a seat in the Commons House. The requirement undoubtedly excluded many men from the assembly, especially in Charles Town, but in view of South Carolina's high per capita rates of income and property ownership, it is possible that nearly half the white adult males could qualify for the Commons House.

The election act of 1721 also set limits on the life of an assembly and established electoral procedures. The law provided for triennial elections; no assembly could sit for more than three years, although the governor could dissolve it sooner. When an assembly was dissolved the governor issued election writs to the churchwardens of each parish, who were responsible for conducting elections. The churchwardens opened the polls at the parish church on the day specified in the writ. The polls remained open two days, and voting was by secret ballot. The churchwardens then announced the results informally and later formally presented both the results and the election writ to the first meeting of the new assembly. The Commons House completed the election procedure by certifying and validating the election returns. The house believed that it had the sole right to judge disputed elections, like the English House of Commons; it investigated such disputes by itself, and neither the governor nor the council had ever really challenged its right to do so.

The newly elected assembly met in Charles Town on the day set by the governor in the writs of election; and as soon as its quorum of nineteen members was present the Commons House began to organize itself. After a quorum had assembled the members of the house

[35] Glen to Bd. of Trade, Dec. 23, 1749, S. C. Pub. Recs., XXIII, 438, S. C. Archives; S-C. Gaz. (Charles Town), Jan. 6, 1748; Edmund Atkin, "Wrong Practices in the Government of South Carolina," in Jack P. Greene, ed., "South Carolina's Colonial Constitution: Two Proposals for Reform," S. C. Hist. Mag., 62 (1961), 76. On headrights, see Labaree, ed., Royal Instructions, II, 564–67, 570.

presented themselves to the governor and took the oath of allegiance to the British Crown. They then returned to their meeting room, and a justice of the peace swore them in as members of the assembly. The governor next directed the house to elect a speaker, and after the election the house presented him to the governor for his approval. In contrast to some of the other colonies, the governor's approval was a formality, for no governor of South Carolina had ever rejected a speaker-elect. The new speaker then requested the governor to allow the Commons House its old privileges and asked that his personal shortcomings not be attributed to the house. This ceremony completed the formal organization of the Commons House, and the assembly was at last ready to go to work.

The Commons House conducted its meetings in a most informal manner. Josiah Quincy, Jr., of Massachusetts observed one of its sessions in 1773 and reported, "The members conversed, lolled, and chatted much like a friendly jovial society." He also said that the members wore their hats while they were sitting and took them off when they rose to speak. They spoke from anywhere in the chamber rather than going to the front. The house still retained one of its oldest and most unusual customs at the time of Quincy's visit: In formal votes the ayes rose to their feet while the nays remained seated.[36]

Josiah Quincy was not impressed with the Commons House, and it seems likely he let himself be misled by its lack of formality. In actual fact, the South Carolina Commons House was probably the hardest working assembly in the American colonies. The election law of 1721 required the assembly to meet at least once every six months, and the governor always called sessions in the winter and fall when planters were in Charles Town for pleasure or business. The winter session was the more important, for the assembly considered the annual tax bill and most of its other regular business at that time. Consequently, winter sessions often lasted from January to June. The governor also called emergency sessions when they were necessary, and as a result it was not unusual for the assembly to sit eight months out of the year. No other colonial assembly endured such long sessions. When in session the Commons House usually met six days a week for at least six hours a day; it normally convened at 9:00 A.M. and sat until 5:00 P.M. with a two-hour break at noon. The length of the sessions made it difficult for planters to attend regularly, and the house had to make

[36] Howe, ed., "Journal of Josiah Quincy, Jr.," Mass. Hist. Soc., *Proceedings*, 49 (1916), 452.

accommodations for them. It often adjourned for one to three weeks in the planting and harvest seasons, and it allowed planters to go home on weekends without penalty, although this made it hard to find a quorum on Fridays, Saturdays, and Mondays.

The Commons House carried on much of its business in committees. Committees were so important that the house would occasionally adjourn for the day and order all committees into session. Among the most important committees were the standing committees, which remained in existence throughout the life of the assembly and dealt with such subjects as privileges and elections, grievances, Indian affairs, trade, religion, the courts, and correspondence with the colonial agents. There were also a number of annual committees, which existed for only a year but performed the functions of standing committees during that time. The most important of them were the financial committees, including those to consider petitions and accounts, to draw up an estimate on the tax bill, and to inspect the accounts of financial officers responsible to the assembly. The speaker also appointed a special committee for every bill that came before the house and for every petition that did not involve the tax bill. When needed he also appointed special conference committees, which met with similar committees from the council. Conference committees were particularly useful, because they enabled the two houses to compose their differences and because they frequently wrote the final drafts of legislation. Finally, there were a few extra-sessionary committees, such as those for Indian affairs and correspondence, which were empowered to transact business on behalf of the assembly during legislative recesses. Although extra-sessionary committees included council members as well as representatives from the Commons House, they were controlled by the lower house because it appointed more members than the council. A variant of the committee system extended even beyond the legislative process. The assembly created many permanent commissions to perform specific jobs, such as stamping and signing paper currency, building and repairing fortifications and roads, and supervising the affairs of the Church of England. Such commissions were supposed to be responsible to the assembly, but commissioners were not paid and the assembly often could not control them.[37]

The most important legislation considered by every assembly was the annual tax bill, which provided the provincial government with its operating income. Import and export duties raised an additional

[37] William Bull, Jr., to Earl of Hillsborough, Nov. 30, 1770, S. C. Pub. Recs., XXXII, 372, 404-5, S. C. Archives; Greene, *Quest for Power*, 93-95, 252-56.

income, but it was permanently earmarked for such specific purposes as the township fund. The South Carolina assembly operated on credit. The tax bill did not appropriate money for the coming year, except for a small contingency fund; it paid off the previous year's debts. Individuals who performed services for the colony or sold goods to it were not paid in cash. Instead they presented petitions to the next assembly in which they requested payment. The committee on petitions and accounts scrutinized each claim on the public and accepted it, rejected it, or accepted it and reduced the amount. The full house then reviewed every item in the committee's report and referred the accepted claims to the committee on the estimate. This committee tabulated the claims and calculated the amount of money needed to pay the colony's debts. Meanwhile a third committee had examined the public treasurer's account and reported on the amount of money still in the treasury. Finally, a fourth committee drew up a tax bill that would make up the difference.[38]

The assembly had not always handled the tax bill in this manner. It had appropriated funds in advance through 1731, but beginning in 1733 it had changed to the credit system. The change increased the assembly's power at the expense of the governor, because the government could not spend any money without the assembly's approval of almost every specific item. The Board of Trade objected to credit financing for this reason, but no governor was ever able to persuade the assembly to relinquish its control. Until 1737 the council had participated equally in writing the tax bill, and all the financial committees were joint committees representing both houses. The council had lost this right in the legislative disputes of the late thirties, however, and in the 1740's it could only suggest amendments or reject the tax bill as a whole. As a result of both developments, the Commons House was able to control the tax bill without effective outside interference.[39]

The contents of the tax bill varied little from year to year, except that taxes rose during wars. Peacetime budgets fluctuated between £30,000 and £40,000 currency per year, while wartime budgets went as high as £60,000. Expenditures for defense and salaries for officials dominated the budget in peace; each accounted for about one-third the total appropriations. In wartime military expenses consumed half

[38] Smith, *S. C. as Royal Province*, 280–82; Greene, *Quest for Power*, 53.
[39] Keith, *First British Empire*, 208; Greene, *Quest for Power*, 53–54; Bd. of Trade to Glen, Nov. 15, 1750, Glen to Bd. of Trade, July 27, 1752, S. C. Pub. Recs., XXIV, 173–74, XXV, 79–80, S. C. Archives.

the budget or more. Tax bills also delineated the type of taxes collected and the method of collection. The bills levied a property tax on slaves and land, appointed appraisers and collectors, and set penalties for non-payment or fraud. Charles Town posed special problems, because the wealth of many of its inhabitants was in personal property and often in money on loan. The assembly estimated that roughly one-sixth of the colony's wealth was owned by residents of the town, and tax bills therefore directed that they pay one-sixth of the taxes. Appraisers for the town calculated the total real and personal estates of each property owner and then apportioned taxes accordingly. If an estimate made by Governor Glen was correct, taxes were light. Glen said that South Carolina taxpayers paid only 2½ to 5 per cent of their annual income in taxes.[40]

The assembly wielded broad powers in many areas besides finances. Members of the assembly considered it the only body with the authority to legislate for South Carolina and recognized few limits on its sphere of activity. The Commons House reiterated again and again its belief that even acts of Parliament were invalid in South Carolina unless the assembly re-enacted them or unless Parliament specifically made them applicable to the colonies.[41] No governor or other royal official had ever attempted to debate the assembly on this point. The assembly's power over the people of the colony was also extensive, especially in economics. Such diverse matters as the regulation of lawyers' fees, building codes for Charles Town, the conduct of seamen, regulation of retail merchandising, the tenure of church pews, and a program of farm subsidies came within the purview of the assembly. The South Carolina assembly typified other colonial assemblies in the scope of its powers, but it also concerned itself with a wide range of strictly local problems that was unusual in the colonies. There was little local government in South Carolina, and the assembly had to become involved in such matters as the operation of ferries and the construction and repair of churches. Other assemblies delegated these problems to county commissions or town meetings, but the South Carolina assembly was reluctant to delegate authority to anyone. As a result it considered more purely local problems than any other colonial assembly.

In spite of the political power vested in the Commons House of

[40] To Duke of Bedford, Oct. 10, 1748, S. C. Pub. Recs., XXIII, 233, S. C. Archives; for examples of tax bills, see Cooper and McCord, eds., *Statutes*, III, 438–48, 472–85, 527–41.

[41] See, e.g., Dec. 10, 1737, Easterby, ed., *Commons Journal, 1736–39*, 356; Mar. 5, 1740, *ibid., 1739–41*, 239.

Assembly, few South Carolinians cared to become members of it. Many of the same men who eagerly solicited council appointments shunned the lower house as much as they could. Josiah Quincy in 1773 reported accurately a sentiment that had prevailed in South Carolina for over three decades. Speaking of the majority of men in the colony, he said, "Political inquiries and philosophic disquisitions are too laborious for them: they have no great passion for to shine and blaze in the forum or a senate." [42] The reasons for such a lack of interest in politics are not hard to find. Legislative sessions were long, and members of the Commons House, like members of the council, served without pay. Perhaps an even weightier reason may be found in a parallel to South Carolina's neglect of intellectual pursuits. Just as the colony's busy social life left little time for reading or study, so it also left little time for public affairs. Whatever the reasons, political apathy was strongest among the wealthy planters. Such families as the Izards, Fenwickes, Blakes, and Warings refused to serve in the Commons House, although earlier generations of the same families had once dominated it. Among the large planters only the Bull family, along with its nearest in-laws, the Draytons and the Middletons, continued to seek public office.

The results of South Carolina's political disinterest were uniformly unfortunate for the Commons House. As several commentators observed, "many Persons of Property and Figure" refused to serve in the house if they were elected to it.[43] Many parishes had to hold elections two or three times before they could find men who were willing to serve, and some assembly seats were never filled. About one-fourth of all the men elected to the assembly in the 1730's and 1740's refused to accept their seats. Moreover, the great majority of men who served in the Commons House sat for one term only, and there was an extremely rapid turnover in the membership of the house. Between 1730 and 1750 a majority of every Commons House was composed of men who had never served in the assembly before and never did so again. The proportion of one-term members occasionally rose as high as two-thirds of the house. The parish of St. James Goose Creek, once the center of political power, exemplified the electoral trends at mid-century. The parish was entitled to four seats in the Commons House, and for the three assemblies that met between 1736 and 1745, the parish elected a total of sixteen men in order to fill all four seats in each

[42] Howe, ed., "Journal of Josiah Quincy, Jr.," Mass. Hist. Soc., *Proceedings*, 49 (1916), 455; see also Greene, *Quest for Power*, 38.

[43] Testimony of Alexander Vander Dussen, Bd. of Trade Minutes, May 25, 1748, S. C. Pub. Recs., XXIII, 15, S. C. Archives; see also *S.-C. Gaz.* (Charles Town), Jan. 6, 1748.

assembly. Six of the sixteen men refused to serve at all, eight served only one term, and only two served two terms.

Other results of the widespread apathy were equally harmful to the Commons House. Although the quorum of the house was set at only nineteen members, less than half the membership, it was often difficult to assemble a quorum. This frequently meant that the public business was delayed, and the governor often had to prorogue the assembly to a better time. Two assemblies, those elected in 1747 and 1749, never managed to muster a quorum and were dissolved by the governor without ever meeting officially.[44] Finally, elections aroused little interest because few men cared enough to campaign for office. The electorate's problem was not choosing between candidates but finding qualified men who would agree to their election. The voters occasionally even elected a man without his knowing it. Few men bothered to vote, and in a few cases assembly members were elected solely by the votes of the two churchwardens in the parish.[45]

Only two parishes in the colony showed any real interest in politics. One was St. Philip's, the Charles Town parish, where there were many merchants and lawyers who wanted to sit in the Commons House. The other was St. Andrew's, which was located just across the Ashley River from Charles Town and was the home of the Bulls, Draytons, and Middletons. These two parishes usually returned the same assemblymen, almost no one refused to sit in the assembly, and elections were contested, often in a spirited manner. In fact, politicians from St. Philip's and St. Andrew's often preferred to avoid campaigns altogether by sitting for other parishes in which they owned land and slaves.

A comparatively few men accepted the burdens of assembly membership willingly, and they became the leaders of the Commons House.[46] Their presence helped to compensate for the rapid turnover in membership, but the South Carolina Commons did not have the continuity of leadership that was common to other colonial assemblies, such as the Virginia House of Burgesses, because many leaders accepted seats in the house only on a sporadic basis. For example,

[44] Glen to Duke of Bedford, Oct. 17, 1748, S. C. Pub. Recs., XXIII, 244–45, S. C. Archives; S-C. Gaz. (Charles Town), Jan. 6, 1748, Feb. 25, 1749.

[45] S-C. Gaz. (Charles Town), Jan. 6, 1748, Mar. 27, 1762.

[46] For a list of these leaders, see Greene, Quest for Power, 475–88. I have omitted the assembly of 1731–33, because it was transitional. The men who had dominated the Commons House in the late 1720's continued to do so in 1731, but in 1732 they began to give way to the younger men who led the house in the 1730's and 1740's. The transition was complete by 1733.

merchant Peter Taylor became an influential leader in the house almost every time he sat in it, but he was not willing to serve regularly. He was an active leader from 1733 to 1739, sat out the assembly of 1739–1742, returned from 1742 to 1745, retired for four years, served in the assembly of 1749–1751, skipped the next two assemblies, and returned to active duty from 1757 to 1762. Other men served more regularly, notably Benjamin Whitaker and Isaac Mazyck, but Taylor's in-and-out pattern of leadership was more common.

The occupations of the leaders in the Commons House differed radically from those of council members. Merchants and lawyers dominated the lower house's leadership, while the great majority of planters were content to remain back-benchers. Twenty-two men emerged as leaders of the Commons House between 1733 and 1751, and in that number there were eleven merchants, six lawyers, four planters, and one physician. Furthermore, saying that four planters became leaders in the house actually exaggerates the importance of the planters. Three of the four planters held positions of leadership for only one year; William Bull, Jr., was the only planter in South Carolina who played a major role in the affairs of the Commons House between 1733 and 1751. As might be expected of a group dominated by townsmen, the leaders of the Commons House owned more personal property but fewer slaves than the members of the council; the average amount of landowning was about the same in both houses. Sixteen house leaders owned an average of 7,600 acres of land. The average value of the personal estates of nine lower house leaders was £11,816 sterling, while seven house leaders owned an average of 121 slaves. Thus, the leaders of the Commons House were probably as wealthy as the members of the council, but they invested more of their capital in personal property than the councilors did.[47]

Merchants and lawyers accepted the responsibilities of assembly leadership for several reasons. Most obviously, the merchants and lawyers lived in Charles Town and found legislative sessions less onerous than planters did. Moreover, lawyers regarded assembly service as a means of social and economic advancement. In South Carolina as in other colonies, law was the profession chosen by many

[47] The 22 leaders were merchants George Austin, Othniel Beale, Jacob Bond, William Cattell, Jr., Daniel Crawford, John Dart, Paul Jenys, Gabriel Manigault, Isaac Mazyck, Benjamin Smith, and Peter Taylor; lawyers James Graeme, Maurice Lewis, James Michie, Charles Pinckney, Andrew Rutledge, and Benjamin Whitaker; planters William Bull, Jr., William Drake, Henry Hyrne, and Henry Middleton; and Dr. John Rutledge. It should be pointed out that the data on the wealth of the Commons leaders are less complete than those for the council.

ambitious young men who lacked family influence. Assembly service was an important step upwards, because it gave a young lawyer a chance both to widen his circle of friends and to prove his political ability and social acceptability. Such families as the Pinckneys and Rutledges acquired social as well as political prominence in the middle of the eighteenth century by advancing through the legal profession and assembly service. Many young merchants also regarded public service as a means of advancement, especially the Huguenots such as Henry Laurens and Gabriel Manigault. In addition, even well-established merchants believed that the mercantile community had special economic interests that must be protected in the assembly. For example, the *South-Carolina Gazette* published in 1741 a long letter from an anonymous correspondent, who pleaded with the voters of Charles Town to elect merchants to represent them in the assembly. He argued that merchants "ought to be better Judges of the Concerns of [Trade], and of the Consequences which flow from particular Laws made relating thereto, than those who are unskill'd in the Practice, and have their Learning therein only from Books and casual Conversation." [48]

The anonymous correspondent was something of an alarmist, for disputes over economic issues became increasingly rare after about 1740. When such issues did appear, however, an interesting thing happened. A majority of the members of the Commons House were planters, but most of the time they were content to remain back-benchers and let the merchants and lawyers control proceedings. When a clear-cut division between trade and agriculture appeared, however, the planters roused themselves and voted down their urban colleagues. Thus, after a committee reported in 1742 that the inhabitants of Charles Town owned one-fifth of the property in South Carolina, the Commons House voted that Charles Town must pay one-fifth of the provincial taxes. Merchants and lawyers objected to the change but were ignored. In 1743 a group of Charles Town merchants and lawyers wanted to operate a silver mine in the Appalachian Mountains. Although several assembly leaders owned shares in the mine, the Commons voted to close it in order to prevent trouble with the Cherokees. In 1748 the assembly reduced the interest on loans from 10 per cent to 8 per cent over the opposition of Charles Town's merchants. The normally acquiescent planters in the Commons House thus proved on each of these occasions that they could revolt

[48] *S.-C. Gaz.* (Charles Town), Nov. 7, 1741, Postscript.

successfully against the merchant-lawyer leadership of the house.[49]

Merchants or planters, leaders or back-benchers, the majority of the members of the Commons House were dedicated to the proposition that the powers of the house should be expanded at the expense of the governor and council. No other fact about the Commons House in the middle of the eighteenth century is so obvious. Indeed, resolutions favoring extension of the house's authority usually passed unanimously. The reasons for what has been called this "quest for power" are less obvious, however, because the members of the house never articulated their goals and motives. The question of purpose and motivation must therefore remain at least partially obscure, but certain observations about the members of the South Carolina Commons House, as well as other colonial representative assemblies, seem valid and pertinent. Both Americans and Britons of the eighteenth century distrusted the concentration of power in a single person or institution, because they feared such power would inevitably be abused. Whenever Englishmen encountered excessive power, whether at home or in the colonies, they wanted to place it under formal, constitutional restraints. The memory of Stuart despotism and the Glorious Revolution of 1688 made it natural for Americans and Englishmen to look with special distrust at the Crown and its representatives. Thus, members of the elected assemblies in South Carolina and other colonies were simply following the example set by Parliament in the previous century by restricting the prerogatives of the Crown and its colonial representatives, the governor and the council. It might be said, in other words, that the colonial lower houses sought to achieve a balance of powers within the imperial framework in which constitutional safeguards would protect local rights and privileges.[50]

Whatever the motives of the assembly members, their drive to extend their authority was overpowering. Members of the house who did not agree with the dominant opinion were forced to go along with the majority in public if they hoped to acquire any political influence at all. For example, Benjamin Whitaker drafted some of the most demanding statements ever written about the rights of the Commons

[49] Mar. 3, 5, 1742, Easterby, ed., *Commons Journal, 1741–42*, 459, 469; Oct. 10–11, 1743, *ibid., 1742–44*, 473–77; Henry Laurens to William Stone, May 18, 1748, "Laurens Correspondence," *S. C. Hist. Mag.*, 30 (1929), 147.

[50] The best discussion of this question is Jack P. Greene's review of F. G. Spurdle, *Early West Indian Government: Showing the Progress of Government in Barbados, Jamaica, and the Leeward Islands, 1660–1783* (Palmerston North, N.Z., 1963), in *Wm. and Mary Qtly.*, 3d Ser., 22 (1965), 146–49.

House, and he occupied the speaker's chair from 1742 to 1744. In private, however, Whitaker believed the assembly possessed no inherent rights; its prerogatives were nothing more than special privileges granted by the Crown. He once wrote, "All Acts of Assembly are made by an Authority derived from the Crown," and he advocated that royal judges review all colonial legislation as soon as it was passed.[51]

IV

While the Commons House of Assembly flourished and expanded its powers, South Carolina's local government and judicial system failed to mature at all. There were few local political institutions, and those that existed depended upon the assembly for their authority and most of their money. Similarly, the provincial court system was centered in Charles Town, and the assembly blocked its expansion.

The parishes of the Church of England were the most important units of local government. Each parish was run by two churchwardens and twelve vestrymen, who were elected every Easter Monday by the voters of the parish. In rural parishes the vestries met only four times a year and had few responsibilities. They did little more than repair church buildings, and they lacked the power to levy taxes or raise money in other ways. The vestries depended upon annual grants from the assembly for their income, and when major repairs or new buildings were needed they petitioned the assembly for additional appropriations. The two churchwardens in each parish had somewhat more power and responsibility. They supervised assembly elections, took care of charity cases, and assessed the parishioners for a poor tax. Churchwardens were not much busier than vestrymen, however, because assembly elections usually came only once every three years and there were normally only two or three charity cases a year.[52] St. Philip's Parish in Charles Town differed from the rural parishes, because the parish was the only form of government in the city. Like rural parishes the city parish cared for the poor and for orphaned or illegitimate children, but charity cases were much more numerous in town. Vestrymen and churchwardens met as often as twice a week, and

---

[51] To [Henry McCulloh], Feb. 3, 1743, S. C. Pub. Recs., XXI, 136–37, S. C. Archives.

[52] Alexander S. Salley, Jr., ed., *Minutes of the Vestry of St. Helena's Parish, South Carolina, 1726–1812* (Columbia, 1919) ; St. Stephen's Parish Vestry Book, 1754–1858, Minutes of the Vestry of St. John's Parish, Berkeley County, 1731–1813, S. C. Hist. Soc. (microfilm) ; see also William Bull, Jr., to Earl of Hillsborough, Nov. 30, 1770, S. C. Pub. Recs., XXXII, 366, S. C. Archives.

they found it necessary to build a workhouse and hospital for the poor, rent an orphanage, and hire a doctor.[53]

The only other unit of local government was the road commission. There was at least one commission in every parish, and the assembly had divided the larger parishes into precincts. The commissions were responsible for building and maintaining all public roads, ferries, bridges, and waterways within their jurisdictions. They had the power to assess taxes for road work and could requisition the services of every slave in the district for six days a year. The authority of the road commissions was limited, however, because the assembly appointed commissioners and many specific questions, such as appointing ferry keepers and setting ferriage rates, were referred to the assembly. In spite of its drawbacks the road system was successful, and South Carolina enjoyed one of the best networks of internal roads in colonial America.[54]

Like other branches of government, the South Carolina judiciary was highly centralized. Three courts sat in Charles Town: the Court of General Sessions, which tried criminal cases; the Court of Common Pleas, which tried civil suits; and the Court of Chancery, which tried cases in equity. The Courts of General Sessions and Common Pleas were presided over by the chief justice and four assistant justices, who were usually laymen and served without pay. The Chancery Court was the governor and council. The Crown had also empowered the Chancery Court to hear appeals from lower courts, but there were no appeals before the 1760's. No courts existed outside Charles Town. There were only a few justices of the peace, who tried cases relating to slaves, misdemeanors, and debt cases of less than £20 currency. The justices of the peace never met together as county courts, they performed no administrative duties except the licensing of taverns, and the office never attained the importance it had in other colonies.[55]

The South Carolina Commons House was entirely satisfied with political centralization and resisted every attempt to strengthen local government. It received many petitions complaining of the hardships caused by the lack of local political institutions from 1740 to 1763, but

---

[53] Minutes of the Vestry of St. Philip's Parish, 1732–1775, St. Philip's Parish House, Charleston; Bridenbaugh, *Cities in the Wilderness*, 396.

[54] Cooper and McCord, eds., *Statutes*, IX, 126–32; Loewald *et al.*, eds., "Bolzius Questionnaire," *Wm. and Mary Qtly.*, 3d Ser., 14 (1957), 227, 232.

[55] William Bull, Jr., to Earl of Hillsborough, Nov. 30, 1770, S. C. Pub. Recs., XXXII, 366, 375–78, 381, 404–5, S. C. Archives; William Simpson, *The Practical Justice of the Peace and Parish-Officer, of His Majesty's Province of South-Carolina* (Charles Town, 1761).

it ignored them all. For example, it rejected a proposal for the local election of road commissioners, it voted against erecting courts outside Charles Town, and it ignored a bill to increase the taxing powers of parish vestries.[56] The Commons House was apparently so jealous of its rights and privileges that it would not share them with anyone, not even a parish vestry. Besides, an extension of local government, especially local courts, would have inconvenienced the influential city merchants and lawyers in the house. The assembly ultimately clung to its power over local affairs too long, for the inadequacy of local government was a major cause of the Regulator movement of the 1760's.

V

The government of eighteenth-century South Carolina operated in a climate of political morality that would not be acceptable today. The difference is, however, not in the behavior of politicians, but rather in the public tolerance of self-seeking ambition. Eighteenth-century politicians admitted their personal motives openly, especially their economic ambitions, and they candidly voiced their belief that a public office was an opportunity for personal profit, not a public trust. English politics frankly depended upon patronage and profits, and colonial politicians accepted English mores with few reservations. Political scandals occasionally developed when someone crossed the thin line separating acceptable and unacceptable use of public office. The best known colonial scandal occurred when Speaker John Robinson of Virginia loaned public funds to his friends, but even Robinson had his defenders. South Carolina never had a scandal of the magnitude of the Robinson affair, but a few of its provincial officials misused public funds.

Financial irregularities in South Carolina almost always involved the office of public treasurer, probably because it was the most profitable office in the provincial government. Three men held the office between 1712 and 1770: Alexander Parris, 1712–1735; Gabriel Manigault, 1735–1743; and Jacob Motte, 1743–1770. Manigault was the ablest by far; his accounts were always in order, and he completed his term without a hint of fiscal irregularity. The same cannot be said of Parris and Motte. It has already been noted that Parris fell behind

---

[56] Jan. 28, 1741, Easterby, ed., *Commons Journal, 1739–41*, 474–75; July 3, Dec. 3, 1741, *ibid., 1741–42*, 259, 297; Apr. 10, 1753, Commons Journal, 401–2, S. C. Archives.

in his accounts during the 1720's and owed the public treasury £40,000 currency in 1731. Although he could not pay his debts, the assembly allowed him to continue as treasurer until his retirement in 1735. The assembly also emitted public orders to cover Parris's debt, orders which were supposed to be retired as Parris and his heirs paid off the debt. The assembly's plan failed, however, when merchant Joseph Wragg somehow acquired control of the Parris debt. According to Henry McCulloh, Wragg appropriated £16,000 in public orders for the personal use of himself and some of his friends. Wragg eventually paid the £16,000 back into the treasury, but in effect he had borrowed money from the public without permission and without paying interest on it. The assembly knew what Wragg had done, but it was satisfied to wait for him to repay the money. As late as 1749 Wragg still owed the public £2,000 currency from the Parris fund.[57]

A new round in the history of the treasurer's office began when Gabriel Manigault, citing the pressures of personal business, submitted his resignation to the assembly on March 23, 1743. The council nominated merchant Othniel Beale to succeed him, and the Commons House countered by nominating merchant Jacob Motte. Neither house wanted to disrupt business but neither wanted to yield to the other, so both houses tendered compromises. The Commons House nominated a third man, merchant William Cattell, Jr., but the council rejected the compromise and suggested that Lieutenant Governor Bull choose between Beale and Motte. At that point Motte began to worry about being cut off from the profits of the treasury. He therefore suggested a deal: If Beale would withdraw from the contest and pay half the salary of the treasurer's clerk, Motte would pay him half the profits of the office for three or four years. Beale agreed and asked the council to withdraw his nomination, and the upper house voted for Motte. Several members of the lower house heard about the deal, and when Motte was questioned he admitted the whole story. A few assembly-men disapproved of Motte's conduct, but a majority of the Commons House saw nothing wrong with the deal and voted Motte into office.[58]

The sequel to Motte's election was equally uninspiring. Motte, a particularly inept treasurer, was habitually late with his accounts, made unauthorized private loans from the treasury, and allowed

<hr/>

[57] McCulloh, "State of the Paper Bills of Currency in South Carolina," Feb. 26, 1743, S. C. Pub. Recs., XXI, 106–8, S. C. Archives; Dec. 1, 1749, Easterby, ed., *Commons Journal, 1749–50*, 309.

[58] Mar. 23, 24, 31, Apr. 28, 30, May 3, 1743, Easterby, ed., *Commons Journal, 1742–44*, 312, 314–15, 349, 404–5, 414–15, 422; Mar. 23, Apr. 28, 29, 1743, Upper House Journal, X, 52–53, 91–94, S. C. Archives.

merchants to delay payment of their import duties.[59] Like other public
officials who handled public money, Motte also failed to distinguish
carefully between public funds and his own money; he used public
funds to pay his personal debts and his own money to pay public
debts. Then a hurricane in 1752 damaged his property so badly that he
could not pay either personal or public obligations. He refused to
honor about £70,000 currency in tax certificates issued before the
hurricane, although refusing to honor them endangered the public
credit at a critical time. The Commons House sympathized with Motte
and postponed an investigation of his affairs, which made Governor
James Glen so mad that he announced he "had washed his Hands" of
the whole business.[60] When the assembly finally took up the question,
further investigation disclosed that Motte did not understand double
entry bookkeeping. He consequently owed the colony an additional
£20,000 currency, which made his total debt £90,000 currency. Motte
turned over his entire estate to trustees appointed by the assembly, and
they sold property until the debt was discharged in 1759.[61] The
assembly still found nothing reprehensible in Motte's conduct and
allowed him to stay in office until his death in 1770.

The South Carolina assembly was as much to blame for the
irregularities in the treasurer's office as anyone. It condoned the
inefficiency of Parris and Motte, the even more dubious conduct of
Joseph Wragg, and the deal between Motte and Beale. By doing so it
showed that South Carolina's political standards were no higher than
those of Great Britain or other colonies.

VI

Colonial South Carolina has often been compared to a city-state,
and the comparison is fitting because Charles Town dominated the
colony's political, social, and economic life. The culture developed
within this colonial city-state was notable chiefly for economic affluence and the almost aggressive gaity of its social life. Although a few

---

[59] June 5, 1747, Easterby, ed., *Commons Journal, 1746-47,* 333; Jan. 28, Mar. 12,
1748, *ibid., 1748,* 19, 164; Dec. 12, 1749, *ibid., 1749-50,* 341-42; Apr. 28, 1750, Mar. 13,
1751, Apr. 17, 1752, Commons Journal, XXV, 523, XXVI, 229, XXVII, 316, S. C.
Archives.

[60] Oct. 7, 1752, Commons Journal, XXVII, 644, S. C. Archives; see also Oct. 5, 7,
1752, *ibid.,* XXVII, 609-10, 640-43.

[61] Nov. 24, Dec. 7, 1752, *ibid.,* XXVIII, 14-16, 95-97; Apr. 7, 1759, *ibid.,* XXXII,
Pt. ii, 225-26; Treasurer's Ledgers, B (1735-73), fol. 48, S. C. Archives; Wills,
Inventories, and Misc. Recs., LXXX-B, 666-82, 1008-63, Charleston Co. Court-
house.

men stood out as exceptions, most South Carolinians devoted their time to their social pleasures and neglected religion, intellectual interests, and government with an equal indifference. Some modern writers might also criticize the colony's political ethics, but in this respect South Carolina was no worse than Great Britain or some of the other colonies.

South Carolina contradicted itself in a sense, for the colony was simultaneously self-contained in some things and responsive to outside influences in others. In government it was remarkably independent. The British Crown was the only outside agency with any real political influence, which it exerted chiefly through the governor and council. In the early 1740's, however, both governor and council enjoyed traditions of freedom from royal interference, and as the Commons House of Assembly increased its powers, English political influence diminished still further. By way of contrast, the provincial economy and society depended upon the outside world. The economy was subject to the demands of the world market, while the people of the colony imitated English fashions whenever possible.

A comparatively small number of men dominated almost every phase of life in South Carolina at mid-century. The wealthy merchants and planters virtually controlled the economy, and the gentry set the tone and pace of social life. Many of the same people also ran the government, but this statement is subject to important qualifications with respect to the Commons House of Assembly. The big planters and merchants controlled the council, along with a few lawyers and royal placemen, but nearly all the planters of South Carolina shunned the Commons House and it was led by the merchants and lawyers of Charles Town. The lower house was also exposed to the influence of voters who did not belong to the gentry, because the colony's election law had set up a very broad franchise. Except in Charles Town, however, this opportunity for the lower classes to exert a political influence was largely negated by the general lack of interest in elections.

CHAPTER XI

TINKERING WITH THE
CONSTITUTION
1743–1749

Throughout the twelve-year administration of Governor James Glen, the political history of South Carolina pivoted upon the constitutional struggles involving the governor and both houses of the assembly. The first half of Glen's tenure, from 1743 to 1749, found each of the rivals contending against both of its competitors. The Commons House of Assembly attacked the governor and the council, Glen fought the council and the Commons, and the council defended itself against the lower house and the governor. Generally speaking, the Commons House tried to encroach upon the prerogatives of its competitors, Glen attempted to regain some of the power lost by previous governors, and the council defended the status quo. The debates usually remained fairly sedate, without stirring up public commotions, but there were two exceptions. In 1745 a dispute between the upper and lower houses kept the assembly from passing a tax bill, and in 1748 Glen lost his temper and prorogued the assembly in the middle of its session. Whether open or behind the scenes, however, the debates of the 1740's caused no real changes in the government, and little was accomplished other than more precise statements of constitutional arguments.

I

From 1743 to 1747 South Carolina's constitutional debates focused upon the council, which was under attack from both the Commons

House and the governor. The Commons House was trying to reduce the upper house's control over money bills still further, while Glen was trying to bring the council under his domination. The council responded sluggishly at first and made little effort to defend itself until 1745. In that year it finally reacted vigorously by rejecting the annual tax bill and by formulating the first comprehensive defense of its constitutional rights and privileges.

The attack on the council originated as part of a general review of the provincial constitution by the Commons House. The lower house was concerned with a number of fundamental issues that did not involve the council at all. For example, the Commons House decided in 1744 to change its name. Members of the house disliked the name "Commons House of Assembly," because it implied that council members were not commoners. The lower house searched royal instructions and provincial statutes for precedents, and it resolved on February 25, 1744, that its name should henceforth be simply "the Assembly." [1] The new name was not accepted in common usage, however, and the house soon reverted to calling itself the "Commons House of Assembly." A second and more basic issue concerned the franchise and assembly elections. Many people believed that the election act of 1721 had set property qualifications for voting and assembly service too low, and the grand jury of the province, meeting at Charles Town in 1742, had requested a new elections law. A bill introduced in 1744 provided that voters must own 300 acres of land or other real estate worth £60 proclamation money and that assembly-men must own 500 acres and 20 slaves or real estate worth £1,000 proclamation money clear of debt. The bill also excluded from the assembly all officeholders who were paid by the public, and it tried to alleviate the inconvenience of legislative service by reducing the duration of assemblies from three to two years. Finally, the bill tried to eliminate religious discrimination by allowing assembly members simply to affirm their loyalty to the Crown instead of taking an oath on the Bible. [2] The house passed the bill promptly and sent it to the council, where it languished for a year before the house needled the council into action.

Other phases of the lower house's constitutional review eventually led to conflict with the upper house, especially when the Commons attacked the council's remaining financial powers and its control of the

[1] Feb. 23-25, 1744, Easterby, ed., *Commons Journal, 1744–45*, 9–10, 13–14, 17.
[2] Nov. 27, 1742, *ibid., 1742–44*, 72; Feb. 22, Mar. 1, 7, 1744, *ibid., 1744–45*, 4–5, 33–34, 35, 39–40, 48.

colonial agent. The first target of the lower house's attack was the council's right to examine petitions and accounts relating to the tax bill. The Commons House did not send the accounts for two items in the tax bill to the council in 1742, and when the upper house complained it replied that it did not have to explain every single appropriation. In holding back a few accounts the Commons House was asserting the principle of its superiority in finances, but the council passed the tax bill anyway. When the Commons House again withheld an account in 1743, the council again passed the tax bill. The next target for the Commons was control of the colony's agent in London. The house resolved in 1744 that its committee of correspondence should correspond with the agent without consulting any members of the council, thus unilaterally abolishing the old joint committee of correspondence.[3]

A different kind of constitutional issue arose in 1744 when the Commons House proposed a change in the tax bill. Every taxpayer was required to swear that his tax returns were complete, but the Commons House suspected that some Charles Town merchants were making false statements about loans they had made. It therefore inserted a clause in the tax bill that would require all residents of Charles Town to take a special oath on the amount of money they had on loan, including bonds and mortgages. Many city merchants resented the indignity of being required to take a special oath, because it seemed to imply they were less honest than other men. Several wrote articles for the *Gazette* arguing that such an oath was contrary to English practice and unconstitutional. The merchant-dominated council also opposed the oath, but when the lower house insisted on keeping the oath the council passed the tax bill. As a last resort a number of merchants petitioned Glen to veto the tax bill, but he, too, approved the bill.[4]

Like the Commons House, Governor James Glen also thought the provincial constitution needed to be reformed, and he showed a particular keenness to reform the council. He thought the governor should be present at the legislative sessions of the upper house, and in one of his first acts as governor he appeared before the council to protest his exclusion. He insisted that the upper house readmit him and record his presence in its journals, but he promised never to enter

[3] Mar. 4–6, 1742, Easterby, ed., *Commons Journal, 1741–42,* 464–65, 469–71, 480, 482; May 5, 1743, *ibid., 1742–44,* 446–47; June 29, 1744, *ibid., 1744–45,* 214–15.

[4] May 25–26, 28–29, 1744, *ibid., 1744–45,* 181, 183, 188, 197–203; *S-C. Gaz.* (Charles Town), June 11, 18, July 4, 1744.

into its debates. The upper house regarded even Glen's compromise as an encroachment on its prerogatives, but it agreed to his demands. It added, however, that if Glen or any future governor ever intervened in its debate it would then be free to expel the governor from its legislative sessions.[5]

Despite the pressure from two sides, the council reacted feebly and made little effort to defend itself until 1744. Its weakness stemmed largely from its lack of unity. Merchant Edmund Atkin had urged stiff resistance to the Commons House and governor ever since 1740; he had frequently voted against bills he disliked and had entered the reasons for his dissent in the journals of the upper house. Atkin could not persuade the other councilors to go along with him, however, and he always voted alone.[6] Atkin was frequently opposed in the upper house by Lieutenant Governor William Bull and Charles Pinckney; Bull had long favored cooperation with the lower house, while Pinckney was a former speaker. With the appearance of the issue of the oath on money on loan, however, Atkin began to gain support. Merchants Joseph Wragg and Richard Hill joined him in voting against the tax bill of 1744, but two other merchants, James Kinloch and William Middleton, voted for it. The upper house passed the bill by a vote of five to three, with Bull, Pinckney, Kinloch, Middleton, and planter Joseph Blake voting aye. Atkin, Wragg, and Hill entered their dissent in the house's journals, in which they accused the majority of "yielding up to the lower house, the Power of two Branches of the Legislature." [7]

The Commons House continued to harass the council in 1745, and the pressure finally forced the entire council to support Atkin's extreme position. On February 16 the Commons House asked the council to expedite passage of the new elections bill, which the council had ignored for nearly a year. When the house did not receive an answer, it sent monthly messages on March 22 and April 29; in the last message it asked the council to explain its failure to act. Taking offense at the persistent pressure, the council accused the lower house of meddling in its affairs. It also resolved that the message of April 29 was "highly contrary to the Usage and essential Privileges of Parliaments," that it had the right to read or not to read any bill as it pleased, that it was not accountable to the Commons for any action it

---

[5] Jan. 20, 1744, Upper House Journal, XII, 7, S. C. Archives.

[6] See, e.g., Sept. 19, 1740, May 6, 1743, *ibid.*, VII, 353–60, X, 109–12.

[7] May 26, 1744, *ibid.*, XII, 79–87; one of the councilors who voted for the bill, probably Kinloch or Middleton, later advised Glen to veto it; Council Journal, May 29, 1744, no. 11, 287, S. C. Archives.

took, and that it would not act on the elections bill at that time. On May 1 the lower house agreed that neither house was accountable to the other and that it had not meant to insult the council.[8]

Neither house took further action or even communicated with the other for the next ten days, and the council used that time to formulate a comprehensive statement of its constitutional rights and privileges. The council had appointed a committee on style, with Edmund Atkin as chairman, when the lower house had tried to change its name, but the committee had never reported. The council now revived the committee, and Atkin submitted on May 7, not merely a report on style, but a fifty-page report on "the Constitution, State and Practice of the Legislature of this Province." Atkin based his report on the premise that the legislature of South Carolina consisted of three separate and distinct branches—the governor, council, and lower house—and that none of them "ought or can mix or blend itself with either of the others, or be set aside by the other two." The governor represented the Crown, the Commons represented the people, and the council represented property. The greatest danger in the encroachments of the Commons House, warned Atkin, was that "Men of *little Estates* may get in [the Commons House], who will have it in their power to oppress the *best*." Atkin devoted most of the report to a chronicle of encroachments on the council's powers by both governor and Commons. He found that a proper balance in government had existed during Bull's administration. He said, "The three Estates in the Legislature were in the Strongest and clearest manner distinguished by every branch of it, and each was generally restrained to it's proper Limits." Under Glen, however, "The Irregularities of long standing . . . are revived," and the council "is reduced to a far worse Situation than ever, being in the most essential points attempted to be set aside." The report warned Glen in particular that the governor "hath no more Right to be present with the Council in their Legislative Capacity, than with the Assembly." The council debated Atkin's report for two days and adopted it on May 10, thus giving its sanction to one of the most complete statements of the council's constitutional position made in colonial South Carolina.[9]

The Commons House broke the silence between the houses on May

[8] Feb. 16, Mar. 22, Apr. 29–May 1, 1745, Easterby, ed., *Commons Journal, 1744–45,* 338, 415, 449–50, 455–56, 458; the quotation is from p. 455.

[9] The report is in May 7, 1745, Upper House Journal, XIII, 118–74, S. C. Archives; the quotations are from pp. 154, 161, 170, 171, 173; see also May 1, 7–10, 1745, *ibid.,* XIII, 109, 175, 183, 188.

10 when it asked for a general conference with the council to dispatch the public business. Although the council did not want to enter into such a conference, it showed its willingness to compromise by promising to act on the elections bill if the Commons would act on the bills before it. The Commons promptly complied and even sent all petitions and accounts when the council asked for them. The council then passed the elections bill with one significant amendment. It deleted the clause permitting religious dissenters in the assembly merely to affirm their loyalty and instead required them to swear upon the Bible. Charles Pinckney opposed the amendment and defended the rights of dissenters, but the rest of the council voted him down. The Commons accepted the amendment and amended the bill itself by further reducing the life of assemblies to one year. The elections bill was then passed without further difficulty.[10]

After a week of productive activity the new harmony was disrupted by the renewal of the dispute over the oath on money at interest. The lower house had included the oath in the tax bill, and the council again tried to delete it. The Commons House decided to retain the oath by a vote of fifteen to fourteen, and so the council rejected the tax bill by a four-to-three majority.[11]

Rejection of the tax bill angered members of the Commons House, and two of them went to Glen with a startling proposition: that he approve the bill without the council's consent. Glen's agreement would have stripped the council of every vestige of its legislative authority, but he turned down the request and the Commons House had to abandon hope for a quick solution to its search for parliamentary supremacy.[12]

The controversy died quickly, because the council had intended its rejection of the tax bill to be merely a show of force, a reminder to the governor and Commons House that it still possessed the authority to strike down laws it did not like. Mercantile opposition to the oath was diminishing because merchants found it less obnoxious than they had feared, and the assembly enacted the same tax bill without delay in

[10] May 10–11, 14–15, 23, 1745, Easterby, ed., Commons Journal, 1744-45, 491–94, 497, 505, 539–40; May 10, 1745, Upper House Journal, XIII, 190–93, S. C. Archives. The final act is in Cooper and McCord, eds., Statutes, III, 656–58.

[11] May 17, 22–23, 1745, Easterby, ed., Commons Journal, 1744-45, 519–21, 533, 541–42; Glen to Bd. of Trade, May 28, 1745, S. C. Pub. Recs., XXII, 102, S. C. Archives.

[12] William Bull, Jr., to Earl of Dartmouth, Sept. 18, 1773, S. C. Pub. Recs., XXXIII, 306, S. C. Archives; Bull was speaker of the Commons House in 1745; see also Wallace, Henry Laurens, 41 n.

January 1746.[13] A few merchants continued their opposition to the oath, including, of course, Edmund Atkin. He still regarded the oath as unconstitutional and voted against every tax bill that included it, even though his votes accomplished nothing.[14]

II

While the special oath imposed upon merchants ceased to be a political issue after 1745, the council was still under pressure from its antagonists. Governor Glen posed a more serious threat, but the Commons House did not neglect the council. It continued to chip away at the upper house's financial powers, and it again withheld accounts in 1746 and 1747. In both years, however, the council apparently asserted itself by amending the tax bill. Exactly what happened to the tax bills of 1746 and 1747 is not clear, but the journals of both houses say that the council passed the tax bills "with Amendments." [15] Neither journal makes any further comment. If the council actually amended the tax bills, it violated the legislative compromise of 1739, but it seems unlikely that the Commons House would have tolerated such an act without a violent reaction. In any case, the two houses found a new issue to argue about in 1747, the council's right to propose methods of raising a revenue. Governor Glen wanted to build a fort in the Cherokee nation, and the council suggested that it be financed by drawing upon the fortifications fund. The Commons House decided that the council's proposal infringed upon its right to frame money bills, especially as the council had not made a formal proposal in this way for several years. The Commons therefore resolved, "His Majesty's Council have no Right to propose any Method of imposing Duties or granting Aids to His Majesty for any Purpose whatever." The dispute ended indecisively, for the council persisted with its suggestion and the Commons House defeated the bill.[16]

[13] Glen to Bd. of Trade, May 28, 1745, S. C. Pub. Recs., XXII, 102, S. C. Archives; Jan. 25, 1746, Easterby, ed., *Commons Journal, 1745–46,* 82–83.

[14] Atkin, "Wrong Practices," in Greene, ed., "S. C.'s Colonial Constitution," *S. C. Hist. Mag.,* 62 (1961) , 75; Jan. 24, 1746, June 28, 1748, Upper House Journal, XIV, 15, XVI, Pt. i, 179–81, S. C. Archives.

[15] Feb. 20, June 7, 1746, Upper House Journal, XIV, 25, 63, S. C. Archives; Feb. 20, June 10, 1746, Easterby, ed., *Commons Journal, 1745–46,* 112, 212; Feb. 12, 1747, *ibid., 1746–47,* 179; on withholding accounts, see June 10, 1746, *ibid., 1745–46,* June 4, 1747, *ibid., 1746–47,* 323.

[16] June 12–13, 1747, *ibid., 1746–47,* 373–75, 386–91; the quotation is from p. 375.

The Commons House was also still tinkering with other political customs that concerned the council less directly. The elections act of 1745 was not living up to the expectations of its sponsors; men still refused to serve in the Commons, and voters disliked annual elections. The assembly therefore passed an additional elections act in 1748 that provided for biennial assemblies. This time the Commons House persuaded the council to allow religious dissenters to make affirmations, rather than swearing oaths. The time spent on the election laws was wasted, however, for the Crown disallowed both new acts because they did not include suspending clauses.[17] In another attempt to make assembly service less time-consuming, the Commons House changed the procedure for enacting laws. In 1748 it adopted Parliament's practice of reading a bill three times in one house before sending it to the other house. The council objected because it anticipated difficulty in amending bills. It suggested that bills be read twice in each house and then sent to the other house; neither house would read a bill the third time until the other house had passed it twice. The Commons House insisted on its new plan throughout 1748, but it went back to the old method of three alternate readings in each house in 1749. It finally accepted in 1750 the proposal the council had made in 1748, and from then on bills were read twice in each house and then sent to the other.[18]

Although the Commons House did not seriously threaten the council after 1745, Governor Glen did. In a letter to the Board of Trade in October 1746, Glen broached a plan for drastically changing the membership of the council. He complained that the council was having a lot of trouble in assembling a quorum for its meetings, because four councilors were in England, three more planned to leave South Carolina, and two lived so far from Charles Town they could not attend regularly. This left only three councilors Glen could rely on. Glen suggested that the Crown appoint new councilors to replace the absentees and nominated seven men, all residents of Charles Town, as suitable replacements. The governor later elaborated on his plan by saying that the council's quorum problems sapped its strength; consequently, its weakness tolerated the growth of irregular political practices.[19]

[17] Cooper and McCord, eds., *Statutes*, III, 692–93; Grant and Munro, eds., *Acts of Privy Council, Col. Ser.*, IV, 49–50, 141.

[18] Feb. 25, Mar. 1, 3, 4, 7, 1748, Easterby, ed., *Commons Journal, 1748*, 66, 88, 106–7, 109–10, 121; May 10, 1749, Jan. 27, Feb. 2, 1750, *ibid., 1749–50*, 357, 384–85.

[19] To Bd. of Trade, Oct. 4, 1746, to Duke of Bedford, Oct. 10, 1748, S. C. Pub. Recs., XXII, 205–8, XXIII, 239–40, S. C. Archives.

Glen's prattle about the council's attendance problems was a sham. Although there were times when the council had trouble assembling a quorum, the late 1740's was not one of them. The lack of a quorum in the upper house kept the assembly from transacting business only once during that period.[20] From four to eight councilors attended meetings regularly, including even William Bull, Sr., who lived fifty miles away. The true reasons for Glen's attempt to change the membership of the council lay elsewhere. In the first place, Glen disapproved of the council's independence and thought it should comply with his wishes more readily. He particularly resented the fact that he could not participate in the legislative debates of the upper house.[21] Glen hoped to increase his influence over the council by filling it with men who would be more responsive to his wishes. Six of the seven men he nominated in 1746 held appointive offices in the provincial government.

A second reason for Glen's dissatisfaction with his council originated in his quarrel with Lieutenant Governor Bull, the council's president and one of its most influential members. According to Glen, part of the trouble was Bull's jealousy. The governor once complained that whenever he tried to change the political customs of South Carolina, he was always opposed by those "who happened to have the management [of the government] before his arrival, by all their friends and relations, and by all those who advised or concurred with these measures, who think themselves impeach'd and their proceedings arraigned by any contrary conduct." [22] The breach between Glen and Bull was widened by a quarrel over the salary the assembly had paid Bull while Glen was in England. Glen claimed half the salary on the ground that Bull had been acting as his deputy, and Bull paid him about a third of his claim. Bull then petitioned the assembly for assistance in paying the rest of the claim but both houses resolved that Bull's income as acting governor was a gift from the assembly, not a salary. Both houses resolved further that Bull therefore should not have to share the money with anyone.[23] Bull apparently did not pay the rest of Glen's claim.

Glen's attempt to revise the membership of the council failed,

[20] Sept. 15, 1746, Easterby, ed., *Commons Journal, 1746–47*, 14.

[21] Glen to Duke of Bedford, Oct. 10, 1748, S. C. Pub. Recs., XXIII, 240, S. C. Archives.

[22] Glen to Bd. of Trade, July 27, 1748, *ibid.*, XXIII, 177.

[23] Jan. 17, Mar. 21, 1746, Easterby, ed., *Commons Journal, 1745–46*, 49, 170–71; Mar. 4–5, 1748, *ibid., 1748*, 110–11, 118–19; Mar. 3, 5, 1748, Upper House Journal, XVI, Pt. i, 67–68, 74–75, S. C. Archives.

because the council members collectively exercised more political influence in London than he did. The Board of Trade did not ignore Glen's nominations, for it appointed five of them to the council during Glen's administration. During the same period, however, it also appointed seven men that Glen had not recommended, of whom three were prominent merchants and three were related to the Bull family. In short, Glen failed to break up the control of the council by the two major power blocs. Glen managed only to achieve a secondary goal of his campaign. His complaints about the excessive number of councilors in England persuaded the Board of Trade to check more carefully on the whereabouts of South Carolina councilors. After that, when the Board found too many councilors in England at the same time, it urged some of them to return to South Carolina. If it discovered that a councilor intended to stay in England it persuaded him to resign, and when councilor John Hammerton refused either to resign or to return to South Carolina it suspended him from the council.[24]

In spite of Governor Glen's protestations to the contrary, the council remained a strong force in the government of South Carolina. In 1747 it could look back upon four years during which it had successfully defended its position against both the Commons House and the governor. Its adversaries could claim only one clear victory over the council between 1743 and 1747: the governor's readmission to the legislative sessions of the upper house. Even that victory turned out to be temporary, however, for the upper house re-excluded Glen in 1750.

III

From 1743 to 1747, while constitutional debates involving the council had dominated politics, the governor and the Commons House of Assembly had kept up a very friendly relationship. Indeed, Glen had even tolerated criticism of his handling of executive affairs in order to remain on good terms with the lower house.[25] The truce between governor and Commons ended in 1748, however, when the house attacked Glen repeatedly and he retaliated by dismissing the assembly. The conflict had its origins in the hardships caused by King George's War, another crisis in Indian affairs which brought an economic recession in South Carolina. The major political issues in

[24] Sirmans, "S. C. Royal Council," *Wm. and Mary Qtly.*, 3d Ser., 18 (1961), 386–87, 392.

[25] See, e.g., Jan. 22, 26, 1745, Easterby, ed., *Commons Journal, 1744–45*, 289, 312–13, 319–20.

1748 all involved wartime spending. Generally speaking, the governor wanted more money to pay the costs of the war, including Indian affairs, while the Commons House insisted on cutting the budget because of the recession. The conflict was not expressed in general terms, however, but rather in a variety of specific issues that were created by South Carolina's efforts to cope with the war and the recession. Moreover, some of the same issues were still alive as late as 1750.

The political crisis of 1748, as well as some later events, was a legacy of the diplomatic and economic crises of King George's War. When France allied itself with Spain in 1743 and declared war on England, the governor of Louisiana began to send agents to all the southern Indian nations. The agents stirred up all the Indians against the English, and even a few of the previously loyal Chickasaws began to raid outlying English settlements. The Chickasaws were put out with Glen because of his stinginess in handing out presents when their chiefs visited Charles Town. The Creeks were upset by the machinations of Mary Bosomworth, a half-breed princess whom the Lower Creeks admired and trusted. A decade earlier, as Mary Musgrove, she had assisted James Oglethorpe in his Indian diplomacy, but she and Thomas Bosomworth, her third husband, were now quarreling with the government of Georgia about land claims. They threatened to lead the Lower Creeks into a French alliance, and they arranged for Malatchi, a young pro-French chief, to become emperor of the Creeks in 1747. The Cherokees, too, were uneasy about their English alliance, and several overhill towns signed a peace treaty with France. The overhill Cherokees were tired of war and hoped to live at peace with both England and France, but South Carolina interpreted their peace treaty as a defection to France. Most Cherokee towns remained loyal to England, but nearly all of them violated the treaty of alliance; they allowed northern Indians, mostly Shawnees and Iroquois, to use their towns as a base of operations against the Catawbas, the only loyal allies of South Carolina.[26]

The English position on the southern frontier deteriorated in 1746, largely because Governor Glen lacked experience in Indian affairs and refused to listen to the advice of others. Convinced that he could persuade the Indians to compose their differences with the English and

[26] Norman W. Caldwell, "The Southern Frontier during King George's War," *Jour. of So. Hist.*, 7 (1941), 42–43, 46–49; E. Merton Coulter, "Mary Musgrove, 'Queen of the Creeks': A Chapter of Early Georgia Troubles," *Ga. Hist. Qtly.*, 11 (1927), 1–30; Corkran, *Cherokee Frontier*, 18–19.

each other, Glen called a series of conferences with the various tribes in the spring and summer of 1746. He even went to the frontier outposts of Ninety Six and Fort Moore to meet the Cherokees and Creeks. His conferences failed, however, because he demanded too much from the Indians, especially by insisting that they attack the French.[27] Glen made Anglo-Cherokee relations still worse in the fall of 1746 by refusing to cooperate with the assembly. The war had disrupted trade with the Cherokees, and the assembly voted to send an agent to the Cherokee nation to reopen trade. Although Glen consented to the assembly's plan, he evidently regarded it as an encroachment on his prerogatives and worked against the agent. He delayed the agent's commission, criticized him publicly, and kept him from exercising any real control over the trade. As a result, the agent could not negotiate with the Indians effectively, and the Cherokees remained at odds with South Carolina.[28]

The balance of power on the southern frontier shifted suddenly in 1746 when the Choctaw Indians revolted against their French allies, but once again Glen muffed a chance to make up for his setback. The headman among the Choctaws, whom the English called Red Shoes, had long been unhappy with the French alliance, and the Anglo-French war provided him with an excuse to revolt against France. Because of the war Louisiana was not able to supply its Indian allies with enough goods to satisfy them, and Red Shoes exploited Choctaw dissatisfaction skillfully. He killed three French traders in November 1746, made peace with the pro-English Chickasaws, and sent a peace mission to Charles Town, which was led by his brother, the Little King. The delegation reached the city on April 10, 1747, and Glen signed a treaty with it eight days later. The Choctaws promised to attack French settlements, and South Carolina promised to open a trade with them and to give them all the arms and ammunition they needed.[29]

[27] Caldwell, "Southern Frontier," *Jour. of So. Hist.*, 7 (1941), 43–44; for Glen's version of the conferences, see Glen to Bd. of Trade, Sept. 29, 1746, S. C. Pub. Recs., XXII, 199–204, S. C. Archives.

[28] Caldwell, "Southern Frontier," *Jour. of So. Hist.*, 7 (1941), 45–46; May 26, 28, 1747, Easterby, ed., *Commons Journal, 1746–47*, 282–83, 296.

[29] Edmund Atkin, "Historical Account of the Revolt of the Choctaw Indians in the Late War from the French to the British Alliance and of their Return Since to that of the French," 1753, Lansdowne Manuscripts, 809, foll. 1–3, Brit. Mus., transcripts in Lib. Cong. The standard source on the Choctaw Revolt is Adair's *Hist. of Amer. Indians*, ed. Williams, 335–76. I have found, however, that Atkin is more reliable than Adair for several reasons: Atkin wrote his account immediately after the revolt, while Adair wrote his nearly 20 years later; Atkin based his conclusions on a careful study of documents relating to the revolt, while Adair relied primarily

It was in supplying the Choctaws with arms, ammunition, and trade goods that Governor Glen bungled the Choctaw revolt. Glen seems to have been in financial trouble in the late 1740's, for at about the same time as the Choctaw revolt he made his claim to half of Lieutenant Governor Bull's salary and asked the assembly for special tax exemptions. Glen therefore tried to make money for himself in the newly opened trade with the Choctaws. He helped one Charles McNair, a newcomer to South Carolina, form a partnership with several old Indian traders, and he promised to grant the new company a monopoly of the Choctaw trade if it would admit his brother, Dr. Thomas Glen, as a partner. The new company was known officially as McNair and Company, but because of the secret deals contemporaries referred to it as the "Sphinx Company." [30] Whatever it was called, McNair and Company displayed a remarkable inefficiency in supplying the Choctaws. The company sent only two pack trains to the Choctaws in three years, and nearly all the goods in the second shipment disappeared mysteriously before they reached the Choctaws. To make matters worse, an unlicensed Chickasaw trader named James Adair made extravagant and unauthorized promises of English presents, a French agent assassinated Red Shoes in 1747, and the Little King died in 1749. By the end of 1749 twenty-two of the forty-six Choctaw towns had renewed their alliance with France, and the remaining English towns were restless. Throughout it all, however, Governor Glen refused to let anyone trade with the Choctaws except McNair and Company. [31]

The initial success of the Choctaw revolt encouraged Glen to formulate a plan for driving France out of the lower Mississippi Valley. In 1747 he proposed that the Creeks, Choctaws, and a small force from South Carolina attack Louisiana from the interior while the British navy launched a simultaneous assault on New Orleans. Glen's plan was basically sound because the French army in Louisiana was small and poorly equipped, but his timing was poor. The English Indians opposed the plan, especially the Lower Creeks who were under the

---

on personal recollection; there is good reason to believe that Adair exaggerated his part in the revolt in order to claim a reward for his services, while Atkin had no such personal interest; and, most important, independent sources support Atkin, not Adair, on disputed points.

[30] Atkin, "Revolt of Choctaw Indians," Lansdowne Mss., 809, foll. 3–4, Brit. Mus.; Adair, *Hist. of Amer. Indians,* ed. Williams, 345–46. It is significant that Atkin and Adair, who disagreed on many other points, agreed on the origin and purpose of this company.

[31] Atkin, "Revolt of Choctaw Indians," Lansdowne Mss., 809, foll. 4–18, Brit. Mus.

influence of the Bosomworths. When the British government also showed no interest in his plan, Glen abandoned the whole idea. As a result, France still exerted a strong influence on the southern frontier when King George's War ended in 1748.[32]

Throughout King George's War Glen's frontier diplomacy was complicated by the economic recession that hit South Carolina in 1744 and lasted until 1748. The war itself caused the recession in South Carolina, for French and Spanish privateers raided the colony's rice ships so often that freight and insurance rates rose to all-time highs. The market value of rice consequently declined from 7½s. per hundredweight in 1741 to 2s. 2d. in 1746. Meanwhile, interference with shipping caused an inflation in the prices of imported food and other goods, while military expenditures nearly doubled provincial taxes. South Carolina's economic distress was partially alleviated by the introduction of indigo as a marketable staple, a development which was due largely to the experiments of Eliza Lucas. Indigo offered many advantages to the planter. It was less bulky than rice and thus less expensive to ship, and planters could easily combine its production with rice growing because the busy season for indigo was an off-season for rice. Most important, Parliament subsidized the cultivation of indigo by paying a bounty on it after 1745, and South Carolina produced nearly 140,000 pounds of it a year in 1747 and 1748. At best, however, the introduction of indigo merely eased some of South Carolina's economic problems; it could not end the recession by itself. As Governor Glen said later, "This Province was brought to the Brink of Ruin by the last French War." [33]

The recession hit the planters particularly hard, and they began to petition the assembly for relief in 1744. Four petitions signed by 519 men complained of the colony's economic hardships, especially a currency shortage, and requested an increase in the local currency. The assembly ignored the petitions in 1744, but two years later it received six new petitions. All the petitions complained of difficulty in paying debts, high interest rates, and the lack of a sufficient currency. This time the assembly acted promptly and passed two bills for

[32] Caldwell, "Southern Frontier," *Jour. of So. Hist.*, 7 (1941), 47, 50–51; Glen to Bd. of Trade, Dec. 1751, S. C. Pub. Recs., XXIV, 421, S. C. Archives.

[33] Glen to Robert Dinwiddie, Mar. 13, 1754, William L. McDowell, Jr., ed., *Colonial Records of South Carolina: Documents Relating to Indian Affairs, May 21, 1750–August 7, 1754* (Columbia, 1958), 478; see also Taylor, "Wholesale Commodity Prices," *Jour. Econ. and Bus. Hist.*, 4 (1932), 358, 360, 372; Charles Boschi to Sec. S.P.G., Oct. 30, 1745, Geiger, ed., "St. Bartholomew's Parish," *S. C. Hist. Mag.*, 50 (1949), 184; C. Robert Haywood, "Mercantilism and South Carolina Agriculture, 1700–1763," *ibid.*, 60 (1959), 15–27; Gray, *Hist. of Agriculture*, I, 290–92.

economic relief. The first act provided for the emission of £210,000 in bills of credit, of which £106,000 would replace old bills and £104,000 would represent an increase in local currency. The second act, called the "justices act," entrusted the trial of debt cases involving £75 currency or less to two justices of the peace and three freeholders, thus reducing court costs and eliminating trips to Charles Town. The assembly passed both bills with remarkably little dissent, as no one in either house, not even Edmund Atkin, raised an objection to either bill. The only opposition came from an anonymous correspondent in the *South-Carolina Gazette,* who condemned the assembly that passed the laws as "the *worst* since his Majesty's Government of us." [34]

The economic relief laws met with a less sympathetic reception in England. The Privy Council disallowed the justices act in 1748, largely because it did not contain a suspending clause. At first the act to emit £210,000 appeared to be headed for approval. The assembly had written it very carefully in order to avoid disallowance on a technical point, and the Board of Trade's legal counsel reported favorably on it in 1747. In the end, however, the Board of Trade's longstanding prejudice against paper money won out, and the Board sent the bill back to its counsel. This time the counsel discovered objectionable features in the bill, and the Privy Council disallowed it in 1754.[35]

IV

Antagonism between Governor Glen and the Commons House of Assembly gradually emerged from the crisis in Indian affairs and the recession. An open break did not take place until 1748, but the first signs of disagreement appeared in 1747 when the Commons House refused to appropriate funds for Glen's plan of invading Louisiana. Later that year Glen proposed that South Carolina build a fort in the Creek nation, and the lower house again rebuffed him on the grounds that the colony could not afford it. When Glen asked the house to reconsider, it agreed to build the fort only if it were financed by issuing an additional £150,000 in local currency. The Commons must have known that the council would never agree to its plan, because the bill to emit £210,000 had been passed the previous year. In any case,

---

[34] May 16, 1744, Easterby, ed., *Commons Journal, 1744-45,* 142-44; Nov. 29, Dec. 4, 1746, *ibid., 1746-47,* 63-68, 81-82; Cooper and McCord, eds., *Statutes,* III, 671-77, 701. The quotation is from *S-C. Gaz.* (Charles Town), Jan. 6, 1748.

[35] Grant and Munro, eds., *Acts of Privy Council, Col. Ser.,* IV, 59-60, 211-12; Brock, Currency of Colonies, 451-53; Jellison, "S. C. Currency Acts," *Wm. and Mary Qtly.,* 3d Ser., 16 (1959), 565-66.

the merchant majority on the council rejected the bill to build the fort.[36]

Governor Glen did not improve matters any when he dissolved a new assembly in the fall of 1747 before it met officially. Acting under the election act of 1745, he dissolved the old assembly in July 1747 and called new elections. The new assembly was supposed to meet in September, but it failed to assemble a quorum then and Glen prorogued it for two months. The Commons House still could not muster a quorum in November, and Glen dissolved the assembly.[37] Glen had every right to dissolve the assembly, but when a new Commons House met in January 1748 a number of its members undoubtedly blamed the governor for the trouble of an extra election.

The first specific conflict between Glen and the Commons House grew out of the French and Spanish attacks on South Carolina shipping. Enemy privateers stepped up their raids in the winter of 1747–1748, and Glen outfitted two sloops to protect ships near Charles Town. The sloops operated effectively and even captured two privateers. The Commons House promised to defray the expenses of the sloops when they were fitted out in January 1748, and it decided to pay for them by issuing public orders. It told Glen on February 27, "We cannot find out any other Means of providing for that Expense." Glen objected to another increase in paper currency, however, and on March 12 he refused to sign a bill to pay for the sloops by emitting £30,000 in public orders, arguing that he would need to obtain the Crown's permission before he could sign such a bill. The members of the Commons House were angry, but they remained quiet for the time being and merely directed the provincial agent to solicit approval of the bill.[38]

The next issue arose when the Commons House tried to increase its control over expenditures for Indian affairs. It did not attempt to interfere directly with the governor's right to formulate Indian policy, but limiting his expenditures would indirectly curtail his policy-making powers. Glen had been buying Indian presents and hiring

[36] Apr. 15, May 16, June 10, 12, 1747, Easterby, ed., *Commons Journal, 1746–47,* 220–21, 225–26, 242–43, 347–49, 373–75; June 11, 1747, Upper House Journal, XVI, Pt. i, 31–32, S. C. Archives.

[37] [George C. Rogers, Jr.], Volume Preface to Easterby, ed., *Commons Journal, 1748,* x.

[38] Jan. 27, Feb. 27, Mar. 5, 12, 1748, *ibid., 1748,* 25–26, 77, 116–17, 168–69; Committee of Correspondence to Peregrine Fury, Mar. 24, 1748, S. C. Pub. Recs., XXIII, 156–59, S. C. Archives; on the operations of the sloops, see *S-C. Gaz.* (Charles Town), Jan. 11, Feb. 15, 1748.

agents without the approval of either house, and the Commons resolved on March 7 not to reimburse any Indian expenditures until it knew who had authorized them. The house explained that the increase in Indian expenses made close supervision necessary. Glen replied that expenses were high because of the war and offered to inspect all Indian accounts himself, but neither his explanation nor his offer satisfied the house. It demanded that Glen send it copies of the orders for all Indian expenditures and complained again of the high cost of Indian diplomacy. Glen ignored the request for copies of his orders; he contradicted his earlier message by arguing that expenses were decreasing; and he criticized the house for sending him an inaccurate and disrespectful message. The Commons answered him on May 16 by saying that its message was accurate and respectful and that it was surprised that Glen thought otherwise. No one said anything more on the subject, but in June the Commons House rejected an Indian account because it did not have a copy of Glen's authorization.[39]

The antagonism between Glen and the Commons House began to build toward a climax in June 1748. The assembly reconvened on June 8 after a three-week recess, and the Commons House promptly tried to reduce Glen's control over Indian expenditures. Catawba and Chickasaw delegations were visiting Charles Town, and Glen had appointed agents of his own to furnish them with food and lodging. The Commons House resolved on June 10 that future delegations must be cared for by the commissary general, an officer responsible primarily to the Commons House. Later that month a delegation of Cherokees arrived in town for a conference with the governor, and both houses of the assembly joined in an effort to dictate a new Cherokee treaty. A conference committee wrote a series of reports that proposed specific terms for the treaty, and the Commons House adopted the reports. The council was still debating them on June 29.[40] Glen may well have resented the assembly's intervention, but it was standard practice for the assembly to offer specific recommendations to the governor in such circumstances.

While the conference committee was working on its reports, the Commons House plunged into still another dispute with Glen. The issue this time concerned an additional bill to the act of 1746 empowering two justices and three freeholders to try small debt suits; the assembly had passed the additional bill, but Glen had not yet

[39] Mar. 7, 12, May 11, 13, 16, June 25, 1748, Easterby, ed., Commons Journal, 1748, 127, 163–64, 235–36, 249–50, 255–56, 359.
[40] June 10, 20, 25, 28, 1748, ibid., 303, 332–36, 356–58, 374–75.

signed it. Glen had received unofficially a copy of the Board of Trade's recommendation that the original justices act be disallowed, and he wrote a letter to Speaker William Bull, Jr., informing him of the recommendation. The lower house reminded Glen that local custom called for him to send a letter to the whole house and asked for a copy of any official messages on the justices act. Glen answered that letters to the speaker were common in England and in other colonies, but he was forced to admit that the Crown had not sent him any official communication. The act was thus still in force and the Commons House wanted Glen to sign the additional bill, along with other bills that the assembly had already passed. Glen refused, because he wanted to wait until the end of the session and sign all bills at the same time. When the lower house insisted, he changed his mind and signed a few bills on June 21. He still refused to act on the additional justices bill, however, and in retaliation the Commons House revived an old issue, introducing a bill to pay for the two sloops by emitting £16,000 in public orders; both houses passed it within a week.[41]

A final conflict between the governor and lower house developed on June 27, when Glen asked the assembly to exempt his house rent and salary from the provincial tax. The next day Glen requested the assembly to increase the allowance for his rent, and he also asked for special compensation because he had relinquished his right to license taverns. A special committee of the house rejected all of Glen's requests and expressed surprise that Glen would ask for special favors when so many people were still suffering from the recession. It also pointed out that Glen had infringed upon the house's privileges by commenting officially on the tax bill before its final passage. The house adopted the committee's report unanimously on June 29.[42]

Almost as an afterthought, the Commons House lashed out at the council as well as the governor. In working on the tax bill the upper house had sent a schedule of proposed amendments to the lower house. The Commons accepted and voted on the council's proposed amendments, but then it suddenly decided that this procedure contradicted its claim to the sole right of framing money bills. It therefore resolved on June 29 that "It is the Opinion of this House that no Agreement should at any Time be made with the Council to countenance or warrant their sending any Schedule of Amendments at any Time to the Tax Bill or Estimate or any Subsidy Bill."[43] In short, the

[41] June 10–11, 13, 20–21, 1748, *ibid.*, 304, 306, 310–11, 337–41.
[42] June 27–29, 1748, *ibid.*, 368, 374, 395–99.
[43] June 29, 1748, *ibid.*, 390–91.

Commons House denied the council's right to suggest amendments to money bills. The tax bill for 1748 had already been passed, however, and the Commons House did not even send a copy of its resolution to the council. It would be the responsibility of other houses in the future to enforce the resolution.

By June 29, 1748, the Commons House had exhausted Glen's patience. It had passed the bill to pay for the two sloops with public orders even though it knew he opposed it. It had demanded that he sign the additional justices bill against his wishes. It had turned down his personal requests for tax exemptions and special appropriations, and it had accused him of infringing its rights. It had complained about the high cost of Indian affairs, and it had reduced his control over Indian expenditures. Glen could not tolerate such behavior any longer. In a long, rambling letter to the Commons House he defended his handling of Indian affairs and argued that expenses were declining. Then he called both houses before him and vetoed both the bill to pay for the sloops and the additional justices bill. Finally he prorogued the assembly until August without giving either house time to return to its chambers. He had the prudence, however, to sign the tax bill.[44]

Glen's action caught his opponents off guard. They had no recourse except to the public press, and Peter Timothy, editor of the *South-Carolina Gazette,* was glad to oblige them. He published protests against the prorogation and a statement that sought to prove that Indian expenses were increasing. Next he printed a series of pointed essays on good and evil magistrates and the capacity of the people to govern themselves. The council, like everyone else, was surprised by Glen, and it took pains to dissociate itself from the governor, inserting a notation in its journals that Glen had committed "so hasty and precipitous an act" without its "Advice or Approbation." It also made sure that the *Gazette* informed its readers that Glen alone was responsible for proroguing the assembly.[45]

The assembly of 1748 did not meet again. The Commons House could not assemble a quorum in August or September, and in November Glen received official notification that the Crown had disallowed the election act of 1745. Glen therefore dissolved the assembly and issued writs for new elections in December. Once again the Commons House failed to assemble a quorum in January 1749. Glen was reluctant to dissolve another assembly before it met officially,

[44] June 29, 1748, *ibid.,* 400–403.

[45] *S-C. Gaz.* (Charles Town) , July 9, 16, 25, 29, Aug. 1, 8, 1748; Council Journal, June 29, 1748, no. 15, 352, S. C. Archives.

but the council urged him to do so. Another house was elected in March 1749, and an assembly finally met officially on March 30, 1749, for the first time in nine months.[46]

King George's War ended long before the new assembly met, and the end of the war removed the causes of friction between Glen and the Commons House. The *South-Carolina Gazette* announced the cessation of hostilities on August 15, 1748, and within a year the southern Indians made peace with England and each other. The Cherokees, Chickasaws, and Catawbas renewed their treaties with South Carolina, and the Cherokees and Creeks agreed to a peace treaty under South Carolina's supervision.[47] Furthermore, the Crown authorized Glen to build a fort in the Cherokee nation at its expense, and it even assumed the financial burden of Indian presents. The Lords of the Treasury granted a total of £6,000 sterling to South Carolina and Georgia for Indian presents in 1749 and 1750. The Crown's plans worked poorly at first, because royal officials tried to control the distribution of presents from London. The South Carolina assembly took over the distribution of presents after 1750, however, and it established a stockpile of non-perishable goods purchased with the Crown's money. It was distributing presents to the Indians from this source as late as 1754.[48] Thus, the Crown relieved one grievance of the Commons House at the same time that the need for Indian presents was diminishing.

The end of the war also brought the return of economic prosperity, which removed the other chief source of friction. With no privateers to threaten shipping, the market value of rice tripled, reaching 9s. sterling per hundredweight in 1749. The good rice market discouraged the cultivation of indigo to some degree, but the Parliamentary bounty kept production at its wartime level. Provincial taxes dropped to £48,000 currency in 1749, and South Carolina entered a decade of prosperity.[49]

The Commons House that met in 1749 lacked the self-assertiveness

[46] *S-C. Gaz.* (Charles Town), Aug. 15, Nov. 7, 1748; Council Journal, Feb. 3, 14, 1749, no. 17, Pt. i, 109–10, 184–85, S. C. Archives; Mar. 28, 30, 1749, Easterby, ed., *Commons Journal, 1749–50,* 3, 12–13.

[47] *S-C. Gaz.* (Charles Town), Aug. 15, 1748; Glen to Bd. of Trade, Aug. 12, 1749, S. C. Pub. Recs., XXIII, 388–91, S. C. Archives; Corkran, *Cherokee Frontier,* 21–22.

[48] Mar. 31, 1749, Easterby, ed., *Commons Journal, 1749–50,* 17–18; Atkin, *Indians of So. Col. Frontier,* 30–33; Memorial of William Henry Lyttelton, [1756], Treas. 1/358, foll. 232–34, PRO; Apr. 29, 1752, Nov. 16, 1754, Commons Journal, XXVII, 395–97, XXX, 50, S. C. Archives.

[49] Taylor, "Wholesale Commodity Prices," *Jour. Econ. and Bus. Hist.,* 4 (1932), 358, 360–61, 372; Gray, *Hist. of Agriculture,* I, 292–93; Brock, Currency of Colonies, 446–47, 456–57; May 24, 1749, Easterby, ed., *Commons Journal, 1749–50,* 188–189.

of its predecessors, and it backed down before both Glen and the council. It gave way to Glen on the question of paying for the two sloops. It abandoned the notion of emitting public orders and voted to pay half the cost of the sloops in the tax bill of 1749 and the other half in the tax bill of 1750. As for the council, the Commons House ignored its resolution of 1748 in which it had decided not to accept the council's proposals for amending money bills. According to the lower house's journals, it even permitted the council to amend the tax bill for 1749.[50]

The Commons House of 1749 had enough spirit, however, to rebuff Glen on two other points. The house decided in May to outfit two scout boats to patrol the colony's southern coast in order to stop runaway slaves. Glen opposed the plan, because the Crown had decided to provide three boats for the same purpose. The lower house thought the need was too urgent to wait for the Crown to act, so it ordered the commissary general to purchase two boats. Glen signed the order, too, thus avoiding another dispute and preserving the form of his authority. The fact remained, though, that the Commons House had made an executive decision and forced the governor to accept it.[51] Later in the session the house opposed Glen again. It had lost confidence in the provincial agent, Peregrine Fury, when he had helped suppress the report on the St. Augustine expedition a few years earlier. In May 1749 it decided to discharge Fury, who was a friend of the governor, and it replaced him with James Crokatt, a London merchant and former resident of Charles Town who did not get along well with Glen. The governor took Crokatt's appointment as a personal insult and told the Commons House, "Gentlemen, If you have any Complaints against your Governor, 'tis possible you could not make Choice of a Person more Proper on that Occasion than Mr. Crokatt." [52]

V

The year 1749 marked the end of six years of inconclusive fussing over the constitution of South Carolina. The Commons House had tried to limit still further the council's power over money bills and the governor had tried to gain control of the council, but both had failed except for the governor's readmission to the legislative sessions of the

[50] May 17, 23, 25, 1749, Easterby, ed., Commons Journal, 1749–50, 118, 173–77, 199.
[51] May 16, 19, 24, 1749, ibid., 109–11, 154, 185.
[52] June 1, 1749, ibid., 276.

upper house. The Commons House had attacked the governor in 1748, but it had backed down in 1749. Its only victory was an increase in its control over expenditures for Indian affairs. In short, important constitutional issues had been raised, but with two minor exceptions, none of them had been settled. Neither the governor, council, nor lower house had amended the provincial constitution; they had merely tinkered with it.

CHAPTER XII

THE DECLINE OF GOVERNOR GLEN

1750-1753

The constitutional debate in South Carolina turned to the office of governor in 1750, and for four years James Glen found himself under attack from three different directions. A revived and reformed Board of Trade began to reduce the governor's autonomy by insisting on a literal obedience of its instructions. Next, the council undertook an investigation of Glen's handling of the Choctaw revolt, and it again raised the issue of the governor's right to sit in on its legislative sessions. Finally, the Commons House of Assembly tried to encroach upon the governor's prerogatives in several different areas. Only an exceptionally astute or influential politician would have been able to defend his rights and privileges successfully, and James Glen was not noted for either his astuteness or his influence.

I

At the end of 1749, just before the first of the attacks upon his constitutional position, Glen stood at the peak of his political career in South Carolina. Earlier in the year he had won a victory over the Commons House by forcing it to accept his plan for financing the two sloops, and he had restored the English system of alliances among the Indians. To consolidate his power still further he began about 1749 to form his own clique of followers in the Commons House. The faction's leader was Chief Justice James Graeme, and two other members were Dr. James Irving and Dr. Thomas Glen, the governor's brother. One of

Glen's opponents said that most of the governor's faction were young men who were susceptible to his "art of winning over youth by his Smile, a Dinner or Glass [of] wine." Because of the importance of Indian diplomacy during Glen's administration, his friends concentrated on the standing committee on Indian affairs; they acquired control of it, and James Graeme became its chairman.[1]

Glen also benefited from a continuation of the truce between the council and the Commons House. Their disputes had disrupted the first years of his administration, but from 1749 to 1753 the two houses merely toyed with each other without really coming to blows. The Commons revived the old issue of the council's right to propose sources of revenue in February 1750, and the upper house relinquished its claims without much of a struggle. The issue arose in debate on a bill to finance the settlement of some recent German immigrants when the council suggested the use of surplus funds in the general treasury. The Commons House reiterated its belief that it had "the sole Right of pointing out and providing ways and means for raising Supplies." The upper house did not even reply to the resolution, and although it later rejected a bill to help the immigrants, it did so only because the lower house turned down a council amendment relating to fees.[2]

The Commons tried a new approach to the reduction of the council's powers in March 1750 by trying to expand the definition of money bills, but this time the lower house backed away from a fight. The assembly had previously defined only the annual tax bill as a money bill, but it now tried to broaden the definition to include any law involving public funds. The council amended a routine bill to offer a bounty for the manufacture of potash, and the lower house expressed the opinion that the potash bill was a money bill and should not be amended by the upper house. Almost every legislative act involved public funds in some way, and surrender to the Commons House on the potash bill would have undermined the council's constitutional position. The council therefore adopted on May 1 a series of resolutions on the definition of money bills. The resolutions pointed out that Parliament defined money bills only as those bills that granted funds to the Crown for general purposes, such as tax bills. The council also noted that Parliament did not consider bills that granted funds for specific purposes as money bills, and it reminded the

[1] William Pinckney to Charles McNair, May 18, 1750, CO 5/373, fol. 51, PRO; see also Mathew Roche to McNair, May 30, 1750, *ibid.*, fol. 54.
[2] Feb. 7, 10, 1750, Easterby, ed., *Commons Journal, 1749–50*, 394, 396–97, 407–8; Mar. 15–16, 1750, Upper House Journal, CO 5/461, 46–47, 49–51, PRO.

lower house that it had amended similar bills in 1747, 1748, and 1749.[3] With both Parliamentary custom and local practice against it, the Commons House abandoned its effort to redefine money bills.

The two houses then laid aside their disputes and did not renew them until 1754. During that time the Commons House allowed the council to exercise all its traditional rights and privileges in peace. For example, the upper house continued to propose amendments to tax bills, and the Commons House received the suggestions and accepted or rejected them on their merits. The lower house even sent the council all petitions and accounts relating to the tax bill.[4]

With the two legislative houses at peace, Glen's position was challenged only by the Board of Trade, but its challenge was one of the utmost gravity. Throughout the 1730's and 1740's the Board of Trade had taken little interest in South Carolina or any other colony. Sir John Monson, president of the Board from 1737 to 1748, had regarded his appointment as a sinecure, and a majority of the Board had followed his example. The Board had allowed the Duke of Newcastle, as secretary of state for the southern department, to take over some of its functions, and it had neglected many of its other duties, including correspondence with the colonial governors. As a result, Glen's predecessors had enjoyed a high degree of independence from interference by the Crown, and they had been free to interpret their instructions liberally and even to disobey them occasionally without being reprimanded or punished. Monson had died in the spring of 1748, however, and other Board members had begun immediately to revive and reform the Board. Monson had been succeeded in the fall of 1748 by the Earl of Halifax, an ambitious politician who knew little of colonial affairs but who sympathized with the reform-minded Board members. During a reshuffling of the British ministry in 1751 Halifax acquired complete control of colonial affairs, including patronage appointments. Consequently, the Board of Trade had more power during his presidency than ever before, and Halifax and the reformers on the Board were determined to use that power to enforce the Crown's policy in the colonies. In particular, they insisted upon a much closer supervision of colonial governors, and they began to scrutinize colonial laws and correspondence with great care. They

<hr />

[3] Mar. 16, 1750, Easterby, ed., *Commons Journal, 1749–50*, 471–72; May 1, 1750, Upper House Journal, CO 5/461, 61–64, PRO.

[4] See, e.g., May 10–11, 1751, Upper House Journal, XIX, 83–84, S. C. Archives; Apr. 13–14, 18, 1751, *ibid.*, XXII, Pt. i, 43–45, 53–54; May 10, 1754, Commons Journal, XXIX, 394–95, 397, 402, S. C. Archives.

demanded that governors adhere to the letter of their instructions, and if a governor ignored his instructions or permitted an assembly to encroach upon the royal prerogative, the Board of Trade promptly corrected him.[5]

James Glen felt the effects of the reform of the Board of Trade sooner than most colonial governors, because he had lost his political influence in England. His original patron, the Earl of Wilmington, and his uncle, the Scottish Earl of Dalhousie, had died during the 1740's, and he had no one to intercede for him at court.[6] To make matters worse, Glen had laid himself open to criticism by neglecting his correspondence with the Board of Trade and by assenting to several laws contrary to his instructions.

The Board of Trade began to reprimand Glen in 1748 and kept up a stream of criticism for the next two years. It started by rebuking Glen for signing the election act of 1745 and the justices act of 1746; it told him, "We much doubt whether any Instances are to be found of a Governor having given his Assent to two Acts more inconsistent with his Instructions [or] tending more to the Destruction of His Majesty's Prerogative."[7] Glen's veto of the assembly's bill for defraying the expenses of the two sloops earned a commendation from the Board, but he was soon in trouble again. In 1749 he prepared a long report on the state of the province at the Board's request, but then he submitted it to the assembly for corrections and suggestions. The Board of Trade reprimanded him for not keeping the report a secret. In November 1750 the Board wrote a long letter in which it recited all of Glen's mistakes, both great and small. It criticized him most for failing to protect the royal prerogative, and it cited as particulars the assembly's custom of itemizing appropriations in the tax bill, the omission of suspending clauses from several bills, and the current militia law, which deprived the governor of the right to order militia out of the colony. The Board epitomized its indictment of the governor by saying, "We have seldom opportunity of Writing to you upon the

---

[5] Arthur H. Basye, *The Lords Commissioners of Trade and Plantations, Commonly Known as the Board of Trade, 1748–1782* (New Haven, 1925), 30–50; Oliver M. Dickerson, *American Colonial Government . . .* (Cleveland, 1912), 35–50, 67.

[6] See G. F. Russell Barker in *DNB* s.v. "Compton, Spencer, Earl of Wilmington"; J. G. B. Bullock, *A History of the Glen Family of South Carolina and Georgia* (n.p., 1923), 8–9.

[7] Bd. of Trade to Glen, Dec. 20, 1748, S. C. Pub. Recs., XXIII, 280, S. C. Archives.

affairs of your Province without being obliged at the same time to complain of some Departure from your Instructions and often of a Notorious Breach of Prerogative." [8] In brief, Governor Glen was in serious trouble with the Board of Trade.

II

While James Glen was still under fire from the Board of Trade, he was confronted by another personal political crisis in South Carolina, precipitated for once by the council. The council had always distrusted Glen, particularly because of his presence at its legislative sessions, and the governor's poor management of the Choctaw revolt gave it an opportunity to embarrass or even disgrace him. In 1749 the council first voiced its suspicions of Glen's handling of the revolt, when it voted unanimously to reject a petition submitted by Charles McNair.[9] A year later it launched a full-scale inquiry into the Choctaw revolt, and the investigation ignited a major dispute with the governor, in which both sides raised fundamental questions about the council's constitutional rights.

About a year before the investigation began, Glen had finally broken off his disastrous association with McNair and Company. When the time had come to send another load of arms and ammunition to the Choctaws in 1749 he had by-passed McNair and selected John Pettycrow, an independent trader who was not associated with McNair. Pettycrow had delivered the goods promptly and efficiently, thus raising the false hope that South Carolina might preserve its Choctaw alliance. Glen abandoned McNair completely in 1750 and told a new story about the Choctaw revolt, which gave most of the credit to one James Adair. According to this new version, Glen had sent Adair into the Choctaw nation in 1744 or 1745 to agitate against the French, and Adair had persuaded Red Shoes to start the revolt. In fact, however, Adair had been an unlicensed Chickasaw trader when the revolt started, and he had apparently done nothing except to go into the Choctaw nation and make extravagant promises of English presents. He seems to have done more harm than good, because when Charles McNair arrived among the Choctaws in 1747 he had discovered that they expected more presents than he could deliver. Adair

[8] Bd. of Trade to Glen, Nov. 15, 1750, *ibid.*, XXIV, 148–77; the quotation is from p. 168; see also Bd. of Trade to Glen, Oct. 26, 1748, Dec. 1, 1749, *ibid.*, XXIII, 250–51, 420–24.

[9] May 27, 1749, Upper House Journal, XVI, Pt. ii, 63, S. C. Archives.

petitioned the assembly in April 1750, asking for a reward for his alleged services, and Glen supported him. Since Charles McNair had returned to England, Matthew Roche, one of his former partners, tried to defend the interests of McNair and Company. He wrote a pamphlet accusing Glen of prevarication and breach of promise, and he submitted the pamphlet and a petition to the assembly on May 3, 1750.[10]

The council appointed a committee to investigate Adair's claims as soon as it received his petition, and it later referred Roche's petition and pamphlet to the same group. The committee of inquiry was headed by Edmund Atkin, the long-time champion of the council's rights and an old foe of the governor. The committee soon reported against both Adair and Roche; it said that Red Shoes had started the revolt by himself and that both petitioners were lying. In its opinion the only Englishman who deserved a reward was John Campbell, a Chickasaw trader who had given presents from his own storehouse to the Choctaws in 1747. The committee also reported that both Adair and McNair had hurt South Carolina's interest among the Choctaws, Adair because of his extravagant promises and McNair because of his incompetence in delivering presents. Finally, the committee condemned Roche's pamphlet as a libel against the governor and recommended that he be arrested for contempt. The council followed the committee's report to the letter. It rejected both petitions and held Roche in custody until he apologized.[11]

The Commons House of Assembly next examined the petitions of Adair and Roche, but the governor's friends in the lower house blocked any criticism of Glen. There was some confusion between the two houses. Atkin's committee walked out of a conference with a committee from the lower house, because the Commons committee had invited Glen to testify without consulting the committee from the upper house. Then the Commons committee inadvertently prevented a witness from testifying before the council committee. Suitable apologies smoothed over the incidents, however, and the Commons House rejected the petitions of both Adair and Roche. James Graeme, the chairman of the Commons committee on Indian affairs and the leader of Glen's faction in the lower house, managed to protect the governor's reputation. His committee criticized McNair severely, but it

---

[10] Atkin, "Revolt of the Choctaw Indians," Lansdowne Mss., 809, foll. 16–21, Brit. Mus.; on Adair's role in the revolt, see Nov. 13, 1747, Council Journal, no. 15, 57–60, S. C. Archives.

[11] May 3, 10, 1750, Upper House Journal, CO 5/461, 72–73, 78–79, 81–91, PRO.

did not even mention Glen in its report and it said as little as possible against Glen's new ally, James Adair.[12]

Rejection of the petitions did not satisfy the council. It wanted to uncover the whole truth about the Choctaw revolt and appointed a committee, again with Atkin as chairman, to investigate all the proceedings of McNair and Company. The committee found itself at a standstill, however, because it discovered that the colony had not preserved its Indian records for the period of the Choctaw revolt. When it turned to the governor for help, he was reluctant to cooperate. Glen apparently was afraid of what the committee might uncover, and he tried to stall it by saying that he had left his copies of the missing Indian records at his home in the country. Fortunately for Glen, the assembly had finished its regular business, and the Commons House adjourned on May 31 until the following November.[13]

The adjournment of the assembly should have ended the investigation by the council, which had been acting as the upper house of the legislature, but several councilors were determined to press on. Regarding adjournment as another of Glen's subterfuges, they decided to continue to sit as the upper house and carry on the investigation. They thus tacitly advanced a constitutional argument that was tenuous at best: that one house of the assembly could transact business while the other house was adjourned. Charles Pinckney and perhaps one or two other councilors rejected this opinion and refused to attend any sessions after May 31. Only three men remained to carry on the inquiry—Edmund Atkin, Hector Beringer de Beaufain, and William Bull, Jr.—but three was a quorum in the upper house.

The comic-opera climax to the struggle between the council and the governor came on June 2, 1750. The three councilors sent a message to Glen on June 1, but he refused to accept it and told the master in chancery not to deliver any more messages from the upper house; Glen went to the council chamber the next morning and told the three councilors they were proceeding illegally because the assembly was adjourned. Glen might have won the argument if he had stopped there, but he went on to revive the issue of the governor's right to sit with the upper house. He said the councilors *"had not a Right even to sit at all as an Upper House, without himself being present."* [14] Glen

[12] May 15, 1750, *ibid.*, 99–101; May 16, 19, 23, 24, 1750, Commons Journal, XXV, 622–23, 660–66, 681–90, 696–99, S. C. Archives; Mathew Roche to McNair, May 30, 1750, CO 5/373, fol. 54, PRO; Atkin, "Revolt of the Choctaw Indians," Lansdowne Mss., 809, fol. 22, Brit. Mus.

[13] Atkin, "Revolt of the Choctaw Indians," Lansdowne Mss., 809, fol. 23, Brit. Mus.

[14] *Ibid.*, italics in original.

then took the seat at the head of the council table and announced that the council was in session to transact administrative business, while the three councilors regarded themselves as the upper house of assembly in session to transact legislative business. The three men therefore resolved that the governor had "put a Stop to the Business before this House" by refusing to receive messages in the customary manner and professed themselves to be "at a loss how to Proceed further." Then everyone sat around the council table without speaking for "some time." Glen finally broke the silence by saying the questions raised were "Matters of great Consequence" and promised to give the councilors an answer that afternoon.[15]

Glen never delivered his answer, however, and the upper house never finished its investigation. Atkin, Beaufain, and Bull met that afternoon and the next three days as well, but Glen did not answer their questions on procedure. The councilors adjourned on June 6, after instructing the committee on Indian affairs to proceed as best it could, but the committee did not submit any further reports.[16]

The council won a major victory as a result of the dispute, however, for Glen abandoned his attempts to participate in the legislative sessions of the upper house. When the assembly reconvened in October, Glen appeared before the upper house and began to read a statement defending his handling of the Choctaw revolt. After the governor had read a few sentences the councilors cut him off because they expected him to criticize their actions. Glen appeared before the upper house for the last time in November 1750 to address both houses and to receive the council's reply.[17] After that, the journals of the upper house never again recorded a governor as being present. Presumably, Glen and his successors as governor did not try to force themselves upon the upper house.

III

After the debacle of the council's investigation of the Choctaw revolt, James Glen altered fundamentally his approach to the governorship. From his arrival in 1743 through 1750, Glen had held himself aloof from existing political groups in South Carolina and tried to build up a party of his own. After 1750, however, he abandoned his

[15] June 2, 1750, Upper House Journal, CO 5/461, 171–73, PRO; see also Glen to Bd. of Trade, July 15, 1750, S. C. Pub. Recs., XXIV, 78–81, S. C. Archives.

[16] June 2–6, 1750, Upper House Journal, CO 5/461, 174–75; Atkin, "Revolt of the Choctaw Indians," Lansdowne Mss., 809, fol. 23, Brit. Mus.

[17] Atkin, "Revolt of Choctaw Indians," Lansdowne Mss., 809, fol. 23, Brit. Mus.; Nov. 22–23, 1750, Upper House Journal, CO 5/461, 177–88, PRO.

independent ways and allied himself with the Bull family. His handling of Indian affairs changed fundamentally, too. He had not previously followed a consistent general policy toward the Indians, but after 1750 he adopted James Oglethorpe's old policy of trying to create an alliance system that included all English Indians. Glen also began to handle Indian diplomacy with greater skill than before, and the last six years of his administration saw him successfully conclude a series of delicate negotiations with the Indians.

Perhaps the reasons for Glen's metamorphosis lay in the reprimands he continued to receive from the Board of Trade. He tried desperately to redeem his reputation in London after 1750, but without any luck. He wrote a long letter in December 1751 defending his management of Indian affairs, but the Board paid little heed to it. He began to veto any bill that appeared to threaten the royal prerogative in any way, even very minor bills, but the Board still seemed oblivious to his efforts. It blamed Glen unjustly for every encroachment upon the royal prerogative that had ever taken place in South Carolina, and it decided in 1754 to replace Glen. The last years of Glen's administration were thus clouded by the realization that he had lost his influence and after 1754 by the knowledge that he was losing his job.[18]

In order to shore up his political influence, Glen formed an alliance with the Bull family about 1751. The Bulls and their in-laws, the Middletons and Draytons, still played an active role in South Carolina politics, and their friendship helped the governor. They were especially strong on the council, and from 1751 to 1756 the council cooperated with the governor rather than opposing him. In return, Glen appointed members of the clans to political offices; William Bull, Jr., represented South Carolina at an Indian conference in New York in 1751, Charles Pinckney, an old associate of the Bulls, became acting chief justice in 1752; and Thomas Middleton became receiver general in 1756. The alliance was consolidated in 1752 by the marriage of Glen's sister to John Drayton; the Bulls and their in-laws had not merely made an alliance with Glen, they had adopted him into their clan. When Glen appointed Thomas Middleton receiver general, Edmund Atkin commented, "This seems to have been a political Step

[18] Glen to Bd. of Trade, Dec. 1751, Bd. of Trade to William Henry Lyttelton, Nov. 9, 1757, S. C. Pub. Recs., XXIV, 389–423, XXVII, 325, S. C. Archives; "Memorandum relating to South Carolina," Mar. 28, 1754, Newcastle Papers, Add. Mss., 33030, foll. 346–47, Brit. Mus.; May 8, 1754, Commons Journal, XXIX, 353, S. C. Archives; on Glen's vetoes, see, e.g., Apr. 24, 1751, Upper House Journal, XIX, 51, S. C. Archives.

in making his [Glen's] Retreat knowing the Connections between the
Bull, Drayton and Middleton Families." [19] Glen himself testified to his
association with the Bull family when William Bull, Sr., died in 1755.
He and the lieutenant governor had battled each other frequently
during the 1740's, but in 1755 Glen delivered a eulogy on the man he
had once accused of unhinging the frame of government. He said, "I
was frequently benefited by following his Advice, more frequently by
imitating his Example, and when I could not equal, I endeavoured to
copy after him." [20]

Even before he formed his alliance with the Bulls, Glen began to
work out a new general Indian policy. He explained his new policy
clearly in 1750 when he said, "I hope . . . that we shall concert a
general Comprehensive Plan of uniting together all the Indians upon
the Continent that are in Treaty or Alliance, or have any dependence
upon the British Government, that as they are all Friends with the
English they may be in perfect friendship one with another." [21] The
idea of uniting all English Indians in a general alliance system had
been originated by Lieutenant Governor George Clarke of New York a
decade earlier and introduced to the southern frontier by General
James Oglethorpe. By 1750 the plan had won the approval of several
colonial governors, including George Clinton of New York. Glen
himself had been trying to make peace between the Creeks and
Cherokees since 1745, but he had not applied the policy to all Indians
before 1750. Glen's adoption of the new policy was founded largely
upon a growing respect for Indians and humanitarian concern for
their welfare. He rejected the common prejudice that they were merely
savages; and he even argued that white men should purchase Indian
land before settling on it. In 1760, when South Carolina was at war
with the Cherokees, Glen opposed the war because he thought
England should try to civilize the Indians instead of fighting them. He
asked at that time, "We call them Savages, have we been at any pains
to civilize them?" [22]

---

[19] To William Henry Lyttelton, May 20, 1756, William Henry Lyttelton Papers,
Clements Lib.; see also Sirmans, "Bull Family," S. C. Hist. Assn., Proceedings, 1962
(1963), 39–40.

[20] S-C. Gaz. (Charles Town), Apr. 3, 1755.

[21] To George Clinton, Sept. 25, 1750, George Clinton Papers, Clements Lib.

[22] To Jeffrey Amherst, Apr. 28, 1760, Amherst Papers, War Office Papers, 34/47,
fol. 11, PRO; see also Glen to the Earl of Holderness and Bd. of Trade, June 25,
1753, S. C. Pub. Recs., XXV, 295–98, 329–30, S. C. Archives. For a completely
different view of Glen, see Adair, Hist. of Amer. Indians, ed. Williams, 298; for a
slightly different interpretation, see John R. Alden, John Stuart and the Southern
Colonial Frontier . . . , 1754–1775 (Ann Arbor, 1944), 25–26.

Glen's management of Indian diplomacy began to improve after he adopted his new policy. It was too late to save the Choctaw alliance, however, and the entire nation returned to the French interest by 1752.[23] On the other hand, Glen helped to persuade the Catawbas and the Iroquois to accept a peace treaty. Both nations were English allies, but the Iroquois had been raiding Catawba towns since 1745. Governor Clinton of New York proposed a general conference of all governors with the Iroquois in 1751 and suggested to Glen that this would be a good time to end the Iroquois-Catawba war. Glen could not attend because of trouble with the Cherokees, but he sent William Bull, Jr., as his representative, along with King Hagler of the Catawbas and five of his braves. Bull and Clinton persuaded the two nations to make peace at Albany in 1751, and the Indians ended hostilities with an exchange of prisoners in 1752. Further mediation was occasionally necessary, but the war did not break out again. For a time Glen also wanted to negotiate a peace treaty between the Iroquois and the Creeks, but the Iroquois rejected his offer of intercession. Fortunately, the distance between the two nations precluded any fighting except occasional skirmishes.[24]

Glen's new policy was tested again by a renewal of the Creek-Cherokee war, which flared up when the Creeks attacked the Cherokees in 1750. The peace treaty of 1749 required Glen to punish the Creeks, but he could do nothing because Georgia refused to cooperate with him. The Cherokees then turned against South Carolina, because they believed, with justification, that South Carolina had defaulted on its treaty obligations. The Cherokees killed and robbed several South Carolina traders in retaliation, and their raids enraged the Commons House of Assembly. The Commons insisted that the Cherokees must be punished and persuaded Glen to embargo all trade with them. Glen finally managed to bring order out of the confused situation, and he negotiated a new Cherokee treaty and reopened trade in November 1751. Nevertheless, the Creek-Cherokee war lasted another year, because the Creeks would not accept a peace treaty. Glen threatened the Creeks with a trade embargo, and the two nations finally agreed on a treaty in October 1752 and did not go to war again.[25]

Although Glen's policy of a general alliance system was working well, it could not solve another major problem involving the Chero-

[23] July 18, 1752, Council Journal, no. 20, Pt. ii, 327–29, S. C. Archives.
[24] Milling, *Red Carolinians*, 243–47; Glen to Clinton, May 21, 1751, George Clinton Papers, Clements Lib.; Clinton to Glen, Dec. 18, 1750, McDowell, ed., *S. C. Indian Documents, 1750–1754*, 9, 204, 214.
[25] Corkran, *Cherokee Frontier*, 23–27.

kees. The nation was split into two factions, one loyal to England and one determined to free the Cherokees from dependence upon any European country, including England. The English faction centered in the middle and lower towns, while the nativistic faction was led by the overhill town of Chota and drew its support mostly from the other overhill towns. Chota had been more or less anti-English since 1738, because South Carolina had ignored its claims and recognized a chief from another town as Cherokee emperor. The Creek war strengthened the Chota faction and discredited the English chiefs, because South Carolina's trade embargo had left the Cherokees unable to defend themselves. Many middle and lower Cherokees blamed South Carolina and its allies for their wartime losses, and they began to turn to Chota for guidance. Glen realized what was happening, and he, too, began to ignore the English chiefs and treated Chota as the leading Cherokee town. The overhill Cherokees accepted Glen's overtures and were willing to renew their alliance with England, but only on their own terms. They particularly wanted Glen to guarantee them an adequate supply of trade goods, and when they conferred with Glen in Charles Town in the summer of 1753, they refused to confirm the alliance until Glen promised to increase their share of the trade. Glen saw, however, that he could not trust the overhill chiefs because of their nativism, so he worked out a plan to counteract their influence. He had been talking for several years about building a fort in Cherokee country to protect the Indians from their enemies, and he now revived the idea for a different reason. If he built the fort in the lower towns, it would be easier to keep the friendship of the lower and middle Cherokees and even to wean them away from Chota. Using money the assembly had appropriated for a fort the previous year, he led an expedition into the lower towns in October 1753. There, near the town of Keowee, he built a fort of earth and wood and named it Fort Prince George in honor of the heir to the British throne. He completed the fort in December and stationed a seventeen-man garrison there before he returned to Charles Town.[26]

IV

After Governor Glen formed his alliance with the Bull family, the center of opposition to him shifted from the council to the Commons House of Assembly. The house found many excuses to complain about Glen's conduct after 1750, but it was fundamentally renewing its drive

[26] *Ibid.*, 38–49.

to increase its powers at the governor's expense. In 1751 and 1752 it challenged his use of the veto power, his right to direct Indian affairs, and his control over fortifications. To make matters worse for Glen, his clique in the lower house dissolved when its leader, James Graeme, moved up to the council in 1751. No one remained in the house to speak for the governor, and the attacks on his rights and privileges came with increasing frequency.

Because of the Board of Trade's criticism, Glen had begun to veto assembly bills that deviated from his instructions, and it was his use of the veto that provoked his first quarrel with the assembly in 1751. The assembly passed a bill that divided St. Philip's Parish in Charles Town into two parishes and established assembly representation for the new parish. Glen vetoed the bill on April 24, because it encroached upon the Crown's authority and because he thought there was no necessary connection between erecting a parish and setting assembly representation. The bill was very popular, and Glen remarked in his veto message that he had heard the assembly would complain to the Crown if he vetoed it. Ten days later, on May 4, he vetoed two other bills, one to revive several expiring laws and one to incorporate the Charles Town Library Society, because he thought they contained technical flaws.[27]

Glen's vetoes outraged the Commons House, and it requested permission to adjourn until October although it had not yet passed a tax bill. The house said it could see no point in continuing its sessions if Glen were going to nullify its "best Endeavours," but the governor denied it permission to adjourn. The assembly was meeting during one of the most violent phases of the Creek-Cherokee war, and it learned on May 8 that the Cherokees had killed four English traders. The Commons House regarded the murders as the final proof of Glen's incompetence, and it resolved on May 10 to petition the Crown in protest against Glen's vetoes and his conduct of Indian affairs.[28]

The threat of a petition to the Crown frightened Glen because of his precarious relationship with the Board of Trade, and he quickly agreed on a compromise with the Commons House. It is impossible to say exactly what happened next, except that the house dropped its petition and Glen signed the disputed bills. Glen prorogued the assembly for three days in order to permit the bills to be reintroduced, and both houses passed the bill to divide St. Philip's Parish and the

[27] Apr. 24, May 4, 9, 1751, Commons Journal, XXVI, 309–15, 402, 420–24, S. C. Archives.

[28] May 7–8, 10, 1751, *ibid.*, XXVI, 407–9, 411–13, 456–58, 461–63.

bill to revive expiring laws without delay. The assembly apparently made a few changes in the bills, but in their final form they still included provisions that Glen had opposed. Glen signed the bills on June 14 and praised the Commons House for not being "a set of stiff positive People." [29]

No sooner had one dispute ended than another one began, this time concerning Indian affairs. The Commons House had supported Glen's Indian policy before 1750, but it opposed his efforts to negotiate alliance treaties among all the English Indians. It hesitated to become involved in intertribal wars, because its members thought the Indians would probably fight among themselves anyway. The house also disliked Glen's plans for building a fort in the Cherokee nation unless the Crown paid for it, and it had turned down Glen's request for an appropriation for the fort in 1750.[30] Peter Timothy, the editor of the *South-Carolina Gazette,* supported the house in its opposition to the governor's Indian policy and accused him of "wretched Management of Indian Affairs." [31]

The controversy over Indian affairs in 1751 began when Glen called the assembly into special session in August. Glen informed the assembly that the Cherokees had agreed to make reparations for the four traders they had killed, and he said the time had come to put Anglo-Cherokee relations on a better footing. He therefore called for money to build a Cherokee fort and for a new law to regulate the Indian trade. The old trade law had just expired, and even the Commons House had admitted earlier that it did not give enough power to the commissioner of the Indian trade. In August 1751, however, the Commons House did not want to be bothered about Indian affairs. The harvest season began in August, and the planters wanted to go home. They agreed to stay only after Glen and the council lectured them on their duty, and even then they were content to pass a temporary ordinance empowering the governor, council, and seven assemblymen to regulate the Indian trade. The house refused to act on the fort unless Glen drew up a prospectus indicating its site, cost, and construction. When the assembly met again in the winter of

[29] May 14–15, June 14, 1751, *ibid.,* 494–95, 612–14; see also May 31, 1751, Council Journal, no. 8, Pt. i, 127–28, S. C. Archives; Cooper and McCord, eds., *Statutes,* III, 751–53, VII, 79–84.
[30] Mar. 15, 17, 1750, Easterby, ed., *Commons Journal, 1749–50,* 467, 481, 483–85; on the Commons' opposition to Glen's general policy, see May 6–8, 1752, Commons Journal, XXVII, 453, 459, 486–87, S. C. Archives.
[31] Timothy to Benjamin Franklin, June 8, 1755, Douglas C. McMurtrie, ed., *Letters of Peter Timothy . . . to Benjamin Franklin* (Chicago, 1935), 14.

1751–1752, it continued to delay action on Indian affairs. It did nothing about a new Indian trade law, and it found a new pretext for not granting money for a fort; it said it thought the lower Cherokee towns might be in North Carolina and nothing should be done until the boundary was settled.[32]

Glen finally prodded the Commons House into action after it reconvened in March 1752, but he was forced to surrender on a constitutional issue before he could do so. When Glen pressed the Commons House about the fort and trade law, the house evaded those issues and raised a constitutional question. Glen had been sending documents relating to Indian affairs only when he wanted appropriations, and even then he had been sending copies instead of the original documents. This practice limited the ability of the lower house to participate in the formulation of Indian policy by restricting its knowledge of Indian affairs. Although the Crown wanted the governor to control Indian policy, the Commons House was not satisfied. It told Glen on March 11 that it expected him to send the original documents "without any delay," but Glen refused because he thought his compliance would infringe upon the royal prerogative. On March 17 the house informed the governor that it must see the original papers in order to form "a true Judgment" of Indian affairs.[33] A stalemate in Indian affairs began at that point and lasted a month and a half; Glen sent the Commons nothing but copies of selected papers, and the house refused to act on the fort or trade law. Then in April Glen learned that Creek Indians had killed five Cherokees, and he was forced to ask the Commons for money to send an agent to the Creeks. Rejecting the request, the house complained on May 1 that it "is kept much in the Dark, relating to Indian Affairs; and cannot help observing that they seldom have any Accounts of them but unless Money is wanted to carry into Execution some Matter recommended by his Excellency." [34] Glen was beaten, and he knew it. On May 5 he began to send original documents to the Commons House "to save the time of copying." Having won its point on the constitutional issue, the house let Glen have his trade law and fort. It passed the law and appropriated £3,000 currency for the fort within two weeks, and it

---

[32] May 17, 26, 1749, Easterby, ed., *Commons Journal, 1749–50*, 126–27, 209, 216; Aug. 28, 30, 1751, Nov. 23, 1751, Jan. 25, 1752, Commons Journal, XXVI, 630–37, 639–52, XXVII, 52–55, 185–86, S. C. Archives; Cooper and McCord, eds., *Statutes*, III, 754–55.

[33] Mar. 11, 13, 17, 1752, Commons Journal, XXVII, 232, 246–47, 267–70, S. C. Archives.

[34] Apr. 29, May 1, 1752, *ibid.*, 401–5, 416–17.

circumvented the boundary question by authorizing Glen to buy the land from the Indians.[35] Thus Glen was compelled to allow the Commons House greater access to Indian documents in order to build the fort and enact the new trade law.

Before the old dispute had disappeared completely a new one began to emerge over the governor's control of fortifications. Glen's commission clearly vested in him "full Power and Authority," with the consent of the council, to build, fortify, and maintain all forts and other fortifications that were necessary to defend South Carolina. The assembly, however, had turned that authority over to a commission of fortifications in 1736.[36] The trouble started on May 5, 1752, when Glen told the Commons House that the commission on fortifications infringed upon the royal prerogative and the act of 1736 must be revised. The lower house objected to Glen's remarks, but it dropped the subject during the summer adjournment. The issue assumed critical importance in September 1752, because a hurricane struck Charles Town and destroyed its military defenses. Glen proposed that the assembly amend the act of 1736 by entrusting control of fortifications to the governor, and he suggested that Charles Town's defenses be completely rebuilt under the direction of John William Gerard De Brahm, an immigrant military engineer from Holland. The Commons House opposed every point of Glen's plan. It insisted that the commissioners of fortifications retain their power, it wanted merely to repair Charles Town's defenses, and it did not trust De Brahm because he was a foreigner. The quarrel dragged on from September to December to the detriment of other public business, but the governor and lower house could not agree on anything. They finally decided in December to petition the Crown for money to rebuild Charles Town's forts, and then they dropped the issue. The city's defenses remained as the hurricane had left them.[37]

The argument over fortifications seems to have exhausted the lower house's capacity for disputation, for it managed to get along with Glen for the rest of his administration without any further serious trouble. Glen vetoed the tax bill in 1753 because it set rates of exchange for foreign coins contrary to the Proclamation of 1704, but the assembly passed a new tax bill without complaint. When Glen built Fort Prince

[35] May 5, 14, 1752, ibid., 444, 552; Cooper and McCord, eds., Statutes, III, 763–71.

[36] Labaree, ed., Royal Instructions, II, 822; Greene, Quest for Power, 254–56.

[37] May 5, 14, Sept. 27, 1752, Commons Journal, XXVII, 434–40, 545–50, 581; Nov. 25, Dec. 7, 13–14, 1752, ibid., XXVIII, 28–31, 83–92, 110–20, 125–33, S. C. Archives; Milligen, Short Description, in Milling, ed., Colonial S. C., 146.

George in 1753 the cost exceeded the amount authorized by the assembly, but the Commons appropriated an additional £5,000 currency, again without complaint. In 1754, when the lower house thought it might be meeting with Glen for the last time, it passed a resolution that praised his management of Indian affairs and referred to "the Happiness we feel and enjoy under your Excellencys mild Administration." [38] Despite all the surface harmony in assembly sessions, an undercurrent of hostility to Glen remained in the Commons House. Henry Laurens, a leader in the house, remarked in 1756 that the prospect of a new governor "puts us in high glee," because "we are much in want of a new Governor we mean a good one." [39]

V

Governor James Glen was still the dominant figure in the government of South Carolina in 1753, but he had suffered considerable damage to his prestige and authority since 1750. The reformed Board of Trade had undermined his independence as governor and reprimanded him repeatedly for disobeying his instructions. The upper house had embarrassed him with its investigation of the Choctaw revolt, and it had excluded him from its legislative sessions. Glen had tried to salvage his position by allying himself with the Bull family, by adopting a more effective Indian policy, and by attempting to defend the royal prerogative against the encroachments of the Commons House of Assembly. He had failed to impress the Board of Trade, however, and his defense of the prerogative had provoked the Commons House. The lower house had clashed with Glen three times in 1751 and 1752, and each time the Commons had beaten him. It had forced him to retract several vetoes, it had gained access to the original documents relating to Indian affairs, and it had frustrated his attempt to regain control of fortifications. By the end of 1753 it was obvious that when Glen stepped down from the governorship, the office would be weaker than when he had assumed it.

[38] May 11, 1754, Commons Journal, XXIX, 423–24, S. C. Archives; see also Glen to Bd. of Trade, July 30, Oct. 25, 1753, Aug. 26, 1754, S. C. Pub. Recs., XXV, 341–42, XXVI, 109, S. C. Archives.
[39] To Devonsheir, Reeve, and Lloyd, Apr. 10, 1756, Letterbooks, II, 217, Laurens Papers, S. C. Hist. Soc.

CHAPTER XIII

THE FALL OF THE COUNCIL

1754–1756

Constitutional developments in general and the rise of the Commons House of Assembly in particular continued to dominate the politics of South Carolina in the mid-1750's, as the lower house persisted in its efforts to accumulate power at the expense of governor and council. The house turned away from the governor in 1754 and shifted its attention to the council, the second obstacle in its path. The attack began with a commonplace disagreement over control of the provincial agent, but it soon expanded into a full-dress constitutional debate. Both houses redefined the provincial constitution in terms that differed radically from their former arguments, and they adhered rigidly to their positions. Neither house would accept a compromise, and even the governor could not break the deadlock. The debate therefore developed into a kind of legislative Armageddon, which could end only in total victory for one house and total defeat for the other.

I

It may seem strange that South Carolina was preoccupied with internal affairs between 1754 and 1756, for during those years France and Great Britain were fighting an undeclared war for possession of the North American continent. Yet the people of South Carolina acted as if the war did not exist, and the records of that period contain only casual mention of such events as the Albany Congress or Braddock's defeat. The chief reason for South Carolina's lack of interest in the Anglo-French contest was Governor James Glen's attitude toward the conflict. Glen believed the reports of French aggression were exaggerated, and he opposed English expeditions into the Ohio River Valley until the Crown ordered him to support them. His procrastination not only kept South Carolina out of the conflict, but it also further damaged his already shaky reputation.

Glen sympathized wholeheartedly with the British effort to control the Ohio Valley, but he had his own plan of expansion, a plan which would give the key roles to South Carolina and to James Glen. He believed the proper way to expand British dominion was by building a series of forts similar to Fort Prince George west of the Appalachian Mountains. He thought a minimum of two forts near the confluence of the Tennessee, Ohio, and Wabash rivers was necessary, and he proposed that the Crown station a regiment of regular troops there. The forts would cut the French empire in two by stopping communications between Canada and Louisiana. Glen's plan required the cooperation of the Cherokees, because the easiest way to reach his proposed fort sites was through the Cherokee nation and down the Tennessee River. To insure Cherokee support, he suggested that the Cherokees acknowledge the king of England as their sovereign and deed their land to the Crown. He further proposed that seven Cherokee chiefs go to England to sign such a treaty, an idea that was favored by Attakullakulla, or the Little Carpenter, who was the sole survivor of the seven chiefs who had visited England in 1730 and the second-ranking chief in the Chota faction.[1]

Glen's plan was sound, except for one thing. He failed to understand the recent shift in the dynamics of the British empire. For many years South Carolina had been left alone to take care of Great Britain's interests on the southern frontier, except for whatever assistance Georgia could contribute. New York had occupied a similar position in the north, and the colonies between New York and South Carolina, settled snugly between the Appalachians and the Atlantic, had taken little part in Indian affairs. New York and South Carolina were interested in the Indians as a source of furs and skins and as a barrier against French invasion. Neither colony wanted to expand English settlement into Indian country. Glen based his plan of expansion on the assumption that the old state of affairs still existed. His plan would strengthen the defensive value of friendly Indians, it would foster the

[1] Glen to Sir Thomas Robinson, Aug. 15, 1754, S. C. Pub. Recs., XXVI, 96–102, S. C. Archives.

Indian trade, and it would leave the Indians in possession of their hunting grounds. Unknown to Glen, however, the nature of England's interest in the Ohio Valley had changed, and new men with new ideas were making policy. The middle colonies had outgrown their old boundaries, and the people there had begun to look to the Ohio Valley for further expansion. The Ohio Company of Virginia was taking the lead in acquiring titles to western land, and Virginia was becoming the center of western land speculation. Lieutenant Governor Robert Dinwiddie of Virginia was assuming the role of spokesman for the new interest in the west and advocating the expansion of English settlement beyond the Appalachians. The activities of the British speculators alarmed the French government, especially the Marquis Duquesne who had become governor of Canada in 1752, and Duquesne began to build and garrison forts in the Ohio Valley. Governor Dinwiddie then had to find a way to force the French out of the Ohio Valley in order to protect the interests of both the Crown and the speculators.[2]

The expansionist policy of Robert Dinwiddie was far removed from the essentially defensive policy of James Glen, and Glen misunderstood Dinwiddie completely. Glen suspected that Virginia's chief interest in Indian affairs was to take the Cherokee trade away from South Carolina, even though only three or four Virginia traders had ever shown an interest in the Cherokees. Glen further suspected Dinwiddie of trying to supplant him as the leading Indian diplomat on the southern frontier. Glen's pride demanded that he must be the spokesman for Great Britain in the south, and he regarded the southern frontier as his private domain; for example, he frequently spoke of the Cherokees and Catawbas as "his" Indians. When Dinwiddie began to spread reports of French activity in the west, Glen thought he was exaggerating those reports in order to create an artificial crisis that would give him a chance to poach on Glen's territory. Glen therefore discounted the reports of French encroachment and ridiculed the urgency of the crisis.[3] Misled by the governor, both the council and the Commons House of Assembly shared Glen's view of the situation. On several occasions during 1753 and 1754 both

<hr>

[2] Lawrence H. Gipson, *The British Empire before the American Revolution*, 12 vols. to date (Caldwell, Idaho, and N. Y., 1936—) , IV, *passim*.

[3] Glen to the Earl of Holderness, June 25, 1753, S. C. Pub. Recs., XXV, 290–302, S. C. Archives; Glen to Dinwiddie, June 1, 1754, McDowell, ed., *S. C. Indian Documents, 1750–54*, 524–28. See also W. Neil Franklin, "Virginia and the Cherokee Indian Trade, 1673–1752," East Tennessee Historical Society, *Publications*, no. 4 (1932) , 3–21; Philip M. Hamer, "Anglo-French Rivalry in the Cherokee Country, 1754–1757," *N. C. Hist. Rev.*, 2 (1925) , 303–22.

houses expressed their doubts about the wisdom of Dinwiddie's policy and their reluctance to send any kind of aid to Virginia.[4]

South Carolina's response to Governor Dinwiddie's appeals for assistance in 1754 and 1755 reflected the colony's distrust of Virginia. In 1754, when Dinwiddie was preparing to send a detachment of Virginia militia under George Washington into the Ohio Valley, he asked the Cherokees and Catawbas to furnish scouts for the expedition. Glen was outraged because Dinwiddie had appealed directly to the Indians without informing him, and the South Carolina governor treated Dinwiddie as a usurper. Glen proposed a conference of all colonial governors before taking any kind of military action—a convenient excuse for doing nothing—and he advised Dinwiddie to defer to his greater experience in Indian diplomacy. Dinwiddie ignored Glen's advice, and when Washington's militia was defeated at Fort Necessity in July 1754, Glen was still talking about a conference of governors. In August Glen received instructions from the Crown to cooperate with Dinwiddie, but he still made only a vague promise of future assistance.[5] Dinwiddie again appealed for help in 1755 to support the campaign of General Edward Braddock, and the South Carolina assembly voted £40,000 currency for Braddock's expedition. Glen vetoed the bill on technical grounds, however, and although the assembly passed a new and acceptable bill at once, the money did not reach Virginia until Braddock's campaign had begun. To make matters worse, Glen spurned Dinwiddie's plea for Indian scouts and kept the Catawbas and Cherokees at home to confer on other matters.[6]

During the summer of 1755, while General Braddock was struggling to outfit his army, James Glen was moving ahead with his own unrelated plans. He had not received official approval of the grand design he had submitted in 1754, but a crisis in the Cherokee nation

[4] June 14, July 3, 1753, Council Journal, no. 21, Pt. i, 484, 499–501, S. C. Archives; Mar. 9, May 10, Sept. 6, 1754, Commons Journal, XXIX, 196–98, 389–91, 470–76, S. C. Archives.

[5] See the correspondence between Glen and Dinwiddie, Jan. 29–June 1, 1754, McDowell, ed., *S. C. Indian Documents, 1750–54,* 472–74, 480–81, 522–28; Glen to Dinwiddie, Aug. 22, 1754, CO 5/14, foll. 247–50, PRO; see also Carter, James Glen, 65–74; Alden, *John Stuart,* 43–44; Louis Knott Koontz, *Robert Dinwiddie: His Career in American Colonial Government and Westward Expansion* (Glendale, Calif., 1941), 266–73.

[6] Carter, James Glen, 76–82; Alden, *John Stuart,* 44–45; Dinwiddie to Glen, Sept. 25, 1755, Virginia Historical Society, *Collections,* 4 (1884), 213; Dinwiddie to William Henry Lyttelton, Sept. 18, 1756, Lyttelton Papers, Clements Lib.

made him decide to go ahead anyway. Northern Indians and French agents were subjecting the Cherokees, especially the overhill towns, to a lot of pressure, spreading rumors of English defeats and urging the Cherokees to abandon their allegiance to England. The undeclared war was interfering with the South Carolina Indian trade, and a conference on trade was desired by the two most powerful chiefs in the nation, Old Hop, the "fire king" of Chota, and the Little Carpenter, his second in command. Glen saw that such a conference could advance his plan, and so he and 500 South Carolinians met Old Hop, the Little Carpenter, and 500 Indians in May 1755 at Saluda Old Town in the backcountry. Glen promised the Cherokees more trade goods and lower prices, and he even pledged his own credit up to £10,000 currency to finance the traders. In return, the Cherokees acknowledged the king of England as their sovereign and ceded the title to all their lands to the Crown. The treaty impressed the people of South Carolina, and even Henry Laurens, an inveterate opponent of Glen, called the land cession "a most charming acquisition." [7] Outside South Carolina, however, the treaty was greeted less favorably. Governor Dinwiddie, for example, called it "a very preposterous, irregular, and inconsistent Step," because he thought the French might cite the land cession as an example of English greed.[8]

The new Cherokee treaty also required South Carolina to build a fort among the overhill Cherokees, but Glen ran into financial trouble and almost alienated the Cherokees. The South Carolina assembly had said long ago that it would not pay for any more forts, and Glen had turned to the Crown for help when he first proposed an overhill fort in 1754. The Board of Trade had approved Glen's project, but Sir Thomas Robinson, the secretary of state for the southern department, had given an ambiguous response. In a letter to Glen on July 5, 1754, Robinson had said that he was sending £10,000 sterling to Governor Dinwiddie for defense and that Glen should apply to Dinwiddie for the money to build the fort. Robinson had not guaranteed that the Crown would pay the entire cost of the fort, but his letter had been misleading. Glen had informed the assembly in March 1755 that Robinson had promised the Crown would pay for the fort, and Glen's successor, William Henry Lyttelton, later said Glen had "very good

[7] Laurens to John Knight, July 10, 1755, Letterbooks, II, 36, Laurens Papers, S. C. Hist. Soc.; see also Corkran, *Cherokee Frontier,* 50–61; for the negotiations at the conference, see "Papers produced by Mr. Glen in Support of . . . his Memorial," [1762], CO 5/377, foll. 99–143, PRO.

[8] To Arthur Dobbs, Sept. 18, 1755, Saunders, ed., *N. C. Col. Recs.,* V, 427.

grounds" for making such a statement.[9] When Glen applied to
Dinwiddie for the money, however, Dinwiddie gave him only £1,000
sterling and Glen estimated the fort would cost about £7,000 sterling.
Glen revised his plan for the fort and reduced the estimate to about
£3,000, but he still could not raise enough money to start work. His
inactivity made the Cherokees restless, and the Little Carpenter led a
delegation of 120 braves to Charles Town in December 1755 in a vain
effort to force Glen into action. The overhill towns then turned to
Virginia for help and negotiated a treaty with Governor Dinwiddie, in
which Virginia promised to build an overhill fort and the Cherokees
promised to furnish scouts for Virginia's raids into the Ohio Valley.
The treaty alarmed Glen more than ever, because the Cherokees
seemed to be slipping away from his control. Glen appealed in
desperation to his assembly, and it agreed to lend him £2,000 sterling
with the understanding that the Crown would repay the loan. In the
spring of 1756, however, the appropriation for the fort became tangled
up in the fight between the upper and lower houses, and in May Glen
still had not started work on the fort.[10]

Glen's pride in his ability as an Indian diplomat caused still another
intercolonial dispute between 1754 and 1756, as he and Governor
Arthur Dobbs of North Carolina argued over the boundary between
the Carolinas. The boundary line did not even exist, except for a
hundred miles near the coast which had been surveyed in the 1730's.
The lack of a boundary did not matter, however, until the 1750's when
white settlers from both Carolinas began to encroach upon land
reserved for the Catawba Indians. The Board of Trade instructed
Dobbs in 1754 to agree on a boundary with Glen, but Glen refused to
cooperate and even suggested that the hundred miles of settled
boundary be discarded. Neither Dobbs nor the Board of Trade could
act without Glen's help, and the Crown was forced to postpone a
settlement as long as Glen remained in office.[11] Glen's behavior in this
affair is almost inexplicable. It seems likely, however, that he feared
that a boundary settlement would place the Catawbas in North
Carolina and thus deprive him of his dominion over some of "his"
Indians.

[9] Robinson to Glen, July 5, 1754, S. C. Pub. Recs., XXVI, 73, S. C. Archives; Mar.
7, 1755, Commons Journal, XXX, 321–24, S. C. Archives; Lyttelton to Sir George
[Lyttelton], July 19, 1756, Newcastle Papers, Add. Mss., 32866, fol. 227, Brit. Mus.
[10] Corkran, *Cherokee Frontier*, 61–74; Alden, *John Stuart*, 46–47; Jan. 23, Feb. 3–4,
Apr. 9, 15, 1756, Commons Journal, XXXI, Pt. i, 47–48, 74, 76, 177, 180, 185–86, S. C.
Archives.
[11] Marvin L. Skaggs, *North Carolina Boundary Disputes Involving Her Southern
Line* (Chapel Hill, 1941), 30–72.

Glen's inability to understand the changed situation on the American frontier and his frantic attempts to repel imaginary encroachments upon his control over the southern Indians demolished the remaining shreds of his reputation. Governors Dinwiddie and Dobbs condemned him for the boundary dispute, his delay in building the overhill fort, and his failure to support Virginia expeditions into the Ohio Valley. Their opinions were shared by no less a person than the Earl of Halifax, the president of the Board of Trade. Halifax regarded Glen as a total incompetent, and he thought Glen had behaved so erratically that England might lose the entire southern frontier.[12]

II

Like most of the assembly's intramural disputes, the controversy that led to the council's downfall began on a minor issue, the question of accepting or rejecting the resignation of the colony's agent. By the time the disagreement expanded fully, the partisans of both houses were attempting to alter the basic structure of the provincial government. Polemicists concentrated primarily on the nature of the council and its rights, but they based their arguments on the broader issues of the rights of the people and the rights of the Crown. With such fundamental questions at stake, it is hardly surprising that Governor Glen could not work out a compromise.

The debate began when agent James Crokatt decided to resign his agency in 1753. Crokatt, who had held the agency since 1749, had not been a very reliable agent, and he had ignored the assembly's wishes on two occasions. He had opposed the assembly's attempts to expand the colony's paper currency, and even though the assembly had rejected a petition by Charles McNair in 1750, Crokatt had supported a similar one which McNair submitted to the Crown because McNair owed him money. Several political leaders had distrusted Crokatt from the day of his election, among them Glen, Edmund Atkin, and Charles Pinckney, but Crokatt retained a loyal following among merchants and members of the lower house. For example, Henry Laurens praised his "unwearied Endeavours to serve us in promoting the Culture of Indigo." [13]

[12] Dobbs to Glen, Mar. 12, 1755, Saunders, ed., *N. C. Col. Recs.*, V, 387–93; Dobbs to William Henry Lyttelton, Mar. 20, 1756, Halifax to Lyttelton, Aug. 13, 1756, Dinwiddie to Lyttelton, Sept. 18, 1756, Lyttelton Papers, Clements Lib.

[13] Laurens to Rawlinson and Davison, Sept. 24, 1755, Letterbooks, II, 78, Laurens Papers, S. C. Hist. Soc.; see also May 27, June 1, 1749, Upper House Journal, XVI, Pt. ii, 61–62, 111, S. C. Archives; Atkin, "Revolt of Choctaw Indians," Lansdowne Mss., 809, foll. 28–29, Brit. Mus.; Crokatt to Henry Pelham, May 18, 1749, Sydney Family Papers, Clements Lib.

Crokatt's decision to resign his office initially provoked nothing more serious than a friendly debate on his successor. Several candidates offered their services, but the leading contender was Charles Pinckney, who had moved to England and had the support of former Speaker Andrew Rutledge and Crokatt himself.[14]

When Crokatt's letter of resignation reached the South Carolina assembly in early 1754, the council accepted his resignation at once, but the Commons House asked Crokatt to remain in office. The Commons House continued to treat Crokatt as the agent, but the council regarded the agency as vacant. The upper house pointed out that the ordinance appointing Crokatt had expired, and it insisted that he could not stay in office without an ordinance or the concurrence of both houses.[15] During 1754 Glen and the council decided to petition the Crown for financial assistance on the overhill Cherokee fort, and they asked Charles Pinckney to present their petition to the Board of Trade. Neither Crokatt nor Pinckney liked the situation, but Crokatt decided to keep his office while Pinckney agreed to represent the colony on the matter of an overhill fort. As a result, South Carolina had two agents in London at the end of 1754, one representing the Commons House and the other the governor and council. Both Crokatt and Pinckney resented the other's presence, and the two men quarreled and refused to cooperate with each other.[16]

The assembly had a chance to settle the question amicably in January 1755, but it failed to do so and the dispute continued. The council learned that Crokatt was still acting as agent and promptly introduced an ordinance to appoint a new agent, but the Commons House rejected the council's ordinance and introduced its own bill for the same purpose. The Commons gave no reason for its action, but it may have thought the nomination of an agent should originate in the lower house. The council voted down the lower house's ordinance on the grounds that it was not proper parliamentary procedure to introduce a new bill similar to one defeated earlier in the same session. The Commons then tried to appoint an agent by a simple resolution of both houses, but the council found this method unacceptable, too,

[14] Andrew Rutledge to Peter Manigault, [1753], Manigault Family Papers, South Caroliniana Library, Columbia, S. C.; S.-C. Gaz. (Charles Town), May 29, 1756.

[15] Jan. 15, Feb. 2, 7–8, 1754, Commons Journal, XXIX, 12, 77–78, 122–23, 128–29, S. C. Archives.

[16] Pinckney to Peter Manigault, Apr. 8, 1756, Manigault Papers, South Caroliniana Lib.; Jan. 14, 1755, Upper House Journal, XXIV, 9–10, S. C. Archives; Edmund Atkin to William Henry Lyttelton, May 20, 1756, Lyttelton Papers, Clements Lib.

and tabled the resolution.[17] Compromise had failed, and each house continued to employ its own agent.

The next round of the controversy, which began in March 1755, expanded the scope of the constitutional debate. The Commons House included a provision for Crokatt's salary in the tax bill, and the council proposed the provision be deleted. The two houses had remained on friendly terms up to that point, but the council's attempt to withhold Crokatt's salary angered the lower house. The Commons not only insisted that Crokatt be paid, but it also injected two new issues into the dispute. First, it revived an old issue by resolving that it would never again submit petitions and accounts to the council. Next, it claimed the exclusive right to nominate the agent, a right which both houses had previously shared on an equal basis. The Commons House explained its resolution by saying that the agent represented the province, and it added, "We conceive the Province should be understood to be the People, and as the People only are to pay for his services it seems just and reasonable that the Representatives of the People should have the nomination of their Agent." [18] The Commons House was thus trying to change the constitutional nature of the agency from the traditional idea that the agent represented the whole assembly to a new conception of the agent as the representative of the people. The council rejected the lower house's innovation and insisted that no one could act as agent unless both houses concurred in his appointment. The council again asked the Commons to amend the tax bill by deleting Crokatt's allowance, and when the lower house refused, the council rejected the tax bill. The lower house offered a slight concession in the form of a resolution to pay Crokatt, but the council tabled it.[19]

By this time tempers were flaring on both sides, and no one but Glen wanted to compromise. As the governor said of the Commons House, "Their whole humours and temper seemed to be soured by the Council." [20] Glen was under pressure from the Crown to obtain an appropriation for Braddock's expedition, and he was anxious to settle the dispute. He prorogued the assembly from April 12 to April 28,

[17] Jan. 14, 1755, Upper House Journal, XXIV, 10, S. C. Archives; Jan. 14–15, 28, Feb. 6, 1755, Commons Journal, XXX, 94, 97, 157, 211, S. C. Archives.
[18] Mar. 22, 1755, Commons Journal, XXX, 410, S. C. Archives; see also Mar. 20–22, ibid., 386, 404–5, 408–11.
[19] Apr. 9, 10, 12, 1755, ibid., 425–28, 438, 454–56; Apr. 12, 1755, Upper House Journal, XXIV, 61, S. C. Archives.
[20] To Bd. of Trade, May 29, 1755, S. C. Pub. Recs., XXVI, 190, S. C. Archives.

which permitted reintroduction of the tax bill, and opened the new session with a plea for harmony. His speech had some effect at first. The council offered to pay Crokatt if the bill did not say the payment was a salary; it thought paying him a salary would imply the lower house alone could appoint the agent. The Commons rejected the offer, but it countered with a promise that if the council gave in on this question it would not be considered as a precedent in the future. Each house rejected the other's offer, and the council rejected the tax bill again on May 13.[21]

The assembly still had not appropriated money for Braddock's expedition, and the pressures of war soon forced the upper house to capitulate. Glen prorogued the assembly again from May 14 to May 15 and went to work on the council. He persuaded the upper house that it must not harm the common cause of the colonies, and it gave in and passed the tax bill, including a salary for Crokatt. It tried to save face by insisting that it was not establishing a precedent but merely yielding to the pressure of an emergency.[22]

The following winter the assembly ended part, but not all, of the dispute by appointing a new agent. The Commons House still preferred Crokatt, but in the interests of harmony it decided to insist only that Charles Pinckney did not get the job. The two houses settled on William Middleton as the new agent. Middleton did not want the job, but he accepted it for the time being in order to keep the dispute from again erupting. There was some disagreement about the wording of Middleton's appointment, but the council agreed finally to let the ordinance say that the agent represented the "inhabitants" of the colony.[23] Middleton's selection settled only one question, however, and other issues remained up in the air. The assembly had not decided whether the council would continue to inspect petitions and accounts, and Crokatt's salary for 1755 had not been paid.

While the legislative dispute lay dormant, the council acquired a new handicap by antagonizing the governor. It thought Glen was moving too slowly on the overhill Cherokee fort, and it asked him on February 19, 1756, to expedite matters by giving it a plan of the fort

[21] Apr. 12, 29, May 1, 2, 13, Commons Journal, XXX, 463–64, 466–67, 488–89, 491–93, 548–52, S. C. Archives; May 13, 1755, Upper House Journal, XXIV, 84, S. C. Archives.

[22] May 14, 19, 1755, Commons Journal, XXX, 557, 577, 580–82, S. C. Archives; Glen to Bd. of Trade, May 29, 1755, S. C. Pub. Recs., XXVI, 189–92, S. C. Archives.

[23] Henry Laurens to Rawlinson and Davison, Dec. 10, 1755, July 7, 1756, Letterbooks, II, 117, 263, Laurens Papers, S. C. Hist. Soc.; Edmund Atkin to William Henry Lyttelton, May 20, 1756, Lyttelton Papers, Clements Lib.; Feb. 18, 21, Mar. 10, 1756, Commons Journal. XXXI, Pt. i, 102–3, 110–11, 115, S. C. Archives.

and an estimate of expense. Glen did not reply, so the council published its appeal in the *South-Carolina Gazette*. Publication was a blunder, because Glen had never been able to tolerate criticism. He finally answered the council on March 26 and said that its request was "not at all necessary." He also complained, "It is the first hint of that kind as far as I recollect that I have ever received during the whole course of my Administration." As for the fort, he said he would submit a plan and estimate when they were ready, but he advised the council that "these matters require some consideration." [24] Thus, the council offended the governor at a time when it needed his support.

In April 1756 the fight between the Commons House and council started again over the same issues as before. The Commons House included an appropriation for Crokatt's salary for 1755 in the tax bill, and it then refused to let the council inspect petitions and accounts. Glen correctly foresaw a new legislative deadlock, and the prospect alarmed him because he needed money to build the overhill fort. On April 21 he begged the Commons House to send the accounts to the council as in the past, and he concluded an impassioned plea for harmony by saying, "For God's sake let us not draw immediate and real Evils upon our Selves for fear of distant perhaps imaginary Dangers." [25] The Commons ignored Glen. When the council realized it would not receive the accounts, it resolved not to act on the tax bill. Glen tried to placate the council by sending for the accounts himself and then offering them to the upper house, but the council would not accept them in that way.[26] The assembly had reached the dangerous stalemate that Glen had feared.

After the impasse developed in the assembly, the controversy turned into a public constitutional debate in the *South-Carolina Gazette*. The Commons House took to the press first with a "Humble Remonstrance" addressed to the governor and presented to him on April 29, 1756. The Remonstrance asked Glen to intervene in the dispute, and in a cleverly designed appeal to his vanity, it said, "There is no one in this Government who knows the *British* Constitution better than Your Excellency." The Remonstrance asked Glen to decide who was at fault in the dispute, and if it were the Commons House, then it asked him to dissolve the assembly and call for new elections. If the council were

[24] Mar. 26, 1756, Upper House Journal, XXVI, 42, S. C. Archives; see also *S.-C. Gaz.* (Charles Town), Mar. 11, 1756.

[25] Apr. 21, 1756, Commons Journal, XXXI, Pt. i, 189–91, S. C. Archives; see also Mar. 30, Apr. 2, 15, 1756, *ibid.*, 161, 167, 185–86.

[26] Apr. 22, 1756, *ibid.*, 192; Apr. 24, 27, 1756, Upper House Journal, XXVI, 55–56, 58–59, S. C. Archives; May 1, 1756, Council Journal, no. 25, 244–45, S. C. Archives.

in error, however, the Remonstrance wanted Glen to suspend the councilors who were responsible. In his reply on May 3 Glen refused either to dissolve the assembly or to suspend members of the council, but he agreed with the lower house that the council was at fault for refusing to pass the tax bill at such a critical juncture. Benjamin Smith, the speaker of the house, predicted the deadlock would continue and asked for an adjournment, and Glen refused. In fact, however, the house was pleased with Glen's reply and ordered both the Remonstrance and the reply printed in the newspaper.[27]

The Humble Remonstrance of the Commons House had not raised any constitutional issues, but an essay in the *Gazette* of May 13 raised some very basic issues indeed. The essay was probably written by Thomas Wright, a member of the assembly, the son of a former chief justice, and the brother of the provincial attorney general. The major point of Wright's essay was his denial of the council's right to act as an upper house of assembly. He said the council's constitutional position was inconsistent and in no way comparable to the House of Lords. He pointed out that the council acted as both a legislative body and a council of state, that members of the council voted in assembly elections, that council membership was not hereditary, and that in each of these respects the council differed from the House of Lords. Wright added that the Crown could not legally create an upper house in a colony, because such an act would imply that the Crown had the right to deprive the people of their rights. Wright's arguments were not new, for the Commons House had briefly considered and then dropped a similar statement the preceding November, but Wright was the first person to deny publicly that the council had legislative rights.[28]

Under attack from the Commons House, the governor, and the public press, the council finally decided to publish its side of the argument; it appointed a committee to write a defense of its proceedings on May 5.[29] The upper house subsequently published a tedious, three-part "Vindication of the Council" in the *Gazette* in late May and early June. The first two installments merely recited the

[27] *S.-C. Gaz.* (Charles Town), May 6, 1756; May 3, 1756, Council Journal, no. 25, 254, S. C. Archives.

[28] *S.-C. Gaz.* (Charles Town), May 13, 1756, Supplement; Nov. 25, 27, 1755, Commons Journal, XXX, Pt. i, 10, 15–16, S. C. Archives. The essay was signed "T___S W___T."

[29] May 5, 1756, Upper House Journal, XXVI, 64, S. C. Archives; Alexander Garden to Cadwallader Colden, Apr. 20, 1756, New-York Historical Society, *Collections*, 54 (1921), 71.

history of the dispute from the council's point of view in great detail. The Vindication tried to show that the Commons House was responsible for the legislative deadlock, it blamed Glen for the delay in building an overhill fort, and it reminded readers that tax bills had been rejected before without harming the province.[30]

The last installment of the Vindication took up the constitutional issues involved, and in it the council attempted to redefine the entire provincial constitution. "This province, and the legislature of it," the council argued, "is entirely subordinate and dependent. Its powers are *derivative* and not *original*. . . . The whole power of legislation here springs from the crown." In other words, the council denied that the people of South Carolina and the provincial assembly enjoyed any inherent political rights; both the people and the assembly possessed only the privileges that the Crown had granted them, and the Crown could abridge or change those privileges whenever it pleased. The council went on to argue that the Crown expressed its will through its instructions to the governor and that the instructions were binding on the entire government. It concluded by observing that the governor's instructions stated explicitly that the council should participate in all legislation on an equal basis with the elected house.[31] The Vindication introduced a radical departure in South Carolina's constitutional debates. By arguing that colonists had no rights except those granted by the Crown, the council adopted an interpretation of the empire's constitution that was more acceptable in London than in America, one which repudiated the council's earlier arguments in defense of its rights, notably in Edmund Atkin's "Report on the Constitution" of 1745. Previously, the council had defended itself by appealing to local custom or by using Atkin's argument that it was the special protector of property rights. In 1756, however, the council based its whole defense on its interpretation of the status of the colonies in the empire and on the governor's instructions.

Perhaps the change in the council's argument was caused by a change in its personnel. Only two councilors who had been active in 1745 were still active in 1756, and Edmund Atkin, the former spokesman for the council's rights, had gone to England. The new spokesman for the council and the probable author of the theoretical part of the Vindication was William Wragg, the son of a prominent merchant who had been educated at the Middle Temple. Wragg was an outspoken conservative who later supported the royal prerogative

[30] *S.-C. Gaz.* (Charles Town), May 22, 29, 1756.
[31] *Ibid.*, June 5, 1756.

more consistently than any other South Carolinian and became a
loyalist during the American Revolution. Under his leadership, the
council had adopted an extremely conservative viewpoint in its
Vindication of 1756.

While Thomas Wright and William Wragg were writing about the
provincial constitution, Governor James Glen was still worrying about
the overhill Cherokee fort. The governor finally decided he could
afford no further delay, so he borrowed £2,000 sterling from private
citizens and without informing the council of his plans, he set off for
Cherokee country on May 19, 1756.[32] Before he reached even the lower
towns, however, a new governor arrived in Charles Town to replace
him. Glen hurried back to town as soon as he heard the news, turned
the government over to his successor, and then retired to his plantation about three miles outside Charles Town. He retired under a cloud
of suspicion, for the Earl of Halifax blamed him even for the dispute
between the council and Commons House, but Glen seems to have been
happy in his retirement. Two years later a friend said of him, "He
enjoy's more happiness than he ever knew in the hurry of business." [33]

III

The new governor of South Carolina, William Henry Lyttelton,
disembarked at Charles Town from H.M.S. *Winchelsea* on June 1,
1756. Lyttelton was a short, slim man with expensive epicurean tastes
and more political influence than any other governor in the history of
the colony. He belonged to the English aristocracy and was related to
the influential Grenville family by birth and to the equally prominent Pitt family by marriage. He had attended Eton, Oxford, and the
Middle Temple and had been elected to the House of Commons at the
age of twenty-four. His older brother, Lord George Lyttelton, was
chancellor of the exchequer and a close friend of the Duke of
Newcastle. Governor Lyttelton himself counted the Earl of Halifax as
a personal friend, and another friend, William Pitt, had discussed the
governorship of South Carolina with Lyttelton and had advised him to
accept it. The Crown had issued his commission as governor on
January 23, 1755, but a series of misadventures had delayed him for

[32] *Ibid.*, May 6, May 22, 1756; June 2, 1756, Council Journal, no. 25, 271, S. C.
Archives.

[33] Henry Bouquet to Col John Forbes, Feb. 1, 1758, Sylvester K. Stevens and
Donald H. Kent, eds., *The Papers of Colonel Henry Bouquet* (Harrisburg, 1940–43),
series 21632, 141; see also Halifax to William Henry Lyttelton, Aug. 13, 1756,
Lyttelton Papers, Clements Lib.

nearly a year and a half. A French squadron had captured his ship in August 1755, and he had thrown his instructions overboard to keep them from falling into enemy hands. Then he had made his way back to England, obtained a new copy of his instructions, and boarded another ship for South Carolina.[34]

Putting an end to the controversy between the two houses of assembly became the first item of business on Lyttelton's agenda. The Board of Trade thought the dispute was keeping South Carolina from its duty of supporting the war effort against France, and it dismissed the issues in the debate as *"trivial points of privilege."* Lyttelton himself was distressed to find the colony "much disturb'd and distracted with intestine dissentions." [35] The council recommended the election of a new lower house, but Lyttelton called the old assembly into session on June 21 and asked it to pass the tax bill. Councilor William Wragg tried to keep the dispute alive, but South Carolina learned on July 2 that war had been declared and the news helped Lyttelton to persuade the rest of the council to postpone further debate. The council passed the tax bill without protest, although the bill included an appropriation for Crokatt's salary and the Commons House had refused to allow the council to inspect petitions and accounts.[36]

Lyttelton next turned his attention to building an overhill fort. Although he personally thought Glen had had good reasons for believing the Crown would build the fort, the Board of Trade had decided that South Carolina should pay for it. The Board ordered Lyttelton to request the money from the assembly, but the Board promised that the Crown would bear the cost if the assembly refused. Lyttelton kept the promise a "profound secret" and asked the assembly for the money.[37] Surprisingly, the assembly voted £9,000 sterling for the fort without quibbling. Lyttelton then hired engineer John

[34] See G. F. Russell Barker in *DNB* s.v. "Lyttelton, George," and J. M. Rigg, in *ibid.*, s.v. "Lyttelton, William Henry, first Baron Lyttleton"; see also Attig, W. H. Lyttelton, 1–6; Lewis M. Wiggin, *The Faction of Cousins: A Political Account of the Grenvilles, 1733–1763* (New Haven, 1958), esp. 163–64. On Lyttelton's adventures in 1755, see Bd. of Trade Mins., Jan. 28, Oct. 9, 1755, S. C. Pub. Recs., XXVI, 132, 145–46, S. C. Archives.

[35] Bd. of Trade to Lyttelton, Nov. 19, 1756, Lyttelton to Bd. of Trade, June 3, 1756, S. C. Pub. Recs., XXVII, 166, 100, S. C. Archives.

[36] Lyttelton to Bd. of Trade, July 19, Dec. 6, 1756, *ibid.*, XXVII, 121–27, 201; Henry Laurens to Foster Cunliffe and Sons, July 19, 1756, Letterbooks, II, 271, Laurens Papers, S. C. Hist. Soc.; June 12, 1756, Council Journal, no. 25, 279, S. C. Archives.

[37] Lyttelton to Sir George [Lyttelton], July 19, 1756, Newcastle Papers, Add. Mss., 32866, fol. 227, Brit. Mus.

William Gerard De Brahm to draw up a plan for the fort and entrusted its construction to Captain Raymond Demeré and 210 troops. The force left Charles Town on September 21, 1756, and when Demeré reached overhill country, he found a small force of Virginia militia already engaged in building a fort. The Virginians finished their fort first, but it accomplished nothing because they did not station a garrison there. Meanwhile, Demeré had to contend with temperamental outbursts from De Brahm, a near mutiny among his troops, and restlessness among the Cherokees. By drawing upon a reservoir of tact, however, Demeré managed to complete the South Carolina fort in April 1757. The fort was named Fort Loudoun in honor of the Earl of Loudoun, the English commander in chief in North America.[38]

Governor Lyttelton had compiled an enviable record in his first month in South Carolina. He had stopped the controversy in the assembly, he had secured the passage of a tax bill, and he had begun construction of the fort. Still, he was worried. The council had said its passage of a tax bill in June was only an expedient, and Lyttelton expected the dispute to flare up again at the first opportunity. William Wragg was still making trouble for the governor, too. He denounced a wartime embargo as unconstitutional, and he opposed Lyttelton on an act for the dispersal of captured Acadians in the colony.[39]

Lyttelton decided in November 1756 to forestall a revival of the controversy by getting rid of the chief troublemaker on the council. The governor suspended William Wragg from the council on November 29, 1756, and told the Board of Trade that Wragg was "an insolent and litigious spirit and very subtle in finding out distinctions to perplex and embroil Publick business." He added, "Altho' he is a zealous stickler for the rights and priviledges real or imaginary of the body of which he is a member because he derives his own importance from it, I have allways observ'd where those rights were not concern'd that he eagerly objected to every thing which seem'd to favour the Prerogative." [40] Lyttelton's description of Wragg was hardly accurate, for Wragg defended all the rights and privileges of the Crown, almost without discrimination. Still, the governor had rid himself of an enemy, and his drastic action served as a warning to the other councilors against renewing their quarrel with the Commons House.

[38] Alden, *John Stuart*, 57–60; Corkran, *Cherokee Frontier*, 75–114; Attig, W. H. Lyttelton, 27–44.

[39] Lyttelton to Bd. of Trade, July 19, Dec. 6, 1756, S. C. Pub. Recs., XXVII, 125, 202, S. C. Archives.

[40] Lyttelton to Bd. of Trade, Dec. 6, 1756, *ibid.*, 201–3.

Lyttelton's suspension of a council member surprised the Board of Trade. It first hinted to Lyttelton that he should restore Wragg to the council and said it would not recommend confirmation of the suspension until it heard more from Lyttelton. Lyttelton replied that Wragg had not changed his attitude and said his own position in South Carolina would be untenable unless the Crown confirmed Wragg's suspension. The Board of Trade accepted Lyttelton's evaluation of the situation without further debate, not only recommending Wragg's dismissal but even praising Lyttelton for his handling of the affair. The Privy Council formally dismissed Wragg on December 6, 1757.[41]

Wragg's suspension produced the results Lyttelton wanted, and the now docile council caused no more trouble. The council did not renew the dispute, and it did not insist that the Commons House send it the petitions and accounts. Thereafter, when the Commons House had completed the estimate and sent the tax bill to the upper house, the governor ordered the public treasurer to lay the petitions and accounts before the council. Thus, although the council continued to inspect accounts, it abandoned its claim of a right to do so.[42]

Although Lyttelton and the Board of Trade accomplished their immediate objections, in the long run the suspension of William Wragg was a blow to the royal prerogative. The Crown itself had punished its most vigorous supporter in South Carolina, but that was not all. In the controversy of 1756 the council had identified its rights with the right of the Crown to control its colonies. Therefore, when Lyttelton and the Board of Trade ignored the council's argument and suspended Wragg, it must have seemed to many people that the Crown had also rejected the council's interpretation of colonial rights as being derived from the Crown. Finally, the victory in the Wragg affair had really been won by the Commons House of Assembly, the potential enemy of the royal prerogative. The only reason for such action was an ignorance of the real issues at stake. Lyttelton and the Board of Trade had looked at the legislative controversy and seen only an impediment to their immediate goals. They had failed entirely to understand that they had damaged the royal prerogative themselves.

After the Wragg affair the council ceased to be an effective force in the government of South Carolina and lost even more of its political

---

[41] Bd. of Trade to Lyttelton, Feb. 10, Nov. 9, 1757, Lyttelton to Bd. of Trade, June 11, 1754, *ibid.*, XXVII, 251, 326, 278–81; Grant and Munro, eds., *Acts of Privy Council, Col. Ser.*, IV, 359–60.

[42] Lyttelton to Bd. of Trade, May 24, 1757, S. C. Pub. Recs., XXVII, 264–65, S. C. Archives; May 12–13, 1757, Upper House Journal, XXVII, 38–39, S. C. Archives.

powers. For four years after 1756 the upper house of assembly did nothing but meet and approve the decisions of the Commons House. In 1760 the council meekly suggested an amendment to the tax bill, and the Commons replied that the mere act of suggesting an amendment constituted an encroachment upon its privileges. The Commons insulted the council by making a verbal reply to the council's written message, but the council passed the tax bill without even requesting an apology. A year later the Commons House forced the council to take down a bar it had erected across the entrance to the council chambers.[43] There seemed to be no end to the indignities the council would tolerate. In 1761, however, the council tried seriously to regain some of its lost powers by amending two bills that indirectly involved taxes; the Commons had tried earlier to define such bills as money bills without any success. Now, when the Commons reproached the council, the upper house revived its claim to the privilege of amending any kind of money bill. Not to be outdone, the Commons House challenged the upper house's right to reject a money bill. Neither house pressed its more extreme claims, and in 1762 the two houses reached a compromise. They decided that the council could not amend the clauses relating to taxes in any bill, but it could amend other clauses. The council allowed this distinction to stand, and thus it surrendered still more of its former powers.[44]

While the Commons House was expanding its control over legislation at the expense of the council, the Crown began to increase its control over the council through the appointment of royal placemen. Planters, merchants, and lawyers had dominated the council prior to 1756, and there had never been more than two placemen on the council at any time. During the late 1750's, however, the Board of Trade began to appoint an increasing number of placemen. Of the ten new councilors appointed between 1756 and 1763, four were placemen and a fifth held a Crown appointment; the Crown also made the superintendent of Indian affairs an extraordinary member of the council with voting rights. At the same time the Crown gave the governor more control over placemen; beginning with Lyttelton, every governor had the power to suspend any royal officeholder. As a result of these two developments, the governor and the Crown acquired more influence with the council than they had ever before known, and in

---

[43] July 18–19, 1760, Commons Journal, XXXIII, Pt. i, 342, 360, S. C. Archives; May 5, 8, 9, 21, 1761, ibid., XXXIV, 62–63, 69–70, 71–72, 82–83.
[44] June 13, 16, July 8, Aug. 6, 1761, ibid., XXXIV, 152–53, 159, 194, 234; May 27–29, 1762, ibid., XXXV, Pt. i, 131–39.

the words of Lieutenant Governor William Bull, Jr., the council became "a dependent body, removeable at pleasure." [45]

There was still another side to the council's fall. As the council lost power and independence, it also lost prestige. After the Wragg affair native Carolinians were less eager to serve on the council. For example, Henry Laurens twice turned down appointments to the council. Furthermore, some of the incumbent councilors did not wish to remain on the council under existing conditions. No one had resigned from the council prior to 1756 unless he moved to England or suffered ill health, but five councilors resigned for other reasons between 1756 and 1762. One of them, George Saxby, went so far as to explain his resignation on the grounds that council service interfered with his duties as receiver general of quitrents. In 1762 Governor Thomas Boone was forced to confess himself "extremely at a loss" to find prospective councilors.[46] William Bull, Jr., later called attention to the fall of the council and said, "It is much to be wished that for the King's Service and the public welfare, the Council were on a more respectable footing." [47]

After William Wragg lost his seat on the council, he was elected to the Commons House of Assembly and became one of its leaders. His move symbolized one of the major changes in the political life of South Carolina in the 1750's: As the council's prestige fell, the prestige of the Commons House rose. South Carolinians began to regard the lower house more favorably than before, and they began to accept seats in it more readily. Two important developments within the house emphasized this change. First, although the turnover in membership continued to be fairly rapid, fewer elected members of the house refused to take their seats. Frequently no more than two or three men in each assembly declined to serve during the 1750's and early 1760's. Second— and perhaps more important—the house began to benefit from a greater continuity in leadership. In the 1730's and 1740's the house had been handicapped by a constant turnover in its leadership, as most leaders had been willing to serve only on an irregular basis. In the 1750's, however, a group of younger men appeared in the house who liked politics and were prepared to accept the responsibilities of

[45] Sirmans, "S. C. Royal Council," *Wm. and Mary Qtly.*, 3d Ser., 18 (1961), 389–90; the quotation is from Bull to the Earl of Hillsborough, Nov. 30, 1770, S. C. Pub. Recs., XXXII, 372, S. C. Archives.

[46] To Bd. of Trade, Sept. 14, 1762, S. C. Pub. Recs., XXIX, 241, S. C. Archives; see also Sirmans, "S. C. Royal Council," *Wm. and Mary Qtly.*, 3d Ser., 18 (1961), 390.

[47] To Earl of Hillsborough, Nov. 30, 1770, S. C. Pub. Recs., XXXII, 372, S. C. Archives.

leadership in session after session. They entered the house in the 1750's, worked their way up to important assignments, and remained leaders in the house until the eve of the American Revolution. Among them were some of the best known politicians of eighteenth-century South Carolina, including Christopher Gadsden, Henry Laurens, Rawlins Lowndes, Peter Manigault, and Charles Pinckney II. They gave the Commons House the kind of uninterrupted leadership that it had not known since the proprietary period.

Despite other changes respecting the Commons House, merchants and lawyers continued to dominate its leadership. Twenty-seven men can be identified as leaders in the house between 1751 and 1763, and fourteen of them were merchants and six were lawyers. Five of the remaining leaders were planters, but three of them were leaders for only one session; one leader was a doctor, and one was a placeman. The same trends appeared among the younger generation of leaders, too. Gadsden and Laurens were merchants, while Lowndes, Manigault, and Pinckney were lawyers.[48]

IV

It is ironical that the South Carolina Commons House of Assembly won one of its most significant victories only because the Crown intervened at a critical point. The dispute over the agency had gone beyond the possibility of compromise in the spring of 1756, and the polemicists on both sides had redefined the provincial constitution in irreconcilable terms. At that critical point Governor William Henry Lyttelton had stepped in and suspended councilor William Wragg. Lyttelton had achieved his short-term goal of maintaining political harmony, but he had also given the council a blow from which it never recovered. It had lost its prestige and independence, as well as additional political powers, and it had ceased to be an effective force in the colony's government. The Commons House benefited most from the fall of the council, as it had acquired the power and prestige lost by the council. Thus, a royal governor had unwittingly aided and abetted the most aggressive enemy of the royal prerogative.

[48] This paragraph and the preceding one are based on a study of the leadership and membership of the Commons House, 1751–1763. As before, the men I refer to as "leaders" are those designated as "first rank" leaders in Greene, *Quest for Power*, 475–88. In addition to those named in the text, the leaders were merchants George Austin, David Deas, John Guerard, Thomas Lamball, Gabriel Manigault, Isaac Mazyck, Robert Pringle, John Savage, Benjamin Smith, Thomas Smith, Peter Taylor, and Paul Trapier; lawyers James Michie, John Rattray, and Andrew Rutledge; planters Henry Hyrne, Henry Middleton, Thomas Middleton, George Gabriel Powell, and William Wragg; placeman George Saxby; and Dr. James Irving.

CHAPTER XIV

FRICTION WITHIN THE EMPIRE

1 7 5 6 – 1 7 6 1

When Great Britain declared war on France in May 1756, the Anglo-French contest for the Ohio Valley expanded from an American struggle into a world war. The British government had never defined precisely the degree of colonial subordination to the Crown, and the pressures of war revealed a divergence of interpretation between South Carolina and Great Britain about the status of the colonies within the empire. When the Crown called upon the colonies for assistance during the war, it found that the colonial assemblies could not be forced to comply and that they often interpreted pleas for cooperation as attempts to infringe upon their rights. The war forced both sides to postpone a resolution of their differences, but an increasing number of political leaders on both sides of the Atlantic became aware of the yawning gulf between colonial practice and imperial theory.

Although South Carolina was far removed from the major battle-fields, the war caused a major shift in the thrust of provincial politics. Constitutional issues had dominated the colony's political history for over a decade, but the war introduced a new element into the constitutional struggle. Previously the Commons House of Assembly had been the aggressor in trying to expand its powers at the expense of the governor and the council, but during the war the Commons House found itself on the defensive. It was forced to defend rights and privileges it had enjoyed for years against encroachment by Crown officials. In short, the initiative passed from the Commons House to the Crown. The conflict between the Crown and the lower house remained muted for most of the war, however, and the house accepted several changes in silence. Open conflict arose occasionally, but it was exceptional.

I

Far removed from the main arenas of fighting, the people of South Carolina lived quietly through most of the French and Indian War. Nevertheless, if periodic outbursts of patriotism and Francophobia are reliable indications of public sentiment, South Carolinians eagerly supported the war effort. Castigations of the French were especially common, probably as a result of South Carolina's long struggle with French agents for control of the southern frontier. Henry Laurens must have expressed the emotions of many other colonists when he denounced "that proud haughty People the French who are the Pest of all human Society in every part of the Globe." He later added, "There is no dealing with that ambitious deceitful People but at the muzzell of our Guns." [1]

The war with France threatened to disturb the peace of South Carolina only twice before the Cherokee War of 1759. During the winter of 1756–1757 the colony was swept by rumors of an invasion by the French and their Creek allies. The rumors frightened the colonists so much that some of them, including Charles Pinckney, almost decided to sell all their possessions in South Carolina and flee to a safer colony.[2] The French attack failed to materialize, however, and so did English plans for an invasion of Louisiana in 1758. William Pitt, the King's first minister, promised Lyttelton that England would invade Louisiana in 1758, but a shortage of supplies and English setbacks in the north forced England to abandon the plan. After that South Carolina remained "free from the Miseries attending the Immediate Scene of Action in War." [3]

In contrast to the preceding war, the economy of South Carolina flourished during the French and Indian War. No foreign privateers

[1] Laurens to John Knight, July 22, 1755, Laurens to Sarah Nickleson, Aug. 1, 1755, Letterbooks, II, 42, 50, Laurens Papers, S. C. Hist. Soc.

[2] Eliza Pinckney to Lady Carew, Feb. 17, 1757, Eliza Lucas Pinckney Letters, Vol. II, Pinckney Papers, S. C. Hist. Soc.; see also Lyttelton to Bd. of Trade, Dec. 25, 1756, S. C. Pub. Recs., XXVII, 205–11, S. C. Archives.

[3] James Wright to Lyttelton, May 14, 1759, Lyttelton Papers, Clements Lib.; see also Pitt to Lyttelton, Mar. 7, 1758, Gertrude S. Kimball, ed., *Correspondence of William Pitt, when Secretary of State, with Colonial Governors and Military and Naval Commissioners in America*, 2 vols. (N. Y., 1906), I, 202–3; Admiral Edward Boscawen to Lyttelton, Aug. 28, 1758, Lyttelton Papers, Clements Lib.

appeared off the coast to harass shipping, and nothing interfered with trade except self-imposed embargoes in 1756 and 1758. The market value of South Carolina's products remained stable throughout the war, except for a slight drop in 1755 and 1756, and rice sold for 7 to 9s. sterling per hundredweight. The production of indigo boomed, and planters demanded more slaves. Henry Laurens complained repeatedly because his correspondents did not send him as many Negroes as he wanted. As a result of the colony's prosperity its paper currency remained stable. Although South Carolina emitted large sums in public orders and tax certificates to pay for wartime appropriations, the exchange ratio remained at about £725 currency to £100 sterling throughout the war.[4]

Although the colony was prosperous and the nearest fighting hundreds of miles away, South Carolinians were constantly reminded of the war by the presence of more than a thousand Acadians. These people were French colonists who had been dispersed throughout the British empire in America after 1755. The English government hoped the Acadians would become useful citizens, but they resisted assimilation and refused to swear allegiance to the English Crown. Their loyalty to France and their Roman Catholicism made the English settlers despise them. The first shipload of Acadians reached South Carolina in November 1755, and within another year about 1,150 of them had landed in the colony. At first South Carolina tried to find some way to deport the Acadians, but the Board of Trade explicitly ordered Governor Lyttelton to keep them in South Carolina. At his suggestion the assembly enacted a law that provided for their dispersal throughout the colony, but the law worked poorly and most of them straggled back to Charles Town. They could not find work, and the overburdened parish vestry of St. Philip's was forced to accept them as charity cases. A few Acadians eventually returned to their old homes in Nova Scotia, but most of them died within a few years of their arrival in South Carolina. By 1760 only 210 of the original 1,150 Acadians were still living in South Carolina.[5]

---

[4] Memorial of Charles Garth, Nov. 12, 1762, Treas. 1/421, fol. 270, PRO; *S.-C. Gaz.* (Charles Town), Oct. 28, 1756, Aug. 11, 1758; Taylor, "Wholesale Commodity Prices," *Jour. Econ. and Bus. Hist.*, 4 (1932), 358, 361; Brock, Currency of Colonies, 460–61; Letterbooks, III, *passim*, Laurens Papers, S. C. Hist. Soc.

[5] Ruth A. Hudnut and Hayes Baker-Crothers, "Acadian Transients in South Carolina," *American Historical Review*, 43 (1938), 500–13; Marguerite B. Hamer, "The Fate of the Exiled Acadians in South Carolina," *Jour. of So. Hist.*, 4 (1938), 199–208; St. Philip's Vestry Minutes, *passim*, St. Philip's Parish House. On the Crown's attitude toward the Acadians, see the Earl of Halifax to Lyttelton, Aug. 13, 1756, Lyttelton Papers, Clements Lib.

II

The French and Indian War affected politics more than any other activity in South Carolina. Although the pressures of war reduced political debate to a minimum, because few men wanted to risk another disruption of the government at a critical juncture, the Board of Trade followed policies that were likely to start a new constitutional struggle. During the presidency of the Earl of Halifax the Board had grown increasingly concerned about protecting the royal prerogative from the encroachments of colonial assemblies. It had revised Lyttelton's instructions in 1755, the first thorough revision since 1720, and it had issued special instructions designed to regain some of the powers the Crown had lost. The special instructions directed Lyttelton to obtain minor reforms in the provincial judiciary, a new elections law, and the transfer of the right to nominate public officials from the assembly to the governor.[6]

The Board of Trade's instructions placed Lyttelton in an awkward position. If he should try to carry out his special instructions by tampering with the courts, electoral procedures, or the assembly's powers, he would undoubtedly provoke another political deadlock. On the other hand, if he did nothing about the provincial constitution he would have to disobey his instructions. Either course would offend the Board of Trade, and even the influential Lyttelton could not afford to alienate Halifax. Lyttelton was an ambitious man who hungered for a more glamorous appointment, preferably the governorship of Jamaica, and Halifax controlled colonial patronage. Lyttelton solved his dilemma with a compromise. He ignored his special instructions and in 1759 even consented to an extension of the elections act.[7] At the same time he persuaded the assembly to relinquish some of its lesser privileges, which enabled him to pose as a defender of the royal prerogative.

Lyttelton launched the more difficult phase of his program, the reduction of the assembly's powers, within six months of his arrival in the colony. In November 1756 the Commons House asked him to send it the current documents relating to Indian affairs, but Lyttelton refused, saying he had not yet received any papers worth communi-

---

[6] Basye, *Board of Trade*, 84–87, 102–5; Lyttelton's general instructions are in S. C. Pub. Recs., XXVI, 269–344, S. C. Archives; the special instructions are in Greene, ed., "S. C. Colonial Constitution," *S. C. Hist. Mag.*, 62 (1961), 79–81.

[7] Cooper and McCord, eds., *Statutes*, IV, 98–101.

cating to the assembly. In February 1757 the Commons appointed a committee to join the governor and council in distributing Indian presents, which was the customary procedure in South Carolina. Lyttelton objected to the committee as an infringement on his powers and persuaded the house not to insist on it; in April he won the right to distribute such gifts at his own discretion. The Commons House said only that the presents must not cost more than £2,500 currency. Lyttelton also appointed a special agent to the Creeks in February without consulting the assembly or explaining his reasons, and in March he refused to let the Commons House examine the council journals and Indian books in order to audit the accounts of the clerk of the council.[8] After April 1757 Lyttelton did not try to force the Commons House to surrender more of its powers; perhaps he thought he had already compiled a sufficiently impressive list of minor reforms. Whatever his motives, the assembly sessions of 1756 and 1757 marked the first time since the administration of Robert Johnson that the Commons House of Assembly had given up any of its rights and privileges.

Lyttelton's decision not to press the Commons House any further was a wise one. He had managed to avoid a split with the house, but he had also stirred up resentment against himself. The Commons House regarded him with hostility for the rest of his administration, although its hostility never reached the point of open controversy. Opposition to the governor appeared as early as February 1757, when the house rejected his proposal to reorganize the militia. In July the house came within two votes of defeating another proposal of his, one which provided for raising a provincial regiment.[9] The opposition to Lyttelton grew so strong that the Commons was able to win back one of the privileges it had surrendered; it forced him to submit all papers relating to Indian affairs to the assembly after May 1757 in order to obtain the appropriations he wanted. Lyttelton continued to have trouble with the Commons House: in 1758 it rejected his plan for raising money to send Cherokees on an expedition against the French; in both 1758 and 1759 it again rejected his plan for reorganizing the

[8] Nov. 16–17, 1756, Feb. 5, 9, Mar. 9, 18, 29, 31, Apr. 1–2, 30, 1757, Commons Journal, XXXI, Pt. ii, 14–15, 37–38, 41, 61–62, 71, 82–83, 86–87, 91, 104, S. C. Archives; Lyttelton to Bd. of Trade, May 24, 1757, S. C. Pub. Recs., XXVII, 261–68, S. C. Archives.

[9] Feb. 11, 1757, Commons Journal, XXXI, Pt. ii, 43, S. C. Archives; Lyttelton to the Earl of Loudoun, Feb. 19, 1757, Loudoun Papers, LO 3293, Huntington Lib.; Lyttelton to Bd. of Trade, July 12, 1757, S. C. Pub. Recs., XXVII, 287–89, S. C. Archives.

militia; and in 1759 it voted to disband the provincial regiment over his objections.[10]

Lyttelton accepted his defeats without making a public issue of them, thereby avoiding more serious trouble, and the outward harmony between governor and assembly was seriously threatened only once, in 1758. Lyttelton wanted to pay a bill submitted by a Charles Town mercantile firm, but the Commons rejected the firm's claim. Lyttelton then paid the bill out of the contingency fund allowed him by the assembly, and the Commons House warned Lyttelton that he was encroaching on its rights and cut the size of the contingency fund in the next tax bill. Lyttelton adhered to his policy of dodging a public argument by accepting the house's action without quibbling.[11] Lyttelton was too prudent a man to commit his feelings about the Commons House to paper, but he may well have shared the opinion of his close friend and confidant, William Knox, who once described the assembly as "the sordid Legislators of Carolina . . . that no King can govern nor no God can please." [12]

The combination of wartime necessity and Lyttelton's determination to sidestep conflict with the assembly thus kept internal dissension in South Carolina to a minimum during the early years of the war. The public face of the colony's politics remained calm except during the winter of 1757–1758, when an army officer started a debate on the Crown's right to quarter troops on civilians. The dispute that followed severely tested Lyttelton's ability to maintain the appearance of harmony, and in order to end the controversy he had to call upon all the influence and restraint at his command.

The quartering controversy began because South Carolina was unexpectedly swamped by more royal troops than the colony could easily provide for. The fortunes of war had turned against England in 1756, and Englishmen everywhere feared a French invasion of the colonies. South Carolina seemed a likely target for an attacking force, and the colony had petitioned the Crown for a garrison of royal troops. William Pitt, the secretary of state in charge of the war,

[10] Mar. 18, May 11, 1758, Commons Journal, XXXII, Pt. i, 146–47, 201, S. C. Archives; Jan. 19, Apr. 4, 1759, *ibid.*, Pt. ii, 82, 198; July 9, 11, 13, 1759, *ibid.*, XXXIII, Pt. i, 14–16, 19–20, 23–25. On the papers relating to Indian affairs, see, e.g., May 10, 1757, *ibid.*, XXXI, Pt. ii, 112; Mar. 13, 1759, *ibid.*, XXXII, Pt. ii, 156; July 11–12, 1759, *ibid.*, XXXIII, Pt. i, 21–22.

[11] Dec. 8, 13, 1758, *ibid.*, XXXI, Pt. ii, 33–37, 45–47; Lyttelton to Bd. of Trade, Apr. 14, 1759, S. C. Pub. Recs., XXVIII, 183–87, S. C. Archives.

[12] Knox to Lyttelton, Mar. 5, 1760, "The Manuscripts of Captain H. V. Knox," Hist. Mss. Comm., *Report on Manuscripts in Various Collections,* 8 vols. (London, 1901–14) , VI, 82.

therefore ordered the First Highland Battalion under the command of Lieutenant Colonel Archibald Montgomery to move from Ireland to South Carolina. At almost the same time the commander of the British army in North America, the Earl of Loudoun—who did not know of Pitt's decision—sent Lieutenant Colonel Henry Bouquet to Charles Town with a detachment of 700 men.[13] In both cases the troops arrived in the province only a few weeks after Lyttelton received notice that they were on the way. By September 1757 more than 1,700 men had landed in South Carolina, and the colony had not prepared quarters for any of them. The presence of so many soldiers without housing raised a ticklish constitutional issue, the right of the Crown to quarter troops in private homes in the colonies without the consent of the owners. The Crown did not have that right in England, but many royal officials thought they had such a right in the colonies. By contrast, most colonists believed they had the same rights as English citizens. In England Parliament had solved the problem by passing the Mutiny Act, which required civilians to supply troops stationed near them with quarters, furniture, blankets, and a few other necessities. Parliament had not specifically extended the Mutiny Act to include the colonies, however, and many colonists believed they were not subject to it. There were thus two constitutional issues involved in quartering troops in the colonies: the Crown's right to assign soldiers to private homes and the extension of the Mutiny Act to the colonies. Disputes involving both issues had already arisen in Massachusetts and Pennsylvania, and Loudoun had warned Bouquet to act prudently on the problem of housing troops.[14]

Colonel Bouquet was not a prudent man, however, and he was dissatisfied with South Carolina's preparations for his troops. The assembly appropriated funds for new barracks as soon as each army detachment arrived, but for the time being the governor and the provincial commissary general had to find temporary quarters in taverns, churches, and schoolhouses. The temporary quarters were painfully inadequate, and the assembly aggravated the situation by refusing to supply the new barracks with furniture and blankets, despite the inclusion of both items in the Mutiny Act. The army officers thought that South Carolina had treated them badly, and both

[13] Pitt to Montgomery and to Loudoun, Mar. 31, 1757, Kimball, ed., *Pitt Correspondence*, I, 27–30; Loudoun to Bouquet, Apr. 24, 1757, Stevens and Kent, eds., *Bouquet Papers*, ser. 21632, 83–84.
[14] Except where otherwise noted, this account of the quartering controversy follows Jack P. Greene, "The South Carolina Quartering Dispute, 1757–1758," *S. C. Hist. Mag.*, 60 (1959), 193–204. I have also given the citations for quotations.

Bouquet and Montgomery complained to Loudoun. Bouquet, the senior officer, thought his men should be quartered in private homes and spoke of the "incontestable right of the King's troops to be billeted in the villages where they are quartered." He added that South Carolinians were *"extremely pleased to have soldiers* to protect their plantations, but will feel no inconveniences from them making no great difference between a soldier and a Negro." [15]

In spite of Lord Loudoun's warning to be prudent, Bouquet argued with the assembly in December 1757 and raised the issue of the Crown's right to quarter troops. The Commons House voted appropriations for barracks furniture and other supplies on November 30, 1757, but for reasons that are not clear it decided simultaneously to discontinue the existing housing allowance for senior officers. The vote enraged Bouquet, and he ordered his senior officers not to pay for their rooms themselves. His order raised a constitutional issue, because after December 1 neither the Crown nor the assembly was paying the rent of eighty-one officers who were living in private homes. Bouquet asked Lyttelton to request the assembly to provide a housing allowance for senior officers as well as more blankets, firewood, and other supplies, but before Lyttelton could act Bouquet began to negotiate secretly with Speaker Benjamin Smith. Bouquet said he would insist only on the housing allowance and additional blankets, and he suggested that South Carolina could reduce its financial burden by requesting the withdrawal of some of the troops. The Commons interpreted Bouquet's suggestions as a sign of weakness, and it voted on December 8 only to provide the extra blankets. Bouquet's direct negotiations made Governor Lyttelton so mad that he asked Lord Loudoun to recall Bouquet. He argued that the assembly would have agreed to all of Bouquet's original requests if he had not tried to settle the matter privately. He then accused Bouquet of trying to enrich himself at the expense of his men, charged that Bouquet and some of his officers were involved in land speculation, and asserted that Bouquet wanted the assembly's friendship so he could stay in South Carolina to look after his interests.[16]

Anxious to avert another quartering dispute, the Earl of Loudoun had begun to formulate a compromise even before Lyttelton asked

[15] Bouquet to Loudoun, July 21, Aug. 25, 1757, Stevens and Kent, eds,, *Bouquet Papers*, ser. 21631, 42, 64; italics in original.

[16] Lyttelton to Loudoun, Dec. 10, 1757, Amherst Papers, WO 34/35, foll. 75–78, PRO; see also Lyttelton to Loudoun, Mar. 21, 1758 (Private), Abercrombie Papers, AB 59, Huntington Lib.; Lyttelton to General [John] F[orbes], May 20, 1758, Lyttelton Papers, Clements Lib.

him to recall Bouquet. Loudoun could not afford to give in openly to colonial demands for the right of freedom from quartering, so he wrote public letters to Bouquet and Lyttelton in which he upheld the power of the Crown to quarter troops on civilians and insisted that South Carolina furnish adequate housing and supplies to the soldiers there. In his public letter to Bouquet he instructed him to quarter troops in Charles Town "by your own authority" if the assembly continued to withhold funds. In a private letter, however, he advised the colonel to "act very Tenderly" in this matter and to remain on good terms with Lyttelton. After receiving Lyttelton's request for the recall of Bouquet, Loudoun decided the governor was right and ordered Bouquet to return to Philadelphia with his detachment.[17] By the time his letters reached South Carolina in February and March 1758, the dispute had already begun to abate because the new barracks had been completed in February.

With the barracks finished and Bouquet recalled, South Carolina was moving toward a peaceful settlement of the controversy, and Governor Lyttelton finished the job with his astute handling of one last flare-up. No one had paid the rent for the senior officers since November 30, and neither the army nor the assembly would recede from its resolutions not to pay it. Bouquet made a final request for a housing allowance for senior officers on February 28, and the assembly again turned him down. Then the Commons House sent Lyttelton a message on March 18 that set forth its views on the King's power to quarter troops, arguing that "Officers and Soldiers cannot be Legally or constitutionally Quartered in private Houses without the Special Consent of the Owners or Possessors of Such Houses." [18] The Commons had raised the constitutional issue clearly and unequivocally, and it wanted to debate the issue further but no one answered. Bouquet left the colony with his troops on March 25, and Lyttelton let the issue drop because "I did not think it prudent to make any reply" to the Commons House.[19] A few months later Loudoun recalled Montgomery, too, but no one ever paid the senior officers' rent for the period from December to March.

The quartering controversy typified Lyttelton's determination to

[17] Loudoun to Bouquet, Dec. 25, 1757 (two letters), Loudoun Papers, LO 5098–99, Huntington Lib.; Loudoun to Lyttelton, Dec. 6, 1757, Feb. 13, 1758, Amherst Papers, WO 34/36, foll. 26–28, 32; see also Stanley Pargellis, *Lord Loudoun in North America* (New Haven, 1933), 203–4.

[18] Mar. 18, 1758, Commons Journal, XXXII, Pt. i, 145, S. C. Archives.

[19] Lyttelton to Bd. of Trade, Dec. 2, 1758, S. C. Pub. Recs., XXVIII, 121, S. C. Archives.

restrain and even stifle political debate, a part of his strategy which contributed greatly to his success as governor. He generally succeeded in holding disputation to a minimum, and to make himself look even better to the Board of Trade he was selective in his reports to the Board. Although Lyttelton kept Loudoun informed on the quartering controversy, he did not mention the dispute to the Board of Trade until December 1758, nine months after it had ended. Furthermore, he told the Board of Trade almost nothing about the opposition to him in the assembly. So far as the Board knew, the assembly had never disagreed with Lyttelton except for the brief argument about his contingency fund in 1758. Even when he had to admit that he had failed to keep the peace Lyttelton found a scapegoat. He blamed the quartering dispute on Bouquet, and he said his trouble with the assembly was caused by James Glen's "unbecoming and unmanly" behavior in failing to protect the prerogative.[20] While he blamed others for his difficulties Lyttelton took full credit for his success in obtaining minor constitutional reforms, and the Board of Trade uncritically accepted his version of what had happened in South Carolina. It praised him for defending the prerogative and for "the Harmony and good will which has, the whole Course of your Administration, subsisted between the different Branches of the Legislature." Lyttelton's performance impressed the Earl of Halifax so much that he promised Lyttelton whatever governorship he wanted, and when the governor of Jamaica died in 1759 Halifax appointed Lyttelton to succeed him.[21]

III

While the French and Indian War changed the political life of South Carolina in many ways, it affected the management of Indian affairs more than anything else. Wartime intrigues and dissatisfaction among the Indians convinced the British government that it must assume a more direct responsibility for Indian diplomacy. At the beginning of the war the state of affairs among the western Indians apparently favored the interests of Great Britain. The Chickasaws remained loyal to England, and it seemed possible that their long years of struggle might soon be coming to an end. The French supply

[20] Lyttelton to Bd. of Trade, May 24, 1757, ibid., XXVII, 268; see also Lyttelton to Bd. of Trade, Dec. 2, 1758, Apr. 14, 1759, ibid., XXVIII, 113-21, 183-87.

[21] Halifax to Lyttelton, Apr. 12, Nov. 15, 1759, Lyttelton Papers, Clements Lib.; the quotation is from Bd. of Trade to Lyttelton, July 24, 1759, S. C. Pub. Recs., XXVIII, 207, S. C. Archives.

of trade goods was again diminishing, as it had during King George's War, and the Choctaws were again making overtures of peace to the English. The Creeks were more troublesome, because, as Governor Lyttelton said, "They mean to hold us in one hand and the French in the other." [22] South Carolina did not need to worry about the Creeks after 1756, however, because the new and able governor of Georgia, Henry Ellis, assumed the primary responsibility for the Creeks. Ellis had a flair for Indian diplomacy, and he quickly proved his ability to manage the Creeks.[23]

South Carolina was much more concerned about the Cherokees, who were repeating their old complaints about the Anglo-Cherokee trade. The Cherokees said they did not receive enough goods, especially ammunition, and they charged that the few whites who traded with them were dishonest and interested mostly in selling rum. The English officers at Fort Prince George and Fort Loudoun also testified that the Cherokees were being shortchanged, cheated, and debauched with rum. The trouble seems to have originated with the credit problems of the Cherokee traders. They could not obtain credit in Charles Town, and they were forced to buy their goods from frontier outposts at high prices. Rum was often the only cargo they could afford.[24] The Cherokees took their grievances so seriously that some of them began to agitate for a French alliance, and one overhill delegation went to New Orleans in 1756 and signed a peace treaty. Most of the Cherokee nation remained loyal to England, however, and about 400 of their braves fought with the Virginia militia in the Ohio Valley in 1757.[25]

Other colonies shared South Carolina's difficulties in managing Indian diplomacy and regulating the Indian trade, and the English government had been convinced for several years that Indian affairs in the colonies needed reorganization. The most conspicuous failures of the existing system arose from conflicting provincial claims over the various tribes. This jurisdictional confusion prevented standard trade regulations, encouraged encroachment upon Indian lands, and made it almost impossible to prevent trade frauds. As early as 1748 men who were aware of these faults had proposed that the Crown reform

[22] Lyttelton to Loudoun, Dec. 18, 1756, Loudoun Papers, LO 2365, Huntington Lib.; see also Lyttelton to Loudoun, Feb. 28, 1757, *ibid.*, LO 29374; Alden, *John Stuart*, 95–97.

[23] W. W. Abbot, *The Royal Governors of Georgia, 1754–1775* (Chapel Hill, 1959), 73–81.

[24] Raymond Demeré and John Stuart to Lyttelton, July 11, 1757, Lachlan McIntosh to Lyttelton, July 21, 1758, Lyttelton Papers, Clements Lib.; Corkran, *Cherokee Frontier*, 133.

[25] Alden, *John Stuart*, 61–64, 67; Corkran, *Cherokee Frontier*, 130–41.

the system by appointing a single superintendent of Indian affairs. Delegates to the Albany Congress in 1754 had supported a similar plan and advocated the appointment of William Johnson of New York as superintendent for the northern colonies. In recognition of the need for reform, the Board of Trade in 1755 had instructed General Braddock to issue a commission to Johnson as superintendent of Indian affairs in the northern colonies. Until that time royal officials had been concerned only with the northern colonies, but in 1756 the Board of Trade decided to appoint a southern agent as well.[26]

For the first superintendent of Indian affairs in the south, the Board of Trade chose Edmund Atkin, the Charles Town defender of the council's rights and privileges. Atkin had been born at Exeter, England, in 1707 and had been active in the South Carolina Indian trade and other mercantile ventures for about twenty-five years. He had been in England since 1750, and during that time he had written two long reports on the Indians in America. One was a history of the Choctaw revolt, the other a general survey of Indian affairs in which he proposed a system of trade reform similar to that adopted by the Crown.[27] Atkin's views on Indian policy closely resembled those adopted after 1750 by James Glen, a man whom Atkin despised. Like Glen, Atkin thought England's policy should be to unite all pro-English Indians in one grand alliance. Atkin said in 1758 that nothing was "of so much Consequence to our American Affairs" as "to promote a Union" among the southern Indians.[28] He was a good choice for the agency in many ways, well educated, intelligent, and experienced in Indian diplomacy, but at the same time he was pompous, slow, and afflicted by rheumatism and gout.

Atkin assumed his duties as southern Indian agent under a number of handicaps. Although such influential men as Halifax and Loudoun supported Atkin's appointment, other officials distrusted him, including the Duke of Newcastle and Henry Fox, the secretary of state for the southern department. Newcastle agreed finally to his appointment and a salary, but he blocked the appropriation of royal funds to pay Atkin's expenses. As a further result of the opposition of Newcastle and Fox, Atkin's powers were more limited than those of William

[26] John R. Alden, "The Albany Congress and the Creation of the Indian Superintendencies," *Mississippi Valley Historical Review*, 27 (1940), 193–210.

[27] This was his *Indians of the Southern Colonial Frontier*, which he wrote in 1755. On Atkin's background, see Wilbur R. Jacobs's introduction to his edition of *ibid.*, and Alden, *John Stuart*, 68–69.

[28] Atkin to General James Abercrombie, May 20, 1758, Amherst Papers, WO 34/47, fol. 204, PRO.

Johnson, the northern superintendent. Johnson's commission made him the "sole" superintendent of Indian affairs in the north, but Atkin was empowered only to make treaties with the southern Indians. The Board of Trade instructed southern governors merely to cooperate with him. The Board's secretary, John Pownall, undercut Atkin's position still further by informing Governor Lyttelton that Atkin's job was simply to gather the information needed for further reorganization of Indian affairs. The Board of Trade gave Atkin a commission and the Treasury issued a warrant for his salary, but both the Board of Trade and the Privy Council told him his instructions would be issued by the Earl of Loudoun. Meanwhile, Fox told Loudoun to replace Atkin if he appeared unsuitable. Atkin knew little of the intrigue against him, but he objected to the formal limitations on his authority, especially the Crown's failure to pay his expenses. He threatened to refuse his appointment, and he changed his mind only when James Crokatt, Charles Pinckney, and other South Carolinians then in England assured him that the South Carolina assembly would pay his expenses.[29]

Besides the ministry's halfhearted support, Atkin was further handicapped by the attitude of the southern governors. Atkin considered trade reforms essential, and he asked the governors of the four southern colonies to give him the sole power to license traders. Only Arthur Dobbs of North Carolina complied with the request, and Robert Dinwiddie of Virginia rejected it completely. Ellis and Lyttelton might also have gone along with the plan if Dinwiddie had agreed to it. In other matters Dinwiddie and Dobbs cooperated closely with Atkin, and Dinwiddie found him to be efficient though tedious. Lyttelton, too, supported Atkin, although Lyttelton thought the job too big for one man. The assemblies of Virginia and South Carolina also cooperated; they supplied him with money, and neither assembly protested Atkin's appointment, although the creation of the superintendency clearly tended to reduce legislative control of Indian affairs.[30] Georgia's Governor Henry Ellis, however, became Atkin's severest critic. Part of the trouble was simply that Ellis did not want to share his authority in Indian affairs with anyone, but a more serious cause of his antagonism was Atkin's Indian policy. Ellis disagreed with Atkin's

[29] Alden, *John Stuart*, 69–70; Atkin to Lyttelton, Mar. 20, May 20, Oct. 15, 1756, John Pownall to Lyttelton, Nov. 7, 1757, Lyttelton Papers, Clements Lib.

[30] Alden, *John Stuart*, 74–76; Dinwiddie to Lyttelton, July 22, Aug. 26, 1757, Va. Hist. Soc., *Collections*, 4 (1884), 673, 689–90; Lyttelton to Bd. of Trade, Aug. 7, 1758, S. C. Pub. Recs., XXVIII, 59–65, S. C. Archives; May 19, 1758, Commons Journal, XXXII, Pt. i, 224, S. C. Archives.

plan of uniting all pro-English Indians in one grand alliance. Georgia was a weak and vulnerable colony, and Ellis thought the best way to protect it was to keep the neighboring Indians so busy fighting each other they would not have time to attack Georgia. Ellis feared that Atkin's negotiations among the Indians would only stir them up against Georgia. Consequently, Ellis opposed Atkin at nearly every turn, and he frequently criticized Atkin as nothing more than a bungling fool.[31]

Edmund Atkin's habit of moving slowly became painfully obvious in his journey from England to South Carolina. Although the Board of Trade agreed to his appointment in May 1756, he did not reach South Carolina until March 1758, nearly two years later. Atkin's delay was not entirely his fault. He was supposed to obtain his instructions from Loudoun, and Loudoun was reluctant to issue them. Atkin followed Loudoun to New York, then to Albany, back to New York, then to Boston, back again to New York, and finally to Philadelphia without receiving his instructions. By that time Atkin had been chasing Loudoun for over four months, and the commander in chief told him to proceed to Virginia and promised he would send the instructions there. Atkin reached Williamsburg in April 1757, and still there were no instructions. Atkin had wasted half a year, and there is no record that he ever received his instructions.[32]

When Atkin reached Williamsburg he found his services were needed at once. Virginia had recruited about 250 southern Indians for service with the militia on the colony's western frontier, and Colonel George Washington, who commanded the militia, could not control the Indians. The Cherokees were running wild, stealing from the white settlers and threatening to kill them. The trouble had started over the shortage of presents for the Indians; Cherokee braves, like mercenary soldiers, expected to profit from war, while the English often acted as if they expected Indians to fight without pay. As a result, the Cherokees and the Virginians were constantly quarreling about gifts, and when the Indians did not receive presents, they thought they had the right to take what they wanted by force. Atkin managed to calm the Cherokees a little by distributing presents, and

[31] Ellis to Lyttelton, Feb. 24, Mar. 13, Aug. 27, 1759, Lyttelton Papers, Clements Lib.; William Knox to ?, May 20, 1760, "Mss. of Capt. H. V. Knox," Hist Mss. Comm., *Mss. in Various Collections*, VI, 84. On Ellis's Indian policy, see Abbot, *Royal Governors of Ga.*, 73–74; Adair, *Hist. of Amer. Indians*, ed. Williams, 300–301.

[32] Atkin to Lyttelton, Oct. 16, Nov. 16, 1756, Jan. 25, Apr. 30, 1757, Lyttelton Papers, Clements Lib.

he appointed a deputy and empowered him to supervise Indian affairs in Virginia during his absence. Atkin then resumed his trip southward in the late fall of 1757, but he suffered an attack of rheumatism in North Carolina and did not reach Charles Town until March 23, 1758.[33]

After Atkin arrived in Charles Town he began to work out his plans for a grand tour of the western Indians, during which he hoped to sign a peace treaty with the Choctaws, bring the Creeks into a closer alliance, and reform the Indian trade. After the South Carolina assembly resolved to pay his expenses, Atkin set off into the wilderness in October 1758. He spent the winter at Augusta, and in the spring he moved to the Creek nation. He made a grand entrance into the Indian country, for in the hope of impressing the Indians with pomp and ceremony he had enlisted a sixty-man honor guard. His negotiations were highly successful from the first. He signed a peace treaty with the Choctaws on July 18, 1758, and unlike James Glen a decade earlier, he made sure that the Choctaws received an ample supply of trade goods and ammunition. Atkin was almost as successful with the Creeks, even though one of them attacked him with a hatchet and nearly killed him. The pro-English Creeks gladly renewed their alliance, and Atkin won over some formerly pro-French chiefs as well. He offended a few of the Lower Creeks, however, and Governor Ellis later had to mollify them with presents. Atkin was least successful in reforming the Indian trade, because the governors would not help him, especially Ellis. Atkin returned to South Carolina in the winter of 1759, leaving the western Indians more solidly in the English interest than ever before.[34]

While Atkin was conducting his negotiations in the west, Indian affairs in the east were rapidly deteriorating. The alliance between South Carolina and the Cherokee nation was falling apart, and by the fall of 1759 the situation had degenerated into open warfare. Although the war eventually pitted South Carolina against the Cherokees, the trouble started in Virginia. Agents from Virginia had recruited over 400 Cherokees in 1758 to accompany General John Forbes on an expedition against Fort Duquesne. The Indians reached Virginia long before Forbes was ready to set out, however, and the restless Cherokees began to drift back to their homes. Forbes enlisted the aid of his cousin, James Glen, but by September only sixty Cherokees remained

[33] Alden, *John Stuart*, 67–68, 71–73; Corkran, *Cherokee Frontier*, 115–29; Atkin to Lyttelton, May 25, Aug. 1, 1757, Lyttelton Papers, Clements Lib.

[34] Alden, *John Stuart*, 97–100. A short report of Atkin's trip is Atkin to Pitt, Mar. 27, 1760, Kimball, ed., *Pitt Correspondence*, II, 268–72; a longer version of the same report is Atkin to Lyttelton, Nov. 30, 1759, Lyttelton Papers, Clements Lib.

with Forbes. Meanwhile, a series of fights had broken out in Bedford County between the Cherokees and Virginia farmers and militiamen. The Cherokees were again disappointed by their presents and were stealing from the whites, while some of the Virginians wanted revenge and others hoped to collect bounties for Cherokee scalps. The most serious incident occurred when a group of white farmers ambushed a party of Indians who were not involved in the Cherokee raids and who had just returned from fighting the French. Three Cherokees were killed in the ambush, and a total of about thirty Cherokees died in Virginia in 1758. The Cherokees were outraged by the deaths of their countrymen. They demanded vengeance, and one or two parties actually set out for Bedford County to get revenge. Governor Lyttelton pacified the Cherokees temporarily by giving them presents in lieu of other compensation. Although some chiefs accepted the gifts, this procedure violated the Anglo-Cherokee treaty, which provided that white men who killed Cherokees must be punished by the whites.[35]

Despite their acceptance of South Carolina's presents as compensation for their losses in Virginia, the Cherokees were still dissatisfied. More and more chiefs, especially in the lower towns, began to demand the blood of white men. The settlers in the backcountry of the Carolinas had not harmed the Cherokees, but like the Bedford County farmers, who did not distinguish between guilty and innocent Indians, the Cherokees did not distinguish between Carolinians and Virginians. A gang of Cherokees raided the back settlements on the Yadkin and Catawba rivers in April 1759 and killed fourteen to nineteen whites. Pro-English chiefs, such as the Little Carpenter and Round O of the middle towns, tried to keep the nation at peace, but sporadic raids continued through the spring and summer. By summer's end, however, the Cherokee thirst for blood seemed to have been slacked. A Cherokee delegation assured the governor of Virginia they wanted nothing more than peace, and Round O persuaded an assembly of lower and middle town chiefs to sue for peace. Apparently, the way was clear for fruitful negotiations.[36]

There can be little doubt that the primary reason for the Cherokee

[35] Corkran, *Cherokee Frontier*, 142–62; Attig, W. H. Lyttelton, 124–30; Forbes to Pitt, July 10, 1758, Kimball, ed., *Pitt Correspondence*, I, 295–97; Forbes to Henry Bouquet, Oct. 15, 1758, Forbes to Gen. James Abercrombie, Oct. 16, 1758, Alfred P. James, ed., *Writings of General John Forbes Relating to His Service in North America* (Menasha, Wis., 1938), 230–31, 233; James Beamer to Lyttelton, Sept. 16, 1758, Lyttelton Papers, Clements Lib.; Lyttelton to Bd. of Trade, Oct. 2, 1758, S. C. Pub. Recs., XXVIII, 79–84, S. C. Archives.

[36] Corkran, *Cherokee Frontier*, 163–77; Attig, W. H. Lyttelton, 139–45.

attack on the Carolina back settlements in 1759 was a desire to avenge the deaths of their tribesmen in Virginia. Dissatisfaction with the English trade had contributed to the deterioration of Anglo-Cherokee relations, but the Bedford County killings precipitated the uprising of 1759.[37] It is true that several chiefs had accepted gifts as compensation for the dead braves, but the offer of those gifts had violated the treaty between the English and the Cherokees. In avenging themselves on innocent whites, the Indians had acted as badly as the Virginia farmers, but the fact remains that white men had killed first. Therefore, Indians as well as whites had legitimate grievances, and the question in September 1759 was whether Governor Lyttelton could work out a peace treaty that would be fair to both sides.

IV

It soon became apparent that Governor Lyttelton would not be able to settle South Carolina's Indian troubles on any basis, much less an equitable one. Lyttelton refused to admit the legitimacy of Cherokee grievances, and his failure to do so—combined with a possible desire for military glory—led South Carolina into a war with the Cherokees. Unlike the Yamasee War of 1715, the Cherokee War did not provoke a revolution, but its political repercussions were numerous. Frequent disagreements between governor and Commons House on the conduct of the war raised again the question of the assembly's right to participate in the formulation of Indian policy.

The memory of the Bedford County ambushes still troubled the Cherokees, and their dissatisfaction increased when the commander of Fort Prince George cut off their trade as a disciplinary measure. Several gangs showed their resentment by renewing their raids, and overhill braves killed three Englishmen near Fort Loudoun and cut off the fort's communications with the outside world. The more responsible chiefs opposed violence, and they hoped they could persuade the governor to restore their trade. Subsequently, two delegations—one from the overhills and one from the lower towns—set off for Charles Town in late September to talk to Lyttelton.[38]

News of the latest Cherokee depradations reached Charles Town on

---

[37] Many contemporaries believed that the Bedford County incidents led directly to the Cherokee War. See, e.g., Atkin to Pitt, Mar. 27, 1760, Kimball, ed., *Pitt Correspondence*, II, 268; Milligen, *Short Description*, in Milling, ed., *Colonial S. C.*, 186–87; Henry Ellis to Lyttelton, Sept. 14 1759, Lyttelton Papers, Clements Lib.

[38] Maurice Anderson to Richard Coytmore, Sept. 12, 1759, Paul Demeré to Lyttelton, Sept. 13, 1759, John Stuart to Lyttelton, Oct. 6, 1759, Lyttelton Papers, Clements Lib.

Sunday, September 30, and for many Carolinians it was the last straw. Lyttelton shared their views, and he proposed that South Carolina should declare war on the Cherokees. Deciding that he would lead an armed expedition against the Cherokees, he convened the council on Monday morning, October 1, and issued a directive for the whole assembly to meet on Thursday. He called out the militia in Charles Town and the back settlements and sent appeals for military assistance to Virginia, North Carolina, Georgia, the Chickasaws, and the Cataw-bas.[39] Lyttelton's decision to go to war was precipitate at best. He did not stop to consider the Cherokee grievances, and he did not wait to hear the delegations that were on their way to see him. Lyttelton had always been a calm, even a cautious governor, and it does not seem possible that he suddenly became a victim of panic. It seems more likely that he had some other motive, perhaps a desire for military glory. He had been denied the chance to lead an invasion of Louisiana, and a Cherokee war may have appeared to him as an ideal substitute.[40]

The first of the many political disputes occasioned by the Cherokee War began early in October, when a strong anti-war party appeared in both houses of the assembly. The council at first supported a declaration of war, but the Commons House unanimously opposed it. The Commons thought a declaration of war would be "attended with the greatest Evils and Calamities," so it asked Lyttelton to withhold a declaration "until all hopes shall be lost of obtaining a reasonable and adequate Satisfaction" from the Cherokees.[41] Lyttelton promised to postpone a declaration of war provided the Commons would appropri-ate the funds necessary for his expedition, but the house cut his requests drastically. Lyttelton complained about "the scantiness and insufficiency" of the appropriation and adjourned the assembly for six months, but he kept his promise not to declare war.[42] A faction opposed to war appeared in the council, too, after the delegations of

---

[39] S.-C. Gaz. (Charles Town), Oct. 6, 1759; Lyttelton to Bd. of Trade, Oct. 16, 1759, S. C. Pub. Recs., XXVIII, 243–49, S. C. Archives; Oct. 1, 4, 1759, Council Journal, no. 28, 122–25, S. C. Archives. For a sample of public opinion in favor of war, see Eliza Pinckney to George Morley, Nov. 3, 1759, Eliza Pinckney Letterbook, 133, Pinckney Papers, S. C. Hist. Soc.

[40] Several of Lyttelton's contemporaries accused him of having this desire; see Milligen, Short Description, in Milling, ed., Colonial S. C., 189–90; Hewatt, Historical Account, in Carroll, ed., Hist. Collections of S. C., I, 444; for a somewhat different view of Lyttelton's ambition, see Attig, W. H. Lyttelton, 149–50 n.

[41] Oct. 11, 1759, Commons Journal, XXXIII, Pt. i, 47–48, S. C. Archives.

[42] Oct. 13, 1759, ibid., 53; see also Lyttelton to Bd. of Trade, Oct. 16, 1759, S. C. Pub. Recs., XXVIII, 243–49, S. C. Archives.

Cherokee chiefs reached Charles Town. Four councilors, half the number then present, proposed an alternative plan that would make an expedition unnecessary. They suggested that the governor arrest some of the visiting chiefs and hold them as hostages until the Cherokees surrendered the Indians who had murdered white men. Lyttelton quite properly rejected the proposal because he had promised the Indians safe conduct through South Carolina. He decided they would accompany his expedition, but for their own safety, not as hostages. The four councilors remained opposed to the expedition, however, while the four other councilors favored it.[43]

Despite the opposition of half his council and all the Commons House, Lyttelton went ahead with his expedition, which was executed as poorly as it had been planned. From the time Lyttelton left Charles Town on October 24 with 1,700 men, everything seemed to go wrong. Lyttelton was short of money, and his soldiers were "miserably cloathed, and worse paid." [44] When measles and smallpox swept through the army, the men began to desert, and by December at least two hundred of them had disappeared. On the way into Cherokee country Lyttelton made one of his worst mistakes; he forgot his promise of safe conduct to the Indians with him and began to treat them as hostages. After his arrival at Fort Prince George on December 9, he began peace negotiations with the Little Carpenter, but he handled the negotiations as badly as the expedition. Although Lyttelton's army was in no condition to fight anyone, the governor insisted on a treaty that favored the white man. Lyttelton persisted in his belief that his presents had compensated for the Cherokees who had been killed in Virginia. He therefore insisted that the Cherokees must atone for the whites they had killed by turning the guilty Cherokees over to him for execution. He had computed the number of dead whites at twenty-four, and he said the Cherokees must surrender twenty-four Indians to him. Until he received the guilty men he said he would continue to hold twenty-four hostages from among the Indians who had gone to Charles Town. He offered nothing in return but a resumption of trade. The Little Carpenter could see no alternative to accepting Lyttelton's terms but war, and so he signed a peace treaty based on Lyttelton's demands on December 26. The Cherokees handed over three murderers to Lyttelton, and he left twenty-one Indian hostages at Fort Prince George and ordered its

[43] Attig, W. H. Lyttelton, 153–59; Oct. 19, 22, 1759, Council Journal, no. 28, 135–39.

[44] S.-C. Gaz. (Charles Town), July 26, 1760.

commander to hold them until the Indians surrendered the rest of the murderers.[45]

Lyttelton marched back to Charles Town in triumph, but his day of glory and his peace treaty were equally short-lived. He arrived in town on January 8, 1760, and accepted congratulatory messages from the council, the provincial clergy, and the Charles Town Library Society the next day. Meanwhile, the Cherokees were plotting revenge. As Governor Ellis of Georgia observed, the treaty was "too mortifying to be observed by the Cherokees." [46] The treaty placed all the blame on the Indians and none on the white man, and Lyttelton had made the Cherokees even madder by breaking his word and arresting the twenty-one hostages. Late in January the lower towns went on a rampage and raided settlements all along the South Carolina frontier. They killed forty or fifty white men, women, and children. Lyttelton heard the news on January 31, and three days later he wrote to General Jeffrey Amherst for troops. A band of Indians attacked Fort Prince George on February 14, hoping to free the hostages there, and during the fight the English soldiers slaughtered every Indian in the fort. Peace was no longer possible after the massacre of the hostages, if, indeed, it ever had been.[47]

The Commons House of Assembly had never joined in the general adulation of Lyttelton, and it soon had a chance to let the governor know how it felt. Lyttelton called the assembly into session on February 6 and asked for money to raise an emergency force to guard the frontier. In its first action of the session the Commons informed Lyttelton that he had insulted the house the previous October with his complaints about the amount of money it had granted him. It also told him, "We never shall implicitly or against our Judgment, comply with any demand made upon the Public even though we were sure of incurring Your Excellency's Censure." [48] This amounted to an open declaration of hostility, but as usual Lyttelton avoided further trouble by saying nothing and the house agreed to his requests for money. The house expressed its resentment only when it rejected a motion to request the governor to take personal command of the militia.[49]

---

[45] The best account of Lyttelton's expedition is Attig, W. H. Lyttelton, 160–67; see also Alden, *John Stuart*, 83–88; Corkran, *Cherokee Frontier*, 178–90; the peace treaty is in CO 5/377, foll. 171–72, PRO.

[46] Ellis to Bd. of Trade, Feb. 15, 1760, Candler and Knight, eds., Ga. Col. Recs., XXVIII, Pt. i, 333, Ga. Dept. of Hist. and Archives; on Lyttelton's triumphant return, see *S.-C. Gaz.* (Charles Town), Jan. 12, 1760.

[47] Alden, *John Stuart*, 101–6; Corkran, *Cherokee Frontier*, 191–206.

[48] Feb. 6, 1760, Commons Journal, XXXIII, Pt. i, 56–57, S. C. Archives.

[49] Feb. 10, 13, 14, 1760, *ibid.*, 69–70, 75–76, 84–85.

Although William Henry Lyttelton had led South Carolina into the Cherokee War, he did not remain in the colony long after the war began. He received word of his promotion to the governorship of Jamaica on February 14, 1760, and he immediately began to prepare to return to England for additional instructions. The Board of Trade appointed Governor Thomas Pownall of Massachusetts to replace Lyttelton, which was considered to be a promotion for Pownall. As the Board of Trade wanted Pownall to return to England for further instructions, it appointed William Bull, Jr., lieutenant governor and entrusted the government of the colony to him. Lyttelton sailed from Charles Town on April 4, and Bull assumed his new post the following day. Bull continued to act as governor for the duration of the Cherokee War. Pownall resigned his office in 1761 without coming to South Carolina, and his successor, Thomas Boone, did not reach the colony until December 1761.[50]

When William Bull assumed the acting governorship of South Carolina, the colony's war policy changed radically. Bull was a realist who, though he lacked James Glen's humanitarian impulses and regarded Indians as "Perfidious Barbarians," always considered practical difficulties and did not worry much about honor or glory. In fact, Bull shared Henry Ellis's cynicism toward those who planned for a grand alliance of English Indians. Like Ellis, Bull believed, "Our true Policy is by dividing to rule these neighboring Indians." [51] Bull had opposed Lyttelton's expedition, largely because he did not think South Carolina was strong enough to subdue the Cherokees by itself. After the war started, he decided that no British force could invade the Cherokee nation successfully because of the mountainous terrain. He therefore argued for a policy of moderation and negotiation, and he hoped for a quick end to the war even if South Carolina had to agree to "terms that perhaps may not be thought suitable, according to the Rules of Honour, observed among Europeans." [52] Bull differed from Lyttelton in another important way, too. He was a former speaker of the Commons House of Assembly, and he quickly restored harmony between the house and the governor by conceding one of the

[50] Halifax to Lyttelton, Nov. 15, 1759, Lyttelton Papers, Clements Lib.; Feb. 14, 1760, Council Journal, no. 28, 169, S. C. Archives; *S.-C. Gaz.* (Charles Town) , Apr. 7, 1760; Bd. of Trade Mins., Mar. 17, 1761, S. C. Pub. Recs, XXIX, 4, S. C. Archives.

[51] Bull to Amherst, June 17, 1761, Amherst Papers, WO 34/35, fol. 202, PRO; see also Bull to Bd. of Trade, Jan. 29, 1761, S. C. Pub. Recs., XXIX, 23, S. C. Archives.

[52] Bull to Bd. of Trade, Aug. 31, 1760, S. C. Pub. Recs., XXVIII, 396–97, S. C. Archives; see also Bull to Amherst, May 8, 1760, Amherst Papers, WO 34/35, fol. 164, PRO; Apr. 28, 1760. Commons Journal, XXXIII, Pt. i, 152, S. C. Archives.

constitutional points Lyttelton had insisted upon. Before the house had time to request permission to inspect Indian records, Bull sent it all the documents relating to the Cherokee War. He told the Commons, "I think it proper to lay them before you, that you may have the fullest information of the State of our Affairs." [53]

Bull took over the government at a difficult time. Upon receiving Lyttelton's call for help, General Jeffrey Amherst had dispatched 1,200 regular troops to South Carolina under the command of Colonel Archibald Montgomery, who had been in the colony during the quartering controversy. Amherst needed the detachment for a campaign into Canada, so he had ordered Montgomery to subdue the Cherokees and return as fast as possible. When Montgomery's troops had disembarked in South Carolina on April 1, however, he found the colony had done nothing to get ready for his expedition. Lyttelton was busy packing, Bull would not do anything until Lyttelton left, and a smallpox epidemic had almost paralyzed the colony. Once Lyttelton was gone, Bull moved swiftly and completed preparations for the expedition within three weeks. The assembly, too, cooperated with the governor by voting the necessary appropriations without delay.[54]

Montgomery's expedition against the Cherokees accomplished little, except possibly to boost Cherokee morale. Montgomery set out from the coast on April 23 and reached the lower Cherokee towns on May 28 without meeting any opposition. His forces attacked and burned several lower towns in early June, still without meeting any real resistance. Montgomery did not want to attempt an invasion of the middle and overhill towns because of the difficult terrain, but when an attempt to negotiate peace failed he decided to strike at the middle towns. The Cherokees ambushed his force near the town of Etchoe, and although British casualties were heavy the army drove the Indians away. Montgomery was burdened with so many wounded men that he decided not to penetrate Cherokee territory any farther. After burning Etchoe he returned to the comparative safety of Fort Prince George. There he decided that he had completed his mission, and he began to prepare to rejoin Amherst. The people of South Carolina were doubly appalled by Montgomery's action. By failing to march into overhill country, as Eliza Pinckney said, "The highland troops under Colonel Montgomery sent by Governor Amherst [have not] done much more

---

[53] Apr. 28, 1760, Commons Journal, XXXIII, Pt. i, 152–53, S. C. Archives.

[54] Alden, *John Stuart*, 106–7; Montgomery to Amherst, Apr. 12, 1760, Amherst Papers, WO 34/47, fol. 4, PRO; May 1, 1760, Commons Journal, XXXIII, Pt. i. 164, S. C. Archives.

than exasperated the Indians to more cruel revenge." [55] Montgomery's decision to withdraw his troops from the colony caused an equal consternation. The people feared a Cherokee attack in retaliation for Montgomery's campaign, and they did not think South Carolina could protect its frontier. Lieutenant Governor Bull convinced Montgomery that a state of emergency existed, and the colonel agreed to leave four companies to guard the frontier. The rest of the detachment embarked for New York in August.[56]

After Montgomery's departure a dispute over war policy arose between the Commons House of Assembly and Lieutenant Governor Bull. The Commons House opposed peace negotiations until the Cherokees had been beaten more decisively, and it wanted to attack the Cherokees at once with a provincial force alone. The assembly therefore voted funds to raise a provincial regiment for an invasion of Cherokee country.[57] On the other hand, Bull believed Montgomery's campaign had proved the folly of trying to invade the Cherokee homeland. Furthermore, the Creeks had murdered some of the English traders in their nation, and both Bull and Governor Ellis were afraid the Creeks might ally themselves with the Cherokees in a joint attack on the English colonies. Under these circumstances both governors opposed offensive action by South Carolina. Bull planned only to defend the frontiers and to try to make peace with the Cherokees. He made no effort to raise the regiment voted by the assembly.[58]

For a time Bull's policy appeared to be succeeding. The Little Carpenter, who headed a peace party among the Cherokees, persuaded the nation to hear the English proposals for a treaty. A majority of the Cherokee nation favored peace, but they no longer trusted the English because of the murder of the hostages at Fort Prince George. Even so, negotiations seemed possible until a band of Cherokees slaughtered the English troops at Fort Loudoun. The Indians had cut its lines of communication and supply, and the English had not been able to relieve the garrison, which surrendered on August 6 with the condition that the Cherokees give the soldiers a guarantee of safe conduct to Fort Prince George. The Indians wanted revenge for the hostages

---

[55] Eliza Pinckney to Mrs. King, July 19, 1760, Letterbook, 171, Pinckney Papers, S. C. Hist. Soc.

[56] Alden, *John Stuart*, 110–13; Corkran, *Cherokee Frontier*, 207–15.

[57] Aug. 5, 14, 1760, Commons Journal, XXXIII, Pt. i, 372–73, 375, S. C. Archives.

[58] Bull to Bd. of Trade, Aug. 31, 1760, S. C. Pub. Recs., XXVIII, 394–400, S. C. Archives; Ellis to Bd. of Trade, Sept. 10, 1760, Candler and Knight, eds., Ga. Col. Recs., XXVIII, Pt. i, 464, Ga. Dept. of Hist. and Archives; Alden, *John Stuart*, 108–10.

killed at Fort Prince George, however, and they ambushed the soldiers on August 10, cutting down twenty, including the commander of the fort, and capturing the rest. Only Captain John Stuart escaped, thanks to the efforts of the Little Carpenter. As soon as Bull heard about the ambush, he abandoned negotiations and gave orders to raise the provincial regiment and on October 19 he wrote to Amherst for help.[59] When the assembly met in October, it did not let Bull forget that his policy had failed; it was "not surprised" at the failure of the "moderate Measures that have been persued" and smugly expressed its expectation that in the future he would always adopt "the most vigorous Councils." Bull's policy had indeed failed, and he could only make what a friend of his called a "long laboriously labored answer." [60]

In response to South Carolina's call for help, General Amherst sent nearly 1,600 regular troops to the colony. Amherst did not need the men in the north this time, and he ordered the commanding officer, Lieutenant Colonel James Grant, to stay in the south until he had defeated the Cherokees. Grant was an able soldier who had served under Montgomery with distinction and had been recommended by Montgomery. Grant was also thin-skinned and quarrelsome, however, and he could not stay out of trouble. He landed early in January 1761, and he soon began criticizing Lieutenant Governor Bull. The first clash between them involved the assembly. King George II had recently died, and Bull was supposed to dissolve the present assembly and issue election writs for a new one. Grant needed supplies at once, however, and it would take two months to elect and convene a new assembly. Grant convinced Bull that an immediate dissolution was not necessary because he had not received formal notification of the King's death. Bull called the assembly into session, and the members approved the necessary expenditures while dressed in mourning clothes.[61] While Grant was still bickering about the assembly, he received a letter from Amherst saying Bull had told him that everything was ready for Grant's expedition. Amherst had simply misunderstood a letter from Bull, but Grant lost his temper again and told Amherst that Bull's promise of complete cooperation "will consist

[59] Alden, *John Stuart*, 114–22; Corkran, *Cherokee Frontier*, 216–25; Philip M. Hamer, "Fort Loudoun in the Cherokee War, 1758–1761," *N. C. Hist. Rev.*, 2 (1925), 442–58; Bull to Amherst, Oct. 19, 1760, Amherst Papers, WO 34/35, foll. 174–78, PRO.

[60] Oct. 10, 13, 1760, Commons Journal, XXXIII, Pt. ii, 8–9, 11–12, S. C. Archives; Alexander Garden to Cadwallader Colden, Oct. 26, 1760, N.-Y. Hist. Soc., *Collections*, 54 (1921), 362–63.

[61] Grant to Amherst, Feb. 3, 1761, Amherst Papers, WO 34/47, fol. 47, PRO; Jan. 16–24, 1761, Commons Journal. XXXIII, Pt. ii, 22–36, S. C. Archives.

in good Wishes only." [62] Grant's temper remained volatile, especially when he thought Bull was trying to usurp his military authority, but Amherst advised him to make his peace with the lieutenant governor and Grant calmed down, virtually ending what had been a one-sided affair from the first.[63]

Grant succeeded where Montgomery had failed, because he kept his troops in Cherokee country until the Indians agreed to a peace treaty. Grant led a force of 2,250 men—1,650 regulars and 600 provincials under Colonel Thomas Middleton—into Cherokee country on June 7. For a while his campaign followed the pattern of Montgomery's expedition; he burned several lower towns without meeting much resistance, but he had to fight off a surprise attack near the town of Etchoe. Where Montgomery had turned back, however, Grant moved forward. He attacked the middle towns in force, burning fifteen and destroying the Cherokees' annual crop of corn. After driving the Indians into the overhill towns, he returned to Fort Prince George on July 9 to wait for the Cherokees to sue for peace. The English cause was helped by the end of the Creek uprising and by the increasing strength of the Little Carpenter's peace party.[64]

South Carolina did not make peace with the Cherokees, however, until there had been one final internal dispute over the terms of the peace treaty. Bull, Grant, and the Commons House of Assembly each had different ideas about the terms of peace. Bull technically had the power to negotiate a peace treaty by himself, but Grant had made contact with the Indians and both the council and Amherst had advised Bull to allow the assembly to participate in negotiations. The Commons House, as usual, was bloodthirsty and wanted to continue the war until the Cherokee nation was virtually exterminated. It said, "We conceive that the only thing in a Cherokee War, that will have any Effect to bring those Savages to a firm and lasting Peace is to destroy as many of their People as we can." [65] Bull and Grant agreed that they should offer reasonable terms to the Cherokees, although Grant, as usual, was critical. He could not understand why Bull should consult the assembly, and he accused him of "conduct so irregular and

[62] Grant to Amherst, Feb. 3, 1761, Amherst Papers, WO 34/47, foll. 46–47, PRO; see also Bull to Amherst, Dec. 27, 1760, Amherst to Grant, Jan. 14, 1761, *ibid.*, 34/35, fol. 187, 34/48, fol. 59.

[63] Amherst to Grant, Feb. 27, 1761, Grant to Amherst, June 2, 1761, *ibid.*, 34/48, foll. 62–64, 34/47, fol. 82.

[64] Alden, *John Stuart*, 126–29; Corkran, *Cherokee Frontier*, 236–54.

[65] Sept. 18, 1761, Commons Journal, XXXIV, 255, S. C. Archives; see also Amherst to Bull, July 2, 1761, Amherst Papers, WO 34/36, fol. 77, PRO; Sept. 10, 1761, Council Journal, III, Pt. ii, 390–91, S. C. Archives.

so unprecedented that I cannot put up with it." [66] At the same time
Grant was also quarreling with the Commons House, in part because
the house thought he should have marched into the overhill towns and
in part because the house sided with Colonel Thomas Middleton in
his personal quarrel with Grant. Middleton had commanded the
provincial regiment in Grant's campaign, and the two men had fallen
out over a trivial issue. Middleton had returned from the expedition
early and attacked Grant in the provincial newspaper. The quarrel did
not end until Grant returned to Charles Town in December and
fought a bloodless duel with Middleton.[67]

Bull and Grant had agreed upon the terms of peace before they
opened negotiations with the Cherokees. Bull had drafted a treaty in
April 1761, in which he proposed the following terms: Cherokee
acknowledgment of English supremacy; an exchange of prisoners;
English re-occupation of Fort Loudoun; election of the Little Carpenter as Cherokee emperor; the execution of four chiefs as a token of
Cherokee guilt; and the recognition of the Twenty-Six Mile River
(near Fort Prince George) as the eastern boundary of the Cherokee
nation. Grant had objected to the boundary clause, however, because
it would have substantially reduced the size of the Cherokee nation
and Bull had deleted it. When a peace delegation headed by the Little
Carpenter reached Fort Prince George on August 28, Grant offered it
the terms he and Bull had agreed upon with one exception. He
omitted the clause relating to the Little Carpenter's election as
emperor, because he thought open English support might undermine
the Little Carpenter's influence. The Cherokees readily accepted most
of Grant's terms, but they knew their nation would never agree to
execute any of its chiefs. They therefore rejected the execution clause,
and Grant sent them on to Charles Town to negotiate this point with
Bull and the assembly. He recommended that Bull omit the execution
clause on the grounds that the Cherokees had been punished enough
by losing their homes and crops.[68]

Bull incorporated Grant's recommendations into the final treaty,
but only after further arguments with the Commons House and Grant
himself. The Commons House met on September 15, 1761, in an ugly
mood. Rather than being glad the war was over, the house was mad
because Grant had not exterminated the Cherokees. It denounced the

[66] Grant to Amherst, Oct. 6, 1761, Amherst Papers, WO 34/47, fol. 108, PRO.
[67] Grant to Amherst, Sept. 3, Dec. 24, 1761, *ibid.*, 34/47, foll. 100, 109; Sept. 18,
1761, Commons Journal, XXXIV, 255–56, S. C. Archives.
[68] Sept. 15, 1761, Commons Journal, XXXIV, 237–42, S. C. Archives; Corkran,
Cherokee Frontier, 258–60.

proposed treaty as "precarious and less honorable than we had reason to expect," but it agreed to accept the treaty if Bull would insist upon the execution of the four chiefs.[69] Bull realized that an attempt to execute the chiefs could easily revive the war, and so he defied the lower house by refusing to reinsert the execution clause. The Little Carpenter was pleased by the omission of the disputed clause and signed a preliminary treaty on September 23. A few weeks later, however, Bull discovered a clerical error in the treaty. He had been ill when the treaty was drafted and he had not had all his papers with him; as a result, he had forgotten that he and Grant had agreed to delete the clause establishing the Twenty-Six Mile River as the eastern boundary of the Cherokee nation, and the clause had been included in the treaty. As soon as he discovered his error, he struck out the clause with the consent of the council. Grant refused to accept Bull's explanation, however, and charged that Bull had deliberately reinserted the boundary clause as a concession to the Commons House. Grant commented to Amherst, "It will appear I dare say extraordinary to Your Excellency, that he should have forgot the only Point of any Consequence which he ever had to settle during the course of the Indian War." [70]

The final round of negotiations took place in Charles Town in December 1761. The Little Carpenter had returned to the Cherokee nation, where the other chiefs had ratified the treaty, and he went back to Charles Town in December with a few other chiefs to sign the definitive treaty. He arrived to find the city in a turmoil. The feud between Grant and Colonel Middleton had reached its height, and the Commons House was outraged with Bull because he had ignored its advice in writing the final draft of the peace treaty. Bull conveniently fell ill again and left final negotiations to Othniel Beale, the president of the council and Bull's father-in-law. Beale and the Little Carpenter agreed on final terms without any trouble and signed the treaty on December 18, 1761. Although satisfied with the treaty, Colonel Grant was still displeased by Bull's performance and hinted that Bull had faked his recent illness in order to avoid public criticism.[71] Bull had the habit of taking to his bed at critical times, but Grant criticized the lieutenant governor too quickly. Bull had been caught in the middle

[69] Sept. 18, 1761, Commons Journal, XXXIV, 255–56, S. C. Archives.

[70] Grant to Amherst, Nov. 18, 1761, Amherst Papers, WO 34/47, foll. 113–14, PRO; see also Grant to Amherst, Oct. 6, Nov. 5, 1761, *ibid.*, 34/47, foll. 108–9, 111–12; Nov. 13, 1761, Council Journal, III, Pt. ii, 412–13, S. C. Archives.

[71] Grant to Amherst, Dec. 24, 1761, Amherst Papers, WO 34/47, foll. 119–20, PRO.

of strong opposing forces, but he had never deviated from what he thought was the practical and proper course for South Carolina to follow.

After more than two years of intermittent fighting the Cherokee War was over. Paradoxically, the colony suffered from more internal dissension at the end of the war than at the beginning. The Commons House persisted in its belief that the treaty was not honorable, and it complained a few months later that the war had "not produced any Real advantage in favour of this province." [72] According to Henry Laurens, who favored the moderate policies of Bull and Grant, it was not until a year and a half after the end of the war that most people began to "open their eyes and acknowledge" that South Carolina had really won the war.[73]

V

In South Carolina during the French and Indian War, as in other colonies, more constitutional issues were raised than settled. Yet neither the failure to settle the issues nor the more dramatic events of the Cherokee War should obscure the fact that important constitutional issues did appear and were debated by the colonists. Probably the two most important questions of the war involved the right of the Crown to quarter troops in private homes and the right of the Commons House to share in the formulation of Indian policy. During the war the Commons House also became aware of the Crown's intention to reform the provincial constitution, and it found itself on the defensive for the first time in a quarter of a century. The thrust of the Crown's reform movement was blunted, however, by the pressures of war and by Governor Lyttelton, who studiously avoided controversy in order to gain advancement. Straightforward constitutional issues thus became rare, and South Carolina's political leaders were more concerned with the Cherokee Indians. Even an Indian war raised political issues, however, and the Commons House struggled to maintain its voice in the decisions of war and peace by opposing both a declaration of war in 1759 and the peace treaty of 1761. Thus, even in the middle of war, the struggle for constitutional supremacy continued.

[72] May 28, 1762, Commons Journal, XXXV, Pt. i, 132, S. C. Archives.
[73] Laurens to Willis Martin, Aug. 29, 1763, Letterbooks, III, 216, Laurens Papers, S. C. Hist. Soc.

CHAPTER XV

THE FRUITS OF WAR
1761–1763

With the ratification of the Cherokee peace treaty in December 1761, South Carolina returned to the sidelines of the French and Indian War. Although the war did not end formally until 1763, South Carolina was at peace for all practical purposes, and peace forced the political leadership of the colony to disinter a set of problems it had postponed for the duration of hostilities. Each of the problems was related to the basic question of South Carolina's relationship to the Crown, and with the exception of a further reorganization of Indian affairs, each of them added to the growing tension between the colony and the home government. Finally, Governor Thomas Boone increased the tension on both sides in 1762 by refusing to recognize some of the most fundamental rights of the Commons House of Assembly.

I

Ratification of the Cherokee peace treaty began a period of improved relations between Englishmen and Indians on the southern frontier. The improvement was made possible by a spirit of cooperation that prevailed in Indian affairs in spite of a lack of harmony in other areas of government. The most remarkable aspect of this unity was the attitude of the South Carolina Commons House of Assembly. It was willing not only to cooperate with other branches of government, but even to surrender part of its traditional political power.

The Commons House had finally realized that one colony could not adequately regulate Indian affairs by itself. Furthermore, the cost of giving presents to the Indians had become an intolerable financial burden on the colony. At Governor Thomas Boone's suggestion, the assembly passed a new law in May 1762, which set up a public monopoly of the Cherokee trade with headquarters at Keowee, near Fort Prince George. Neither the assembly nor the Cherokees liked the new law, and on orders from the Commons House, provincial agent Charles Garth asked the Board of Trade to establish uniform trade regulations in the south. Garth simultaneously requested the Lords of the Treasury to assume the financial burdens of Indian diplomacy.[1] The willingness of the Commons to surrender its authority over the Indian trade was unique; it was the only recorded occasion when the house volunteered to reduce its powers.

As the South Carolina assembly retired to a subordinate position, the Crown appointed a new Indian superintendent and increased his powers. The first superintendent, Edmund Atkin, had never exercised much authority because the Crown and the governors had not supported him, and he had lost all his influence on Indian policy after the beginning of the Cherokee War. Governors Bull and Ellis had ignored his advice whenever he offered it, and when the South Carolina council had also ignored him Atkin had resigned from the council. Atkin had died at his plantation at Mars Bluff on October 8, 1761, a lonely and forgotten old man.[2] The new governor of South Carolina, Thomas Boone, recommended John Stuart to General Amherst, and with Amherst's support Stuart obtained a commission as Atkin's successor on January 5, 1762. Stuart, a Scot with a flair for adventure, was born in Inverness in 1718. He had sailed around the world with Admiral George Anson during King George's War and then joined a mercantile firm in Charles Town. After his firm had gone bankrupt, he had received a commission as captain in one of the independent companies stationed in South Carolina. During the Cherokee War he had been posted at Fort Loudoun, where he had displayed a talent for Indian negotiations, and he was the only person in the garrison who escaped both death and capture in 1760.[3]

When Stuart took over the superintendency, the southern Indians

[1] Cooper and McCord, eds., *Statutes*, IV, 168–73; Memorial of Garth, Nov. 1762, S. C. Pub. Recs., XXIX, 259–64, S. C. Archives; Memorial of Garth, Nov. 12, 1762, Treas. 1/421, foll. 270–71, PRO.

[2] Atkin to Amherst, Nov. 20, 1760, Apr. 4, 1761, Amherst Papers, WO 34/47, foll. 218–23, PRO; Nov. 1, 1760, Council Journal, CO 5/477, 45, PRO; *S.-C. Gaz.* (Charles Town), Oct. 17, 1761.

[3] Alden, *John Stuart*, 48, 83, 118–19, 135–36, 156–75.

were in a rebellious temper. The Cherokees disliked South Carolina's public trade, and they also protested against white settlement on their land, a complaint which was echoed by the Catawbas. The Choctaws and Chickasaws were uneasy but hopeful of a profitable trade with the English. The most serious complaints came from the Creeks. For decades they had held the balance of power on the southern frontier, and they had derived great pleasure from playing off England and France against each other. The French and Indian War had eliminated France as a competitor in North America, and the Creeks realized they could no longer engage in balance of power diplomacy. One pro-French chief named The Mortar tried to organize a conspiracy against England, but the other Indian nations refused to cooperate and his scheme collapsed.[4]

Officials in England as well as the colonies recognized the need to pacify the southern Indians, and so the four southern royal governors and Stuart met Indians from the five major nations in a general conference at Augusta, Georgia, in 1763. Henry Ellis, the former governor of Georgia, had proposed the conference, and it was approved in March 1763 by the Earl of Egremont, the secretary of state for the southern department. Egremont ordered Stuart and the governors to forgive the Indians for their past misdeeds and to promise them trade and redress of grievances. He also arranged for Stuart to distribute presents worth £5,000 sterling.[5] The governors disagreed about the site for the conference, but the Creek Indians settled the argument by refusing to travel beyond Augusta. The conference therefore opened at Augusta on November 5, 1763, and made rapid progress. Stuart distributed presents to 846 Indians who were, in his words, "incessant" in their "Demands for Rum, Pipes, and Tobacco."[6] The delegates signed a treaty on November 10, in which the English promised the Indians more trade goods and the Cherokees and Creeks made generous concessions on boundaries and promised not to molest existing white settlements.[7]

Both Stuart and the governors were pleased by the success of the conference, although they were worried because they had not settled

4 *Ibid.*, 175–81.

5 *Ibid.*, 181; see also circular letter of Egremont, Mar. 16, 1763, Sir Jeffrey Amherst Papers, I, fol. 12, Clements Lib.

6 Stuart to General Thomas Gage, Dec. 31, 1763, Thomas Gage Papers, American Series, Clements Lib.; see also Stuart's list of presents distributed at the Congress, Nov. 19, 1763, Amherst Papers, VII, fol. 95, Clements Lib.

7 Alden, *John Stuart*, 183–85. For contemporary accounts of the Congress, see the letter of Stuart and the governors to Egremont, Nov. 10, 1763, CO 5/65, 285–88, PRO; *Journal of the Congress . . . at Augusta, 1763* (Charles Town, 1764).

the Indian trade. Like the South Carolina assembly, they believed general trade rules enforced by the Crown were necessary. Egremont and other British officials shared this opinion, but the Crown did not adopt official trade regulations until 1768.[8] In the meantime, however, South Carolinians could agree with Henry Laurens, who said that because of the Augusta Congress, "We have some prospect of being at Peace with those very troublesome Neighbours for some Years to come."[9]

II

For a few months in 1762 the political leaders of South Carolina dared to hope that the spirit of cooperation in Indian affairs might carry over into other areas of government. Their optimism was occasioned in large part by the appointment of a native South Carolinian, Thomas Boone, as governor of the colony. Boone was the nephew of Joseph Boone, who had been active in politics a half-century earlier as a leader of the dissenter and anti-proprietary factions. Educated at Eton and Cambridge, Thomas Boone had inherited his uncle's considerable landed estate. He had been living in South Carolina in 1759, when the Crown had appointed him governor of New Jersey. After a successful term there of eighteen months, he had been promoted to the governorship of South Carolina. When he came home as governor in December 1761, the assembly welcomed him and expressed its satisfaction at the appointment of a native son.[10]

Despite the hopes of the local politicians, Thomas Boone gravely disappointed South Carolina. He had little talent for politics, and he involved the colony in several unnecessary controversies. Although he was responsible for starting at least two disputes, many of his troubles were not his fault. He had the misfortune to inherit a set of unsolved problems that his predecessors had been able to ignore because of the Cherokee War.

One of the most vexing of Boone's inherited problems was that of recruiting men for service in the royal army. Early in the war William

[8] Alden, *John Stuart*, 185–86; see also Amherst to Stuart, Apr. 16, 1763, Amherst Papers, WO 34/48, fol. 103, PRO; Bd. of Trade to Stuart, Aug. 5, 1763, S. C. Pub. Recs., XXIX, 345–47, S. C. Archives.

[9] Laurens to Richard Oswald and Co., Dec. 3, 1763, Letterbooks, III, 248, Laurens Papers, S. C. Hist. Soc.

[10] Dec. 24, 1761, Commons Journal, XXXIV, 271–72, S. C. Archives; Jack P. Greene, "The Gadsden Election Controversy and the Revolutionary Movement in South Carolina," *Miss. Valley Hist. Rev.*, 46 (1959), 470.

Pitt had devised a plan, called the requisition system, for recruiting troops in the colonies for service in North America. Pitt set a quota of recruits for each colony every year, but South Carolina had never once met its quota. The assembly generously appropriated money for recruiting, but the overall record remained poor. A chief reason perhaps was South Carolina's fear of a slave rebellion. The Negro population was twice the size of the white population, and the colonists were afraid that if large numbers of white men went off to serve in the army the slaves would start an insurrection.[11] The assembly had voted money for a South Carolina regiment of 700 men in 1757, but only 300 men enlisted in it. The colony fared even more poorly in raising troops for other commands. For example, in 1760 the Crown assigned South Carolina a quota of 500 recruits and it failed to enlist a single man.[12]

The recruiting problem became more acute after the Cherokee War ended. The Crown had not insisted that South Carolina meet its recruiting quotas while the Indian war was going on, but when it ended royal officials began to demand that the province fulfill its obligations. The assembly outraged General Amherst by disbanding the provincial regiment at the end of Grant's expedition in 1761, and Amherst gave Governor Boone a personal lecture on the need for recruits before Boone left New Jersey.[13] Boone tried hard to speed up enlistments and the assembly helped him, but he fared as badly as his predecessors. Amherst therefore decided to make one final attempt to raise troops in South Carolina. He sent three recruiting officers to the colony in the summer of 1762, including the well-known Captain Robert Rogers of the Rangers, who had a reputation as one of the most effective recruiters in North America. Rogers and his fellow officers failed miserably; they enlisted only fifty-seven men, and most of them came from North Carolina.[14] After that it was clear that soldiers could not be enlisted in South Carolina, and the colony's failure in

[11] See, e.g., Lyttelton to Loudoun, Nov. 5, 1756, Amherst Papers, WO 34/35, fol. 63, PRO; Bull to Bd. of Trade, Jan. 29, 1761, S. C. Pub. Recs., XXIX, 20–21, S. C. Archives; on the requisition system in general, see George Louis Beer, *British Colonial Policy, 1754–1765* (N. Y., 1907), 52–71.

[12] Lyttelton to Bd. of Trade, Aug. 7, 1758, S. C. Pub. Recs., XXVIII, 52, S. C. Archives; Return of the S. C. Regiment, Jan. 31, 1760, Amherst Papers, WO 34/35, fol. 151, PRO; Return of Troops, 1760, Treas. 1/423, fol. 36, PRO.

[13] Bull to Amherst, Dec. 5, 1761, Amherst to Bull, Dec. 20, 1761, Amherst to James Grant, Jan. 2, 1762, Amherst Papers, WO 34/35, fol. 209, 34/36, fol. 84, 34/48, fol. 94, PRO.

[14] Boone to Amherst, Mar. 15, 1762, W. Ramsay to Amherst, June 28, 1762, *ibid.*, 34/35, foll. 217–18, 34/47, foll. 122–23; State of Recruits, 1762, Treas. 1/415, fol. 132, PRO.

recruiting gave it a reputation for being delinquent in supporting the war effort.

Largely as a result of its shortcomings in recruiting soldiers, South Carolina also failed to collect financial compensation from the Crown. As an inducement to the colonies to raise troops, the English ministry had begun to grant money to the colonies in 1756 to compensate for their expenditures in the war effort. The first grant had gone to several northern colonies, and upon receiving an application from the agent of Virginia and North Carolina, Parliament had voted £50,000 sterling for Virginia and both Carolinas in 1757. South Carolina received £11,714 from the grant. From 1759 on Pitt had annually promised the colonial governors that he would request financial compensation if they would meet their recruiting quotas. Parliament had made annual appropriations of £200,000 sterling from 1759 to 1761, and in both 1762 and 1763 it voted £133,333 annually for this purpose.[15]

It is impossible to say exactly how much South Carolina spent for military purposes during the war, but the total amounted to more than £200,000 sterling, or £6,500,000 currency. The assembly emitted a total of £699,593 currency in public orders earmarked for the war effort; to that amount should be added the major portion of £880,755 in tax certificates, which were not specifically designated for defense but most of which was spent for that purpose.[16] The cost of Lyttelton's expedition alone eventually added up to £751,789 currency. While the colony borrowed time by emitting paper money and redeeming it after the war, taxes still rose higher than ever before. One resident said they had quadrupled. He may have exaggerated, but after 1756 the annual tax bill never fell below £100,000 currency, and in 1761 it went over £300,000.[17] The entire colony would have agreed with William Bull, Jr., who said, "When the greatness of our Expence, and the smallness of our numbers are considered, this Province will appear to have exerted her utmost endeavors in her defence."[18]

Despite the heavy financial burdens of the war, South Carolina collected almost no compensation from Parliament. The Lords of the

[15] Beer, *British Colonial Policy*, 53–57; Keith, *First British Empire*, 329–30; Memorial of James Abercrombie and James Wright, [1758], Treas. 1/372, fol. 201, PRO.

[16] Brock, Currency of Colonies, 460 n, Table XXVI.

[17] Alexander Garden to Sec. S.P.G., S.P.G. Mss., B5, no. 216; Cooper and McCord, eds., *Statutes*, IV, 34, 45, 53–73, 103, 128–43, 155, 179. On the cost of Lyttelton's expedition, see Feb. 22, 1762, Commons Journal, XXXV, Pt. i, 24, S. C. Archives.

[18] To Bd. of Trade, Jan. 29, 1761, S. C. Pub. Recs., XXIX, 28, S. C. Archives.

Treasury decided to peg reimbursements to recruiting and repaid each colony on the basis of the number of recruits it had enlisted. This plan discriminated against South Carolina, which had technically recruited very few men for the King's regular army, although it had enlisted hundreds for the Cherokee expeditions. The assembly decided to try to persuade the Treasury to set aside its rule, and at its request Governor Boone and agent Charles Garth petitioned the Treasury for compensation in 1762. British policy required each colony to defend its own coast, so the petitions of Boone and Garth listed only the money spent for the Cherokee War and frontier defense. They figured the total spent to defend frontier settlements at £751,769 currency, or about £108,000 sterling.[19] The Treasury insisted on its rule about recruiting, however, and South Carolina collected only £285 sterling, the bounty for the fifty-seven men enlisted in 1762.[20] If the Crown had a legitimate grievance against South Carolina for its failure to recruit soldiers, South Carolina thus had an equally valid grievance for its failure to receive financial compensation.

A third source of conflict during Boone's administration was illegal trade. It never became a serious problem in South Carolina, but there were indications that South Carolina, like other colonies, did not want to prosecute those who disobeyed the Navigation Acts. The merchants of South Carolina had usually obeyed the trade laws in the past, because they had not been tempted to break them. They dealt chiefly in the profitable and legal staple products of the colony, not in rum or foodstuffs, the usual items in illegal trade.[21] During the war, however, the situation changed. It became profitable to trade with French colonies through the neutral Spanish ports of Pensacola and Monte Cristi. The trade was quite small, especially in comparison with that carried on by northern merchants, but the Court of Vice-Admiralty in Charles Town refused to condemn vessels caught in the trade.[22] The assembly was reluctant to take action, too, but Governor Boone was determined to stop the trade with the enemy if he could. He persuaded

[19] May 20, 1761, Commons Journal, XXXIV, 73–74, S. C. Archives; Memorials of Boone and Garth, Feb. 28, Sept. 21, 1762, Treas. 1/415, foll. 113–15, 134–35, PRO.

[20] "Apportionment amongst the Colonies," 1762, Treas. 1/415, fol. 111, PRO.

[21] Commissioners of Customs to Lords of Treasury, Jan. 2, 1750, S. C. Pub. Recs., XXIV, 261–62, S. C. Archives; Sellers, Charleston Business, 178–81; no one complained of smuggling in South Carolina until 1753, when James Glen said a small illegal trade existed; see Glen to Bd. of Trade, Mar. 1753, S. C. Pub. Recs., XXV, 174–214, S. C. Archives.

[22] Bull to Pitt, Feb. 18, 1761, Kimball, ed., Pitt Correspondence, II, 394–96; Beer, British Colonial Policy, 72–131; Keith, First British Empire, 331–34; Bridenbaugh, Cities in Revolt, 66.

the assembly in 1762 to enact a law designed to reduce smuggling, but the statute merely tightened up regulation of the coastwise trade and ignored the basic problem of trading with the enemy through neutral ports. The act displeased Boone, who insinuated the assembly was protecting illegal traders and called the law "fruitless and ineffectual." Nevertheless, he approved the act on the grounds that it would be difficult to get a better one.[23]

Thomas Boone was not responsible for South Carolina's difficulties in recruiting, finances, or illegal trade, but his own lack of foresight started a new dispute with Georgia in 1763. Boone announced on April 5, 1763, that he would accept applications for land grants in the area south of the Altamaha River. That land now belongs to Georgia, but in 1763 South Carolina could reasonably claim it, since the land was included in the Carolina charters of 1663 and 1665 and the Georgia charter of 1732 had set the Altamaha River as the colony's southern boundary. Nevertheless, the Crown had never recognized South Carolina's claim to the area, and it certainly had not authorized Boone to grant land there. In spite of the confused legal situation, Boone's announcement appealed to the speculative instincts of South Carolina. The colonists organized land companies and applied for grants in droves; even the self-righteous Henry Laurens fought down his scruples against speculation and invested in a land company. Within a month Boone approved 418 warrants for a total of 513,000 acres of land south of the Altamaha.[24]

Governor James Wright of Georgia objected violently to Boone's conduct, and he managed to block the land speculators. Wright peppered the Board of Trade and the secretary of state with angry letters, in which he charged that Boone was allowing his friends to monopolize the land warrants. He said surprisingly little about South Carolina's claim to the Altamaha region. The Board of Trade listened to Wright sympathetically, promising that it would place the disputed region under his jurisdiction and would help him find a way to invalidate the warrants Boone had already issued. Actually, the Board of Trade did not help Wright very much. It merely censured Boone and told him not to sign any more warrants. In July 1763 the South

[23] Cooper and McCord, eds., *Statutes*, IV, 173–76; May 29, 1762, Commons Journal, XXXV, Pt. i, 143, S. C. Archives.

[24] Apr. 5, 1763, Council Journal, no. 29, 43–50, S. C. Archives; Laurens to John Rutherford, Apr. 4, 1763, Letterbooks, III, 135–36, Laurens Papers, S. C. Hist. Soc.; Laurens to Lachlan McIntosh, May 4, 1763, Letterbook, 1762–1766, 38–42, Laurens Papers, Hist. Soc. of Pa.; Egerton Leigh, "Warrants granted . . . to the Southward of Altamaha river . . . 1763," Shelburne Papers, XLIX, 239–53, Clements Lib.

Carolina council suspended action on all land claims in the area, because it thought the land might belong to Indians. The Board of Trade, however, neither invalidated the existing claims nor annexed the Altamaha region to Georgia.[25]

III

When Governor Boone started the quarrel over the Altamaha lands, he was already engaged in a much more serious dispute at home, the Gadsden election controversy. The controversy began in September 1762, when Boone challenged the right of the Commons House of Assembly to determine the validity of assembly elections. Before it ended, the assembly had ceased to function for a year and a half. Disputes over constitutional issues were all too common in South Carolina, but no other governor had shown the determination that Boone did.[26]

As early as January 1762 Boone told a friend that he thought the lower house had assumed too much power, and he implied that he expected to become involved in disputes with it.[27] As a first step in his campaign to reduce the authority of the Commons House, Boone acquired more control over assembly meetings. The Commons had controlled the duration and time of its meetings for many years by asking the governor's permission to adjourn to a specific date. Previous governors had always agreed to such house requests unless they had special reason not to. Boone, however, refused to let the assembly adjourn itself. Whenever the lower house requested permission to adjourn, Boone rejected the request and prorogued the assembly to a date he had selected.[28] In another minor reform Boone also emulated Lyttelton by refusing to allow a committee of the Commons House to help supervise the distribution of Indian presents.[29] The lower house accepted both changes in silence.

[25] Abbot, *Royal Governors of Ga.*, 100–102; Bd. of Trade to Boone, May 30, 1763, S. C. Pub. Recs., XXIX, 329–31, S. C. Archives; July 4, 1763, Council Journal, no. 29, 75, S. C. Archives.

[26] Except where otherwise noted, this account of the Gadsden dispute follows Greene, "Gadsden Election Controversy," *Miss. Valley Hist. Rev.*, 46 (1959), 469–92. I have also given the citations for quotations.

[27] Thomas Boone to ?, Jan. 17, 1762, Miscellaneous Manuscripts, P 2465, South Caroliniana Lib. For a different view of the cause of the Gadsden dispute, see Richard Barry, *Mr. Rutledge of South Carolina* (N. Y., 1942), 84–86; Barry suggests that Boone started the dispute because he was angry at the assembly leaders and their wives for snubbing his mistress.

[28] May 29, July 9, Aug. 9, 1762, Commons Journal, XXXV, Pt. i, 143, 152, 153, S. C. Archives.

[29] May 29, July 9, 1762, *ibid.*, 137–38, 152.

The election dispute began when Governor Boone proposed a new elections law. The assembly had passed an additional elections act in 1759, which had made minor changes in the requirements for the franchise and assembly membership, but the Crown had disallowed it because it did not include a suspending clause.[30] Disallowance of the 1759 law led Boone to re-examine the elections act of 1721, and he found it virtually useless because it was "so loose and general, so little Obligatory on the Church Wardens, and so difficult in prescribing the forms to be observed."[31] He therefore recommended a new elections act to the assembly, but the Commons House turned down his recommendation in March 1762, and decided to keep the old law. Boone, offended by the rejection of his proposal, decided to teach the Commons House a lesson by demonstrating the flaws in the act of 1721 at the next opportunity.

Boone's chance came in September 1762, when the voters of St. Paul's Parish chose Christopher Gadsden to represent them in the Commons House. There were irregularities in the election—the churchwardens had neglected to take a required oath and they had filled out the election return improperly—but after an investigation the Commons decided the spirit of the elections law had not been violated. The house voted to seat Gadsden on September 13 and then sent him to Governor Boone to take his oath. Boone had learned of the irregularities in Gadsden's election, and he refused to administer the oath of office. The governor lacked the power to vacate a single election, so Boone dissolved the assembly and issued writs for new elections.[32] In dissolving the assembly Boone remarked, "To a rigid execution of [the elections law] your Body owes, or ought to owe, its existence."[33]

Boone's actions and remarks raised two important constitutional issues. First, by refusing to let Gadsden take his seat in the assembly, Boone had challenged the Commons House's right to exercise one of the basic privileges of Anglo-American parliaments: the sole right of the elected assembly to determine the validity of elections. The House of Commons in England had successfully claimed this right a century and a half earlier, and colonial assemblies had freely exercised it from their beginnings. Only one previous governor of South Carolina,

[30] Cooper and McCord, eds., *Statutes*, IV, 98–101; Grant and Munro, eds., *Acts of Privy Council, Col. Ser.*, IV, 487–89.

[31] Mar. 19, 1762, Commons Journal, XXXV, Pt. i, 41, S. C. Archives.

[32] Boone to Bd. of Trade, May 31, 1763, S. C. Pub. Recs., XXIX, 335, S. C. Archives.

[33] Sept. 13, 1762, Commons Journal, XXXV, Pt. i, 158, S. C. Archives.

Francis Nicholson, had ever tried to deny the right of the lower house to arbitrate elections. Nicholson had refused to swear in an elected member of the assembly in 1725, because the man was under indictment for a felony. A month later, however, Nicholson had conceded the point and administered the oath. None of Nicholson's successors had tried to interfere with the assembly's control of assembly elections. Second, Boone's remark that the assembly owed its existence to the elections act of 1721 had even more serious implications. He seemed to be saying that the assembly existed, not because of the rights belonging to the inhabitants of South Carolina, but because the Crown had sanctioned a specific law. Such a belief would in turn have implied acceptance of the doctrine that colonial rights were granted by the Crown and could be changed whenever the Crown pleased.

When the new assembly convened in November 1762, it angrily defended its rights and attacked the governor. Thirty-seven of the forty-eight members had served in the previous assembly, and they had not yet had a chance to answer Boone. The Commons House instructed its committee on privileges and elections to prepare a report on Boone's proceedings, and it adopted the committee's report with minor amendments on December 3. The report denied Boone's assertion that the assembly existed solely because it was created or recognized by the elections act of 1721. It said, "The right of the Inhabitants of this Province, to be represented in the Legislature, is undeniably founded not upon that act but in the known and ancient Constitution of our mother Country." As the representatives of the people, the house claimed the exclusive right to judge assembly elections. The report then defended the previous assembly's action in validating Gadsden's election. It said that Gadsden had been elected by a large majority of the voters of St. Paul's Parish, none of whom had complained about the election, and it added that churchwardens had implicitly sworn to obey the elections law by the act of taking office. The house later adopted a series of resolutions and a remonstrance to the governor which mostly reiterated the previous arguments. One resolution, however, denounced the dissolution of the last assembly as "a most precipitate, unadvised, unprecedented Procedure, of the most dangerous Consequence." [34]

The Commons House presented its report, resolutions, and remonstrance to the governor on December 6, and it heard his rebuttal the next day. Boone defended his actions and statements only insofar as they related directly to Gadsden's election and the dissolution of the

[34] The quotations are from Dec. 3, 1762, *ibid.*, XXXV, Pt. ii, 27, 28.

assembly. He declared again that Gadsden's election violated the law, that the Commons House did not possess the sole right to judge elections, that he held the exclusive privilege of dissolving assemblies, and that he was answerable only to the King in such matters. In addition, he insisted that his silence on other issues should not be interpreted as agreement with the house. Boone believed that all the assembly's rights, even its existence, were *"granted* and *given"* to it by the Crown, but he said so only in a letter to the Board of Trade.[35] As a result, the broader constitutional issue raised by the house disappeared from the debate.

The Commons House first assigned to Christopher Gadsden himself the task of answering the governor's message, and Gadsden simply restated the earlier arguments of the house. When Boone received Gadsden's statement, his only response was to refer the lower house to his reply of December 7. Convinced that it could not otherwise obtain satisfaction from Boone, the Commons House resolved on December 16, 1762, by a vote of twenty-four to six not to transact any further business "until his Excellency shall have done justice to this House." [36]

In January 1763 the debate moved from the state house into the public press. Most of the essays published by the *South-Carolina Gazette* and its competitor, the *South-Carolina Weekly Gazette,* added little to the constitutional debate. For example, assemblyman William Wragg criticized the resolution of the Commons House to transact no further business, but on the ground that it would inconvenience the colony. Only Christopher Gadsden found anything new to say. In an essay published on February 5, he said that neither the Board of Trade nor any other agency of the Crown could arbitrate the dispute because it "can be *constitutionally* decided only by a British parliament." Gadsden seemed to imply that Crown officials had a limited jurisdiction over the colonies at best and that only Parliament was superior to the colonial assemblies. Gadsden also suggested that the American colonists unite in the appointment of a single agent to protect the *"natural* privileges they are *all* entitled unto as British subjects." [37] The newspaper debate disturbed Boone, and he stopped it in April by ordering the editors "to Publish Nothing in their Gazettes that might appear to be injurious to the Powers and Authority of this Government." [38]

---

[35] Boone to Bd. of Trade, Dec. 17, 1762, S. C. Pub. Recs., XXIX, 279, S. C. Archives; italics in original. His reply to the Commons House is in Dec. 7, 1762, Commons Journal, XXXV, Pt. ii, 35–37, S. C. Archives.

[36] Dec. 16, 1762, Commons Journal, XXXV, Pt. ii, 48, S. C. Archives.

[37] *S.-C. Gaz.* (Charles Town) , Feb. 5, 1763.

[38] Apr. 5, 1763, Council Journal, no. 29, 51, S. C. Archives.

While individual South Carolinians were carrying on the debate in the newspapers, the governor and Commons were appealing to the Board of Trade. The Board received a letter from Boone giving his side of the quarrel on March 9, 1763, but Boone's arguments failed to impress his superiors. Although the Board declined to comment on the constitutional merits of the assembly's argument, it decided that Boone's dissolution of the assembly in September 1762 was unjustified. Meanwhile, the committee of correspondence of the Commons House had prepared a long report of the controversy, which it sent to the provincial agent, Charles Garth, along with instructions to print the account and to circulate it among English officials. Garth was in an awkward position because Boone was his cousin and had helped him to obtain his appointment. Therefore, although he had the report printed, he did not submit it to the Board of Trade until July 1764.

In South Carolina the Commons House adhered to its resolution not to do business with the governor. Boone called the assembly into session in March and April 1763, but not enough members turned up to convene the house. A smallpox epidemic struck the colony during the summer, and contributors to the *Gazette* criticized the house for not meeting to deal with this crisis. Even then the legislators ignored Boone's call for an assembly in August.[39] Finally, in September 1763, the Commons agreed to meet with Boone because the Creek Indians seemed to be on the verge of an uprising. The session was short and unproductive. Boone antagonized the Commons still further by personally checking the credentials of members chosen in by-elections, and the Commons devoted its time to preparing a petition to the Crown. The petition reasserted the house's constitutional claims, blamed Boone for the breakdown in government, and asked for the redress of the assembly's grievances. The house approved the petition on September 13, 1763, exactly one year after Boone had dissolved the assembly. Most of the members then went home, and the house was unable to muster a quorum. With the assembly's petition on its way to England, Boone once more restated his position and asked for support from the Board of Trade.

The contest dragged on through the rest of 1763 and half of 1764. Boone tried to reconvene the assembly in January and March 1764, but the Commons still refused to do business with him. In April Boone decided to return to England, and he sailed from Charles Town on May 11, 1764, leaving the colony in the hands of Lieutenant Governor William Bull, Jr., who recalled the assembly and quickly restored amicable relations between Governor and Commons. Boone

[39] *S.-C. Gaz.* (Charles Town), Apr. 2, July 2, 16, Aug. 20, 1763.

appeared in a hearing before the Board of Trade on July 13, and the Board handed down its verdict three days later. It found Boone guilty of "Conduct highly deser[v]ing his Majestys Royal displeasure," but it also criticized the Commons House for refusing to transact business.[40] The decision was a victory for the Commons House. The Board of Trade made no comment on the constitutional issues involved, and the house resumed its former practice of judging elections without royal interference. Boone appealed the Board of Trade's decision, but when it was upheld by the Privy Council Boone did not return to South Carolina. Two years later the Crown replaced him with a new governor.

IV

The Gadsden election controversy clarified the nature of the constitutional crisis in South Carolina more than any other political dispute before 1763. It came at the end of a series of lesser conflicts—such as those involving recruiting, finances, and smuggling—and thus it increased the existing strain between the provincial government and the Crown. Most of the earlier disputes had dealt with peripheral issues, however, while the election controversy went right to the heart of the matter. Governor Boone had challenged an ancient right of the elected assembly, the right to judge elections, and he had even implied at one point that colonial rights were derived solely from the Crown. The stubborn defense which the Commons House then made, appealing to the rights of South Carolinians as Englishmen, thus foreshadowed the stout resistance to the new imperial policy initiated after 1763, a resistance that would ultimately unite thirteen colonies in rebellion against the nation to which they proudly traced the origins of their liberties. Indeed, the Gadsden election controversy differed from later conflicts, such as the Stamp Act crisis and the issues in the coming of the Revolution, in only two respects. The dispute involved only one colony, and the Crown failed to support the royal governor.

When the French and Indian War ended in 1763, the issues in the constitutional struggle in South Carolina were more clearly defined than ever before, and the colonists sensed that long-established rights now seemed to be seriously challenged. Perhaps the final emphasis after a survey of a century of South Carolina politics belongs to the self-serving ambitions of Governor Boone, who anticipated the future

[40] "Governor Boone's State of the Dispute," Hardwicke Papers, Add. Mss., 35910, foll. 241–42, Brit. Mus.; I have used the transcripts in the Lib. Cong.

trend of policy by inviting a contest on grounds that the lower house found quite acceptable. Or perhaps the emphasis belongs rather to the fact that the Board of Trade at this critical turning point in the history of the English-speaking people upheld the position taken by the lower house of assembly. Whatever the emphasis, the Commons House of Assembly had achieved a new confidence, a new rationale for its powers, a redefinition of its constitutional position in the empire; it would oppose any new challenge to its rights with the same vigor which characterized the Gadsden election controversy. But in 1763 the course which history was destined to take had yet to be determined.

BIBLIOGRAPHICAL ESSAY

BIBLIOGRAPHICAL ESSAY

Governor James Glen said in one of his reports to the Board of Trade, "I turned over with great labour most of the old Journals of the Council and Assembly and as they have no Indices I was obliged to submit to the drudgery of reading many of them a sort of Study in which there is neither Entertainment nor Instruction." [1] The modern historian must sympathize with the governor, for there are many "old Journals" to be "turned over" in studying the political history of colonial South Carolina and few of them yield much entertainment. There are even times when their instructive value becomes dubious.

The place to begin turning over old journals is the manuscript collection known as Records in the British Public Record Office Relating to South Carolina, 1663–1782, 36 volumes, in the South Carolina Archives Department, Columbia, South Carolina. These records are transcripts that were made in 1895 under the direction of W. Noel Sainsbury of the Public Record Office; they are occasionally cited as the "Sainsbury Transcripts." The records consist primarily of correspondence between officials in South Carolina and those in England, but they also encompass a great variety of other materials. The collection includes nearly all the South Carolina material in the Colonial Office Records, Series 5, vols. 13–20 (Plantations General), vols. 286–292 (Carolina, Proprietary), vols. 358–411 (South Carolina), and vols. 1257–1279 (Proprietary Governments); Series 324/49–50 (royal patents); and Series 391/1–89 (Journals of the Board of Trade). It omits only a few enclosures and some previously published items from the proprietary period; the historian must consult the original Colonial Office Records for the enclosures, while the proprietary records are in the sources described later. The first five volumes,

---

[1] "An Attempt towards an Estimate of the value of South Carolina," Mar. 1751, S. C. Pub. Recs., XXIV, 303–4.

covering the years 1663 to 1710, have been published in a facsimile edition (Columbia, 1928–47).

The South Carolina Public Records should be supplemented by the following published collections of official British Records: W. Noel Sainsbury *et al.*, eds., *Calendar of State Papers, Colonial Series, America and the West Indies, 1574– —,* 43 vols, to date (London, 1862– —); Joseph Redlington, ed., *Calendar of Treasury Papers, 1557–1728,* 6 vols. (London, 1868–89); William A. Shaw, ed., *Calendar of Treasury Books and Papers, 1729–1745,* 5 vols. (London, 1897–1903); W. L. Grant and James Munro, eds., *Acts of the Privy Council of England, Colonial Series, 1613–1783,* 6 vols. (Hereford and London, 1908–12); Leo F. Stock, ed., *Proceedings and Debates of the British Parliaments Respecting North America, 1542–1754,* 5 vols. (Washington, 1924–41); and Leonard W. Labaree, ed., *Royal Instructions to British Colonial Governors, 1670–1776,* 2 vols. (New York, 1935). Manuscript collections in the British Public Record Office that are particularly useful to the student of colonial South Carolina include CO 5/64–66, which contains the correspondence of the Superintendents of Indian Affairs for the southern colonies; CO 324–48, a list of members of and nominations for the councils in the royal colonies; Treasury Papers 1/319–426, covering the period 1745–1763; and the Amherst Papers, War Office Papers 34/1–103, which are indispensable for the French and Indian War.

Second in importance only to the South Carolina Public Records are the colony's legislative and administrative journals. The most valuable journals are those of the Commons House of Assembly, which include not only the proceedings of the assembly but also many petitions that illuminate the political, economic, and social life of the colony. The lower house journals include Alexander S. Salley, ed., *Journal of the Commons House of Assembly, 1692–1735,* 21 vols. (Columbia, 1907–46), an incomplete and rather unsatisfactory edition; The Journal of the Commons House of Assembly, 1705–1775, in the South Carolina Archives; and J. H. Easterby and Ruth S. Green, eds., *The Colonial Records of South Carolina,* Series I: *The Journal of the Commons House of Assembly, 1736–1750,* 9 vols. (Columbia, 1951–62), an excellent editorial job in every way. The Journal of the Upper House, 1721–1774, South Carolina Archives, contains the legislative proceedings of the council, and its administrative records from 1721 to 1733. Although it frequently duplicates the journal of the Commons House, it includes material not available elsewhere and is especially useful for the legislative decline of the council. The Journal of His Majesty's

Honourable Council, 1734–1774, South Carolina Archives, which is the record of the council's executive proceedings, covers matters that usually did not concern the assembly. It is most helpful on the problems created by the land boom of the 1730's.

The official records of the proprietary period are somewhat erratic. *The Shaftesbury Papers and Other Records Relating to Carolina and the First Settlement on Ashley River prior to the Year 1676,* ed. Langdon Cheves, South Carolina Historical Society, *Collections,* 5 (1897), is an excellent collection of letters and journals covering the activities of both the proprietors and the first settlers. After 1676, however, the proprietary records are scattered and incomplete. Alexander S. Salley has edited two useful collections, *Journal of the Grand Council of South Carolina, 1671–1680, 1691–1692,* 2 vols. (Columbia, 1907), and *Commissions and Instructions from the Lords Proprietors of Carolina to Public Officials of South Carolina, 1685–1715* (Columbia, 1916). A few documents not available anywhere else will be found in the appendix to William James Rivers, *A Sketch of the History of South Carolina to the Close of the Proprietary Government by the Revolution of 1719* (Charleston, 1856). A few additional references to South Carolina are in the John Locke papers in the Lovelace Collection, Bodleian Library, Oxford University, and in the Shaftesbury Papers in the British Public Record Office.

As for the official records of the colony itself, Thomas Cooper and David J. McCord have edited the colonial laws in *The Statutes at Large of South Carolina,* 10 vols. (Columbia, 1836–41). Their compilation inexplicably omits a number of important acts, however, and the historian must supplement it by consulting Governor Archdale's Laws, 1696, and Proprietary Session Laws, 1696–1719, in the South Carolina Archives, and Acts Passed at Different Dates, 1721–1770, CO 5/412–424. The land records of South Carolina are important because land problems became major political issues in the 1690's and again in the 1730's and 1740's. The most useful land records are the Memorial Books, 1711–1775, 15 vols., in which landowners listed their grants and other land claims, and the Quit Rent Books, 1733–1774, 5 vols., which recorded quit rent payments. Grants, [1670]–1775, 46 vols., and Plats, 1731–1775, 23 vols., are more difficult to use. These records are all located in the state archives. For land sales, the historian must refer to Mesne Conveyances, 1719–1800, 156 vols., Office of Register of Mesne Conveyances, Charleston County Courthouse, Charleston, South Carolina. Many of these volumes are missing, and I have relied on the index to the Mesne Conveyances, which is complete. The only published land records are in Alexander S. Salley, ed., *Warrants for Land in South Carolina, 1672–1711,* 3 vols. (Columbia, 1910–15).

Since Indian affairs so often occupied the attention of the government of South Carolina, the colony's Indian records have been valuable for the periods in which they were kept. William L. McDowell, Jr., has compiled two well-edited volumes as Series II of *The Colonial Records of South Carolina;* they are *Journals of the Commissioners of the Indian Trade, September 20, 1710—August 28, 1718* (Columbia, 1955), and *Documents Relating to Indian Affairs, May 21, 1750—August 7, 1754* (Columbia, 1958). At present Mr. McDowell is preparing an edition of the remaining unpublished Indian records, the Indian Books of South Carolina, nos. 5–6, 1754–1760, South Carolina Archives. The Treasurer's Books, 1725–1773, 4 vols., were helpful for the information they contain on the various scandals involving the Public Treasurer and for their record of duties paid on imports and exports. Another valuable source is St. Philip's Parish Vestry Books, 1732–1774, 2 vols., St. Philip's Parish House, Charleston; Charles Town had no government before the Revolution, and the vestry of St. Philip's was forced to perform many of the functions of a city government. The colony's legal records, however, were not very useful for the present study. These records include the Records of the Proceedings of the Court of Common Pleas: Judgment Books, 1733–1791, 16 vols.; Court of Ordinary Records, 1672–1692; and Mortgage Books, 1734–1766, 15 vols., all in the South Carolina Archives; and the South Carolina Admiralty Records, 1716–1763, 5 vols., Federal Records Center, East Point, Ga. Useful for their biographical data on individuals were Anne King Gregorie, ed., *Records of the Court of Chancery of South Carolina, 1671–1779,* in *American Legal Records,* VI (Washington, 1950), and Wills, Inventories of Estates, and Miscellaneous Records [title varies], 1671–1868, 100 vols., Office of the Judge of the Probate Court, Charleston County Courthouse.

The records of neighboring colonies have often helped to fill in the gaps in the records of South Carolina. The records of North Carolina are invaluable for the proprietary period. Every draft and revision of the Fundamental Constitutions, as well as every charter issued by the Crown, is in Mattie Erma Edwards Parker, ed., *North Carolina Charters and Constitutions, 1578–1698* (Raleigh, 1963). Many other proprietary documents are in William L. Saunders, ed., *The Colonial Records of North Carolina,* 10 vols. (Raleigh, 1886–90). The records of Georgia are most useful for the 1730's and 1740's, when Georgia and South Carolina became involved in a series of disputes. The basic Georgia source is Allen D. Candler and Lucien L. Knight, eds., *The Colonial Records of Georgia,* 25 vols. (Atlanta, 1904–16) ; vols. XX and XXVII–XXXIX have never been published and are available in typescript at the Georgia Department of History and Archives, Atlanta, and at the Georgia Historical Society, Savannah. An invaluable supplement to the *Colonial Records* are the Egmont Manuscripts, 1732–1743, University of Georgia Library, Athens. The *Colonial Records* and the Egmont Manuscripts duplicate each other to some extent, but each contains material the other does not; both have many references to events in South Carolina. As for unofficial Georgia records, an indispensable source for the history of South Carolina are the *Manuscripts of the Earl of Egmont: Diary of Viscount Percival, Afterwards First Earl of Egmont, 1730–1747* (Historical Manuscripts Commission, *Sixteenth Report,* 3 vols. [London, 1920–23]). The *Collections* of the Georgia Historical Society (1840– —) are most useful for the letters of James Oglethorpe in vol. III and for the letters relating to Oglethorpe's siege of St. Augustine in 1740 and the Spanish invasion of Georgia in 1742, which are in vol. VII. The Wormsloe Foundation has also published several volumes that refer frequently to South Carolina; they include E. Merton Coulter, ed., *The Journal of William Stephens, 1741–1745,* 2 vols. (Athens, 1958–59) ; Robert G. McPherson, ed., *The Journal of the Earl of Egmont, 1732–1738* (Athens, 1962) ; and E. Merton Coulter, ed., *The Journal of Peter Gordon, 1732–1735* (Athens, 1963). Although Virginia was less concerned with South Carolina than either North Carolina or Georgia, the *Collections* of the Virginia Historical Society (1882–92) contain the correspondence of Governor Alexander Spotswood (vols. I–II) and Robert Dinwiddie (vols. III–IV), including their correspondence with governors of South Carolina.

Perhaps the greatest frustration endured by the historian of colonial South Carolina is the almost total absence of private or semi-official papers before 1740. There are only three small collections worth mentioning: "Letters from John Stewart to William Dunlop," *South Carolina Historical and Genealogical Magazine,* 32 (1931), 1–33, 81–114, 170–74, which are excellent for the administration of Governor James Colleton; John Archdale Papers, 1690–1706, Manuscripts Division, Library of Congress, Washington, D. C.; and Documents Relating to the Case of Thomas Nairne, Henry E. Huntington Library, San Marino, California. In addition, a few letters from

Edward Randolph on South Carolina are in the Randolph papers in Prince Society, *Publications,* 24–28, 30–31 (1898–99, 1909). There are also a very few scattered references to South Carolina before 1740 in the Shelburne Papers and Sydney Family Papers in the William L. Clements Library, Ann Arbor, Michigan, and in the Newcastle Papers and Sloane Manuscripts in the British Museum, London. Nearly all the Sloane Manuscripts relating to South Carolina have been published in *S. C. Hist. Mag.,* 21 (1920), 3–9, 50–51; 55 (1954), 59–70. The lack of private papers before 1740 is partially compensated for by the Manuscripts of the Society for the Propagation of the Gospel in Foreign Parts, Office of the Society, London, and the Fulham Palace Manuscripts, Fulham Palace, London. The S.P.G. sent many missionaries to South Carolina, and they often commented on political events in their letters to the Society and the Bishop of London. These collections are very helpful on the first twenty years of the eighteenth century, particularly on the establishment of the Church of England. Religious issues disappeared from politics after South Carolina became a royal colony, however, and clergymen rarely discussed the government after about 1720. Frank J. Klingberg has edited the letters of two leading S.P.G. missionaries in *Carolina Chronicle: The Papers of Commissary Gideon Johnston, 1707–1716* (Berkeley, 1946), and *The Carolina Chronicle of Dr. Francis LeJau, 1706–1717* (Berkeley, 1956). Other selections from the S.P.G. Manuscripts have appeared in *S. C. Hist. Mag.,* 4 (1903), 221–30, 278–85; 5 (1904), 21–55, 95–99; 50 (1949), 173–203.

After 1740, however, there is an abundance of private and semi-official papers. One of the most important collections are the William Henry Lyttelton Papers, 1751–1760, Clements Library. The collection consists almost entirely of letters to Lyttelton, and it is particularly valuable on the origins of the Cherokee War. There are also many references to other phases of political life during Lyttelton's administration. A second collection of equal value are the various papers of Henry Laurens. The bulk of the Laurens Papers covers the years from 1747 to 1792 and is located in the South Carolina Historical Society, Charleston. This collection consists of copies of letters from Laurens to his business associates outside South Carolina; most of the letters refer only to business affairs, but they include a number of comments on politics, especially after Laurens was elected to the assembly in 1757. Joseph W. Barnwell and Mabel L. Webber have edited some of this correspondence and published it in the *S. C. Hist. Mag.,* 28–31 (1927–30). The Historical Society of Pennsylvania in Philadelphia owns a

Letterbook of Laurens, 1762–1766; it includes copies of Lauren's personal correspondence, mostly to persons living in South Carolina or Georgia. The South Carolina Historical Society's collection of Pinckney Papers is only slightly less important for this study than the Lyttelton and Laurens Papers. The Pinckney Papers are most useful in the period before 1763 for the letters of Eliza Lucas Pinckney, who commented frequently on the social and intellectual life of South Carolina but only occasionally on its political life.

Many other private and semi-official papers refer occasionally to South Carolina after 1740. The Abercromby Papers and Loudoun Papers in the Huntington Library are valuable for the quartering dispute of 1757–1758. The George Clinton Papers in the Clements Library contain the correspondence between Governors Clinton and Glen on Indian affairs in the 1750's, and there are a few references to South Carolina in the Jeffrey Amherst Papers, 1758–1764, and the Thomas Gage Papers, American Series, 1755–1775, in the same repository. The Hardwicke Papers in the British Museum also refer occasionally to South Carolina. The Manigault Family Papers, 1750–1844, in the South Caroliniana Library, Columbia, are valuable chiefly for several letters relating to the agency dispute of 1754–1755. Mabel L. Webber has edited and published some of Peter Manigault's letters in the *S. C. Hist. Mag.*, 15, 31–33 (1914, 1930–32). Published correspondence for the 1750's and 1760's also includes the following: Sylvester K. Stevens and Donald H. Kent, eds., *The Papers of Colonel Henry Bouquet*, 19 mimeographed vols. (Harrisburg, 1940–43), useful for the quartering dispute of 1757–1758; the *Colden Papers* in the New-York Historical Society, *Collections*, 50–56, 67–68 (1917–23, 1934–35), which contain several letters from South Carolinians, notably Dr. Alexander Garden; Alfred P. James, ed., *Writings of General John Forbes Relating to His Service in North America* (Menasha, Wis., 1938); Historical Manuscripts Commission, "The Manuscripts of Captain H. V. Knox," *Report on Manuscripts in Various Collections*, 8 vols. (London, 1901–1914), VI, 81–296, which includes some correspondence between William Knox and William Henry Lyttelton; Douglas C. McMurtrie, ed., *Letters of Peter Timothy . . . to Benjamin Franklin* (Chicago, 1935), which includes Timothy's criticisms of Governor James Glen; and Gertrude S. Kimball, ed., *Correspondence of William Pitt when Secretary of State, with Colonial Governors and Military and Naval Commissioners in America*, 2 vols. (New York, 1906).

The historian of colonial South Carolina is fortunate in the number and quality of contemporary narratives and descriptions relating to the colony, and I have depended greatly on those accounts. A particularly useful compilation of such writings is Bartholomew Rivers Carroll, ed., *Historical Collections of South Carolina* . . . , 2 vols. (New York, 1836). It contains Alexander Hewatt, *An Historical Account of the Rise and Progress of the Colonies of South Carolina and Georgia,* 2 vols. (London, 1779), the first complete history of the colony and still one of the best, despite Hewatt's lapses into plagiarism. The collection also includes Francis Yonge, *A Narrative of the Proceedings of the People of South Carolina in the Year 1719* (London, 1721), which is the best and indeed almost the only source on the overthrow of the proprietary government. Another valuable compilation is Chapman J. Milling, ed., *Colonial South Carolina: Two Contemporary Descriptions* . . . (Columbia, 1951), which includes the two best contemporary accounts of the colony in the middle of the eighteenth century, James Glen's *A Description of South Carolina* (London, 1761) and George Milligen's *A Short Description of the Province of South Carolina* (London, 1720). A third very helpful collection is Alexander S. Salley, ed., *Narratives of Early Carolina, 1650–1708,* in J. Franklin Jameson, ed., *Original Narratives of Early American History* (New York, 1911). The most useful narratives in it are Samuel Wilson, *An Account of the Province of Carolina* (London, 1682); John Ash, *The Present State of Affairs in Carolina* (London, 1706), a dissenter's protest against the establishment of the Church of England; and John Archdale, *A New Description of That Fertile and Pleasant Province of Carolina* (London, 1707), in which Archdale discusses some phases of his administration as governor. Two less useful compilations are Newton D. Mereness, ed., *Travels in the American Colonies* (New York, 1916) and P. G. J. Weston, ed., *Documents Connected with the History of South Carolina* (London, 1856).

As for individual narratives, there are three excellent histories of paper currency in South Carolina. They are [William Bull, Sr.], "An Account of the Rise and Progress of the Paper Bills of Credit in South Carolina" [1739], in Cooper and McCord, eds., *Statutes,* IX, 766–80; *An Essay on Currency, Written in August 1732* (Charles Town, 1734); and *The Report of the Committee of the Commons House of Assembly of the Province of South-Carolina on the State of the Paper-Currency of the Said Province* (London, 1737), reprinted in Easterby, ed., *Commons Journal, 1736–39,* 291–320. An interesting and detailed picture of the colony around 1700 can be gathered from [John]

Lawson's History of North Carolina . . . , ed. Frances Latham Harriss (Richmond, 1937) ; [Thomas Nairne], *A Letter from South Carolina* (London, 1710) ; and John Norris, *Profitable Advice for Rich and Poor* (London, 1712). Edmund Atkin wrote two scholarly studies relating to Indian affairs in the mid-eighteenth century; they are his "Historical Account of the Revolt of the Choctaw Indians in the Late War from the French to the British Alliance and of Their Return Since to That of the French," 1753, Lansdowne Manuscripts, vol. 809, foll. 1–32, British Museum, and *Indians of the Southern Colonial Frontier: The Edmond Atkin Report and Plan of 1755,* ed. Wilbur R. Jacobs (Columbia, 1954). I have also consulted the following narratives and descriptions, which are arranged in chronological order: John Crafford, *A New and Most Exact Account of the Fertile and Famous Colony of Carolina* (Dublin, 1683) ; *Carolina Described More Fully Than Heretofore* (Dublin, 1684) ; Francis Yonge, *A View of the Trade of South-Carolina with Proposals Humbly Offered for Improving the Same* [London, 1722?]; *An Apology or Vindication of Francis Nicholson, Esq.; His Majesty's Governor of South-Carolina, from the Unjust Aspersions Cast on Him by Some of the Members of the Bahama-Company* (London, 1724) ; John Norris, *The Liberty and Property of British Subjects Asserted in a Letter from an Assembly-man in Carolina to His Friend in London* (London, 1726) ; [Fayrer Hall], *The Importance of the British Plantations in America to this Kingdom* (London, 1731) ; *Report of the Committee Appointed to Examine into the Proceedings of the People of Georgia, with Respect to the Province of South-Carolina, and the Disputes Subsisting between the Two Colonies* (Charles Town, 1736) , reprinted in Easterby, ed., *Commons Journal, 1736–39,* 72–157; [Benjamin Whitaker], *The Chief Justice's Charge to the Grand Jury for the Body of this Province* (Charles Town, 1741) ; J. H. Easterby, ed., *The St. Augustine Expedition of 1740: A Report to the South Carolina Assembly,* introduction by John Tate Lanning (Columbia, 1954) , reprinted from Easterby, ed., *Commons Journal, 1741–42;* Klaus G. Loewald *et al.,* eds. and trans., "Johann Martin Bolzius Answers a Questionnaire on Carolina and Georgia," 1751, *William and Mary Quarterly,* 3d Ser., 14 (1957) , 218–61; 15 (1958) , 228–52; William Simpson, *The Practical Justice of the Peace and Parish-Officer, of His Majesty's Province of South-Carolina* (Charles Town, 1761) ; *Journal of the Congress of the Four Southern Governors, and the Superintendent of that District, with the Five Nations of Indians, at Augusta, 1763* (Charles Town, 1764) ; and Mark A. DeWolfe Howe, ed., "Journal of Josiah Quincy, Junior, 1773," Massachusetts Historical Society, *Proceedings,* 49 (1916), 424–81. Two other contemporary accounts must be used with care. For reasons explained in Chapter XII, [James] *Adair's History of the American Indians,* ed. Samuel Coles Williams (Johnson City, Tenn., 1930), is not reliable on the Choctaw revolt; Adair is trustworthy, however, when discussing the Cherokees and Creeks. David Ramsay's *The History of South Carolina, from Its First Settlement in 1670, to the Year 1808,* 2 vols. (Charleston, 1809), is useless for the period before 1763. Ramsay said that he relied on Alexander Hewatt for the pre-Revolutionary era, and this meant in practice that Ramsay simply plagiarized or summarized Hewatt's work.

There are a few other sources that should be mentioned. The *South-Carolina Gazette* (Charles Town, 1732–1776) has been helpful in several ways. It occasionally printed local political news, although not too often; it published the governor's proclamations; and, most important, political essayists used it to express their views on current disputes. Elizabeth Donnan, ed., *Documents Illustrative of the History of the Slave Trade to America,* 4 vols. (Washington, 1930–35), is an excellent compilation. Jack P. Greene, ed., "South Carolina's Colonial Constitution: Two Proposals for Reform," *S. C. Hist. Mag.,* 62 (1961), 72–81, shows how the Board of Trade and the conservative Edmund Atkin wanted to change the provincial government.

Like so many other historians today, I have relied extensively on microfilm, transcripts, and other reproductions of manuscripts. The Library of Congress has microfilms or transcripts of all the British records listed above except the Lovelace Collection and Shaftesbury Papers. The bibliographers for this material are Grace G. Griffin, *A Guide to Manuscripts Relating to American History in British Depositories Reproduced for the Division of Manuscripts of the Library of Congress* (Washington, 1946), and Lester K. Born, *British Manuscripts Project: A Checklist of the Microfilm Prepared in England and Wales for the American Council of Learned Societies, 1941–1945* (Washington, 1953). These bibliographies should be used in conjunction with Charles M. Andrews, *Guide to the Materials for American History, to 1783, in the Public Record Office of Great Britain,* 2 vols. (Washington, 1912–14), and Charles M. Andrews and Frances G. Davenport, *Guide to the Manuscript Materials for the History of the United States to 1783, in the British Museum, in Minor London Archives, and in the Libraries of Oxford and Cambridge* (Washington, 1908). The legislative journals, administrative journals, statutes, and Indian records in the South Carolina Archives are available on microfilm; they are listed in William Sumner Jenkins, *A Guide to the Microfilm Collection of Early State Records* (Washington, 1950). The South Carolina Public Records and the *South-Carolina Gazette* are available on microfilm, too, and there are microprint editions of the contemporary narratives and descriptions listed in Charles Evans, *et al.*, *American Bibliography*, 14 vols. (Chicago and Worcester, Mass., 1903–59), and Thomas D. Clark, ed., *Travels in the Old South: A Bibliography*, 3 vols. (Norman, Okla., 1956–59). I have used Philip M. Hamer, *A Guide to Archives and Manuscripts in the United States* (New Haven, 1961), as a guide to manuscripts that have not been microfilmed or otherwise reproduced, and for bibliographies of published sources. I have also relied on J. H. Easterby, *Guide to the Study and Reading of South Carolina History: A General Classified Bibliography* (Columbia, 1950), and Jack P. Greene, "The Publication of the Official Records of the Southern Colonies," *Wm. and Mary Qtly.*, 3d Ser., 14 (1957), 268–80.

Among the secondary works on colonial South Carolina, several of the general studies of the American colonies have been especially helpful to me. Charles M. Andrews, *The Colonial Period of American History*, 4 vols. (New Haven, 1934–38), contains a good account of the proprietors and the issuance of their charters; George Louis Beer, *British Colonial Policy, 1754–1765* (New York, 1907), is still one of the best studies on the friction within the British empire during the French and Indian War; Wesley Frank Craven, *The Southern Colonies in the Seventeenth Century, 1607–1689*, in Wendell Holmes Stephenson and E. Merton Coulter, eds., *A History of the South*, I (Baton Rouge, 1949), is helpful on the English background, the first settlements, and the headright system; Lawrence Henry Gipson, *The British Empire before the American Revolution*, 12 vols. to date (Caldwell, Idaho, and New York, 1936– —), is valuable for the French and Indian War; Arthur Berriedale Keith, *Constitutional History of the First British Empire* (Oxford, 1930), is excellent on constitutional issues in general and on the French and Indian War in particular; Leonard W. Labaree, *Royal Government in America* (New Haven, 1930), is useful as background for the constitutional struggle in South Carolina; and Herbert L. Osgood, *The American Colonies in the Seventeenth Century*, 3 vols. (New York, 1904–1907), and *The American Colonies in the Eighteenth Century*, 4 vols. (New York, 1924), contains a fairly good political narrative of South Carolina from 1670 to 1743, but Osgood's interpretation is not reliable and he neglects the years after 1743. Michael G. Hall, *Edward Randolph and the American Colonies, 1676–1703* (Chapel Hill, 1960), is good on the reorganization of colonial government in 1696, including the creation of the Board of Trade, while Arthur H. Basye, *The Lords Commissioners of Trade and Plantations, Commonly Known as the Board of Trade, 1748–1782* (New Haven, 1925), and Oliver M. Dickerson, *American Colonial Government . . .* (Cleveland, 1912), are helpful on the reformation of the Board of Trade in 1748 and its subsequent policy.

Previous political histories of South Carolina have their respective merits and faults, but they all share one common failing. They all neglect the period from about 1740 to 1763, probably because there were no major crises then, and thus they omit much of the drama of the rise of the Commons House of Assembly. Edward McCrady, in *The History of South Carolina under the Proprietary Government, 1670–1719* (New York, 1897), and *The History of South Carolina under the Royal Government, 1719–1776* (New York, 1899), relies on a straight chronological narrative. As a former officer in the Confederate army, McCrady was deeply loyal to his native state and suspicious of any political authority above the provincial level, including the proprietors and the Crown. He was often surprisingly perceptive in his interpretation of politics, but his approach was too legalistic; he occasionally made inferences that his evidence would not support, and he neglected Indian affairs. William Roy Smith's *South Carolina as a Royal Province, 1719–1776* (New York, 1903), is useful on constitutional issues and the history of paper currency, but his rigidly topical organization is often misleading. The best of the older histories are David Duncan Wallace's *The History of South Carolina*, 4 vols. (New York, 1934), and his *South Carolina: A Short History, 1530–1948* (Chapel Hill, 1951). Wallace was a meticulous worker and absolutely reliable on specific facts, but his interpretation follows McCrady too closely, especially in his treatment of the proprietors. There have been very few political studies of colonial South Carolina in recent years. The only important recent book, Jack P. Greene, *The Quest for Power: The Lower Houses of Assembly in the Southern Royal Colonies, 1689–1776* (Chapel Hill, 1963), was not published until I had substantially completed this study; I have tried to incorporate as many of Mr. Greene's findings into the final draft as possible. There have been a few recent articles on the political history of South Carolina, and I have relied extensively on Jack P. Greene, "The South Carolina Quartering Dispute, 1757–1758," *S. C. Hist. Mag.*, 60 (1959),

193–204; the same author's "The Gadsden Election Controversy and the Revolutionary Movement in South Carolina," *Mississippi Valley Historical Review*, 46 (1959), 469–92; and my article on "The South Carolina Royal Council, 1720–1763," *Wm. and Mary Qtly.*, 3d Ser., 18 (1961), 373–92.

There are a number of very helpful studies dealing with the early proprietary period, in addition to the works of Andrews and Craven already cited. Louise Fargo Brown, *The First Earl of Shaftesbury* (New York and London, 1933), discusses Shaftesbury's colonial interests and ventures in detail. Maurice Cranston, *John Locke: A Biography* (New York, 1957), and Peter Laslett's introduction to his edition of Locke's *Two Treatises of Government* (Cambridge, Eng., 1960) are helpful on the Fundamental Constitutions. Herbert R. Paschal, Jr., Proprietary North Carolina: A Study in Colonial Government (unpubl. Ph.D. diss., University of North Carolina, 1961), describes the work of the proprietors more fully than any other study. William S. Powell, *The Proprietors of Carolina* (Raleigh, 1963), is a compilation of biographical data on the individual proprietors, while Alexander S. Salley, *The Early English Settlers of South Carolina* (Columbia, 1946), provides biographical information on the more prominent settlers from England. For the important Barbadian background to the colonization of South Carolina, I have relied on Vincent T. Harlow, *A History of Barbados, 1625–1685* (Oxford, 1926), and John P. Thomas, Jr., "The Barbadians in Early South Carolina," *S. C. Hist. Mag.*, 31 (1930), 75–92.

The social development of South Carolina has attracted the attention of several able historians. The best description of the mature society of the colony is in Carl Bridenbaugh, *Myths and Realities: Societies of the Colonial South* (Baton Rouge, 1952). Also useful for social history are Bridenbaugh's *Cities in the Wilderness: The First Century of Urban Life in America, 1625–1742* (New York, 1938) and *Cities in Revolt: Urban Life in America, 1743–1776;* Thomas Jefferson Wertenbaker's *The Golden Age of Colonial Culture*, 2d rev. ed. (New York, 1949) and *The Old South: The Founding of American Civilization* (New York, 1942); and Frederick P. Bowes, *The Culture of Early Charleston* (Chapel Hill, 1942). For questions relating to slavery and servitude, I have relied on Almon W. Lauber, *Indian Slavery in Colonial Times within the Present Limits of the United States* (New York, 1913); Warren B. Smith, *White Servitude in Colonial South Carolina* (Columbia, 1961); and my article on "The Legal Status of the Slave in South Carolina, 1670–1740," *Journal of*

Southern History, 28 (1962), 462–73. Edward McCrady, "Slavery in the Province of South Carolina, 1670–1770," American Historical Association, *Report, 1895* (Washington, 1896), is out of date and contains serious errors of fact. A useful related work is Frank J. Klingberg, *An Appraisal of the Negro in Colonial South Carolina: A Study in Americanization* (Washington, 1941), which, despite its title, is primarily a study of the S.P.G.'s activities in the colony. Other studies of religion include Babette M. Levy, "Early Puritanism in the Southern and Island Colonies," American Antiquarian Society, *Proceedings,* 70 (1960), 69–348; Frederick Dalcho, *An Historical Account of the Protestant Episcopal Church in South-Carolina* (Charleston, 1820); and George Howe, *History of the Presbyterian Church in South Carolina,* 2 vols. (Columbia, 1870–83).

Historians have also shown a particular interest in the economic growth of South Carolina. Several of the best studies are concerned with the colony's paper currency. They are Curtis P. Nettels, *The Money Supply of the American Colonies before 1720* (Madison, Wis., 1934); Leslie Van Horn Brock, The Currency of the American Colonies, 1700 to 1764 (unpubl. Ph.D. diss., University of Michigan, 1941); and two articles by Richard M. Jellison, "Paper Currency in Colonial South Carolina: A Reappraisal," *S. C. Hist. Mag.,* 62 (1961), 134–47, and "Antecedents of the South Carolina Currency Acts of 1736 and 1746," *Wm. and Mary Qtly.,* 3d Ser., 16 (1959), 556–67. As for the colony's trade, two indispensable statistical compilations are George Rogers Taylor, "Wholesale Commodity Prices at Charleston, South Carolina, 1732–1791," *Journal of Economic and Business History,* 4 (1932), 356–77, and Charles Joseph Gayle, "The Nature and Volume of Exports from Charleston, 1724–1774," South Carolina Historical Association, *Proceedings, 1937* (1940), 25–33. Leila Sellers, *Charleston Business on the Eve of the Revolution* (Chapel Hill, 1934), is useful but not entirely reliable in its description of the merchants. The authority on agriculture in the colony is Lewis Cecil Gray, *History of Agriculture in the Southern United States to 1860,* 2 vols. (Washington, 1933). Also useful are Alexander S. Salley, *The Introduction of Rice Culture into South Carolina,* South Carolina Historical Commission, *Bulletin,* 6 (1919) and C. Robert Haywood, "Mercantilism and South Carolina Agriculture, 1700–1763," *S. C. Hist. Mag.,* 60 (1959), 15–27. Regrettably, there are no studies of South Carolina's land system, but Henry A. M. Smith has written several articles on land ownership in specific areas for the *S. C. Hist. Mag.,* of which the most important is "The Baronies of South Carolina," *S. C. Hist. Mag.,*

11–18 (1910–17). There is also a revealing study of Henry McCulloh, the Crown's special commissioner of quit rents for the Carolinas, in Charles G. Sellers, Jr., "Private Profits and British Colonial Policy: The Speculations of Henry McCulloh," *Wm. and Mary Qtly.*, 3d Ser., 8 (1951), 535–51.

Probably no other single factor influenced the government of South Carolina more than its position on the frontier of the British empire, and studies of the southern frontier therefore assume an unusual importance. The two standard works on the subject are Verner W. Crane, *The Southern Frontier, 1670–1732* (Durham, 1928), and John R. Alden, *John Stuart and the Southern Colonial Frontier . . . , 1754–1775* (Ann Arbor, 1944). Both books are excellent, meticulous in their attention to detail and sound in their interpretation, and the historian's major task is to fill in the twenty-two year gap between them. David H. Corkran, *The Cherokee Frontier: Conflict and Survival, 1740–1762* (Norman, Okla., 1962), fills the gap well for the Cherokees and presents the Indian's point of view more effectively than any other work. Other occasionally helpful studies are Norman W. Caldwell, "The Southern Frontier During King George's War," *Jour. of So. Hist.*, 7 (1941), 37–54; John Pitts Corry, *Indian Affairs in Georgia, 1732–1756* (Philadelphia, 1936); Amos A. Ettinger, *James Edward Oglethorpe, Imperial Idealist* (Oxford, 1936); John Tate Lanning, *The Diplomatic History of Georgia: The Epoch of Jenkins' Ear* (Chapel Hill, 1936); and Trevor R. Reese, *Colonial Georgia: A Study in British Imperial Policy in the Eighteenth Century* (Athens, 1963). For the period after 1750, anyone interested in the southern frontier should read William W. Abbot's instructive and well-written *The Royal Governors of Georgia, 1754–1775* (Chapel Hill, 1959). Also useful on the southern frontier in the 1750's is Louis Knott Koontz, *Robert Dinwiddie, His Career in American Colonial Government and Westward Expansion* (Glendale, Calif., 1941). Two helpful general works on the southern frontier are Chapman J. Milling, *Red Carolinians* (Chapel Hill, 1940) and John R. Swanton, *The Indians of the Southwestern United States* (Smithsonian Institution, Bureau of American Ethnology, *Bulletin*, 137 [Washington, 1946]). Herbert Eugene Bolton and Mary Ross, *The Debatable Land: A Sketch of the Anglo-Spanish Contest for the Georgia Country* (Berkeley, 1925), emphasizes Spain's role on the southern frontier before 1732. Charles W. Arnade, *The Siege of St. Augustine in 1702* (Gainesville, 1959), is the best study of that subject.

Biographies of colonial South Carolinians are rare. David Duncan

Wallace, *The Life of Henry Laurens* . . . (New York, 1915), is the only full-length published biography; it is good on Lauren's personal life and political career but weak on his business interests. Three recent doctoral dissertations have discussed the careers of colonial governors of South Carolina. Clarence J. Attig, William Henry Lyttelton: A Study in Colonial Administration (unpubl. Ph.D. diss., University of Nebraska, 1958), is the best of them. Mary F. Carter, Governor James Glen of Colonial South Carolina: A Study in British Administrative Policies (unpubl. Ph.D. diss., University of California, Los Angeles, 1951), and Richard P. Sherman, Robert Johnson: Proprietary and Royal Governor of South Carolina (unpubl. Ph.D. diss., University of Southern California, 1951), are helpful but do not cover their subjects thoroughly enough. Important additional biographical information on Governor Lyttelton can be found in Lewis M. Wiggin, *The Faction of Cousins: A Political Account of the Grenvilles, 1733–1763* (New Haven, 1958).

Finally, there are four specialized studies relating to South Carolina that have been invaluable for the present work. Charles C. Crittenden, "The Surrender of the Charter of Carolina," *North Carolina Historical Review*, 1 (1924), 383–402, is a first-rate article. Arthur H. Hirsch, *The Huguenots of Colonial South Carolina* (Durham, 1928), is perceptive on the political role of the Huguenots in the late seventeenth century. Shirley Carter Hughson, *The Carolina Pirates and Colonial Commerce, 1670–1740* (Baltimore, 1894), demonstrates the connections between pirates and colonists in the 1680's. Hirsch and Hughson have been unfairly criticized by native South Carolinians. Robert L. Meriwether, *The Expansion of South Carolina, 1729–1765* (Kingsport, Tenn., 1940), is local history at its best. It gives an excellent, detailed account of the settlement of Governor Johnson's townships and the backcountry.

INDEX

INDEX

S

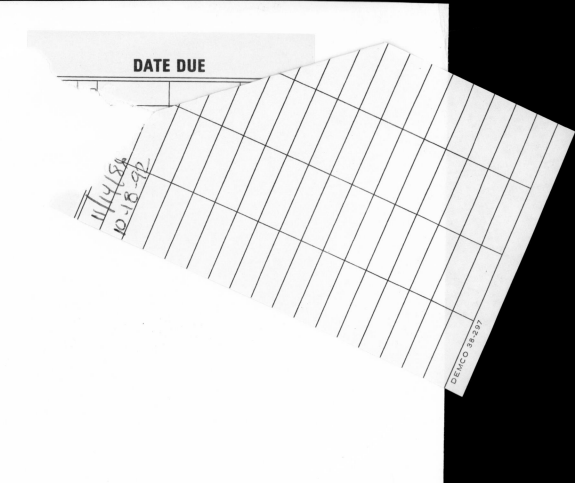

Colonial South Carolina
1763

OVERHILLS

LOWER

Estatoe

Ft. Loudoun

Chota

MIDDLE

Ft. Prince
George

SOUTH

Hiwassee

Tellico

Etchoe

Keowee

ST. MARK'S

Broad River

Wateree River

PARISH

Saluda

CHEROKEES

Ninety Six

River

Saxe Gotha

CRAVE

CAROLI

BERK

Augusta

Fort
Moore

COLLETON Co.

Edisto R.

River

Savannah River

GRANVILLE Co.

Ocmulgee River

Oconee River

Ogeechee River

Beaufort

Coweta
Town

Purrysburg

Sayannah

Chattahoochee

Altamaha River

Satilla River

Site of
Ft. King George

Frederica

St. Mary's River

Fort
St. George

Ft. Diego

Ft. St. Francis

Ft. Picolata

St. Johns River

St. Augustin